Feminist Theorists
Three Centuries of Key Women Thinkers

Edited by Dale Spender
Introduction by Ellen Carol DuBois

 Pantheon Books, New York

This book is dedicated to
DORA RUSSELL
one of the best feminist theorists

Library of Congress Cataloging in Publication Data
Main entry under title:

Feminist theorists.

   Reprint. Originally published: Women's Press, 1983.
With new introd.
   Bibliography: p.
   1. Feminists—Biography—Addresses, essays, lectures.
I. Spender, Dale.
HQ1150.F46   1984   305.4′2′0922   83-47747
ISBN 0-394-53438-7
ISBN 0-394-72197-7 (pbk.)

Manufactured in the United States of America
98765432

Feminist Theorists

Contents

Introduction   ix
Ellen Carol DuBois

Foreword   1
Dale Spender

Aphra Behn: A Scandal to Modesty   8
(1640–1689)
Angeline Goreau

Mary Astell: Inspired by Ideas   28
(1668–1731)
Joan K. Kinnaird

Mary Wollstonecraft: Sexuality and Women's Rights   40
(1759–1797)
Miriam Brody

Harriet Martineau: A Reassessment   60
(1802—1876)
Gaby Weiner

Margaret Fuller: Feminist Writer and Revolutionary   75
(1810–1850)
Marie Mitchell Olesen Urbanski

Barbara Bodichon: Integrity in Diversity   90
(1827–1891)
Jacquie Matthews

Lucy Stone: Radical Beginnings   124
(1818–1893)
Leslie Wheeler

Matilda Joslyn Gage: Active Intellectual   137
(1826–1898)
Lynne Spender

Josephine Butler: From Sympathy to Theory   146
(1828–1906)
Jenny Uglow

Hedwig Dohm: Passionate Theorist   165
(1833–1919)
Renate Duelli-Klein

Millicent Garrett Fawcett: Duty and Determination   184
(1847–1929)
Ann Oakley

Charlotte Perkins Gilman: The Personal is Political   203
(1860–1935)
Ann J. Lane

Emma Goldman: Anarchist Queen   218
(1869–1940)
Alix Kates Shulman

Olive Schreiner: New Women, Free Women, All Women   229
(1855–1920)
Liz Stanley

Vida Goldstein: The Women's Candidate   244
(1869–1949)
Gaby Weiner

Christabel Pankhurst: Reclaiming Her Power   256
(1880–1958)
Elizabeth Sarah

Alice Paul: The Quintessential Feminist   285
(1885–1977)
Jean L. Willis

Virginia Woolf: The Life of Natural Happiness   296
(1882–1941)
Naomi Black

Vera Brittain: Feminist in a New Age   314
(1896–1970)
Muriel Mellown

Mary Ritter Beard: Women as Force   335
(1876–1958)
Ann J. Lane

Simone de Beauvoir: Dilemmas of a Feminist Radical   348
(1908–   )
Mary Evans

Modern Feminist Theorists: Reinventing Rebellion   366
Dale Spender

Bibliography   381

Biographical Notes on Contributors   399

Acknowledgments

I would like to thank all the contributors to this volume; it has not been an easy one to put together (the correspondence related to it is greater than the manuscript) and there have been many delays borne with much patience. I would also like to thank Ros de Lanerolle of the Women's Press for her integrity, care and concern.

Introduction

The biographies in these pages demonstrate the complexity of feminism, and of feminists. Somewhere in this collection of twenty-one lives, there is a woman for every taste, and an example to prove – or disprove – every psychological theory of what "causes" feminism. There are women who were educated and encouraged by their fathers (Barbara Bodichon, Margaret Fuller) and those who were thwarted and tyrannized by them (Lucy Stone, Mary Wollstonecraft). There are women with inspiring mothers (Christabel Pankhurst) and those with mothers who tried to break their spirit (Charlotte Perkins Gilman). There are women, like Mary Wollstonecraft, who experienced crushing personal disappointments, and others, like Josephine Butler, whose lives were contented in the most conventional sense. Some were happily married (Mary Beard), some were happily unmarried (Mary Astell, Alice Paul), and others were not quite either (Simone de Beauvoir). Some are feminists about whom most readers will know nothing, while others represent familiar lives brilliantly retold. What is really remarkable, given this personal variety, is that each individual found in her experience some reason to challenge the existing position of women, and some basis of commitment to other women sharing that goal.

The political and intellectual approaches of these twenty-one figures are as varied as their lives. They range from the remarkable breadth of feminists who attempted to comprehend the female dilemma in all its many facets, to the single minded leadership of others dedicated to eliminating one small element of women's oppression. Emma Goldman, the radical anarchist; Millicent Garrett Fawcett, the conservative nationalist; Harriet Martineau, the classic liberal; Simone de Beauvoir, the modern existentialist – each found a different way to describe and explain women's consistent subordination. With so many disparate forms of feminism, the effect of the whole is one of a political tradition that is extremely complex, progressing unevenly and sometimes through the contradictions of its parts. As Alix Kates Shulman writes of Emma Goldman:

We must understand that feminism is not a monolith. There are and always have been different strands of feminist politics: economic issues, issues of sex and the family, legal and constitutional issues, woman-centredness; and these strands aggregate in different patterns of overlap and exclusion, depending on the time and place and the individuals who embrace them (223).

Above and beyond the individual biographies, this collection raises two important sets of questions. The first one has to do with "theory" and its role in the project and annals of feminism. The other has to do with "history" and what it means to regard feminism as a political and intellectual tradition over time.

The question to which this book implicitly responds is, why have there been so few feminist theorists? The answer it gives is that there have been many. It does so by defining just what a feminist theorist is in a very expansive way. Three different kinds of feminists fall under its rubric. First, there are the women whose primary life-work was to think and write about the oppression and liberation of their sex; these were theorists in the most classic sense. Then there are the political figures, whose activism reveals underlying, informing ideas about women. Finally, there are the working intellectuals, women who made their living from ideas on many topics, but about women in particular.

This inclusive approach seems appropriate, given what we learn in these pages about how feminist theory reaches out to movements for political change on the one hand; and reaches within, to the inner reality of women's lives, on the other. Because of its relation to feminist politics, feminist theory has often taken a less abstract form than other theory. In Jacquie Matthews's words, it is more likely to be "clothed in a few pamphlets" than "housed in vast tomes of authoritative and often turgid prose" (94). Politics has also been the medium within which feminist theory has been tested, and the major force by which it has advanced. Jenny Uglow shows us how Josephine Butler's efforts to reform mid-nineteenth–century legislation about prostitution revealed the major "minefields" in Victorian feminist thought, and in some cases exploded them (162). As Alix Kates Shulman writes of Emma Goldman, "Attempting to separate [her] ideas from her deeds is a futile task, for in her the two were inextricably linked" (222). All these women were "political" thinkers whose reason for investigating what it meant to be a woman was, above all, to change it. This more than anything distinguished them from their male contemporaries, with whom they often shared intellectual assumptions and approaches.

Women's lives, when women strive to understand and change them, have always been the source of feminism's most profound insights. This is why the form these essays takes is to interweave personal and intellectual biographies. "Self-experienced truths are beyond scrutiny," asserted nineteenth-century German feminist Hedwig Dohm (166). Nowhere is this link more dramatically demonstrated than in the example of Charlotte Perkins Gilman, whose unexcelled theoretical contributions were based in her own fearless and brilliant analysis of her turbulent emotional life. Gilman had the courage to "plumb her own emotions," to tell the truth about what she felt and feared, and to make profoundly original theory out of it. "With . . . Gilman the body of her work came almost directly out of her personal struggles," writes Ann J. Lane. "We cannot comprehend the scope, the power or the limitations of her ideas without a close understanding of her life" (202). "Until we see what we are," wrote Gilman, speaking for feminist theorists in general, "we cannot take steps to become what we should be" (215).

The oppression of women has been, to some degree, a matter of ideas, ideas about women held by men and women alike, which keep women "in their place." Perhaps this is why the struggle for education, for the tools to think and write, was feminism's first great organized effort. The ideas women have about themselves, this volume argues, can make them powerless or powerful, depending on how these ideas lead us "to make sense out of the world and act upon that reality" (368). What can women do? What have women done? What is the truth about women? The feminist theorists in these pages have all sought to alter existing ideas about women, to explain female subordination on grounds other than natural inferiority, and to set the record straight about what women can and have done. What Ann J. Lane writes about Mary Beard is true of all of them: they "recognized that the success of revolution, any revolution, depends on changed consciousness, on the ability to shatter . . . the inner tyrants, the ones we internalise" (346). These pages are full of examples, from Mary Wollstonecraft to Simone de Beauvoir, of women whose ideas literally changed the lives of all women.

If the importance of ideas is one of the major themes of this book, the significance of history is the other. This collection approaches feminist theory historically. It chronicles "three centuries of women's intellectual traditions." Because there is always something very timeless in feminist perception, the historical dimension of feminist thought can easily be overlooked, but these essays demonstrate how much we would lose were we to do so. Unless we place even the most visionary of these thinkers in their own times and places, we will be either mystified or disappointed by aspects of their thought. An historical approach makes it possible to understand how Victorian feminist Josephine Butler could be both a political activist and a believer in Christian destiny, a defender of personal liberty and a guardian of public morals. Presumably contemporary feminist theory is equally contradictory and just as marked by its own historical epoch. Changing historical circumstances also explain much of the variety among feminist theorists, particularly, it seems, in the area of sex and the family. For instance, as bourgeois culture was struggling to overcome aristocratic ways of life, Mary Wollstonecraft argued that the emancipation of women depended on the establishment of the middle-class family ideal; a century later, speaking for an insurgent working class, Emma Goldman saw the same sexual and family order, now dominant, as women's greatest enemy. To appreciate how these two women could be equally radical, equally feminist, and even equally correct in their analyses, we must, in Liz Stanley's words, "resist temporal chauvinism" (231). In recovering the history of feminist theory, cautions Miriam Brody, "be wary . . . not to superimpose upon it ideas current and connected to our historical condition" (43).

Even on the basis of these twenty-one essays, it is possible to propose a division of the history of feminist theory in England and the United States into several periods. As Mary Astell's biographer points out, there was a feminist intellectual tradition before Mary Wollstonecraft, which "preached not women's rights but women's duties, at a time when women were not thought worthy of duties," especially with respect to children (37). A second period, extending to about the middle of the nineteenth century, featured thinkers of exceptional breadth, such as Wollstonecraft and Margaret Fuller, and concentrated on establishing the abstract equality of the sexes; its characteristic focus was on education, but it also gave some attention to elevating women's place in the family. The emergence of an activist women's movement about mid-century inaugurated a third period in feminist theory, which focused on political equality and economic independence. As Leslie Wheeler observes of Lucy Stone, the need to mobilize large numbers of women and to focus on discrete political goals exercised a conservative influence on feminist thought in this period; even so, individuals like Gilman and Goldman continued to expand the frontiers of theory. Winning the vote in England and the U.S. signaled the beginning of a fourth period, as did the traumatic discovery, during World War I, that all women were not inherently opposed to war or possessed of special moral attributes. From that point until the beginning of our own time, feminist thinkers grappled especially with the question of whether women and men were truly different in character and personality; and sex and psychology became much more important to feminist thought in this period. As we learn more about our past, and about the many feminist thinkers not included in these pages, we will be able to modify these necessarily sketchy periodizations and refine our sense of the stages, changing emphases, and achievements in our intellectual traditions.

Indeed, the more we learn about feminist thinkers of the past, the more we can really say we have a history. A people has a history when they know their past, and we are still learning about ours. In these pages there are occasional examples of women building on the thought of their predecessors, but far too few. Instead, the long process of developing feminist ways of thinking has repeatedly been interrupted and even reversed, as women, forced into ignorance of their own traditions, have had to rethink ideas their predecessors have already thought. Pioneers like Mary Wollstonecraft, Margaret Fuller, and Olive Schreiner have been discredited on sexual and psychological grounds, so that later generations were afraid to read their books or recognize their achievements. The pathbreaking theoretical discoveries of Charlotte Perkins Gilman, a woman with "an enormous international reputation in her lifetime" (211), were lost and forgotten within twenty years of her death. Mary Beard, whose life work was to remedy women's historical invisibility by establishing the record of their many contributions to history, herself became historically invisible, listed in her obituary chiefly as the wife of an historian. Will our daughters be ignorant of the work of Simone de Beauvoir, or even of our own?

There is reason to hope not. The intent of this collection is to halt the process of historical denial by establishing the breadth of the feminist theoretical tradition and developing the record of women's intellectual history. In doing so, *Feminist Theorists* is helping to ensure that feminism will never be without a history again. Theory needs history. With a history, a past of which we are conscious and from which we have learned, our understanding of ourselves as women and what it will take to transform our place in human society will grow by leaps and bounds, and our victories will increase.

Ellen Carol DuBois
August 1983
Buffalo, New York

Foreword

Dale Spender

Theorising is something that men do – so they say: the contributions in this volume suggest otherwise. Theories are also something male theorists have used to justify numerous forms of oppression: the contributions in this book suggest that theories can also be used in the interest of liberation. So, from the outset we confront a problem. While both sexes may have been making theories for as far back as we can trace, only one sex is seen as the theorists, one sex has its theories accepted as legitimate, only one sex *owns* the realm of theory.

This is not surprising: only one sex controls information in our society. Totalitarian regimes are in a position to put forward their own version of the facts, and to suppress alternative – subversive – versions. And patriarchy is a totalitarian regime. It is the dictatorship of the male. It can put forward its version of the facts and erase alternatives: it can even insist that its propaganda is the 'truth'. This is why highly political theories formulated by men which legitimate inequalities of sex, race, and class, can be judged to be *neutral*, while theories put forward by those who are not men can be judged to be political and subversive. The dictatorship of men makes up not just the theories but the values attached to them and it attaches far more value to its own.

This is why for women one of the central issues in theories for liberation is who controls the channels of communication, who is it who decides what we know?

Given that women have been around for quite as long as men, it is little short of astonishing to recognise that while we are surrounded – or even inundated – by books by men about their theories (including their theories of women) one would be hard-pressed to stock even a small shelf with books containing the theories of women. Even the shelves of the British Library are much as Virginia Woolf described them almost 60 years ago: the place abounds with books by men while the women – the minor literary or intellectual figures – are hidden from view more often than not off the premises and in the depots.

One could of course *leap* to the immediate conclusion that women are absent as knowledge-makers and theorists because women have not made knowledge and theories. Such a leap is fostered by patriarchy which stands to gain if women come to believe in their own inferiority and to accept that they have nothing worthwhile to contribute. To come to such a conclusion, however, is to be completely (albeit conveniently) misled. For this volume – one of the few to declare that women are full creative and intellectual beings – defies the propagandising of patriarchy and demonstrates unequivocally that women have had much of value to contribute. It also helps to demonstrate that men have often had good reason to fear what women will say.

If we live in a society where women's knowledge and theories are notable by their absence, in which women's ideas are neither respected nor preserved, it is not because women have not produced valuable cultural forms but because what they have produced has been perceived as dangerous by those who have the power to suppress and remove evidence.

All of the women in this volume are critical of male power. All of them have described and explained male power as a problem. All of them have persuasive arguments against it and suggest sensible methods for ending it. In the circumstances it is understandable that men should not want this subversive literature widely distributed. They are being nothing less than logical when they appreciate the advisability of keeping such revolutionary literature out of the hands of young women.

Men have recognised that when women *know* the arguments against male power, women are different. Men have recognised that women are much less manageable when they learn that for centuries there has been a long and honourable tradition of women who have resisted and protested against men and their power. The reason that men understand this is because the women within these pages have told them.

All of these women in some way started from the position of feeling that they were perverse. Without the knowledge that women of previous generations had protested and without the understanding that women of their own generation shared their experience of dissatisfaction, they invariably felt themselves to be misfits. They often doubted the reality of their own pain and anger, for if it were real why were there no other women who expressed similar feelings? So the knowledge that other women did indeed feel the same way – knowledge gained by communication with other women – was a source of strength: the discovery that women of the past had been through the same process helped to remove the doubts and increase the confidence.

Because they experienced this absence of knowledge about women's lives and feelings many of these women were centrally concerned with the issue of women's invisibility: this is why they generated ideas and formulated theories about the way women's words are censored and deleted in a male-dominated society. Their passionate explanations were forged from their own experience, which led them to believe that to be deprived of a past was to be deprived of power in the present. Women wanted to reclaim their own traditions because such knowledge made them feel good, because it enriched their lives, illuminated the world, offered options and facilitated growth and a sense of self esteem: women wanted to know their past as protesters against patriarchy, and to tell other women, because it provided a basis for action and resistance. Such knowledge told them they were right to rebel, that their grievances were real and their resistance reasonable.

And it is for these very same reasons that men have denied women the knowledge of their own heritage. For these very same reasons that men have erased the presence of women's *action*. Through their practice of censorship they have produced a history which is virtually womanless, or where it does admit the existence of women it is in a *passive* form. In this way women's purpose and power is undermined.

It is one of the most tragic ironies that many of the women who appear in the following pages were women who urged the importance and necessity of the visibility and accessibility of women's tradition as active, creative and intellectual beings; and were women who became victims of the process of elimination which they had identified and described. Most of them have been removed from the record, becoming the 'minor' writers stored in the basement and available only to the determined few who have the resources – and the resilience – to locate them.

This cycle of women's voices bursting forth only to be interrupted and silenced, says Michelle Cliff (1979), *is* women's tradition. This censoring and suppression of women's words of protest, time after time, is the common heritage of women. As men erase the subversive thoughts of women from the traditions which are transmitted from one generation of women to another, we must begin anew. With no received history of resistance and rebellion, state Anna Coote and Beatrix Campbell (1982), each generation must start again and re-invent its own.

And it all takes time.

Born into a society in which their plentiful theories are the framework for making sense of the world (and this includes 'making sense' of women in relation to themselves), men have their confidence boosted, their assurance reinforced, their authority confirmed. They have possession of their 'glorious' and active past: they are in a position to take and build on what they have received. But this is not the case for women.

It is not simply that women must start from the beginning: they must first unlearn what a patriarchal society has taught them about themselves. Having been initiated into a male-dominated society they have been well instructed in the art of woman-devaluation, and if they have learnt their lessons well women will have emerged with their confidence undermined, their assurance dissolved and their sense of self debased. It is from this position that they must start to reject the prevailing wisdom and begin afresh to construct the meanings which are consistent with their own experience. Women are often late starters. The act of questioning, rejecting, seeking and reconceptualising often comes after marriage, or after the children, or after the children have left home: this helps to account for the pattern noted by Ann J. Lane, that women's creative efforts defy the model men have made for themselves with the peaks in youth and middle years. The work done by many women is often late in life – as in the cases of Mary Ritter Beard, Hazel Hunkins-Hallinan, Dora Russell and Elizabeth Cady Stanton for example, all of whom stand in stark contrast to the notion that human beings become conservative with age!

But what all of these women have done has all been done before. It has 'disappeared'. So while men proceed on their developmental way building on their inherited tradition, women are confined to cycles of lost and found, only to be lost and found again – and again.

Why men do what they do is a question not difficult to answer and Mary Beard has provided a comprehensive analysis of the way women's capacity for action and existence as a force is denied, so that women can come to accept the 'reasonableness' of their own oppression (she even includes an assessment of education as the institutionalisation of men's good opinion of themselves, and like Virginia Woolf counsels women to remain educational 'outsiders'. When an institution provides only propaganda *against* one's interests it is as well not to immerse oneself in it or to start producing it). That women have not created the culture, not built communities, acquired skills, made discoveries or inventions, constructed value systems, developed insights and understandings, been poets, philosophers or artists, was the propaganda of the absurd, argued Beard – and women believed it at their peril!

But such explanations do not necessarily account for *how* men do what they do, and it is here that Matilda Joslyn Gage's theories come to the fore. Men, she insists, *rob* women of their labour, *all* their labour, their physical, emotional and intellectual labour. This means that women do not *own* the ideas they produce: it means that men can take the creative and intellectual energy of women and use it to their own ends. By stealing women's labour men are then in a position to assert that women have no creative and intellectual resources of their own.

Many women have provided case studies which fit readily into Gage's thesis. Ruth Hubbard (1979) has shown how Rosalind Franklin's ideas were *stolen* by the men in the work on the double-helix: Hilary Simpson (1979) has shown how some of the 'major' writers like D. H. Lawrence, William Wordsworth and F. Scott Fitzgerald have taken over, wholesale, the writing of women and called it their own. The phenomenon of women's intellectual energy being the raw material which men transform into the finished product – sometimes with the simple addition of their name – is familiar to many research assistants, and few are the women who have not experienced the appropriation of their ideas by men.

Gage's thesis – the product of years of study outside educational institutions – is as central and illuminating on the 'woman question' as Karl Marx's is on the 'class question', but while Marx has been reprinted (and reprinted), Gage has been out of print this century until very recently: while there are volumes devoted to Marx, there is none on Gage. More than most other women who have analysed women's invisibility, Gage explored and documented the practice and put forward strategies for change: more quickly and more effectively than most other women has she been removed from the record. Writing less than 50 years after Gage and on comparable issues, the historian Mary Ritter Beard makes no mention of her.

The precise details of men's theft of women's ideas provide the basis of two (astonishing) accounts in this book. Marie Mitchell Olesen Urbanski's essay reveals that the propaganda and censorship employed in relation to Margaret Fuller suggests that in the name of male scholarship there are no limits to which men will not go to discredit a woman, banish her to the periphery and make her a 'minor' writer so that within a short space of time she slips over the edge into oblivion. Elizabeth Sarah has shown how one man can minimise a movement of thousands of women, even to the extent of enlisting women in the task, and how, despite abundant contrary evidence, proceed to provide an 'authoritative' history in which women are negated. By classifying Christabel Pankhurst's political protest as hysterical outburst we lose her power and are denied her positive presence: when we mock Christabel Pankhurst in a society in which men control knowledge we are the living evidence of the colonisation of our minds.

When we have believed that Harriet Martineau was a crank, Josephine Butler a saint, Millicent Garrett Fawcett a boor and Lucy Stone a prude, and when we find none of these attributes attractive and have no desire to know anything more about the 'minor' characters who possessed them, we are behaving in the required manner in a patriarchal society.

The contributions in this book are interesting and illuminating in their own right, but they also have a political purpose. They defy the classification of 'woman' in a patriarchal society. They stand as a testimony that women have actively resisted male domination for at least three centuries: they stand as a testimony that women have a powerful intellectual tradition. They repudiate the rationale that women are without resources and that men are the rightful theorists.

It has not been easy to bring together these contributions, and while what is here is cause for celebration, what is absent from this record is a matter for much regret. All of these women theorists are white: I would dearly loved to have included accounts of Ida B. Wells, of Josephine Ruffin, Sojourner Truth and Harriet Tubman, to name but a few (for further discussion see Dale Spender 1982(b)). Missing too are women outside the English speaking world and Hedwig Dohm alone cannot begin to indicate the richness of the tradition which encompasses Alexandra Kollontai, Frederika Bremer, Olympe de Gouges, George Sand, Rosa Luxembourg and Clara Zetkin.

Crystal Eastman almost entered the pages, and the omission of 'Sophia, a person of quality' who in 1739 wrote *Woman Not Inferior to Man* is most unfortunate.

That Catharine Macaulay to whom Mary Wollstonecraft owed so much, and Mary Hays who owed so much to Mary Wollstonecraft, are absent, deprives us of some of the understandings about the communities of women of the past. To not have included Frances Wright – who I see as the mother of women's studies – or Anna Wheeler, the Grimke sisters, Harriet Taylor and Frances Power Cobbe is to omit much of value. And to have put together a volume of women theorists (and how many such volumes are there?) *without*

Elizabeth Cady Stanton is to commit a grave sin of omission.

But this book is a *beginning* and not an end. In many ways it constitutes an appeal (as many women within its pages have previously appealed) for women to reclaim and celebrate our past, as a political act. It is an appeal to women to be suspicious of what we have been taught under a male dictatorship and to recognise that we have been victims of a massive propaganda campaign. It is an appeal to develop our own channels of communication and to distribute our own alternative theories and truth.

Not all of the articles in this book reflect my views or share my assessments of the women concerned. This is not a disclaimer but how it should be. While criticising the way men have silenced the voices of women which do not support their own, I am hardly in a position to exclude the voices of women which are not consistent with my own. On the contrary, I welcome the diversity of interpretation and the opportunity for debate. Neither now nor in the past has feminism been a monolith and while there is no question that for as long as men have held power, women have protested, that protest has taken many different forms and for many different reasons. Part of women's tradition is the acknowledgement of authenticated differences within the shared framework of oppression.

This then is a glimpse of some of women's intellectual traditions over the last three centuries. It is a glimpse however, which patriarchy would prefer us to do without. We can see that what we are doing today is not something new but something old: this is a source of strength and power.

Aphra Behn:
A Scandal to Modesty
(c. 1640–1689)

Angeline Goreau*

'Masterpieces are not single and solitary births,' wrote Virginia Woolf in *A Room of One's Own*, 'they are the outcome of many years of thinking in common, of thinking by the body of the people, so that the experience of the mass is behind the single voice. Jane Austen should have laid a wreath upon the grave of Fanny Burney, and George Eliot done homage to the shade of Eliza Carter . . . all women together ought to let flowers fall upon the tomb of Aphra Behn, for it was she who earned them the right to speak their minds' (1928, 1963, p 65).

Aphra Behn was the first Englishwoman to become a professional writer. Certainly other women before had written poems or a play or a tract, and a few had even published under their own names, but Aphra was the first to leave aside the claim that she merely scribbled to amuse herself in private hours, and insist upon a literary identity of her own. She successfully forced the men who dominated the jealous circle of letters in Restoration England to recognise her as an equal. In a London that boasted only two theatres, she had 17 plays produced in 17 years. She wrote 13 'novels' (30 years before Daniel Defoe wrote *Robinson Crusoe*, generally termed the first novel), and published several collections of poems and translations. Her *Oroonoko* contained one of the earliest literary portrayals of the horrors of slavery. It was widely read in her time, and reprinted for years after the scandalous name of its author had once again been returned to the anonymity thought proper to a woman of her generation.

Aphra Behn, though she did not and could not know it then, would signal a turning in feminine history, augur a whole new spectrum of possibility for her sex. Her example demonstrated that a woman – if

* The Author gratefully acknowledges the generous permission of Oxford University Press in allowing her to reprint extracts from *Reconstructing Aphra: A Social Biography of Aphra Behn* (1980).

lucky, if willing to surrender respectability, comfort, approval, perhaps even love; if prepared to risk ridicule, loss of reputation, vilification or attack – might declare her autonomy and make a living by writing in an age when her only social and economic alternative was to marry or to find a wealthy 'protector'. She was both sign and cause: the wave of women writers who came after would have inevitably come, but for her immediate successors the ground she gained was important. Mary Manley, Mary Pix, Eliza Haywood, Catherine Trotter, Arabella Plantin, Penelope Aubin, Elizabeth Rowe, and others could look back to her – though history would forget those early lady writers of the eighteenth century almost as quickly as it forgot Aphra Behn herself. Still, they formed a tradition, if largely invisible, that securely established the woman writer as a literary 'fact'.

The life Aphra Behn led would have been extraordinary in any age, but for a woman of the seventeenth century it was virtually unheard-of. Aphra was an adventuress who undertook the long and dangerous voyage of the West Indies, became involved in a slave rebellion there, and visited a tribe of Indians who had never before seen Europeans. She was a spy for Charles II against the Dutch. She was a debtor imprisoned for expenses incurred in the service of the king. She was a feminist who vociferously defended the right of women to an education, and the right to marry whom they pleased, or not at all. She was a sexual pioneer who contended that men and women should love freely and as equals. Finally, she was a political activist who argued the royalist point of view at Will's Coffee House and from the stage of the Drury Lane Theatre.

In an age when popular wisdom held that the 'domestic sphere' ought to represent the circumference of a woman's experience, the very catalogue of Aphra Behn's life represented a radical violation of the territory deemed suitable to her sex. Concern for reputation, added to the restraints exercised by husband or family, usually provided a strong argument to keep a woman within her proper bounds, but Aphra may well have started out in life with a peculiar advantage in this respect. Though the actual circumstance of her birth remains a subject of much debate, it is generally agreed that she was not born to either fortune or position – and may well have even been illegitimate. [1] As she tells it in *Oroonoko*, her father died during the ocean voyage to the West Indies, leaving her mother and Aphra (along with a sister and brother) to fend for themselves. Later, on her return to London, Aphra was forced to find a way of supporting herself. Her brief marriage to a mysterious (and still unidentified, if indeed he ever existed) Mr Behn seems to have little altered her desperate circumstances, and her career as a spy ended in debtor's prison. She was in her late twenties when she began to write professionally for the theatre.

The first recorded production of Aphra Behn's work was the play *The Forced Marriage; or, the Jealous Bridegroom*, which was performed on Tuesday, 20 September 1670, at Lincoln's Inn Fields. Under the inscription, '*Va mon enfant! Prend ta fortune*', the prologue to this first effort frankly declared the author's sex:

> Women those charming victors, in whose eyes
> Lie all their arts, and their artilleries,
> Not being contented with the wounds they made,
> Would by new strategems our lives invade.
> Beauty alone goes now at too cheap rates;
> And therefore they, like wise and politic states,
> Court a new power that may the old supply,
> To keep as well as gain the victory:
> They'll join the force of wit to beauty now,
> And so maintain the right they have in you.
> If the vain sex this privilege should boast,
> Past cure of a declining face we're lost.
> You'll never know the bliss of change; this art
> Retrieves (when beauty fades) the wandring heart;
> And though the airy spirits move no more,
> Wit still invites, as beauty did before.
> Today one of their party ventures out,
> Not with design to conquer, but to scout.
> Discourage but this first attempt, and then
> They'll hardly dare to sally out again.[2]

Both author and audience were well aware that *The Forced Marriage* represented a break from tradition: Aphra is transgressing and chooses to acknowledge it openly. She has also chosen not to present herself as an exception to the rule but as speaking on *behalf* of her sex, declaring her entry into the hitherto masculine domain of literature as a step for all women. She is aware of the symbolic significance of her act. The statement delineates the spheres thought proper to masculine and feminine enterprise – 'wit' and 'beauty' – and justifies the woman writer's 'invading' property historically not her own. The language of the statement borrows 'masculine' metaphors of battle: artilleries, wounds, strategems, politic states, power, victory. But at the same time, the borrowed aggression is contradicted by 'feminine' retreat – the offensive has its source in women's desire to please, to retain masculine affection and desire rather than infringe upon prerogative. The deliberate ambiguity is no doubt in part a device to attract the attention of a fickle audience and to disarm her ready critics, but it also seems to represent a fundamental division in Aphra's attitude. Her fighting declaration of entry into the sphere of the wits is equivocated by her (not unjustified) fear of being considered unfeminine.

Though unwise to read material of this sort as direct autobiographical statement, it is at least arguable that Aphra's preoccupation here with the ephemerality of feminine beauty is not uninfluenced by her being nearly 30 in a world where women's attractiveness supposedly ended at 25. This does not seem to have prevented Aphra from carrying on a love life that was thought of by some as scandalous, but she nevertheless felt, and resented, the pressure that the double standard of sexual aging imposed on women. 'You'll never know the bliss of change,' she warns the men of the audience, implying that by depriving women of mind in favour of body, they condemn themselves to endless repetition.

Behind the burlesque of the teasing prologue, another more general problem is raised: that of the increasingly vulnerable and contingent position of women in Restoration society. 'Beauty alone goes at too cheap rates,' accurately describes the world of the wits and rakes who frequented the theatre. The easy availability of sex took its toll of the way women were treated in general. Aphra's argument ironically recalls an economic reality: if the value of women's principal commodity is debased, they must find a new way to attract men. Aphra's way would be to establish the base for her own autonomy. With difficulty.

The relative success of her first play encouraged Aphra to submit a second. Only six months later, on 24 February 1671, *The Amorous Prince* went on the boards. The prologue assumes more confidence than that of the first play, and indeed takes on a bantering tone of assault:

> Well! you expect a prologue to the play,
> And you expect it to petition-way;
> With *chapeau bas** beseeching you t'excuse
> A damn'd intrigue of an unpractised muse.

* hat in hand

Aphra goes on to tally up the objections that will be brought against her play. One group of critics, she says, will condemn it because it does not conform to the classical rule for heroic tragedy but is defiled by comic action: 'You grave Dons,' she writes, 'who love no play/ But what is regular, great Jonson's way;/ Who hate monsieur with the farce and roll,/ But are for things well said with spirit and soul.'

In the guise of a sardonic prologue, Aphra was taking her position in the war of opinions, as Dryden called it, that divided the theatrical coterie as well as the learned critics of her day. The factions were the 'Ancients' and the 'Moderns': for 'regular' plays that kept to the Aristotelian unities of time, place, and action – or for 'natural' ones that did not; for rhymed verse or for prose; for tragedy or for comedy; for moral instruction or for amusement. Aphra's mockery of 'You grave Dons. . .' was, at least in part, an attack on Dryden. He had been made Poet Laureate the year before (1670) and Aphra was a neophyte in the theatre – worse still, of the wrong sex. The parody in her prologue must have seemed effrontery.

She appears to have been very much under attack herself, however. Her third play, *The Dutch Lover*, produced on 6 February 1673, carried an 'Epistle to the Reader' which ridiculed her detractors and further defended the position she had taken in the ideological fray going on in the theatre. 'Good Sweet, Honey, Sugar-Candied Reader,' she began in a sarcastic imitation of current literary flattery, 'Which I think is more than anyone has called you yet, I must have a word or two with you before you do advance into the treatise; but 'tis not to beg your pardon for diverting you from your affairs by such an idle pamphlet as this is . . . for I have dealt pretty fairly in the matter, told you in the title-page what you are to expect within.'

Having taken a dig at her literary colleagues, Aphra goes on to ridicule the ponderous logic and pretentious language that academic pronouncements on drama were couched in: 'Indeed, had I hung a sign of the immortality of the soul, or the mystery of godliness, or of ecclesiastical policie, and then had treated you with indiscerptibility and essential spissitude (words, which though I am no competent judge of, for want of languages, yet I fancy strongly ought to mean just nothing) . . . or had presented you with two or three of the worst principles transcribed out of the peremptory and ill-natured (though prettily ingenious) Doctor of Malmesbury [Hobbes]. . . I were then indeed sufficiently in fault; but having inscribed comedy on the beginning of my book, you may guess pretty near what penny-worths you are like to have, and ware your money and your time accordingly.'

Next, she lampoons certain members of the Royal Society who

disparaged plays as a lesser art: 'I would not yet be understood to lessen the dignity of plays, for surely they deserve among the middle if not the better sort of books; for I have heard the most of that which bears the name of learning, and which has abused such quantities of ink and paper, and continually employs so many ignorant, unhappy souls of ten, twelve, twenty years in the University (who yet poor wretches think they are doing something all the while) as logick etc. and several other things (that shall be nameless lest I misspell them) are much more absolutely nothing than the errantest play that e'er was writ.'

Finally, pretending to apologise for her presumption in joining an argument outside her 'sphere', Aphra attacks the new science that pretended to classify both literature and language into a system of rules: 'Take notice, reader, I do not assert this purely upon my own knowledge, but I think I have known it very fully proved, both sides being fairly heard, and even some ingenious opposers of it most abominably baffled in the argument: Some of which I have got so perfectly by rote, that if this were a proper place for it, I am apt to think myself could almost make it clear; and as I would not under-value poetry, so neither am I altogether of their judgement who believe no wisdom in the world beyond it. I have often heard indeed (and read) how much the world was anciently obliged to it for most of that which they called science, which my want of letters makes me less assured of than others happily may be: but I have heard some wise men say that no considerable part of useful knowledge was this way communicated, and on the other way, that it hath served to propagate so many idle superstitions, as all the benefits it can be guilty of, can never make sufficient amends for; which unaided by the unlucky charms of poetry, could never have possessed a thinking creature such as man.'

Literature in the English language had rarely, if ever, seen such a diatribe in print with a woman's name signed at the bottom. Something had made Aphra very angry indeed, and from the text, one might guess that she had been told that her 'want of language' or 'want of letters' disqualified her from taking a position in the dispute over the rules that ought to govern the writing of plays. Of course it was true that her sex had excluded her from the academies, and it was also true that, unlike Dryden, she could not read Aristotle and the 'Ancients' for herself. She insists, however, that she is not asserting her position 'purely on my own knowledge', but has listened very carefully to both parties presenting their platforms and has memor-ised the arguments. Defiantly sarcastic, she is first of all refusing to be intimidated into a sense of inferiority because of her sex's ignorance, and second, dismissing the much-vaunted 'learning' that she has been denied as so much 'academic frippery'. This stance, as comments she later made would bear out, did in fact mask a certain sense of deprivation, but she was at this point determined to hold her own among her male colleagues no matter at what disadvantage.

The wits and fops and critics and writers might have been amused and titillated by the innovation of a woman writing for the theatre when she produced her first play, but when a second appeared in rapid succession and then *The Dutch Lover*, it must have become apparent that she intended to establish herself as a permanent competitor. To make matters worse, she had dared to throw herself into a debate over the function and nature of theatre that was beyond her education or proper sphere. According to Aphra, a deliberate effort was made to sabotage, discourage, and eliminate her from the stage. Her 'Epistle to the Reader' recounts:

> Indeed that day 'twas acted first, there comes me into the pit, a long, lither, phlegmakick, white, ill-favour'd, wretched fop, an officer in masquerade newly transported with a scarf and feather out of France, a sorry animal that has nought else to shield it from the uttermost contempt of all mankind, but that respect which we afford to rats and toads, which though we do not well allow to live, yet when considered as a part of God's creation, we make honourable mention of them. A thing, reader – but no more of such a smelt: This thing, I tell ye, opening that which serves it for a mouth, out issued such a noise as this to those that sat about it, that *they were to expect a woeful play, God damn him, for it was a woman's.* Now how this came about I am not sure, but I suppose he brought it piping hot from some who had with him the reputation of a villanous wit: for creatures of his size of sense talk without all imagination, such scraps as they pick up from other folks. I would not for a moment be taken arguing with such a propertie as this: but if I thought there were a man of any tolerable parts, who could upon mature deliberation distinguish well his right hand from his left, and justly state the difference between the number of sixteen and two, yet had this prejudice upon him; I would take a little pains to make him know how much he errs. For waving the examination why women having equal education with men, were not as capable of knowledge, of whatsoever sort as well as they: I'll only say as I have touched before, that plays have no great room for that which is men's great advantage over women,

that is learning. We all well know that the immortal Shakespeare's plays (who was not guilty of much more of this [learning] than often falls to women's share) have better pleased the world than Jonson's works, though by the way 'tis said that Benjamin was no such Rabbi neither, for I am informed that his learning was but Grammar high (sufficient indeed to rob poor Sallust of his best orations) . . . and for our modern [dramatists], except our more unimitable Laureate, I dare to say I know of none that write at such a formidable rate, but that a woman may hope to reach their greatest heights. Then for their musty rules of unity, and God knows what besides, if they meant anything, they are enough intelligible and as practible by a woman.

All pretence of apology or feminine coquetry has evaporated in the heat of Aphra's fury at being discriminated against because of her sex. Her anger at the reception of *The Dutch Lover* finally outweighs the hesitant sense of transgression that tempered her boldness at her literary debut. The sense of the argument is twofold: first, Aphra implies that it is not any lack in women's innate capacity for knowledge that has kept them from the pen but a double standard in access to learning; but secondly, she asserts that the 'learning' denied to her sex is in no way essential to the writing of plays. As before, in the same breath that she protests women's exclusion from the possession of 'knowledge', she denies that her present activity requires it in the form it was presented. There is some confusion between her stated position against the writing of plays being governed by erudition and the separate issue of women's relation to knowledge. Apparently, the criticisms that had had such a radical-ising effect on her had further entrenched her self-doubt at the same time that they had strengthened and given the force of anger to her nascent feminism. But whatever the contradictions of her 'Epistle to the Reader', it was as close to a manifesto as a female author writing for a popular audience had come.

The full risk and radical nature of the literary stance Aphra Behn had taken can only be realised when understood in the context of what other women wrote, how they viewed their own writing in relation to the world, and what significance they chose to give the act itself. In the generation just before Aphra's, two women writers emerged who published a body of literary work under their own names, breaking with a long tradition of feminine anonymity. They were Katherine Philips, the 'Matchless Orinda' (1631–1664), and Margaret Cavendish, the Duchess of Newcastle (1624?–1664).

Katherine Philips was part of a literary 'society of friends' which included the poets Jeremy Taylor and Henry Vaughan, Sir Edward Dering, Katherine's husband, and several ladies under pastoral pseudonyms. They wrote each other elevated verse celebrating honour, virtue, and the modest life, and espoused platonic friendship. Katherine's poems were handed about in manuscript and had acquired quite a reputation when, at the encouragement of the Earl of Orrery, she began the translation of Corneille's *Pompey*. Though it was widely known among her friends to be her work, she shrank from the idea of signing her name to a published text: she wrote to Sir Charles Cotterel, whom she called 'Poliarchus': 'I would beg leave publickly to address it [Pompey] to the Duchess, but that then I must put my name to it, which I can never resolve to do; for I shall scarce ever pardon myself the confidence of having permitted it to see the light at all, tho' it was purely in my own defence that I did; for had I not furnished a true copy, it had been printed from one that was very false and imperfect. But should I once own it publickly, I think I should never be able to show my face again' (Philips, 1705, pp 127–8). Not wishing to involve herself directly in the business of publication, Orinda confided the affair to Sir Charles Cotterel, with only one stipulation: 'I consent to whatever you think fit to do about printing it,' she wrote a little later, 'but conjure you by all our mutual friendship, not to put my name to it, nay, not so much as the least mark or hint whereby the public may guess from whence it came' (p 152).

A few months later, an edition of Katherine Philips's poems was published in London, without her knowledge, according to the indignant letter she wrote to Poliarchus: 'The injury done me by that printer and publisher surpasses all the troubles that to my remembrance I ever had . . . who never writ a line in my life with the intention to have it printed . . . you know me, Sir, to have been all along sufficiently distrustful of whatever my own want of company and better employment, or the commands of others have seduced me to write, and that I have rather endeavoured never to have those trifles seen at all, than that they should be exposed to all the world . . . sometimes I think that to make verses is so much above my reach, and a diversion so unfit for the sex to which I belong, that I am about to resolve against it forever; and could I have recovered those fugitive papers that have escaped my hands, I had long since, I believe, made a sacrifice of them to the flames. The truth is, I have always had an incorrigible inclination to the vanity of rhyming, but intended the effects of that humour only for my own amusement in a retired life, and therefore did not so much resist it as a wise woman would have done' (pp 227–9, p 234).

There was hardly anything shocking in the published verses. The people the poems were addressed to were disguised under names like Lucasia and Silvander, the subject matter of the highest virtue, and the style so literary that one wonders if they were in fact *not* written with publication in mind. Katherine Philips unquestionably harboured literary aspirations and found it perfectly natural that the *male* poets of her group should publish their works; but whether or not she really believed it was unthinkable for a woman to make herself 'public' in this way, she nevertheless wrote to all her friends to disclaim responsibility for the publication and ask them to spread the word. To Dorothy Osborne she complained: 'I must never show my face among any reasonable people again, for some most dishonest person hath got some collection of my poems as I hear, and hath delivered them to a printer who I hear is just upon putting them out and this hath so extreamly disturbed me, both to have my private folly so unhandsomely exposed and the belief that I believe the most part of the world are apt enough to believe that I connived at this ugly accident that I have been on the rack ever since I heard it. . . .'[3]

Mrs Philips even went so far as to claim that this event had thrown her into a 'fit of sickness'. She finally succeeded in having the edition suppressed, and forced the printer, Marriott, to apologise and publicly announce his intention to withdraw the book in an advertisement in the London *Intelligencer* of 18 January 1664. Six months later, Mrs Philips died of smallpox. Her poems were posthumously re-edited, with her disclaimer of responsibility and her assertion that the activity of writing verses was 'unfit for her sex' prefacing the new edition. She was thereafter held up as an example to her sex, a proof that women might have 'wit'. She was often referred to as the 'Chaste Orinda', and future defenders of women's right to the muse would cite her as a paragon for imitation, passing over Aphra Behn. Mrs Philips had, in fact, succeeded in preserving the character Sir Edward Dering had given her in his epilogue to her translation of *Pompey*: 'No bolder thought can tax, those rhymes of blemish to the blushing sex; As chaste the lines, as harmless is the sense, as the first smiles of infant innocence' (Philips, 1705, p 232).

Margaret Cavendish, the Duchess of Newcastle, was equally eager to guard her reputation for virtue, and in her autobiography, appended to the life of her husband, plainly told the reader: 'I am chaste, both by nature, and education, inasmuch as I do abhor an unchaste thought' (Cavendish, 1667, 1907, p 176). She does not seem to have regarded the publishing of her writings as a blight on her reputation, however, and even went so far as to insist that she wrote for 'fame' and 'eternity itself'. At the same time, she constantly reminded the reader not only of her own incompetence in the field of 'learning', but of her sex's general incapacity in that field of endeavour: 'Women's minds are like shops of small-wares,' she commented to another lady, 'wherein some have pretty toys, but nothing of any great value' (Cavendish, 1664, (a), p 14).

A young lady, apparently encouraged by seeing another woman venture into print, wrote to the Duchess and received the following reply: 'Madam, you wrote in your letter that I had given our sex courage and confidence to write, and to divulge what they writ in print; but give me leave humbly to tell you, that it is no commendation to give them courage and confidence if I cannot give them wit' (1664, (a), p 225).

Margaret Cavendish was married to the powerful and wealthy Duke of Newcastle. He was many years older than she, and they lived in a great, empty country estate and had no children. To keep her occupied, and doubtless also away from other men, he encouraged her, as she tells it, 'in my harmless pastime of writing'.[4] He paid printers to publish lavish editions of her writings and protected her by writing introductions for nearly all of them, defending her. His commendation would be followed by a letter from her thanking him for permission to publish – a favour, she noted, few men allowed their wives. She was always careful to signal her proper position of inferiority and wrote of her husband: 'He creates himself with his pen, writing what his wit dictates to him, but I pass my time rather with scribbling than with writing, with words than with wit . . . I am so far from thinking myself able, to teach, as I am afraid I have not capacity to learn, yet I must tell the world, that I think that not any hath a more abler master to learn from, then I have, for if I had never married the person I have, I do believe I should never have writ so, as to have adventured to divulge my works' (Cavendish, 1655, unpaginated).

Despite the Duchess's humility about her own abilities, her evident desire for recognition and eagerness for literary fame scandalised her contemporaries. She was thought bold even to madness: when her first book of poems was published in 1653, Dorothy Osborne wrote to her fiancé, William Temple, to ask him to send her the curiosity, commenting, 'Sure the poor woman is a little distracted, she could never be so ridiculous else as to venture at writing books and in verse too. If I could not sleep this fortnight I should not come to that' (Osborne [Temple], 1914, p 82).

Dorothy Osborne was a young woman with an evident gift and urge to write – for seven whole years she kept up a steady stream of letters to her lover, articulate with descriptions of the countryside around her, of her reading, of whatever gossip she could garner in her isolated corner. The idea of a woman's employing her pen for a public, however, seemed outrageous to her: 'You need not send me my Lady Newcastle's book,' she wrote to William Temple a few weeks after she had asked him to get her a copy of the newly published work, 'for I have seen it, and am satisfied that there are many soberer people in Bedlam, I'll swear her friends are much to blame to let her go abroad . . . there are certain things that custom has made almost of absolute necessity, and reputation I take to be one of those: if one could be invisible I should choose that, but since all people are seen and known, and shall be talked of in spite of their teeth's, who is it that does not desire at least that nothing of ill may be said to them . . . no not [even] my Lady Newcastle with all her philosophy' (Osborne [Temple], 1914, p 100, 218).

Dorothy Osborne was only expressing the general opinion of her day in condemning Margaret Cavendish's rash adventure: her act of publication earned her the title 'Mad Madge', and she shut herself away in the countryside, receiving only visitors who flattered and approved her, often in hopes of finding a generous patron. The Duchess's eccentricities did in fact become more and more pronounced, though whether it was a natural evolution or the effects of the conflict of her ambitions and her sex is not clear. Her husband might subsidise the publication of her philosophical works or poems, but her plays, which were all intended for the stage, went unacted.

The intensity of Katherine Philips's anguish over having her name attached to a published work and the violence of the reaction to the Duchess of Newcastle's publicly acknowledging the authorship of her work serve as in index of the strength of opposition a woman writer of that time might encounter. Orinda had the support of a circle of friends; the Duchess of Newcastle had the privilege of great wealth; and both had the approval and encouragement of affectionate husbands. Aphra Behn had none of these advantages: she was alone and had a living to make. Perhaps, though, necessity freed her. If she had no one to protect her or to fall back on, she also was the guardian of no one's honour but her own.

The two principle inhibitions, then, that kept women from writing and from publishing their writing in the seventeenth century and before, were the sense that wit belonged to the masculine province and the fear of violating feminine 'modesty'. The first is clear enough, but the second is less immediately evident. Its source lies in the complex interaction of symbolic and concrete interpretation of the concept of feminine sphere. This division of masculine and feminine spheres of experience separated 'the world' from 'the domestic circle', the public from the private arena; women were denied access to the former and confined to the latter by 'custom'. The social hegemony of modesty and its attributes – virtue, honour, name, fame, and reputation – served to police the segregation by ascribing a sexual significance to any penetration, either from within or without, of a woman's 'private circle'. To publish one's work was to make oneself 'public': to expose oneself to 'the world'. Women who did so violated their feminine modesty both by egressing from the private sphere which was their proper domain and by permitting foreign eyes access to what ought to remain hidden and anonymous.

Katherine Philips's near-frantic fear of being 'exposed' to the world through the publication of her poems takes on a more logical aspect in this perspective. Dorothy Osborne's casual wish to become invisible in order to protect her reputation unwittingly expresses the impulse that must have made countless women choose anonymity over publicity. The unidentified female author of a feminist tract published in 1696 states quite explicitly her reasons for keeping her name a secret: 'I presume not so far upon the merits of what I have written, as to make my name public with it', she said, adding, 'nothing could induce me to bring my name upon the public stage of the world . . . the tenderness of reputation in our sex . . . made me very cautious, how I exposed mine to such poisonous vapours. I was not ignorant, how liberal men are of their scandal, wherever provoked, especially by a woman (Anon, 1696, iv–vi). Anna von Schurman, in a letter she reprinted in her book *The Learned Maid or, Whether a Maid may be a Scholar?* specifically asks her fellow-scholar Johannes Beverovicius (author of *The Excellency of the Female Sex*, 1639) not to dedicate his book to her because it might damage her reputation: 'I do heartily entreat you, yea by our inviolable friendship I beseech you, that you would not dedicate this book to me', she writes, 'for, as you are not ignorant, with what evil eyes the greatest part of men do behold what tendeth to our praise' (von Schurman, 1641, p 38). She was afraid that malicious tongues would call her his mistress. The title page of Anna von Schurman's learned treatise announces that it was written by 'a Virgin', and the author of the prefatory 'Epistle to the Reader' praises her extensive mastery of learning, but further states that 'these gifts are far inferior to those which she accounteth chief: piety without ostentation, modesty beyond example, and most exemplary holiness of life and conversation'. It seems that even those women who were strong enough and educated enough to argue against male prerogative in the domain of knowledge still felt they had to protect the reputation for modesty that was such an important reinforcement of the 'feminine sphere'. This constraint created a split in women of literary ambitions that forced some into anonymity, others into denial of responsibility for publication, and still others into constant apology and humble appeal. It is this tradition of invisibility that makes Aphra's open demand for literary equality and recognition so impressive.

Perhaps Aphra Behn might not have had the courage or stamina to defend such a position had the Restoration not created a favourable climate. It was generally acknowledged among both proponents and opponents that there had been what might be called a 'sexual revolution' in the 1660s. Charles II's return to the throne effected an abrupt and deliberate reversal of Puritan ethic. His need to distinguish himself in every way from his predecessors – added to his natural inclination – created an atmosphere in which promiscuity, systematic frivolity, and extravagance were adhered to as a social norm almost as dogmatically as the more severe of the Puritan party had adhered to godliness. Adultery was part of the calling of a gentleman, as essential to his place in society as fluency in French, a wig, or a sword at his side. The king set the tone by openly keeping several mistresses, carrying on numerous chance affairs, and bestowing titles, estates, and fortunes on his women and bastards. The 'new' libertinism primarily affected the fashionable society of London – the court and aristocratic circles, the playhouse, the coffee-houses, and ordinaries – but, as these were both the most visible and the most influential groups, they seemed to dominate the rest.

The shift in sexual ethos was very much in evidence in the social milieu Aphra Behn moved in – the courtiers, wits, poets, theatre-goers, fops, actors and actresses. A character in her play *The Amorous Prince* (1671), remarks that 'there is nothing but foutering* in this town' – a play on words that covered both the sexual sense and also meant, in the slang of the day, to waste time and tongue doing nothing. There are several references to the vogue for libertinism and the new breed of wild gallant who seduces wherever he likes. At one point, the hero chastises a lady he is trying to persuade to bed by telling her that her concern for her reputation is out of date: 'Fy, fy, Laura', he says, 'a Lady bred at court, and yet want complaisance enough to entertain a gallant in private! This coy humour is not

---

* fornicating

à-la-mode. . .' Another hesitant young lady in a poem of Aphra's is informed 'this nicety's out of fashion'.

The wits had announced the demise of feminine chastity and a fashionable following had ostensibly rejected traditional restrictions, but the influence of modesty had far from departed. It had, in a sense, gone underground. The libertine bent every effort to seduce a lady to his bed, but once she was there, he despised her for it. The expression of desire on the part of a woman still violated too many taboos – the woman who was kind (in both senses of the word) was sure to be rejected: 'My love she did retard, prevent,/ Giving too soon, her kind consent,' wrote Wycherley (1924, vol I, p 24). A woman had to be distant in order to be attractive. 'The Forsaken Mistress' who speaks in Etheredge's poem of that name has understood too late the sexual politics behind the seduction she has given in to: 'Tell me, gentle Strepthon, why,' she begs her lover, 'You from my embraces fly?/ Does my love thy love destroy?/ Tell me, I will yet be coy' (1963, p 42). Whether or not it was fear, the wits generally took flight in the face of feminine response. Ismena, a young woman in Aphra Behn's second play, remarks to a typical Restoration rake: '. . . as most gallants are, you're but pleased with what you have not; and love a mistress with great passion, 'till you find yourself beloved again, and then you hate her.'

Despite their profession of sexual liberty, the promiscuous gallants of the Restoration still more or less unconsciously held on to the very ideas about woman's modesty they had loudly repudiated. This double impulse put women in an impossible position. Aphra Behn, in a poem 'To Alexis, in answer to his Poem against Fruition', complained:

> Since Man with that inconstancy was born,
> To love the absent, and the present scorn,
> Why do we deck, why do we dress
> For such short-liv'd happiness?
> Why do we put attraction on,
> Since either way 'tis we must be undone?
> They fly if honour take our part,
> Our virtue drives 'em o'er the field.
> We lose 'em by too much desert,
> And Oh! they fly us if we yield.
> Ye Gods! is there no charm in all the fair
> To fix this wild, this faithless, wanderer?

The contradictory position that the demands of modesty had

always put women in needed no external reinforcement from men, however, for whatever libertine ideology might proclaim, the 'fair sex' was still very much subject to them. Women of Aphra Behn's generation had been educated to modesty, and it remained a powerful force whether they chose to conform to its dictates or defy them. Countless remarks in letters, poetry, and drama suggest that it was rare for a woman to renounce entirely at least the appearance of feminine virtue – Wycherley's reference in a preface to one of his plays to that 'mask of modesty' all women 'promiscuously wear in public', is characteristic. This self-image was so deeply ingrained that often even women of notorious reputation made an attempt at pretence. If they acknowledged their own sexuality and acceded to it, they violated the essential element of what they had been brought up to believe was their femininity: virtue. On the other hand, if they held to honour, they sacrificed desire. Numerous poems written by the wits and libertines who were Aphra Behn's friends record this ambiguity on the part of their women – Wycherley's 'A Song to an incredulous dissident Mistress, who said, she was resolved to keep her reputation, in spite of her love', among them.

Since few seventeenth-century ladies discussed such matters in personal correspondence, it is difficult to document fully the female point of view, but what little surviving evidence there is testifies to the toll this conflict took on women. Aphra Behn herself wrote at the end of her life (in one of the last works she composed) of the mind/body split that the feminine education of her age necessarily produced: '. . . 'tis the honour of our sex to deny most eagerly those grants to lovers, for which most tenderly we sigh, so contradictory are we to ourselves, as if the deity that made us with a seeming reluctancy to his own designs; placing as much discord in our minds, as there is harmony in our faces. We are a sort of airy clouds, whose lightning flash out one way, and the thunder another. Our words and thoughts can ne'er agree.' (*Works*, Vol V, pp 404–5).

Like her literary colleagues Rochester, Wycherley and Etheredge, Aphra Behn wrote poetry and plays which dealt openly with sex. Like them also, she regarded marriage as a repressive institution and embraced an ideal of sexual freedom. But there the similarity ended. Aphra's conception of the way affairs ought to be carried on between the sexes differed profoundly from that of her male friends and professional peers. Alone, she defended the feminine point of view in her writing; but the source of difference between Aphra and the wits was not merely a shift in perspective or power (male to female) – it had to do with her vision of love itself.

Aphra detested the Restoration 'game of love' and passionately desired sincerity. She had a reputation for 'plain-dealing' and expected the same from men. In a poem she wrote to a man she was in love with (probably a lawyer and 'wit-about-town' named John Hoyle), she expressed disdain for the sexual politics of the market-place that Restoration love had become:

> Take back that heart, you with such caution give,
>   Take the fond trifle back;
> I hate Love-Merchants that a trade would drive,
>   And meanly cunning bargain make.
>
> I care not how the busy market goes,
>   And scorn to chaffer for a price:
> Love does one staple rate on all impose,
>   Nor leaves it to the trader's choice.
>
> A heart requires a heart unfeigned and true,
>   Though subtly you advance the price,
> And ask a rate that simple love n'er knew,
>   And the free trade monopolise.

Aphra's lover, according to her, had asked 'more for his heart than 'twas worth'. His condition was that she remain faithful to him, while he reserved the liberty to make love to other women. She was to give herself entirely, while he was to fit her into the interstices of these other affairs. 'Every hour still more unjust you grow,/ . . . freedoms you my life deny,' Aphra protests. She does not herself feel either need or desire for the same promiscuity that he claims as his privilege, but she will not be denied equal possibility in principle. Free love demands equality, she tells him: 'Be just, my lovely swain, and do not take/ Freedoms you'll not to me allow;/ Or give Amynta so much freedom back:/ That she may rove as well as you./ Let us then love upon the honest square,/ Since interest neither have designed,/ For the sly gamester, who ne'er plays me fair,/ Must trick for trick expect to find.' (*Works*, Vol VI, p 204).

Exploitation, said Aphra, had forced the sexes into a merry-go-round of self-interest: men using women who were obliged to use men. Furthermore, the double-standard imposed on women pressed them into still more degrading hypocrisy and deceit: 'This unlucky restraint on our sex makes us all cunning,' says one of her female characters. Aphra partly blamed social convention for this state of affairs; but that she also saw men as having a large responsibility in the reinforcement of that convention – despite their rhetoric – is clear from many statements she made in her literary and other texts. 'In vain, dear youth, you say you love,/ And yet my marks of passion blame,' she wrote in answer to a lover who had sent her 'some verses on a discourse of love's fire'. He had evidently given her notice that it was man's nature to let his fancy wander where it might and that it was not woman's place to object. Her answer implies that he is merely using other women to escape intense involvement with her. The 'love's fire' he is offering her is only a pale imitation of the real thing: 'A fancy strong may do the feat,' she tells him; 'Yet this to love a riddle is,/ And shows that passion but a cheat;/ Which men but with their tongues confess.' (*Works*, Vol VI, pp 196–7).

For Aphra, sexual desire was naturally a part of love's expression, but if isolated from feeling, it atrophied into an endless repetition. Sexual freedom, without love, was no freedom at all, to her mind. The social modes of the 1660s and 1670s had produced a new sort of narcissism – the highest form of which was a phenomenon which Aphra called 'the fop in fashion'. Incapable of any real passion or feeling outside of self-adoration, 'hardened and incorrigible', the fop valued only the constant change of fashion. Aphra, in a caustic aside, describes the way a Restoration fop behaved himself in a love affair: '. . . by a dire mistake, conducted by vast opinatrety [*sic*], and a greater portion of self-love . . . he believes that affectation in his mein and dress, that mathematical formality in every action, that a face managed with care, and softened into ridicule, the languishing turn, the toss, and the back-shake of the periwig, is the direct way to the heart of the fine person he adores. . . This is he, of all human kind, on whom love can do no miracles. . . Perhaps it will be urged, since no metamorphosis can be made in a fop by love, you must consider him one of those that only talks of love . . . wanting fine sense enough for the real passion. . .' A fop was a silly imitation of a wit – but an accurate reflection nevertheless of fashionable behaviour. Aphra's conclusion makes the connection clear: these pretences of love, she says, 'reach the desire only, and are cured by possessing, while the short-lived passion betrays the cheat'. Fashion had left love form without substance. (*Works*, Vol V, p 72).

The vision of free love that Aphra opposed to the wits' libertinism was based on a philosophical system that underlies much of her writing: social convention, she held – whether the convention of modesty or that of liberated conformity – had denatured instinct. Aphra's moral system defined what was right as what came naturally. Society and its morality, based on false assumptions, were responsible for the corruption of relations between the sexes. And she was quite sure which sex was responsible for the false assumptions and the conventions.

This logic is very much present in Aphra's play, *The Amorous Prince*. The heroine is a young woman, Chloris, who has been brought up in the country, away from all society, in perfect innocence. She is seduced by a prince, Frederick, who promises to marry her but leaves on the excuse that business at court requires him. Chloris is so naïve that she is not even aware that she has done anything wrong. When another woman friend asks her whether she has given up her 'maidenhead', Chloris replies: 'What's that?' 'A thing young gallants long extremely for', the worldly-wise Lucia tells her, 'and when they have it too, they say they care not a daisy for the giver.' Indeed, it very soon appears that the prince is the model of a Restoration gallant – he had cynically used Chloris and now moves on to other seductions. What is more, he looks down on her because she has neither title nor fortune to barter for marriage. He repents his hard-hearted behaviour, however, when he receives the false information that Chloris has committed suicide. Once he believes her dead, his affection blossoms. When she makes an unexpected and sudden return, the prince is prevailed upon by her brother to marry her. The moral of the story is stated in the epilogue. Addressing the women of the audience, Chloris makes an apology for her lack of modesty: 'Ladies, the Prince was kind at last,/ But all the danger is not past;/ I cannot happy be till you approve/ My hasty condescension to his love./ 'Twas want of art, not virtue, was my crime;/ And that's, I vow, the author's fault, not mine./ She might have made the women pitiless,/ But that had harder been to me than this:/ . . . simple nature never taught the way/ To hide those passions which she must obey.' Aphra's point is that Chloris's virtue is actually far superior to that of her lover, who has after all only acted according to its customs. The degrading intrusion of economic consideration into relations between the sexes would prove a familiar theme in all of Aphra Behn's work.

In addition to inventing herself as the first woman to make a profession of writing in the English language, Aphra also proved to be the first woman to openly discuss sexual matters in print. The position she had taken against the double-standard, as well as her espousal of sexual freedom for women, would make her name a scandal to the generation that came after. In the next 100 years, the principle that what was not decent ought not to be read came to dominate, and Aphra's works fell out of currency. It was not until the beginning of the twentieth century that any work of hers came reasonably within the reach of a curious reader who might have come across her name and wish to read something she had written. In 1905, Ernest Baker published some of Mrs Behn's novels under the imprint of a collection called 'Half-Forgotten Books'. Predictably, most of the titles in this collection were by women. Mr Baker's preface to Aphra Behn's novel explained that since the relaxing of moral strictures in the last few years had made the author's work 'less offensive to modern taste', it could now be reprinted without creating great scandal.

How fortunate we are to have her back among us now.

Notes

1   See my argument concerning the contradictions in accounts of Aphra Behn's birth, in *Reconstructing Aphra: a Social Biography of Aphra Behn*, Oxford University Press, Oxford, 1980.
2   Aphra Behn, *Works*, ed Montague Summers, London, 1913. All further quotes from Aphra Behn's works are from this edition.
3   Letter to Dorothy Osborne [Temple], printed in *Martha, Lady Gifford: her Life and Correspondence (1664–1722)*, ed Julia Longe, London, 1911, pp 38–42.
4   Margaret Cavendish 'To the Lord Marquis of Newcastle' prefacing *Philosophical Letters*, London, 1664, unpaginated.

Mary Astell:
Inspired by Ideas
(1668–1731)

Joan K. Kinnaird*

In 1675 Mrs Hannah Woolley, schoolmistress and writer of books on cookery and household management, published *The Gentlewoman's Companion*. Her introduction contains this unexpected diatribe:

> The right Education of the Female Sex, as it is in a manner everywhere neglected, so it ought to be generally lamented. Most in this depraved later Age think a Woman learned and wise enough if she can distinguish her Husbands Bed from anothers. Certainly Mans Soul cannot boast of a more sublime Original than ours, they had equally their efflux from the same eternal Immensity, and (are) therefore capable of the same improvement by good Education. Vain man is apt to think we were meerly intended for the Worlds propogation, and to keep its humane inhabitants sweet and clean; but by their leaves, had we the same Literature, he would find our brains as fruitful as our bodies. Hence I am induced to believe, we are debar'd from the knowledge of humane learning lest our pregnant Wits should rival the towring conceits of our insulting Lords and Masters. (1675, p 2)

Mrs Woolley's complaint was intended for a female audience only, but the themes of her indictment – male oppression, the equal intellectual capacity of the sexes, the injustice of barring women from higher learning – appear openly and often in the literature of Restoration England. Rebellious daughters and emancipated wives, 'she-philosophers' – all rebels against male authority – crowd the Restoration stage. So many took up the cause of women in the 'Battle of the

* An earlier version of this article, entitled 'Mary Astell and the Conservative Contribution to English Feminism' appeared in *The Journal of British Studies* Volume XIX, Number 1, Fall 1979, pp 53–75. The generous permisson to reprint here is gratefully acknowledged.

Sexes' in the last decades of the century that A. H. Upham (1913) has found in the pamphlet literature of the time 'a large and well defined movement, an early "liberation war" of the sex' (p 262). Finally, in 1694 – after numerous other comparable claims had been made by women – Mary Astell, self-styled 'Lover of Her Sex', published the first considered plea by an Englishwoman for the establishment of an institution of higher learning for women, *A Serious Proposal to the Ladies for the Advancement of Their True and Greatest Interest.*

Criticism of women's education was not new; it had been growing since the sixteenth century, and others before Mary Astell had claimed women's right to higher learning. Most notable among them were Anna Maria von Schurman, whose work appeared in English translation in 1659 as *The Learned Maid*; or, *Whether a Maid May Be a Scholar*, and Mrs Bathsua Makin, author of *An Essay to Revive the Ancient Education of Gentlewomen in Religion, Manners, Arts and Tongues* (1673).[1] But Mary Astell alone proposed an *institution* of higher learning, for von Schurman spoke of private education and Mrs Makin of boarding schools for 'gentlewomen' of eight and nine years of age.

Confronting the understanding that as early as the Restoration period there were *many* women active on behalf of their sex, women who were challenging the entrenched beliefs about female inferiority – particularly intellectual inferiority – and who were protesting about women's exclusion from learning, raises numerous questions. First, there is the question of the origin of their ideas; by what means did they come to see through the prevailing 'truths' and to find grounds for the formulation of their own rebellious alternatives? Second, if there was 'a large and well defined' women's movement during the Restoration period, could it be that it was the 1600s and not the 1960s that was the era in which feminism was born? And third, what is the significance of this omission of women's protest from the mainstream historical records; what process of selection has been at work – and why – that we could have been led to believe that feminism is a fairly recent invention?

Tracing the sources of the ideas of these 'zealous feminists' of the Restoration is no simple task and not just because there are always difficulties in attempting to determine the origin of an individual's consciousness; in this case it is complicated by the fact that some of the 'explanations' that have been put forward to account for women's protest seem inadequate and inappropriate.

Briefly, within 'conventional' sources it has been suggested by those such as George Ascoli (1906), Jean Gagen (1954), Lawrence

Stone (1977) and Keith Thomas (1968) that the period was one in which many established traditions were being questioned, where secular sanctions were being substituted for divine ones, and where women's protest was part of an overall process of questioning the basis of existing social arrangements. But as is so often the case when attempts are made to fit women into the schemata designed primarily to describe and explain men's actions, this proves to be an unsatisfactory interpretation of women's actions.

For example, Mary Astell, considered to be the first major English feminist for her defiant praise of women, who challenged many of the concepts about women and their capabilities, had little or no sympathy with Puritanism, secularism, or Lockean political thought, despite the fact that these constituted the basic framework in which existing traditions were being questioned. It becomes something of a puzzle, then, to see how Astell's protest can be explained as part of this movement with which she had no sympathy. For far from following the libertarian or anti-establishment trends, Astell reveals that she was a staunch loyalist and a fervid defender of the Church of England. So, paradoxical as it may seem in 'conventional' terms, it is more likely that feminism in its early phase, owed as much, if not more likely that feminism in its early phase owed as much, if not authoritarian and secular impulses in Restoration culture.

Mary Astell, her eighteenth-century biographer George Ballard observed, loved obscurity, 'which she courted and doated (*sic*) on beyond all earthly blessings', and was 'ambitious to slide gently through the world, without so much as being seen or taken notice of' (1775, p 308). A suitably worthy aim for a modest woman of her time. As far as her private life is concerned, she almost did succeed in this wish for very little is known about her personal history. She was born at Newcastle in 1668 into a gentry family of royalist sympathy that included lawyers and clergymen, as well as merchants. Ralph Astell, a clergyman uncle, supposedly educated the bright young girl until his death in her early teens. In her twenties, orphaned after the death of her mother, she left home – even though a brother, Peter, continued to live in Newcastle – and moved to London. By 1695 she was settled in Chelsea. For a time she was an independent householder but later joined the household of the daughter of the Earl of Ranelagh, Lady Catherine Jones, with whom presumably Mary Astell lived until her death in 1731. Mary Astell never married; George Ballard reports that she was disappointed by the breakdown of marriage negotiations with an eminent clergyman (p 449–50); her own writing indicates that she was extremely critical of the institution of marriage.

Her circle consisted mainly of Anglican divines whom she joined in theological debate and in literary warfare against the Dissenters, earning thereby a reputation as an 'ingenious' lady and a formidable polemicist. (One obituary notice in 1731 describes her as 'a Gentlewoman very much admired for several ingenious Pieces . . . in the cause of Religion and Virtue' and praises her 'elevated mind' and 'Turn of Genius above what is usual in her own Sex, and not unworthy of the most distinguished Writers of the Other', Salter, 1915, p 426.)

She attracted the friendship of a number of brilliant young women. Besides Lady Catherine Jones, her feminine disciples included Lady Elizabeth Hastings (she who inspired the compliment, 'To love her is a liberal education'); Lady Elizabeth's four half sisters; Lady Ann Coventry, author of devotional tracts; and Catherine Atterbury, wife of Frances Atterbury the prominent Tory and high church divine. There was Elizabeth Elstob,[2] the Anglo-Saxon scholar, who came from Newcastle and probably knew the Astell family there. During her years in London, Elizabeth Elstob visited Mary Astell frequently and later furnished George Ballard with many details on Mary Astell's life. Twenty years younger, but especially dear to Mary Astell, was the future Lady Mary Wortley Montagu, who in later life testified to the influence Astell had upon her during her early years.

There are fleeting glimpses of the feminist's life in Chelsea. Spying from her window idle visitors come for 'chatt and tattle' she leans out to announce that 'Mrs Astell is not at home' (Ballard, 1775, p 309), not suffering such triflers to make inroads upon her more serious hours. More graciously she receives the young antiquarian, Ralph Thoresby, who had come with the 'obliging Mr Croft, the minister who introduced me to the celebrated Mrs Astell' (Hunter, 1830, p 161). At dinner she argues divinity with Dean Atterbury, no stranger to polemics, who admires her intellect but admits ruefully, 'I dread to engage her' (Ballard, 1775, p 312). At tea she sits with the ladies reflecting on the memoirs of her Chelsea neighbour, the Duchess of Mazarin, who serves 'as an unhappy Shipwreck to point out the Misfortune of an ill Education and unsuitable Marriage' (p 312). An interest in science prompts a visit to Sir Hans Sloane to see his curios and to show him some of hers. She walks through the fields of Chelsea with Lady Elizabeth Hastings to consider possible sites for a school for girls. Dramatically she confronts Lady Mary Wortley Montagu with the promise that she will return from the dead, if possible, to prove the truths of the Christian religion to her sceptical young friend (Halsband, 1956, p 118). And on many a Sunday morning, despite inclement weather, she is seen walking from

Chelsea to St Martin's to hear a celebrated preacher. In the last years, too, there are moving glimpses of Mary Astell stoically enduring an operation for cancer and dying some time later (in 1731) alone – having barred her friends in the last days – with a coffin and shroud set by the bed to fix her mind upon eternity (Ballard, 1775, pp 315, 317).

The glimpses are few for a life that spanned 65 years. But if obscurity cloaked her personal life, it certainly did not hide her militant views. In 1695 the Platonist divine, John Norris, rector of Bemerton, won her permission to publish their correspondence, *Letters Concerning the Love of God*, so long as he did not reveal her identity. Mary Astell had initiated that correspondence two years before, and in her first letter struck a note of feminine assertiveness that would echo through all subsequent writings:

> Sir,
> Though some morose Gentlemen wou'd perhaps remit me to the Distaff or the Kitchin, or at least to the Glass and the Needle, the proper Employments as they fancy of a Woman's Life; yet expecting better things from the more Equitable and ingenuous Mr Norris, who is not so narrow-Soul'd as to confine Learning to his own Sex, or to envy it in ours, I presume to beg his Attention a little to the Impertinencies of a Woman's Pen. (*Letters*, pp 1–2)

The early correspondence with Norris reveals as well an identification with her sex as a whole and a personal commitment to the advancement of women that mark the feminist. It is these characteristics which distinguish the feminist from the two other related species – on the one hand, the 'learned lady' who, while often critical of males, is concerned only with her own pursuits; and on the other hand, the dissident or unconventional woman whose behaviour may violate society's norms but who feels no need to protest or improve the conditions of women in her society. By contrast, Mary Astell was a feminist, a woman with a mission; 'Fain wou'd I rescue my Sex' she declared resolutely, 'or at least as many of them as come within my Sphere from that Meanness of Spirit into which the Genrality of 'em are sunk' (*Letters*, p 49).

Dean Atterbury once regretted that Mrs Astell had not the 'most decent manner of insinuating what she means, but is now and then a little offensive and shocking in her expressions'; she lacked, he found, 'a civil turn of words' (Ballard, 1775, p 312). Nowhere are the directness and asperity of which Atterbury complains more apparent than in her censure of meanness of spirit in the female sex. Mrs Astell upbraided the gentlewomen of her day, all too many of whom were 'content to be Cyphers in the World, useless at the best, and in a little time a burden and nuisance to all about them'. Their conversation was insipid, 'idle twattle and uncharitable Remarks', and their company tedious. Preoccupied with fashion, their bodies were 'Glorious Temples which enshrine no better than Aegyptian Deities'; they were like to the 'garnish'd Sepulchre, which for all its glittering, has nothing within but emptiness or putrefaction!' In her ire, the metaphors spill forth in reckless profusion. 'How can you be content' she rails, 'to be in the World like Tulips in a Garden, to make a fine shew and be good for nothing?' Women must wake to a new consciousness of their worth:

> For shame let's abandon that *Old*, and therefore one wou'd think, unfashionable employment of pursuing Butter-flies and Trifles! No longer drudge on in the dull beaten road of Vanity and Folly which so many have gone before us, but dare to break the enchanted Circle that custom has plac'd us in. (*Serious Proposal*, part 1, p 6; part 2, p 131; part 1, p 3)

Perhaps not Atterbury's 'civil turn of words' – but confused metaphors notwithstanding, a dramatic manifesto.

But before Mary Astell could rescue other women, she herself had to be freed. What had liberated her own consciousness and empowered her to break through custom's 'enchanted Circle'?

The answer perhaps startles the modern reader – at first – for other than feminism we are not used to seeing systems of thought as effectual agents of change. Yet the magic charm for Mary Astell was nothing less than philosophy. 'I have courted Truth', she exulted, 'with a kind of Romantick Passion' (*Letters*, p 78). And the truth that she courted and that made her free was a heady blend of Cartesian and Platonic principles.

The Cartesian philosophy fostered an introspective psychology, a radical consciousness of self – important to the growth of feminism – by its insistence on the thinking *I* as the touchstone of all knowledge and even of existence. Here was a philosophy that began not with revelation or the wisdom of the ancients or even with nature and sense experience but with consciousness itself. And here was a philosophy not presented in elaborate academic discourse but in a personal memoir of autobiographical fragments, anecdotes, observations and reflections.

The parallels with contemporary feminist philosophy are quite remarkable and the method seems to have been just as effective then as it is today.

Descartes had argued that reason was by nature equal in all men, for since reason alone distinguished men from brutes it must be found complete in each individual. It was this notion that the feminists seized upon so avidly. Mary Astell boldly proclaimed the radical thesis that God had given all mankind the same intellectual potential – whether ancient or modern, rich or poor, male or female. Circumstances determine the extent to which men and women may exercise their rational faculties, but the faculties are present in all, at least as 'sleeping powers' (*Serious Proposal*, part 1, p 29).

Descartes had also decided that it was necessary to sweep away the rubble and begin anew with the knowledge tested in the crucible of self discovery, and for women like Astell, who had not enjoyed the same educational opportunities as men, this was indeed an attractive philosophy for it made her lack of formal education no disadvantage. Such a theory not only bolstered Astell's confidence, she was also able to use it to bolster the confidence of other women.

Mary Astell's third debt to Descartes was in the realm of methodology for she was won to the cause of 'right thinking', to the pursuit of rigorous analysis and orderly progression of thought that made it possible to sweep away misconceptions, prejudices and outworn beliefs. And so fortified with faith in the equal intellectual capacity of the sexes and the authority of the thinking self and secure in a supportive methodology, Mary Astell could dismiss with almost flippant ease conventional arguments about the inferiority of women. To those who argued that men were physically superior to women and that strength of mind accompanied strength of body, she responded wryly, 'tis only for some odd Accidents which philosophers have not yet thought worthwhile to enquire into, that the sturdiest Porter is not yet the wisest Man!' (*Some Reflections*, p 86).

If women did not appear often in the pages of history perhaps it was because men, not women, wrote those histories. And on the rare occasions where they condescended to record the great and good actions of women, men usually said that such women acted above their sex, as much as to say that not women but 'Men in petticoats' had performed them (*Christian Religion*, p 206). An unbiased review of nations past, she contended, would reveal that nations, especially the English, had flourished more under feminine than under masculine governance; her seventeenth-century understandings have modern overtones.

Mary Astell prided herself on her modernity and her self-reliance, and that pride shines through her account of how she had ventured forth, unaided by authority, on the doubtful mission of rescuing her sex; she could see full well the flighty existence that women led but asserted that there was an alternative. That was why she wanted an institution of learning for women.

Some of her ideas, of course, we would not find so very attractive today, for while she wanted women to withdraw from the superficial social life they enjoyed and to set their minds upon higher things, she does not go so far as to argue for women's acceptance in public life. She was scornful of the ornamental role that women played, but not of their characteristics of being the mainstay of the private sphere.

That she herself had no time for the niceties of fashionable elegance is revealed by an incident when a commentator, discussing *A Serious Proposal* (and obviously experiencing a mind-set about women), referred to her as a 'fair and elegant lady of quality' to which Lady Louisa Steuart (Lady Mary Wortley Montagu's granddaughter) responded with derisive glee:

> This fair and elegant lady of quality was no less a person than Mistress Mary Astell, of learned memory, the Madonells of the Tatler, a very pious, exemplary woman and a profound scholar, but as far from fair and elegant as any old schoolmaster of her time; in outward form, indeed rather ill-favoured and forbidding, and of a humour to have repulsed the compliment roughly had it been paid to her while she lived. (Quoted in Smith, 1916, pp 15–16)

Lady Louisa's description rings true, and it finds an echo in other biographical accounts. There one feels with an absolute certainty is the Mary Astell who in *Bart'lemy Fair* could denounce with waspish severity the Earl of Shaftesbury and the dissolute wits of the Kit-Kat Club. There is the Mary Astell who could needle Richard Steele – no foe to women's rights – into ungenerous satire in *The Tatler*.[3] There too is the fearsome polemicist who trounced Daniel Defoe for his dissenting views. Dean Atterbury, who had winced often enough beneath her criticism ('She strikes me very home, you see'), would recognise *that* Mary Astell (Ballard, 1775, p 312).

Mary Astell was often very critical of men; she chided women for deriving their image of self worth from male esteem and for failing to realise that they were 'capable of Nobler Things than the pitiful Conquest of some worthless heart'. Men, she was fond of declaiming, had for centuries deliberately kept women sunk in folly and ignorance that they might tyrannise over them. Yet despite her anger against men she never challenged their God given right to rule the family, and the seventeenth-century view that the wife belonged to her husband echoes in many of her statements. Not the least of matrimony's advantages, Mrs Astell tartly observed, is the preparation it offers long suffering women for sainthood.

The rights Mary Astell recognised for women with respect to matrimony applied *before* women were married: a woman had the right to reject a suitor whom she could not in good faith hope to love, and the right to remain single. Like other feminists and moralists of her time, she spoke out against the 'marriage market' and the practice of parents and guardians who were so concerned with property settlements or social advantage that they forced their unwilling charges into marriages with detested partners. 'They only who have felt it, know the Misery of being forc'd to marry where they do not love' (*Some Reflections*, p 7). More poignantly still she depicted the plight of the aging unmarried woman in a society that afforded women no real alternative to matrimony. All too often lacking spiritual and intellectual resources to draw upon, the 'superannuated virgin' was a tragic figure to contemplate. This was one of the reasons for her desire to establish a women's college, where such women would find a place and a purpose – much like the nunneries of old, but free from compulsory vows.

To Mary Astell, England's institutions were admirable, but unfortunately human nature – or at least male nature – was not. When Mary Astell reviewed the social order she found noble institutions and noble aims corrupted by ignoble men. The institution of marriage was to her reasonable, for example, but certain 'abuses' had arisen which needed to be eliminated. England lived in a degenerate age, and reform would come not with a change in institutions but with a change in hearts. What was needed was a moral reformation and in that reformation English gentlewomen would have a mission to perform. If they gave up their frivolous and ornamental lives and began to acquire knowledge and virtue (through education) their wisdom would help to counter the growing degeneracy.

Their sphere of action would be the family. Mary Astell was not interested in freeing women from domestic tyranny to send them forth into the world. The ladies in her opinion were too much in the world already. Rather she was intent on summoning them home – home from the play houses and pleasure gardens, from the tea tables and card tables – home to their proper sphere, the family and the hearth.

While she espoused the values of the family she was anything but a traditionalist in her concept of the gentlewoman's role within the patriarchal structure. She belongs in the ranks of those seventeenth-century reformers who promoted an enlightened ideal of marriage as rational and companionate and who elevated the status of women in marriage by assigning to them responsibility for perpetuating those values and virtues that can alone sustain society. Much more than other reformers, however, Mary Astell insisted on the need to educate women to their responsibilities in marriage. Men acted against their own best interest she argued when they set up 'the Scare-Crow of Ridicule to fright women from the Tree of Knowledge', for only a woman of ingenious education could build a strong and happy marriage. Such an education would also produce effective mothers. Astell decried the seventeenth-century practice of the wealthy of turning the young over to wet nurses and servants and in the new reform tradition urged women to nurse their infants and to watch over their children in the formative years. The proper rearing of children was a noble calling she argued, and it was the mother's prime responsibility.

> For Fathers find other business. They will not be confined to such laborious work, they have not such opportunities of observing a child's temper, nor are the greatest part of 'em like to do much good, since precepts contradicted by Example seldom prove effectual. (*Serious Proposal*, p 38)

Mary Astell could never resist the feminist barb!

This was her feminist vision; a mingling of radical feminist zeal with a conservative programme. Her feminism was not born of liberal impulses but of conservative values. She preached not women's rights but women's duties – at a time when women were not thought worthy of duties and when they were accorded no role in the transmission of social values to the young.

A review of her career makes it possible to comment on the nature and scope of English feminism or protofeminism. Feminism associated with the late nineteenth century is the doctrine of the complete equality of the sexes. Such seventeenth-century protofeminists as Mary Astell, Hannah Woolley and Lady Mary Chudleigh made no such claim; they preached the equality of 'souls' (as did Mary Wollstonecraft who made a transition to also preaching equality of rights), and hence according to the understandings of the time, equality of the rational faculties. As a matter of course they seem to have accepted the idea of masculine and feminine natures. Men and women differed physically and since emotions were rooted in the body, it followed that the two sexes enjoyed different temperaments, different sensibilities and different gifts. In short, the sexes were equal in dignity and in moral responsibility, but different in their equivalence – and so in their appointed tasks.

Imbued as she was with the corporate view of society, believing firmly in the legitimacy of degree, priority and place in the social order, enthralled with the rational design of the universe, Mary Astell preached the authority of the thinking self only to free women from the tyranny of ignorance and social frivolity so that they might realise in their sphere their full potential as wives, mothers and teachers of the young. That later generations might use the arguments to *challenge* the established order was beyond the reach of her imagination. In the nineteenth century feminists would spurn the notion of distinct natures and distinct spheres as they claimed for women the right to participate fully in public life; by that time they would look upon domestic duties and virtues as a mark of the subjugation of women. And in our time they have attacked 'the feminine mystique' as an expression of male chauvinism, quite unaware that this mystique had been, to a large extent, the conscious creation of the early English feminists. Ironically, if inevitably, many of the origins of feminism have been obscured and we have been prevented from recognising that it was not only the 'radical' movements among men but more importantly the 'conservative' movements among women which promoted the dignity of women, educational reform and the ideal of companionate marriage as one stage in the development of women's struggle for emancipation. Yet the seventeenth-century words of Mary Astell still have the ring of relevance.

Notes

1   For further discussion of these women, see J.R. Brink, (1980).
2   *An Essay in Defence of the Female Sex*, 1696, now generally attributed to Judith Drake rather than Astell, see Florence Smith, 1916, app II pp 173–182.
3   For reprints of some extracts see Katharine M Rogers, 1979

Selected Works of Mary Astell

A Serious Proposal to the Ladies for the Advancement of Their True and Greatest Interest, London, 1694, 1697, 1701.

Letters Concerning the Love of God Between the Author of the Proposal to the Ladies and Mr John Norris, London, 1695.

Some Reflections Upon Marriage, London, 1700.

Moderation Truly Stated: or a Review of a Late Pamphlet Entitul'd Moderation a Vertue with a Prefatory Discourse to Dr D'Avenant Concerning His Late Essays on Peace and War, London, 1704.

A Fair Way with the Dissenters and Their Patrons, London, 1704.

An Impartial Enquiry into the Causes of Rebellion and Civil War in This Kingdom, London, 1704.

The Christian Religion as Profess'd by a Daughter of the Church of England, London, 1705

Bart'lemy Fair or an Enquiry after Wit, London, 1709.

Mary Wollstonecraft:
Sexuality and Women's Rights
(1759–1797)

Miriam Brody

Ironically Mary Wollstonecraft's *Vindication of the Rights of Woman*, an argument advocating the supremacy of reason in guiding human affairs, was buried under a torrent of abuse, directed less at the writing than at the writer. Wollstonecraft's work, written at the time of the French Revolution, urged the liberals of her day, compatriots in the great task of overthrowing what they believed together was decadent aristocratic privilege, to extend the rights of man – citizenship – to women. It is perhaps understandable that her conservative political enemies reacted vituperatively, as did Horace Walpole who thought the idea of women's rights to be so unnatural that its advocate must be herself a 'hyena in petticoats', or as did Hannah More, who helped to bolster the somewhat shaking ranks of privilege in the English countryside with her dissemination of evangelical tracts. More declared the idea of women's rights to citizenship – to vote, to perhaps even hold public office – was so inherently ridiculous, she would not bother to read the *Vindication*.

What is perhaps more surprising to the contemporary reader is that Wollstonecraft's ideas appeared tainted to so many feminists throughout much of the century which followed their publication. For while she was invoked occasionally, with enthusiasm by her contemporary, Abigail Adams, with eulogies as a martyr by Elizabeth Cady Stanton, with admiration by Virginia Woolf, for the most part the women's rights campaigns in the nineteenth and twentieth centuries ignored their indebtedness to this brave and early argument.

Wollstonecraft's life overshadowed her argument. To assuage his own great grief, her husband, the political philosopher William Godwin, published shortly after her death his own candid memoirs of her life, making public to a large reading audience her long and unhappy love affair with Gilbert Imlay, the birth of their child, her desperate suicide attempts. The affront to conventional morality which was Wollstonecraft's life easily fanned the fires of conservative opposition to women's rights. To be a Mary Wollstonecraft and to advocate women's rights was to forsake all conventional virtues, was to shake the foundation of the family itself.

In fighting for limited reforms, the vote, admission to university, reform of marriage laws, feminists abandoned Wollstonecraft so as not to bring down upon their own heads the opprobrium of being thought sexually wanton. Ironically, to read the *Vindication of the Rights of Woman* is to discover Wollstonecraft is as careful and restrained in her description of sexual virtue as a Hannah More could have wished her to be. At the same time, to her everlasting credit and distinguishing herself from legions of female reform-advocates who preceded her, Wollstonecraft makes abundantly clear that a 'morality' which depends upon the violation of women's rights is no morality at all.

The issue raised by the virtual disappearance of Mary Wollstonecraft until recent years is very much still with us. Feminists who enter this debate over ideas ignore this equation at their peril. For once again anti-feminists raise the spectre that the advocacy of women's rights is the advocacy of wanton hedonism, of selfish abandonment of socially-necessary responsibilities. Mary Wollstonecraft, could she answer her detractors, would never yield the argument that all moral evil begins in patriarchy, that it is to feminists we must look to carve out an ethical standard for our human community.

The 'Dolphin' and the Moralist – the Wollstonecraft Problem

There are two Mary Wollstonecrafts – one who loved and one who was contemptuous of love. The first is the woman Virginia Woolf called a 'dolphin', a creature who 'rushed Gilbert Imlay through the waters until he was dizzy and only wanted to escape' (1932, p 160), the same woman who would attempt suicide to end the despair of her unrequited love for him. The second is the woman who wrote the feminist argument of the *Vindication*, recommending passionless friendship between husband and wife, hoping that the fires of sexual love will cool by the time the marriage is well established so the couple can get on with the rest of their life. Not this prim moralist, but the despairing, love-stricken Wollstonecraft of the *Love Letters* (1908) has won the sympathy and excited the imagination of our twentieth-century contemporaries. That vision of Wollstonecraft was also useful to the anti-feminist moralists of her own time and of the nineteenth

century, moralists who were pleased to affirm that the wages of sin
and of pernicious feminist doctrine had taken so painfully their toll on
Wollstonecraft's life.

Indeed the nineteenth-century readers, who had been presented
almost exclusively with the popular image of Wollstonecraft as despairing social pariah, found when they came of their own accord to
the *Vindication* a mild surprise that the 'other' Wollstonecraft existed
at all – moral, judicious, and, it would appear, carefully sceptical of
any intrinsic value in sexual pleasure for its own sake. It is tempting to
dismiss this apparently prudish Wollstonecraft of the *Vindication* and
dwell on the self-evidently significant argument of the substance of
the work – the extension of the Enlightenment credo of the rights of
man to woman. But what seems to be a paradoxical relationship
between the two Wollstonecrafts is an interesting incongruity to
question, particularly because in the questioning we may come closer
to an understanding of the possibilities a feminist thinker has in her
own time for constructing a theory of sexuality and family life.[1]

Wollstonecraft was not alone, of course, in arguing that romantic
love is dangerous – to individuals, to society; but it was for
Wollstonecraft to argue that such love posed a particular danger for
persons who wished to advance women's rights. While for individuals
romantic love might indeed lead, as it did in her own life, to despairing attempts at self-destruction, or to other abuses of reason,
Wollstonecraft comes to argue in the *Vindication* that insofar as
society is concerned, romantic love, based as it is in sexual passion,
can undermine and corrode the order on which civil and egalitarian
relationships are to be based.

When Mary Wollstonecraft moves within her own argument to
suggest restraint and control over sexual energy, she advances the
supremacy of reason and rational behaviour as if the elaborate edifice
of society and the intricacies of relationships between the sexes within
this edifice would remain in a workable functional balance only if
sexual passion were allowed its brief intense moment – and then were
heard from no more. There was no need for her to justify the brief
reign of 'passion'; for it to die soon was in her vocabulary 'natural',
unless one was 'vitiated' by improper education. To understand the
degree of disorder which she envisioned would or did flow from
unrestrained sexuality, and its harmfulness to women's rights, we
must know more about the source of these ideas and the rich tradition
which gave them voice before Wollstonecraft. In caring so deeply for
order and writing implicitly as if an abyss of chaos yawned just
beneath a homestead founded and maintained on sexual feeling,

Mary Wollstonecraft was helping to pass on a set of attitudes inherited from her puritan forebears and Enlightenment contemporaries.

She did not, however, pass these ideas on unaltered. The *Vindication of the Rights of Woman* is more than simply an assault on the conventional belief in the double standard of sexual behaviour writ large in eighteenth-century sexual ideology. Wollstonecraft's argument advances a theory of human sexuality such that she may incorporate into the human social scheme the imperative of women's education, the beginning point, she believed, for women's ultimate civic and political emancipation.

To read Wollstonecraft fully and to appreciate the linkage of her ideas on sexuality and women's rights, readers must also come to the argument aware of it as a feminist response to a particular set of historical conditions, material and ideological – and we must be wary, in our search for its contemporary significance, not to superimpose upon it ideas current and connected to our own historical condition. This understanding of the historical relativity of ideas is important insofar as feminist historians have been much interested in concepts of public and private spheres in interpreting women's history. A close reading of the *Vindication* reveals that Wollstonecraft makes also a particular use of notions of public and private spheres, but in a manner appropriate for her own argument and her own times. Contemporary interpretations of 'public' as 'in the marketplace' and 'private' as 'in the home' blur the way these realms were related for her and conceal her particular assault on patriarchal ideology.

In connecting the issue of sexuality to feminism, Wollstonecraft does not argue for the sexual liberation of women; her contribution to feminist argument was to use traditional and contemporary notions of disdain for sexual passion to forge a new interpretation of the civic significance of domestic life.

This reading of the *Vindication* suggests that Wollstonecraft's interpretation of domestic life eschews rigid boundaries between public and private life, arguing instead that domestic life be newly understood as connected to the political life of the state. By working to weaken these boundaries, Wollstonecraft is claiming the needs of the state are the needs of the home – rational inhabitants. The particular 'right' of women, for which Wollstonecraft argues, is the right to be educated; but the roots of this privilege extend deeply into the foundation of society, into the relationship of home and state, as Wollstonecraft conceives human social life. The acknowledgement of this single right brings into a new focus the social vision of family life.

Giving a new focus to public and private spheres, Wollstonecraft is making a more important argument than traditional criticism has implied in seeing her essentially as a reformer who accepted the patriarchal sexual division of labour. Rather than simply a traditional liberal feminist, Wollstonecraft exposes a more radical dimension in her argument; for in the sharp dichotomy she draws between public and private, it is the life of passion outside the body politic which becomes the antithesis of the life of reason. In particular it is male passion, or sensuality, which she identifies as responsible for the political subordination of women, moving closer as she makes this argument to the more radical feminist analysis of women as a sex class and implying that the sexual politics of domestic life must be inevitably oppressive to women in patriarchal societies.

Advancing a definition of public and private spheres which makes sense for the *Vindication*, Wollstonecraft makes her argument on sexuality compatible with an idea of human virtue – an idea which is itself a blend of Enlightenment notions of woman as citizen and romantic notions of woman as mother. If, as some critics have suggested, the contemporary feminist debate suffers from a failure to make progressive arguments on a theory of sexuality and the family, leaving only the anti-feminists to compose models for these issues, we might turn once again to admire Mary Wollstonecraft: she did not falter from an attempt to make of these ideas a feminist argument.

The Tie is Equal: Puritan Restraint, Romantic Feeling, and Enlightenment Reason

The traditions which inform Wollstonecraft's work are Enlightenment, early Romanticism (she appears to anticipate the Romantic movement and is contemporary with the strain in eighteenth-century society which was sympathetic to it) and Puritan. Her Enlightenment convictions tell her that all is possible for human societies if we strive mightily to discover truth through reason; her early Romantic sympathies that 'sensibility is the most exquisite feeling of which the human soul is susceptible' (Wollstonecraft, 1788, p 145), reminding us that she accepted with the poets who would follow her that a higher form of truth was available through the exercise of imagination. Any reader of Wollstonecraft recognises the theme running through all her work which celebrated nature and delighted in effusions of sentiment. *The Vindication of the Rights of Woman*, though it is not the work in which this feeling is most evident, does bear the imprint of her early Romantic sympathies in its recommendations for the education of children and, most significant for us, in its descriptions of domestic life. By keeping these sympathies carefully subordinated to her

Enlightenment respect for reason she provides in fact a living example of the very hierarchy she would recommend as consistent with human virtue. But Wollstonecraft is not simply an austere Enlightenment philosopher – she both connects to and distinguishes herself from the Romantic tradition which followed her, particularly as this tradition shaped attitudes towards women in the home.

Both the Enlightenment and early Romantic traditions are at play with each other in the pages of the *Vindication* as Wollstonecraft works to discover an ideal of virtuous behaviour which is appropriate for both sexes. This ideal comes to understand sexual and family life as bearing a relationship to each other so that the whole of society will benefit; setting forth this relationship, she brings into focus older themes of Puritan ideology.

The double standard of sexual morality, presumably to maintain family inheritance to property without the aspersion of illegitimacy, is acknowledged in much eighteenth-century literature as sound and proper morality. But such advice, even as it has held sway into our own time, has always been at odds with Christian doctrine. As Puritan writers interpreted such doctrine, they wrote: '. . . think not thy husband tied to this rule, O Woman; nor thou the wife tied, O Husband, and the other free: the tie is equal.'[2] Wollstonecraft descends directly from Puritan orthodoxy in this matter, even as do other Christian reformers. In their common inheritance, Wollstonecraft and evangelical contemporary Hannah More can sound much like each other as they condemn sexual profligacy and moral degeneration, even though they take their arguments to quite divergent ends with regard to the civic and political emancipation of women (see More, 1799).

At one with the Puritan reformers in attacking the double standard, Wollstonecraft differs with them on what comprises the governing impulse to behave morally. The just civic order which would reasonably be the creation of moral citizens was not merely an ideal, but a workable construction, she argued, for which all citizens are eligible, by virtue of having been born with the capacity to reason.

But in the call to arms to build this civic order, Wollstonecraft once again identifies older Puritan values and distinguishes a model of respectable behaviour to be cast in the eighteenth-century reformist literature as separate from aristocratic viciousness. This literature describes the nascent beginnings of the idea of middle-class respectability, a doctrine of moral behaviour which despised sexual promiscuity as identifiably aristocratic behaviour. Industry, enterprise, self-denial as one made one's own way upward in society were values antipathetical to the expense of time, money, and emotional energy involved in sexual license. If the best of the aristocratic tradition of love was embodied in the medieval notion of courtly love, such a tradition had been distinctly at odds with hopes for love in married life – a relation of property at best. By contrast, the middle-class ideology of marriage begins to invest expectation of emotional satisfaction in married life and imposes sexual boundaries to safeguard these expectations.[3]

In Wollstonecraft's descriptions of married bliss we see the unfolding of the new middle-class idea: husband and wife sufficient unto each other, engaged in great enterprise for the family and the society's order and prosperity. Rather than sexual adventure outside marriage, the ideal demanded fidelity and chastity for men and women. In discussing the ideal of chastity, however, moral reformers differed from Wollstonecraft both in their idea of female purity and in their assessment of whose chastity, male's or female's, must necessarily come first.

The ideal of female purity was slowly taking form out of a welter of Jacobean and Augustan misogynist literature degrading to women. Respect for the property of middle-class men translated historically into respect for the chastity of their daughters and wives. While the *Vindication* concerns itself with the idea of chastity, the argument parts company dramatically with the new feminine ideal, embodied in such a heroine as Pamela, 'delicate, insipid, fainting . . . and void of all feeling until marriage' (Thomas, 1959, p 207). Even while Wollstonecraft reacts to and against the degradation of woman's sexuality in eighteenth-century literature, she posits a distinctive model separate from that of such contemporary reformers of manners as Richardson. Indeed, it is argued impressively that much of the relief with which women may have acquiesced in notions of their own sexual apathy – which prevailed in the nineteenth century – stems from the alternative apparently being only to be degraded as a sexual object (see Nancy Cott, 1978).

But Wollstonecraft is not arguing that women are passionless, as in the direction of the new ideology of middle-class respectability. Nor does she argue that women are responsible for the sexual purity of men, as implied by the Christian moral reformers or as evidenced in the heroic withstanding of the muchly-sought-after Pamela, whose final reward by her would-be seducer whom she therefore saves from sin, is marriage to him. Wollstonecraft believes in sexual feeling in women. Indeed it is axiomatic in her work that men and women are created alike in regard to sexual feeling, as they are in rational capacity. Rather than claiming for women the responsibility of reforming men, Wollstonecraft argues that female purity is unattainable as a social ideal without male chastity preceding it.

What Wollstonecraft comes to in the *Vindication* is a vision of reality which satisfies her Romantic sympathies, her training in Enlightenment philosophy and is consistent with the Puritan values that helped to define the anti-aristocratic ideology of the new middle class. The model of order which she creates is of an ideal family life, throwing into new perspective, as she does so, our notions of what constitutes for her public and private spheres. It is the family which will channel feeling, without which life is soulless, diffuse passion, so feeling may be governable, and act as the foundation stone for moral order, such that reason may produce a perfectable society. Without the primacy of reason, there can be no emancipation for women. In the *Vindication of the Rights of Woman* these ideas are woven into a single fabric.

'Forgets the Pleasure of an Awakening Passion': Sexuality and Rational Order in the Vindication

Wollstonecraft's ideas about sexual life between men and women are clear and straightforward: sexual feeling by itself is 'appetite'. 'What are cold, or feverish caresses of appetite,' she asks, 'but sin embracing death, compared with the modest overflowings of a pure heart and exalted imagination?' (1792, 1978, p 316). Sexual feeling is at best transitory, she says '. . . without virtue, a sexual attachment must expire, like a tallow candle in the socket, creating intolerable disgust' (p 317). Such feeling is implanted by nature in us to perpetuate the species '. . . nature by making the gratification of an appetite . . . a natural and imperious law to preserve the species, exalts the appetite and mixes a little mind and affection with a sensual gust' (p 248).

In the *Vindication* Wollstonecraft frequently describes the transmutation of appetite into feelings which alone can lay the foundation for a reasonable and virtuous relationship between the sexes. But before such relationships become possible, men and women must be capable of subordinating the call of appetite to the sovereignty of reason. They must, if need be, exercise self-denial, the traditional Puritan virtue, and overcome sexual feeling, if such feeling is incompatible with what their reason tells them is virtue. In her letters to Gilbert Imlay, Wollstonecraft unhappily found herself frequently needing to deliver him sermons on love and constancy. On one such occasion she wrote:

> The common run of men I know, with strong health and gross appetites, must have variety to banish ennui, because the imagination never lends its magic wand, to convert appetite into love, cemented by according reason . . . They do not exist (these more elevated emotions) without self-denial . . . (they) are the distinctive characteristic of genius, the foundation of taste, and of that exquisite relish for the beauties of nature, of which the common herd of eaters and drinkers and child-begetters, certainly have no idea. (*Letters*, p 101–2).

The capacity to deny appetite or sexual feeling is, then, the foundation of genius; such capacity distinguishes between superior and inferior persons. In her own life time, Godwin wrote, she kept an earlier relationship with the Swiss painter Fuseli platonic because he was married, 'Being true to her own principles that the mind can control sensual pleasures' (1927, p 61).

It is in self-denial that one becomes virtuous, in discovering one's duties over one's pleasures. The control of appetite is linked to the performance of duty, duty which is intrinsically social and links individuals to the social institution of family life. This performance ultimately brings a satisfaction which is its own reward. In understanding the particular emphasis she places on family duties, the connections she will make between domestic duties and civic responsibilities are uncovered. In her most despairing personal moments with Gilbert Imlay, Wollstonecrft applied a measure of virtuous practice to her own life and observed:

> I meet with families continually, who are bound together by affection or principle – and when I am conscious that I have fulfilled the duties of my station, almost to a forgetfulness of myself, I am ready to demand, in a murmuring tone of Heaven 'Why am I thus abandoned?' (*Letters*, p 148)

The transformation of appetite, into a more enduring sentiment, assisted by such 'forgetfulness' of self, binds families together. The transformation established in persons the principles which will insure they will respond to domestic duties. Reading Wollstonecraft on these descriptions of domestic harmony is understanding in her language that there is a social contract among individuals in a family, much as her Enlightenment philosophy tells her there is a social contract among citizens in the state. Just as reason, guiding what is inevitably understood as mutual self-interest among citizens, brings assent to the social contract, so too reason insists that the sentiments which spring forth from and are transmuted from appetite will operate in such a way as to ensure the happiness of individuals in family life. Reason must enable one to foresee this mutual benefit or reason should advise one to foreswear any temporary gratification from appetite. In a more resolute moment, speaking out of conviction and anger, Wollstonecraft wrote to Imlay:

> . . . your attention to my happiness should arise as much from love, which is always rather a selfish passion, as reason – that is, I want you to promote my felicity, by seeking your own . . . there are qualities in your heart which demand my affection; but unless the attachment appears to me clearly mutual, I shall labour only to esteem your character instead of cherishing a tenderness for your person. (*Letters* pp 41–2)

The relations of husband and wife to each other and of parents to children are relations governed by principles cemented by affection; but the reason these feelings will endure is that they are based in rationality. The association between reason and feeling is central to Wollstonecraft's argument for the rights of women; but to understand the significance of family life for her, it should be appreciated that Wollstonecraft – very much the Enlightenment empiricist – understands that these governing principles of family life become inculcated by reason in the very operation of domestic work of the family. They do not spring airily from a natural source. One becomes a parent from parenting, and in parenting one binds oneself to the social order. Domestic relations transform sexual feelings into feelings of family community:

> The feelings of a parent mingling with an instinct merely animal, give it dignity; and the man and woman after meeting on account of the child, a mutual interest and affection is excited by the exercise of a common sympathy. (p 248)

In a letter to Imlay, Wollstonecraft speaks of her growing affection for their infant daughter. What had begun in reason has ended in feeling. Domestic experience has been the catalyst, but only because a sense of reason had set the wheels in motion:

> I write in a hurry, because the little one, who has been sleeping a long time, begins to call for me. Poor thing. When I am sad, I lament that all my affections grow on me, till they become too strong for my peace, though they all afford me snatches of exquisite enjoyment. This (my feelings) for our little girl was at

first very reasonable – more the effect of reason, a sense of duty,
than feeling – now she has got into my heart and imagination, and
when I walk out without her, her little figure is ever dancing before
me. (*Letters*, p 42).

Eventually these family relations inflate and overcome the passion
which may have initiated them in the union between man and woman.
The domestic sphere, representing community and a network of
inter-relationships with children, the civic responsibility of caring for
and educating them, becomes a paradigm of social order. Thus we
can see the reasonableness with which Wollstonecraft argues the
apparently astonishing advice:

> In order to fulfil the duties of life . . . master and mistress of a
> family ought not to continue to love each other with passion – not
> indulge those emotions which disturb the order of society, and
> engross the thoughts that should be otherwise employed. (p 114)

'*Different Duties to Fulfil*' – the Family and Civic Life
Before continuing with Wollstonecraft's analysis of the interplay
between sexuality and reason, we should observe the image of family
life emerging from the pages of the *Vindication*; in constructing a
particular ideology for the family, Wollstonecraft lays the basis for
arguing for the rights of women in the only terms which enable her to
confront the prevailing ideology of her time, an ideology which
accepted women's inferiority as 'natural', 'divinely intended', and
serving the needs of men for light companionship and amusement.
Based on her understanding of the family, Wollstonecraft argues
women's equal intellectual capacity as 'natural', 'divinely intended',
and serving the needs of citizens for order and governance.

Her model of the family is not the refuge from the competitive toil
and duress of the marketplace, as such a model grew out of the
romanticised depiction of the domestic sphere in the nineteenth
century. Wollstonecraft, for all of her sympathies for Romantic
sentiment, must be sharply distinguished from those after her who
eulogised the 'angel by the hearth'. In the *Vindication* husband and
wife are impelled toward a joint performance of duty subordinating
for the mutual benefit of their eventual happiness and for their
dependent children any wayward sentiments which, unsupported by
reason, do not serve this social end.

However, in her own fashion she does sentimentalise the home.
Both in her private correspondence with Imlay and throughout all her

writing, she depicts the family gathered around the hearth with an exaggerated fondness, such that one may excuse her excess only by remembering that she never needed to compare her mental image to any actual domestic reality she superintended. But the sentimental-ising of the home which would achieve mythic proportions in the nineteenth century is in the *Vindication* only decoration, not a foundation stone. The gathering around the hearth is the fruit of labour, the reward to be reaped after the work is done. The work itself is rational work, the performance of duty, in the manner of the citizen to the state; husband and wife who have honourably 'ceased to love each other with passion' go on to 'fulfil the duties of life'. Rather than as refuge from the state, home is a continuation of the state. The same virtues describe the behaviour of husband and citizen, mother and citizen. There is no natural distinction between the two roles.

This reading of the relationship of home and community is not to say Wollstonecraft did not recognise the civic existence of a state beyond the home. She recognised it sufficiently to argue in the pages of the *Vindication* that women should have a political existence in it (p 262). But the recognition of the 'public' life of the state should not make automatically a private life of the home. If one needs an 'other' sphere, so that the mutual exclusiveness of two spheres is more apparent, the 'private' sphere in the Wollstonecraft vision is sexual appetite, which throws into sharp relief the public sphere of com-munity life. And as 'private' and separated from the rational governance of duty in community life, sexual appetite – the anarchy of feeling in self – is always dangerous. Wollstonecraft in seeing the domestic and civic sphere through one lens distinguishes between the public life of the citizen and the private life of the 'passionate self'. Her ragbag of discarded sentiments, useless and profitless feelings, not needed in the marketplace, as some have described the home in post-industrial societies, is the 'self' when the self has yielded to appetite.

Like the 'common herd of eaters and drinkers and child-begetters' she scorns in the *Letters to Imlay*, Wollstonecraft implies the sensualist is beyond the body politic, lost to the Enlightenment of reason or the elevation of poetic imagination; what is worse, she implies in this description of the uselessness of being engrossed by 'love' that it is by its very nature a social evil:

> Love from its very nature, must be transitory. To seek for a secret that would render it consistent, would be as wild a search as for the philosopher's stone, or the grand panacea; and the discovery

would be equally useless, or rather pernicious, to mankind. (p 113)

The trouble with love is, as she had written earlier, it is always 'rather a selfish passion', it is anti-social, it is in its earliest form 'appetite' and anti-rational.

Wollstonecraft makes a necessary 'other' out of appetite, justifying the domestic sphere as part of the civic sphere, moving next to her argument for the rights of women. If she cannot, or will not, move women out of the home, she will move the home, with the woman in it, toward the state:

> When I treat of the peculiar duties of women, as I should treat of the peculiar duties of a citizen or father, it will be found that I do not mean to insinuate that they should be taken out of their families, speaking of the majority . . . (p 155)

We see that what she is precisely doing is speaking of these duties as she would speak of citizenship, of parenthood. As for the distinctiveness of work in the home, Wollstonecraft acknowledges:

> Women, I allow, may have different duties to fulfil but they are *human* duties, and the principles that should regulate the discharge of them, I sturdily maintain, must be the same.

> To become respectable, the exercise of their understanding is necessary, there is no other foundation for independence of character; I mean explicitly to say that they must only bow to the authority of reason . . . (p 139)

The 'different duties' are of course domestic duties, now categorised as 'human' – or the universal duties of responsibility to reason, the duties of the citizen.

Such merging of the domestic with the civic sphere was easier for Wollstonecraft, of course, in that the two spheres were never seen as so rigidly separated as they became with progressive industrialisation. Although one does not wish to posit any mythic golden age for women in pre-industrial societies, still we must distinguish between the weaker boundary between home and work that existed in Wollstonecraft's England and what we think of today when we speak of 'private' and 'public' spheres. Indeed, illustrative anecdotes Wollstonecraft has left us in the pages of the *Vindication* describe the work of childcare easily blended with paying work in the community with the woman either behind a shop counter with her children at her feet or working for cottage industries in the home. With a model of home blended with the economic life of the community, Wollstonecraft's description of it on models of citizenship and contract is plausible, as well as being importantly serviceable for her arguments for women's rights.

'Private Vice is a Public Pest': Sensuality and the Body Politic
The life of the sensualist is the private life of sexual feeling, unconnected to social relationships which, by their definition, promote order in the discharge of duties. Wollstonecraft's vision of the private world of passion is doubly dangerous: dangerous to the rational order of society, to the happiness of citizens, and dangerous to women and to their rational expectations of the rights of citizens.

There is a danger to women alone and to their hopes to become part of the rational fellowship of citizens because men as sensualists have degraded and debauched women, their bodies and their minds. Saying 'all the causes of female weakness, as well as depravity . . . branch out of one grand cause, want of chastity in men' (p 249), Wollstonecraft writes in response to a flood of advice literature to young women, advice which assumed the actual inferiority of their sex and recommended, rather than a rational education, a curriculum in 'feminine' arts which, Wollstonecraft believed, could only serve to further corrupt them. Raised to believe they can have authority only insofar as they dissimulate, flatter, and manipulate the sex which has power over them, young girls become foolish women. 'Men,' writes Wollstonecraft '. . . have too much occupied the thoughts of women . . . and . . . they cannot live without love' (p 224). 'Pleasure', she writes, 'is the business of woman's life . . . and while it continues to be so, little can be expected from such weak beings' (p 145).

What is worse is that this corrosion incapacitates women as rational citizens and apparently justifies their subordination:

> Modesty, temperance, and self-denial, are the sober offspring of reason; but when sensibility is nurtured at the expense of understanding, such weak beings must be restrained by arbitrary means. (p 179)

There is, then, a direct link between the inculcation of sensibility in women by sensualist men and the subordination of women. And it is again the sensualist who, standing outside the community of rational fellowship, excludes women from membership therein as well.

> The sensualist, indeed, has been the most dangerous of tyrants, and women have been duped by their love, as princes by their

ministers, whilst dreaming that they reigned over them. (p 107)

The sensualist makes the false argument for femininity which denies women education, the education which would make of their domestic work the moral work of the citizen-mother.

> In the regulation of the family, in the education of children, understanding, in an unsophisticated sense, is particularly required – strength both of body and mind; yet the men who, by their writings, have most earnestly laboured to domesticate women, have endeavoured by arguments dictated by a gross appetite, which satiety has rendered fastidious, to weaken their bodies and cramp their minds. (p 155)

But the sensualist prevents more than the birth of the citizen-mother; he prevents as well the birth of the citizen-father in himself. Wollstonecraft asks that 'The father of a family will not . . . forget in obeying the call of appetite the purpose for which it was implanted' (p 89). No one embodied more dramatically for Wollstonecraft a slave to sensuality than Jean Jacques Rousseau whose *Emile* she could partly admire, but whose education of Sophie she despised. Sophie is raised to be a paragon of feminity, a creature naturally incapable, according to Rousseau, of Emile's capacity to reason. Rousseau was blinded, responded Wollstonecraft, by his own excess of sensibility:

> He was afraid lest the austerity of reason should disturb the soft playfulness of love. The master wished to have a meretricious slave to fondle, entirely dependent on his reason and bounty; he did not want a companion, whom he should be compelled to esteem, or a friend to whom he could confine the care of his children's education, should death deprive them of their father, before he had fulfilled the sacred task. (p 204)

The sensuality of the father robs the children of their mother, even if he himself were able to fulfil 'the sacred task' with whatever store of reason he had left untainted by sensuality. If left unchecked the private life of the sensualist invades and corrodes the public sphere of the citizen-parent. The corrosion is invisible when it is the corrosion of the mind; but for Wollstonecraft the corrosion does not end there. Wollstonecraft also makes a eugenic argument. The private life of the sensualist corrodes public health; 'private vices' she argues, become 'a public pest' (p 282).

The sensualist opposes the citizen-father not only in failing to educate the citizen-mother, but in discouraging her from nursing her babies, a practice Wollstonecraft argues has invidious social repercussions. She deplored, as did other reformers of her time, the common practice for mothers to send their babies out to be wetnursed.

In addition to dissuading women from nursing and thereby rendering 'the infancy of man a much more perilous state than that of brutes', she asks 'in how many ways are children destroyed by the lasciviousness of man?' (p 297). The sensualist is more than the enemy of his lover, he is the poisoner of the society he should have worked to improve. Speaking of the great importance of male chastity, Wollstonecraft asks:

> And what nasty indecent tricks do they not also learn from each other, when a number of them pig together in the same bed chamber, not to speak of vices, which render the body weak whilst they effectually prevent the acquisition of any delicacy of mind. [It] produces great depravity in all the relationships of society . . . love that ought to purify the heart and first call forth all the youthful powers and prepare the man to discharge the benevolent duties of life is sacrificed to premature lust; but all the social affections are deadened by the selfish gratifications, which very early pollute the mind, and dry up the generous juices of the heart. (p 282)

Wollstonecraft claims the sensualist sacrifices mind to passion, the reversal of the ethic she espouses, the private relations spoiling the public.

The conviction that social disorder attends excess of sensuality stems from more, we see, than simple Christian orthodox inheritance. Wollstonecraft turns on its head here the anti-feminist argument that education for women will, by causing indelicacy in females, render them immoral and family life precarious. She responds:

> It is the want of domestic taste, and not the acquirement of knowledge, that takes women out of their families, and tears the smiling babe from the breast that ought to afford it nourishment. (p 285)

The want of domestic taste, we have come to see, is not a natural failure; it is a corruption for which the male sensualist is responsible, responsible in encouraging excess of sensibility in women, responsible in depriving women of education which would allow their reason to assume their governance.

The ultimate disorder, the irreversible poisoning of the social order, occurs when male sensuality creates an appetite which cannot ultimately be satisfied, such that the sensualist begins to crave 'even equivocal beings', or has 'promiscuous amours' with women which produce a 'destructive barrenness'. (p 250)

> The weak enervated women who particularly catch the attentions of libertines, are unfit to be mothers, though they may conceive; so that the rich sensualist, who has rioted among women, spreading depravity and misery, when he wishes to perpetuate his name, receives from his wife only an half-formed being that inherits his father's and his mother's weakness. (p 249)

This is a rich depiction of social disorder, of relationships askew, men and women exhausting each other, forsaking responsibilities to children, begetting children, who – if born at all – are born infirm, the victim of the venereal disease of their parents. Whereas if men and women submitted to the duties of their station in life, submitted by virtue of the authority of reason, the domestic peace which would ensue would include the advantages of a small family size, as well as the inculcation of principle so necessary to civic order.

> Formed thus by the discharge of the relative duties of her station, she marries from affection, without losing sight of prudence, and looking beyond matrimonial felicity, she secures her husband's respect before it is necessary to exert mean arts to please him and feed a dying flame, which nature doomed to expire when the object became familiar, when friendship and forebearance take place of a more ardent affection. This is the natural death of love, and domestic peace is not destroyed by struggles to prevent its extinction. I also suppose the husband to be virtuous; or she is still more in want of independent principles. (p 138)

Perhaps nowhere else in the *Vindication* are the roots of domestic order so carefully exposed in the control of sensuality.

'Stalking Mischiefs' and the Authority of Reason: Sexuality and the Rights of Women

We come to the final question in understanding the relationship in Wollstonecraft's writing between sexuality and the rights of women. We understand these rights to be the freedom from the corrosive influence of male sensuality, that they will be educated to do the rational civic work of the home. But before women can enjoy these rights, men must be persuaded to be virtuous.

It is important to understand, in order to appreciate the inter-relatedness between Wollstonecraft's ideas, that the *Vindication of the Rights of Woman* is indeed an argument. There is at the base of her writing a claim: women should be treated as men are. The claim rests on an assumption:

> . . . if any class of mankind be so created that it must necessarily be educated by rules not strictly deducible from truth, virtue is an affair of convention. (p 182)

For virtue to be an 'affair of convention' is itself so unacceptable an idea, it must be rejected: 'I could not believe what my reason told me was derogatory to the character of the Supreme Being' (p 175). Therefore, 'To render mankind more virtuous, and happier of course, both sexes must act from the same principle; but how can that be expected when only one is allowed to see the reasonableness of it?' (p 293).

The argument is written so it is seen to proceed from basic principles, one leads logically to the next. Women must be educated so they may be reasonable, reasonable so they may be virtuous, virtuous so that all of society may be happier. There is no call to arms in the *Vindication*, no call to take power. The argument rests on the belief that reasonable people can perceive the validity of self-evidently reasonable ideas. If the *Vindication* tirelessly reiterates the primacy of reason and subordinates its enemy, sensuality, it is because without this primacy, there is no hope for women. Such is its logic. If men will not be reasonable, they will be sensualists. If they will be sensualists, women will be their slaves.

> Let us . . . submit to the authority of reason . . . if it be proved that this throne of prerogative only rests on a chaotic mass of prejudices, that have no inherent principle of order to keep them together – they may escape who dare to brave the consequence, without any breach of duty, without sinning against the order of things. (p 201)

As the eternal foe of reason,

> Love is, in a great degree, an arbitrary passion, and will reign like some other stalking mischiefs, by its own authority, without deigning to reason. (p 222)

On the possibility of a moral order under the governance of reason, on the possibility of governing this 'stalking mischief' love, Wollstonecraft places her hopes for women's education – for her the key to their emancipation. Sexual life, insofar as she can include it within the moral order, must remain under the careful regulation of virtuous individuals engaged in duties which are domestic. As citizen-parents, educated, virtuous, governing the potentially disruptive work of 'appetite', men and women may make an improved society. For Wollstonecraft to have done otherwise, to have vindicated sexual feeling or found a place for passion for its own sake in her moral order, would have been to undermine the possibilities for women's emancipation as she understood them.

The argument of the *Vindication* must see a primacy of reason in the moral order. The citizen-parent reigns in the public life of the home as community, over the lover-sensualist in the private life of passion. In working to include women in the equality of the rights of man, Wollstonecraft excludes the sexual life of both.

It was an old hierarchy, reason over passion, but one advanced for new purposes – to advance the cause of women. It was not a hierarchy particularly easy to translate into a governing ethos over one's own emotional life, as Wollstonecraft discovered in her own relationship with Gilbert Imlay. Unlike her contemporaries, Wollstonecraft laboured to argue men must reform themselves before women could be reformed. Unlike those who came after her, Wollstonecraft argued men and women must control their sexuality, rather than that women had none at all to control. Unlike the theorists of family life who followed, she argued that domestic work is civil work, subject to the same principles, worthy of the same right to be performed by educated citizens.

Nor was it a theory without problems, particularly in the cold-bloodedness with which she describes 'the natural death of love'. Yet it is an attitude one can understand against the particular conditions of her time. Elaborating a morality for sexual life which included women and men sharing responsibilities and arguing for a public definition of family life which would give women the inherent right to be educated as citizens, Mary Wollstonecraft constructed a model of personal and civic life, to advance the rights of women. We are still working, in our own time, to do the same.

Notes

1 Not that the woman herself needs vindicating; but it might stand as a footnote to this reading that rather than having to accept, as one of her more virulent detractors wrote of her, that in bowing to Gilbert Imlay she sunk

lower than any other woman, feminist or no, we can come instead to understand that the writer of the *Vindication*, in so mistrusting sexual feeling could have predicted her own narrowly missed demise; to have understood and to have even theorised about one's precarious condition in relation to sexual feelings saves one, we can say for Wollstonecraft, from being entirely its victim.

2 *Matrimonial Honour*, 1642, London p 181–2 as quoted in Keith Thomas, 1959, 'The Double Standard', *Journal of the History of Ideas*, 20, p 201.

3 For a fuller analysis of Puritan attitudes towards morality and the beginnings of middle-class respectability, see Keith Thomas, 1959.

Harriet Martineau:
A Reassessment
(1802–1876)

Gaby Weiner

Harriet Martineau wrote her first article in 1822 at the age of 20, became nationally famous at the age of 30 when she published a series on political economy, and by the time of her death at the age of 74, had produced over 50 books (or series of books) and pamphlets. As a journalist for the *Daily News*, she wrote 1,642 articles in her 14 years' employment there, and also contributed to a further 50 or more periodicals including the influential *Edinburgh* and *Westminster Reviews*.

She was an important national figure for over 40 years; a feminist who had immense influence as a writer, and was thus able to offer considerable support to some of the radical causes of the time. What was less well-known in Britain but more so in the United States, was that in addition to achieving fame as a writer and raconteur on most topics of contemporary interest, Harriet was a perceptive observer and an incisive analyst of the political scene, making particularly sharp commentaries on the role and political status of women in European and American society. She travelled widely and used what we would now recognise as sociological observation techniques, to gather data on a wide range of public and social institutions which provided materials for her books. She also wrote, in 1838, a hand-book for travellers, which clearly laid out her own strategies for objective observation.

Considerable though her contribution was to nineteenth-century ideas, both in this country and in the United States, Harriet Martineau has not achieved a principal place in modern nineteenth-century historical texts. She is to be found in most textbooks, but usually subsumed in the footnotes.

There are paradoxes in Harriet Martineau's existence for she was a single, middle-class woman who held deep convictions on a number of radical issues and yet who needed social approval in order to achieve economic independence and personal survival. It is interesting therefore to examine how she came to be in this position, and to assess her historical contribution, particularly on feminism and social analysis; and it is also interesting to attempt to identify the reasons for her neglect by historians, educationalists, sociologists, economists and philosophers – for she was all of these and made a contribution to all these areas. Harriet's economic position necessitated that she write for a living, and in order to do so, she needed to gain the approval of the important publishers and editors of the day. Yet, for a woman to have a successful career and be accepted into middle-class Victorian society was a situation of great contradiction.

So differentiated were the perceived roles and limitations of men and women in the nineteenth century that since career orientation was couched in male terms, those women who sought to break into this territory could not, by definition, be *proper* women. As far as the Victorians were concerned, *proper* womanhood could only be satisfied by maternal and domestic duties and those who stepped outside the normal sphere were regarded as abnormal and deficient. It was assumed that women who were satisfied with their sexual identity would be unlikely to be attracted by activities which took them away from domestic duties.

'Women who are happy in all home ties and who amply fill the sphere of their life and love, must in the nature of things very seldom become writers'. (Massey, 1962, p 271)

Conversely, for a woman to gain entry into Victorian society, she needed to acquire respectability in terms appropriate to social expectations; namely she needed to display *proper* womanliness. For married career women, this proved difficult yet it was possible in a few cases; for instance Elizabeth Gaskell was able successfully to fulfil her domestic role, pursue a literary career, and retain her social standing in middle-class Manchester society. However, for single career women, who in general were regarded as bookish, barren spinsters and therefore *improper* women, this was almost impossible.

Harriet Martineau attained great fame, social recognition and intellectual esteem during her lifetime. In order to achieve this she was obliged to satisfy the requirements for social acceptability but at the same time, to hold on to her political and social principles, many of which remained unaltered during her long career. This conflict led her into situations which seemed oddly paradoxical; for instance, whilst she campaigned vigorously and publicly for female education for many years, she refused to become identified, in any way, with the early women's movement. As a Victorian intellectual in a male world, she could not afford to allow herself to become too identified with women's issues, neither would she tolerate in her own or in other people's writing, excessive emotions or passions which, she felt, had a specific female orientation.

She publicly sought the company and patronage of men, particularly early in her career, and when she lived in London, quite soon after her first literary success, the most eminent came to visit her – Thackeray, Carlyle, Dickens, Malthus, Darwin, Landseer etc. She used a male pseudonym in her earliest writing and in common with other female contemporaries who were also breaking new ground as female role innovators, eg Florence Nightingale and Angela Burdett, contributions were made in the prevailing mode of the dominant (male) tradition rather than in offering any radically new form.

On the other hand, whilst she rejected the means by which feminists in the past had sought to achieve change in the status of women, criticising, in the oft-quoted comment, Mary Wollstonecraft for being 'a poor victim of passion with no control over her own peace, no calmness, content', she nevertheless recognised the extent of female oppression in nineteenth-century England (and America) and argued frequently for the necessity of change; through example rather than by legislation:

> Nobody can be further than I from being satisfied with the condition of my own sex, under the law and custom of my own country. . . The best advocates (of the course) are yet to come – in the persons of women who are obtaining access to real social business – the female physicians and other professors in America, the women of business and female artists in France; and the hospital administrators, the nurses, the educators and substantially successful authors of this country . . .
>
> The time has not come which certainly will come, when women who are practically concerned in political life will have a voice in making the laws which they have to obey; but every woman who can think and speak wisely, and bring up her children soundly, in regards to rights and duties of society is advancing the time when the interests of women will be represented as well as those of men. (Martineau, 1877, p 400)

In several of her books she allocated chapters to a plea for extending the employment and political rights of women and campaigned actively for female education, not exclusively for middle-class women but for the 3 million women who were working full-time and yet had received no education:

> So far from our country-women being all maintained as a matter of course by us, the breadwinners, 3 million out of 6 (million) adult Englishwomen work for subsistence; and two out of three for independence – we must improve and extend education to the utmost; and then open a fair field to the powers and energies we have educed. This will secure our welfare nationally and in our homes. (Martineau, 1859, p 336)

The education of women was a life-long consideration of Harriet's emanating from her observations of the differential treatment of girls and boys, regardless of intellect, when she was in the school-room, receiving a classical education alongside her sisters and brothers.

She had the fortune to be born, in 1802, into a Unitarian family, the sixth child out of eight of Thomas and Elizabeth Martineau of Norwich. Both her parents were from the Norwich manufacturing classes, descendants of Huguenots driven from France after the revocation of the Edict of Nantes in 1685, which has allowed non-Catholics freedom of worship. At the time of her birth, Harriet's father was a manufacturer of Bombazines (twilled or corded silk or cotton). Later the failure of the business and his subsequent death was a major contributory factor in her adoption of a literary career.

Most Unitarians, contrary to the accepted tenets of the time, believed that women had intellectual capacities equal to men's (though physiological differences gave them different roles) and wished to educate them accordingly. Also, as Harriet drily pointed out, education and study was felt to be a hedge against destitution.

> The remarkable feature of the family story in those days, was the steady self-denial and clear, inflexible purpose with which the parents gave their children the best education which they could, by all honourable means, command. In those times of war and middle-class adversity, the parents understood their position, and took care that their children should understand it, tell them that there was no chance of wealth for them and about an equal probability of a competence or of poverty; and they must therefore regard their education as their only secure portion. (Martineau, 1876, p 2).

Although Harriet described her childhood as extremely unhappy, portraying her younger self as sickly, dyspeptic and full of fears – a difficult child whom nobody loved or wanted to be with – her parents made sure that she received a good and broad education. In addition to two years' excellent co-educational schooling in Norwich at the school of Isaac Perry, where she received a thorough grounding in Latin, French and English composition, Harriet received a home education similar to other Unitarians in the nineteenth century. There was much reading aloud and discussion in the cultural family circle as well as social exchanges with the intellectual leaders of local society. Harriet was also sent away to study with Lant Carpenter, the Unitarian minister and educationalist, in Bristol, as much to increase her physical fitness as to further her studies.

> Lant Carpenter . . . postulated that physical education was at the heart of both intellectual and moral excellence though detrimental if pursued as an end itself, just as mental and moral culture would defeat their own ends if pursued without reference to physical health. Girls, like boys, required sensible clothing, fresh air and exercise. (Watts, 1980, p 279)

She was frequently dispatched to relatives in the country in the hope of improving her health but despite her declared unhappiness at home, was always frantically homesick. In addition to her existing afflictions, during her adolescence, another more serious was added. She became increasingly deaf though she retained sufficient hearing later in life to communicate with the aid of an ear trumpet.

Though Harriet had reservations about her mother's feelings for her, being convinced that her oldest sister Rachel was much preferred, she developed a very strong attachment to her younger brother by three years, James (later to become an important Unitarian minister), studying with him whenever she could, writing to him regularly when he was away from home, and generally consulting him on all matters. It was at James's suggestion that Harriet first began to write and when, at the age of 17 he met and fell in love with his future wife, Harriet was deeply hurt.

> In the history of human affections, of all natural relations the least satisfactory is the fraternal. Brothers are to sisters what sisters can never be to brothers as objects of engrossing and devoted affection. (Bosanquet, 1928, p 22)

At the end of her formal education, Harriet continued to read and study, often getting up very early in the morning and reading long into the night, to allow for the completion of her daytime domestic duties. At the age of 19 or 20, when girls of a similar age thought mainly of prospective suitors or marriage, Harriet became deeply interested in religious and philosophical questions. She was, at about this time, converted to 'necessarianism', a philosophy deriving from the ideas of arch-Unitarian Joseph Priestley, which held that individuals must act according to the laws of their own natures, rather than as a result of any mystical direction. This belief formed the basis for Harriet's commitment to social and political reform in later years.

Characteristically her first published works, in the radical Unitarian journal, the *Monthly Repository*, were concerned with women. The first two were on the subject of 'Female Writers of Practical Divinity', and the third, produced a year later at the age of 21 and entitled 'Female Education', called for educational equality for girls. She argued, as she was to do so often in later life, that it could only be beneficial to women to receive an equal education to that of men. Using the male pseudonym 'Disciplus', she wrote that in her experience, when girls and boys studied the same topics, their progress was equal; however boys were encouraged to complete their education whereas girls were restricted by their social duties and then condemned for their lack of achievement.

> She is taught to believe that solid information is unbecoming her sex, almost her whole time is expended on light accomplishments and thus before she is sensible of her powers, they are checked in her growth, chained down to mean objects, to rise no more; and when the natural consequences of his mode of treatment arise, all mankind agree that the abilities of women are far inferior to those of men. (Martineau, 1823, p 22)

Harriet's first book, on a more 'appropriate' subject, appeared under her own name in Autumn 1823, and was a volume of *Devotional Exercises; Consisting of Reflections and Prayers for the Use of Young Persons*. It met with a favourable response and quickly went into a second edition.

Whilst contemplating the start of a new book, the peaceful pattern of family life, which had improved for Harriet since her late teens, was shattered by three events. First, her oldest brother died in Madeira; then her father's business failed in the great crash of 1825, causing his health so to deteriorate that he died a year later. Finally, a young theological student friend of her brother, John Hugh Worthington, to whom Harriet had become engaged despite James's opposition, died of 'brain fever' within months of their engagement. Thus at the age of 24, Harriet's comfortable though not luxurious middle-class life-style was destroyed. The possibility of marriage no longer existed, although according to her autobiography, this was welcomed with some relief by Harriet:

It was happiest for both of us that our union was prevented by any means. I am, in truth, very thankful for not having married at all. I have never since been tempted, nor have suffered anything at all in relation to that matter which is held to be all important to women, love and marriage. (Martineau, 1877, p 131)

The main consideration which now faced Harriet and her remaining family was economic, and the education, so painstakingly acquired by the girls, proved to be the mainstay of family survival. Only three daughters, Rachel, Harriet and the youngest, Ellen, now remained at home with the formidable Mrs Martineau. Since teaching was the most suitable employment for educated middle-class women, Rachel acquired a post as a governess and later became headteacher of the Liverpool Girls' School, to which Mrs Gaskell sent one of her daughters; Ellen was assigned to teach the children of the extended Martineau family and the virtually deaf Harriet was deputed to stay at home with her mother.

Harriet decided to try and earn a living by writing, and experienced some success over the next few years, by contributing regular articles to the *Monthly Repository* and winning prize money in Unitarian essay competitions. However, financial liberation was not achieved until she hit upon the idea of using fictional illustration to describe the principles of political economy for the masses, to make what had been 'specialised' knowledge, available to all. Her scheme was to produce monthly stories, which though fictional in theme and content, explained clearly the principles of political economy as understood by those who supported the *laissez-faire* or Free Trade policy. The science of political economy, of popular interest to the Victorians, undertook to define the changing relationships between wealth, labour and production in terms of 'natural' and therefore immutable laws which governed market forces and which, if allowed unrestricted freedom, would act for the benefit of all classes. Her attitude to the task of writing a popular series on this subject was essentially practical, as was her approach to most of the activities undertaken by her in the course of her career. (This practical bias of her work may have been one of the causes for her neglect by historians.)

She acknowledged the value of the existing published works on political economy adding:

These are very valuable, but they do not give us what we want – the science in a familiar, practical form. They give us its history; they give us its philosophy; but what we want is its PICTURE. (Martineau, 1832, p xi)

Although it took her two years to complete, the series *Illustrations of Political Economy*, was an enormous success from the first volume and Harriet achieved a degree of financial security and national fame at one stroke.

> I remember walking up and down the grass-plat feeling that my cares were over. And so they were. From that hour, I have never had any other anxiety about employment than what I choose, nor any real care about money. . . I think I may date my release from pecuniary care from that 10th of February 1832 (the publishing date of the first volume). (Martineau, 1877, p 178)

As a consequence of her literary success, Harriet became 'lionised' by London society. She had moved from Norwich to London to research and write the series, and was forced to exercise considerable self-discipline in the face of numerous social invitations and requests to visit her home, in order to complete the regular production of the monthly volumes. In two and a half years, she produced three series of tales on political economy and further commissioned works on Taxation and the Poor Law, 34 volumes in all, at the same time as enjoying a hectic social life in London.

She met and corresponded with many famous artists and writers and was consulted by several government ministers about reform measures being considered for legislation, including the 1832 Reform Bill.

When the last volume was completed, Harriet decided to use some of the £2,000 eventually earned by the series, to finance a two-year trip to the United States. She was one of the first English women to travel independently to America, and with only a female companion and a vast number of introductory letters, she travelled widely and was very well received wherever she went – that is until she declared herself in sympathy with the abolitionist cause. She was not then made quite so welcome as she had been before.

She was eager to see as much of America as she could in the time allotted and though before she left England she had refused to commit herself to a publication on her travels, she wished to keep accurate records of her American experience. Whilst on the long voyage across the Atlantic, she addressed herself to the problems of what, whom and how to observe. She later published her ideas in a small neglected volume, *How to Observe; Morals and Manners* (1838) which could today be described as one of the first introductions to sociological methodology.

She opted for a scientific approach to observation and discussed the similarities between scientific exploration and discovery and the observation of social manners and morals. She argued that the observer should be objective, impartial, and aware of his (*sic*) own prejudices.

She stated that the observer needed to be clear about the aims of observation and should adopt a relative rather than a moral analysis of social institutions.

> The observer who sets out with a more philosophical belief, not only escapes the affliction of seeing sin wherever he sees a difference, and avoids the suffering and contempt and alienation from his species but, by being prepared for what he witnesses and aware of the causes, is free from the agitation of being shocked and alarmed, preserves his calmness, his hope, his sympathy; and is thus far better fitted to perceive, understand, and report upon the morals and manners of the people he visits. (Martineau, 1838, pp 22–3)

She listed those social and political institutions which were indicative of a country's social characteristics and therefore worthy of observation; and finally recommended useful practical tips for observers. These included directions on the preparation of questions and the desirability of a daily journal; and explicit instructions, ie always to have a notebook at hand and never to take notes during an interview.

Before travelling to America, Harriet had been optimistic about the position of women in the young democracy. On arrival, therefore, she was particularly critical in her observations of the ambiguities of the American Constitution and the social and political roles of American women. She did not voice her criticism publicly whilst in America, but when she returned home and wrote her excellent analysis, *Society in America*, she commented on the absurdity of a democracy that held 'that governments derive their just powers from the consent of the governed', and yet did not enfranchise women.

> The democratic principle condemns this as all wrong; and requires equal political representation for all rational human beings. Children, idiots, criminals . . . are the only fair exceptions. (Martineau, 1837, p 200)

She described the state of American women as politically non-existent and invisible, and strongly condemned among others Jefferson and James Mill who opposed political rights for women on the grounds that their interests lay with their fathers or brothers rather than with the ballot box. A firm believer in self-determination for women she argued that it was up to women to decide whether or not their domestic roles and political representation were incompatible and not for others to make these decisions on their behalf.

Harriet's theoretical approach to 'the Woman Question', formed in her youth and shaped whilst in America, was similar in analysis to her attitude towards slavery. Her perception of these two issues, which concerned her more than any other during her lifetime, was based upon an unswerving commitment to the freedom of the individual and the removal of limitations on political representation, employment and social involvement.

She held to the principle that 'real' freedom meant that individuals should be able to exercise control of their lives and destinies, and that if restrictions were removed from women, they would eventually achieve power and status within society.

> It is pleaded that half the human race does acquiesce in the decision of the other half, as to their rights and duties. . . Such acquiescence proves nothing but degradation of the injured party. It inspires the same emotions of pity as the supplication of the freed slave who kneels to his master to restore him to slavery, that he might have his animal wants supplied, without being troubled with human rights and duties. (Martineau, 1837, p 203)

> That woman has power to represent her own interests no one can deny until she has been tried. . . The principle once being established – the methods will follow easily and naturally. (Martineau, 1837, p 206)

The book, and another more travel orientated volume, were published amid great acclaim in her home country but in America, many thought that Harriet had abused their hospitality and were quick to deride her woman's perspective.

> Does a woman of circumscribed education and recluse habits feel herself competent to teach a whole nation – a nation that did not think the wisest and greatest in *her* land capable of giving them sound instruction. (Chapman, 1877, p 175)

On her return to England, Harriet published several books including the two on America, the handbook on observation and a novel *Deerbrook*. In 1839, her health finally collapsed due, so it is said, to overwork, and she spent five years in Tynemouth as an invalid until she made a celebrated recovery through mesmerism (or hypnotism – a popular Victorian preoccupation). She retired to Ambleside in the Lake District, where she built a house and continued to produce books and articles on a wide range of contemporary issues.

In 1861 she was asked to contribute regular leaders to the Liberal paper, the *Daily News*, and from then to a few years before her death, she wrote up to six leaders a week from her home in the Lake District. She was a brilliant journalist, clear, knowledgeable and perceptive and 'thoroughly in accord with the canons of the fine journalistic style of the middle of the century' (Webb, 1960, p 42). So persuasive was she as a journalist, that Florence Nightingale used Harriet's influence to achieve certain cabinet appointments and one of Harriet's major articles, in the *Edinburgh Review* in 1859, resulted in a fundamental public reappraisal of the role of women in Victorian society. This article, entitled 'Female Industry', drew upon the 1851 Census returns to demonstrate that as there were at least half a million more women than men, marriage for a considerable number of women was out of the question. As already quoted she also showed that of the 3 million women currently in employment, half worked for subsistence and two-thirds independently of their families. She criticised her contemporaries for not recognising the changes in society or appreciating the industrial and commercial contribution made by women, and argued vigorously for higher wages and the expansion of opportunities for women.

> In a community where a larger proportion of women remained unmarried than at any known period; where a greater number of women depend on their own industry for subsistence; where every pair of hands, moved by an intelligent head, is in request; and where improved machinery demands more and more skilled labour which women can supply, how can there be doubt that women will work more and more. (Martineau, 1859, p 322)

In the same article, she wrote once more on the necessity for expanding female education, this time judiciously orientating her justification for this long held principle in terms of improvement of workforce potential and increased domestic skills which would ultimately improve the quality of family life.

> We believe that the conclusion of the best observers will be that it is not the labour of the factory which hardens and brutalises the minds of men or women – but the state of ignorance in which they

enter upon a life of bustle and publicity. (Martineau, 1859, p 323)

Another consequence of her article in the *Edinburgh Review* was that the Society for Promoting the Employment of Women was established at Langham Place. Although she was not one of that circle and remained unwilling to identify herself too closely with any women's rights movement, Harriet supported all attempts to achieve female suffrage and was also actively involved, though quite elderly at the time, in the campaign, led by Josephine Butler, to repeal the Contagious Diseases Acts. In fact opposition to the acts originated from articles written by Harriet in the *Daily News* in 1863 but no concerted action was taken to get them repealed until the 1870s.

Harriet lived until she was 74, despite her debilitated childhood and two periods of invalidism during middle-age when she was convinced that death was imminent. In addition to her trip to America, she made an extended visit to the East and also travelled through Ireland, writing books and articles on her experiences. Though she never married, Harriet took the prefix of Mrs during middle-age, indicating the way it was used at the time when she stated that the title of Mrs was more appropriate to a woman of maturity than the implicitly youthful Miss.

The fact that Harriet Martineau has no major place in modern texts on nineteenth-century history may have, perhaps, more to do with the way in which women have been defined in history, and their comparative neglect, than with the value of her particular contributions to mid-Victorian social and political life.

It has been suggested that where women have a place in history as actors (rather than wives, daughters, mistresses etc), the standard measurement is male and thus they are seen as honorary, pseudo or deficient males.

> For as Simone de Beauvoir pointed out years ago, throughout most of written history, at least, the standard of humanity has been male. Women who act in the world have been seen as men 'manqués' – males with something missing. And in case anyone wondered what was missing, Sigmund Freud told us. (Degler, 1974, p 4)

While historical eminence has been defined in male terms, women such as Harriet – and many others in this volume – have been eliminated because their contribution, their lives and their experience cannot be conveniently placed in the existing categories. The criteria by which historical significance in the past has been judged and then ascribed are numerous. They include power, innovation, creativity, genius, public office, skill in warfare and diplomacy, philosophical or theoretical advancement, single-mindedness, being at the right place at the right time, and so on.

When we consider Harriet Martineau, we see that although immensely famous in her time, she does not fit the female role cast by history, ie she was neither a wife, mother or mistress; neither does she fit the male role cast by history in the way that perhaps some eminent women did (for instance, Queen Victoria who held public office). And as this volume testifies there has been no category of women intellectuals.

Harriet Martineau was an interesting and knowledgeable political economist. However she had no chance of entering politics, no patron or other means of financial support, and so she made use of a practical rather than theoretical approach to promote political understanding* and at the same time earned her own living.

She was an acute social observer, capable of making considerable theoretical contributions to socio-methodology, but because she worked alone, and outside the established circles of power it was relatively easy for her work to remain hidden and fail to be absorbed into the sociological tradition.

She was a brilliant writer but the judgement of her is that she was descriptive and interpretative rather than essentially creative. She campaigned vigorously with the aid of her pen, wrote critical and inspirational articles on a number of subjects, and her autobiography, published after her death, is a candid and fascinating portrait of mid-Victorian, middle-class society.

As a journalist she translated difficult and obscure themes for popular reading – yet because the topics she chose were not those generally associated with 'women's' subjects (eg children's books, domestic considerations), she was labelled by historians as second-rate and bookish.

She supported many radical movements in her time (eg abolition, women's suffrage, the expansion of education), but because she could not *afford* to stop writing in order to support a cause (her income depended almost entirely on regular commissions), she has not been characterised as a social reformer. She could not take time off from her work to become a leader of any of the movements she

* Editor's Note: One could argue simply that her theories were not those of men and therefore were deemed not to exist; I see Harriet Martineau as an intensely theoretical person – who grasped the intellectual principles of the problems she tackled and was able to translate them into accessible forms.

supported. Nevertheless, as previously mentioned, several of her articles initiated national radical movements.

She was never in public office, and indeed turned down three offers of a small government pension in order to keep her political independence, though she was consulted on various occasions by Ministers of State. She was interested in and wrote on many different subjects. Yet as she had specialist knowledge in a number of areas and did not restrict herself to one specific cause or activity with which she alone could be identified, historians have viewed her as superficial and pedantic.

Harriet Martineau was an outstanding woman of her day. Because she was a woman, she took the woman's perspective on many issues and fortified by her social training, was particularly concerned about social and political reform. While she was deeply committed in her beliefs (or lack of them – she became an atheist late in life), she placed little importance on the value of her work and was modest in her claims to posterity. In fact she understood the social mores perfectly. Anticipating her historical assessment she wrote of herself (in the third person and for her own obituary in the *Daily News*):

> Her (Harriet's) original power was nothing more than was due to earnestness and intellectual clearance within a certain range. With small imaginative and suggestive powers, and therefore nothing approaching genius, she could see clearly what she did see, and give a clear expression to what she had to say. In short she could popularise, while she could neither discover or invent. . .
>
> The function of her life was to do this and, in as far as it was done diligently and honestly, her life was of use, however far its achievements may have fallen short of expectations less moderate than her own. (Martineau, 1876, p 2)

Yet her writing remains. When read today, her clear, uncluttered journalistic style and total candour reveal fascinating accounts of the social and political events of the nineteenth century, as well as providing a fascinating account of this remarkable woman, who in many respects, still remains an enigma. Further reclamation, further study, discussion and debate on her work and that of other women like her – of the type afforded to her contemporary, John Stuart Mill – is part of our task of reclaiming our history.

Select Bibliography of Harriet Martineau

Books:
Devotional Exercises, 1823.
Illustrations of Political Economy, (9 vols), Charles Fox, London, 1832–34.
Society in America, (3 vols), Saunders & Otley, New York, 1837.
How to Observe; Morals and Manners, Charles Knight, London, 1838.
Retrospect of Western Travel, (3 vols), Saunders & Otley, London, 1838.
Deerbrook, Edward Moxon, London, 1839.
Harriet Martineau's Autobiography with Memorials by Maria Weston Chapman, (3 vols), Smith, Elder & Co, London, 1877.

Articles:
Articles in the *Monthly Repository*, 1822, 1823, 1827–9.
'Female Industry', *Edinburgh Review*, vol 109 (p 298), 1859.
Leaders in the *Daily News*, May 1852–April 1866, (I, 642 publ. art.).
Obituary, *Daily News* (p 2), 29 June 1876.

A full bibliography of Harriet Martineau's published works is in *The Life and Work of Harriet Martineau*, by Vera Wheatley, Secker and Warburgh, London, 1957.
Valerie Kossew Pichanick has also written a biography, *Harriet Martineau: the Woman and her Work*, Univ. of Michigan Press, 1980.

Margaret Fuller: Feminist Writer and Revolutionary
(1810–1850)

Marie Mitchell Olsen Urbanski

Margaret Fuller was the major inspiration of the American feminist movement. She was born in 1810 to Margaret Crane and Timothy Fuller in Cambridgeport, Massachusetts. Fuller's family background was distinguished. Her father, a somewhat independent member of New England's intellectual élite, was a Harvard graduate, a lawyer, and for a time, a member of the United States House of Representatives.

After Timothy Fuller had recovered from his disappointment that his first-born was female, he came to realise she was precocious, and he began to tutor her when she was three. Although he later fathered males, he continued to educate his daughter. He taught her Latin at age six, demanding that she translate her lesson in Horace or Virgil to him without mistake or hesitation. Later she was to study Greek, Italian, and French in Dr Park's school in Boston and Miss Prescott's school in Groton. Although her family background was intellectual, it was still Calvinist; as a child, she was punished for reading *Romeo and Juliet* on a Sunday when she should have been studying the Bible. Some years later, she became interested in Goethe and taught herself German well enough to publish translations.

Despite her rigorous intellectual education, Margaret Fuller was just as much aware as any other girl of the social importance of being pretty. There are conflicting accounts of her appearance. From the few dissimilar portraits extant it is impossible to describe her accurately, but it is important to piece together what details of appearance are available because scholars hostile to the feminist movement have used reports of Fuller's lack of conventional beauty to discredit her ideas. What does seem clear is that as an adolescent Fuller did not *think* she was pretty, so she took great pains with her appearance. Thomas Wentworth Higginson's biography contains a frequently repeated description of sixteen-year-old Margaret at a ball Timothy Fuller gave for President John Quincy Adams. Fifty-eight years after the party, an old woman remembered Margaret as a girl with 'a plain face, half-shut eyes, and hair curled all over her head; she was laced so tightly . . . by reason of stoutness, that she had to hold her arms back as if they were pinioned; she was dressed in a badly-cut, low-necked pink silk, with white muslin over it . . .' (Higginson, 1884, p 29). It is not surprising the Higginson's unnamed, disapproving source opined that Margaret danced quadrilles 'very awkwardly'. This old informant could have had a faulty memory; or she could have been influenced by the descriptions she had read in the *Memoirs*. Another possibility is that even at 16, Fuller was so imposing that she had made an indelible, unsettling impression on another girl at the ball. A revealing anecdote in Fuller's autobiographical 'Mariana', depicts her unconventional persona wearing rouge in the face of great hostility, because she thought it made her 'look pretty'. Both accounts show a determined girl, willing to lace herself beyond pain, wearing hair curlers all day, and trying to improve her looks by unacceptable means – decolletage and rouge.

As Fuller matured, her adolescent awkwardness and self-consciousness were replaced by graceful carriage and an acute expression that pierced disguises. Edgar Allan Poe described her bluish-grey eyes as full of fire, her sensuous mouth as beautiful or sneering, her hair as lustrous and profuse, and her voice as musical. Frederic Henry Hedge wrote she was not beautiful, but not plain, with a face that 'fascinated without satisfying'.[1] A woman who attended her seminars said Margaret 'appeared positively beautiful in her intelligent enthusiasm' (Howe, 1883, p 110). When the famed Polish poet, Adam Mickiewicz, wrote her from Paris urging her to think of herself as beautiful, Fuller had become attractive enough to enjoy as her lover a handsome Italian nobleman 11 years her junior. In the twentieth century, Harvard Scholar Perry Miller (1905–63) was to assert that she was 'phenomenally homely', but he was so virulently anti-feminist and disturbed by her forceful presence that he either altered or ignored what descriptions were available.

Liberal newspaperman Horace Greeley admired Fuller's dramatic ability and thought that, if she had 'condescended' to be an actress, she would have become the first lady of the American theatre. Fuller's dramatic style and growing reputation for brilliance both repelled and fascinated an ever-widening circle of friends. After seeking an invitation to visit Ralph Waldo Emerson, the leading radical thinker of the day, she became a member of the American Transcendentalist literary and philosophical movement. At first, she idealised Emerson and found in him the mentor she had long sought. Their intense intellectual exchanges gradually became emotionally charged. Although Emerson was married, they grew obsessed with each other, exchanging many carefully composed letters, quarrelling, reconciling, and continuing their discussions in their journals. Living within the constraints of the ideal of spiritual love became too much of a conflict, and they came to deny their feelings. Emerson transmuted his ambivalent emotions to poetry, and Fuller turned to other men.

A long-standing argument that Margaret Fuller and Emerson never resolved concerned his failure to admit the great difficulty a lady faced in being self-reliant and earning a living. After Fuller's father died, she had to make money to help her widowed mother and her younger brothers and sister. Because her brothers were not of legal majority, control of her father's estate went to a hated uncle, an arbitrary and narrow man who valued money above education. Fuller worked so resolutely to help educate her siblings that she gave up a long-desired trip to Europe with visiting feminist Harriet Martineau.

After an intense but frustrating stint of school teaching, Fuller found a means to make money that became very important in the history of the feminist movement. Fuller proposed a series of seminar-style Conversations which leading Boston women paid to attend. As she wrote in her letter of prospectus in 1840, her conversations would supply 'a point of union to well-educated and thinking women . . . where many of mature age wish for some place of stimulus and cheer . . . and for those younger, a place where they could state their doubts and difficulties, with a hope of gaining aid from the experience or aspirations of others' (Higginson, 1884, p 113). Unlike those who favoured traditional social gatherings, she wished to avoid the 'commonplace and personalities', and to 'systemise thought'. Her Conversations remained popular until she moved to New York. As 'consciousness-raisers', they influenced a nucleus of liberal thinkers who became leaders of the subsequent feminist and abolitionist movements in the United States.

Although her Conversations lasted five years, there is only one published account of a series, reconstructed from notes by a participant. After hearing that Fuller's Conversations were brilliant, comparable to Platonic dialogues, readers of 'Ten Conversations' generally react with disappointment. The discussions of 'Mythology of the Greeks and Its Expression in Art' are rather dry. Significantly, this was the only series to include males. One should consider recent scholarship which documents that conversations among women change when men are present. It is no surprise that Caroline Healey Dall explains in her preface that Margaret 'never enjoyed this mixed class, and considered it a failure so far as her own power was concerned. She and Mr Emerson met like Pyramus and Thisbe, a black wall between' (Dall, 1895, p 13). Dall also notes Emerson's interruptions and egotism: 'Emerson pursued his own train of thought. He seemed to forget that we had come together to pursue Margaret's' (p 46).

Dall's record reveals how Fuller dealt with overbearing men – with irony: 'Margaret said archly that she had thought the presence of gentlemen would prevent the wandering and keep us free from prejudice' (p 46). She smiled when rebuking William White, and at times, capitulated: 'Margaret wanted to pass on to Diana, but there were too many clergymen in the company' (p 117).

Although it is regrettable no one recorded a series of Conversations in which only women were present,[2] what does remain is evidence of Fuller's tactful handling of group discussions. Dall's record is at variance with Fuller's ill-deserved reputation for narcissism, which Emerson helped to create.

During the years that Fuller held her Conversations, she devoted the major part of her thought to writing. In 1840 she became the first editor of the *Dial*, the Transcendentalist literary and philosophical journal. Having to rely on unpaid contributors, she was often compelled to fill out her issues with essays she wrote in great haste. After relinquishing the *Dial* to Emerson in 1842, she took a westward journey on the Great Lakes and travelled by wagon into the Illinois prairie. Her narrative of this expedition, *Summer on the Lakes*, impressed Horace Greeley, who offered her a job as literary critic and feature writer on his New York *Tribune*, which she accepted. She finished writing her masterpiece, *Woman in the Nineteenth Century*, which was published in February, 1845, soon after she began work for Greeley. From this time on, she continued to support herself by writing. After less than two years in New York, she persuaded Greeley to let her become his foreign correspondent. She wrote dispatches for the *Tribune* from Great Britain, France and Italy.

In Italy she met Marquis Giovanni Angelo Ossoli, who eventually became her lover. A member of the nobility attached to the papacy, Ossoli joined the revolutionaries led by Giuseppe Mazzini, who sought to overthrow papal and foreign control of the various Italian states in order to unite Italy as a republic. During this period of unrest, Fuller gave birth to a son, Angelo. Not long afterwards, armed revolution broke out. Ossoli fought for the republic in the front lines, and Fuller directed the Fate Bene Fratelli hospital in Rome that received the wounded and the dying. After the collapse of the revolution in 1849, Fuller and Ossoli fled to Florence with their baby, and then sailed for the United States. The family drowned at sea, when their ship struck a reef during a storm off Fire Island, New York.

Much has been made of Fuller's dramatic life, and she does leave behind her the legend of a woman who lived in accordance with her beliefs and who influenced many American thinkers of her time. However, her richest heritage for the twentieth century is to be found in her writing. Even Perry Miller, one of her worst detractors, conceded that a remark Emerson alleged she made – 'I now know all the people worth knowing in America, and I find no intellect comparable to my own' (*Memoirs*, 1, p 234), may well have been true. Fuller was a genius whose writing is not yet fully appreciated. Although her inspiration began in the Transcendental well-spring of truth, the divine intuition, her vision accelerated to the universe – 'It is a constellation, not a phalanx, to which I would belong'. There is an often repeated story that Fuller told Thomas Carlyle in London in 1846 that she accepted 'the universe'. Whether or not this anecdote is approcryphal, it is true in spirit. Fuller was a comprehensivist. Although she began with the Transcendentalist dicta of self-reliance, her perspective included teleology. When an individual adhered to principle, then growth would take place. Not only would a transformation of the individual occur when connection was made, but correspondingly of society. Her vision is synergistic; human regeneration can take place when the individual monad fuses with the universal divine spark. Then, society catches fire and is transformed. Those who are receptive to 'lyric glimpses' and 'third thought' can become a part of the 'subtle and indirect motions' of the universe. As an incarnation of the Transcendental spirit, she is a precursor of contemporary thinkers, such as her grandnephew, Buckminster Fuller, who fuse the illumination of the mystic with the reason of the scientists.

During Fuller's lifetime, the United States was suffering from a parochial cultural outlook. Not unlike other young countries, America was self-consciously calling for an independent expression of its own culture while at the same time emulating traditional English literature. More than any other figure of her time, Fuller was instrumental in educating Americans to develop a more cosmopolitan artistic taste. As editor of *Dial*, and later as literary critic and feature writer for the *Tribune*, she was able to reach a wide audience. At a time when Emerson considered the ballet immoral and Nathaniel Hawthorne objected to undraped statues in Europe, Fuller defended dancing, acting, music, and considered the human body beautiful. Like a cultural missionary to a society still fettered to its Puritan past, she sought to establish the concept that an artist's personal life should not keep readers away from his or her work. Of the notorious George Sand Fuller wrote: 'It is her works, and not her private life, that we are considering.' And of Goethe (considered corrupt and sensual by Americans), some might call *The Elective Affinities* an 'immoral book', but she considered it 'a work of art'. As a literary critic, she set high standards and made powerful enemies when she wrote unfavourable reviews of the poetry of such reigning giants as James Russell Lowell and Henry Wadsworth Longfellow. An independent editor, she accepted Henry David Thoreau's first published poem, an essay advocating women's rights, and wrote many psychologically probing, experimental tales and essays, which helped to lessen America's cultural insularity.

As many other Americans of her time, Fuller was optimistic about the future greatness of the American republic 'if she has but the soul to will it'; but she also understood the power of a narrow-minded majority to corrupt. If a writer or book reviewer feared censure from the public, he would 'find the ostracism of democracy far more dangerous than the worst censure of a tyranny.' Moreover, unlike most of her contemporaries, Fuller welcomed 'a fusion of the races', including the African. Then, if the atmosphere were free with the 'winds from all quarters of the globe' bringing seed enough, there would be a new and golden harvest. For the full flowering of American genius, a polyglot society was needed. She foresaw the American people liberated by means of technology. When the nation was 'studded with towns, broken by the plow, netted together by railways and telegraph lines', then there would be leisure for original ideas (Fuller, 'American Literature', *Papers on Literature and Art*, 1846).

Despite Fuller's optimistic vision of the future, her articles reflected increasing awareness of social and economic inequities. In New York she celebrated Christmas in prison with thieves and prostitutes, and Valentine's Day at a dance in an insane asylum. However, it was not until she reached England that she felt the full horror of poverty.

Her 33 dispatches for the *Tribune*, written from 12 August 1846 to

6 July 1849, reveal a growing indignation at the plight of the oppressed. Coupled with her anger was a presentiment of impending revolution: '. . . all that pomp and parade of wealth and luxury in contrast to the misery, squalid, agonising, ruffianly, which stares one in the face in every street of London, and hoots at the gates of her palaces more ominous a note than ever was that of owl or raven in the portentous time when empires and races have crumbled and fallen from inward decay' (Fuller, *At Home and Abroad*, 1856, p 170). It was impossible, she wrote, to enjoy cultural life in the manufacturing towns, 'burning focuses of grief and vice', where she was appalled at the drunken women, the beggars, the filth, and the polluted air. Fuller visited some tourist attractions but she was mostly concerned with exploring how the people lived. She visited factories, schools, and, long before Zola wrote *Germinal*, descended on a bucket into a coal mine at Newcastle. She pitied the draft horses dreaming of green pastures, who were condemned never to see the day again. She noted upper-class means of social control in which a gentleman was 'cut' by the local gentry for his opposition to the oppressive Corn Laws. Although she had an entrée to some homes of the upper class, she deplored 'the shocking inhumanity of exclusiveness', and hoped for the 'day when the noblest commoner shall be the only noble possible in England' (p 188). In her letters for the *Tribune*, she not only deplored the condition of the poor, but openly advocated a more equitable distribution of wealth.

Other letters to New York reveal extraordinary powers of observation as she described visits with famous writers: Harriet Martineau, Thomas DeQuincey, Joanna Baillie, and William Wordsworth. At Thomas Carlyle's home, she met Giuseppe Mazzini, the exiled Italian revolutionary. Her interest in Mazzini and his cause was immediate. After a sojourn in Paris, where her friendship with George Sand and the Polish poet Adam Mickiewicz influenced her to liberate herself emotionally, she travelled to Italy.

With vivid prose she wrote home to the States of the burgeoning unrest in Rome. At first, she believed Pope Pius IX, who controlled the papal state that cut through the Italian peninsula and encompassed Rome, was sincere in his efforts to liberalise the theocratic state. However, unwilling to accept any loss of his temporal power, Pius had a change of heart and fled the Vatican disguised as an ordinary priest. His return to power was brought about by French and Austrian troops, and followed by the abortive uprising led by Mazzini. Her dispatches to the *Tribune* pleading for American help met with some sympathy, but when Horace Greeley learned of her liaison with Ossoli, he refused to accept any more of her work. Yet, a year after her death, Greeley published articles sent by Marx and Engels from Germany.

In assessing Fuller's accomplishments as a social thinker, it is impossible to separate her feminist theory from her writing on any subject. When she discussed the problems of poverty, she never forgot that the plight of women was especially difficult. She described ways to alleviate their labour – day-care centres, public laundries and baths. Many impoverished women suffered working as prostitutes: 'I have seen them under the thin veil of gayety, and in the horrible tatters of utter degradation' (p 211). She came to see a prostitute as the paradigm for all women, as she noted numbly that in Lyon women worked as weavers or prostitutes, and that in Rome mothers and wives were beaten by their men for their drunken diversion. Her initial thinking, stimulated by interaction with women who attended her Conversations, was crystallised in her formal feminist treatise, *Women in the Nineteenth Century.* She continued the arguments introduced by this key work in much of her subsequent writing.

Preceded by Mary Wollstonecraft's *A Vindication of the Rights of Woman* (1792), Fuller's *Woman in the Nineteenth Century* (1845) deals with many of the feminist issues delineated by Wollstonecraft, but it differs in tone. Wollstonecraft wrote in indignant anger, whereas Fuller wrote in a Transcendental mood of optimism.

In the United States, Fuller's work was preceded in 1837 by Sarah Moore Grimké's *Letters on the Equality of the Sexes and the Condition of Women.* Grimké devotes considerable space to Biblical exegesis, to prove that, within the sight of God, men and women are equal. She also discusses education for girls, the inequality of pay for men and women, (citing an inequity not too dissimilar from the current US ratio of 59 percent to 100 percent), and the sexual exploitation of the black slave. On other issues, Grimké is less advanced, but, nevertheless, her series of 15 letters published in the Boston *Spectator* is an important precursor to Fuller's work.

A concept Fuller suggests in *Woman in the Nineteenth Century* is the idea of sisterhood. No matter how noble the man is, or how good his intentions are, he cannot understand a woman's needs or adequately represent her. Therefore, Fuller argues, women must band together to help each other. In her introduction to *A Vindication of the Rights of Woman,* Wollstonecraft states that most writers address their instruction to *ladies* but that hers is intended for the members of the *middle class,* who live in a more 'natural state' than the corrupt aristocracy. Fuller, on the other hand, assets that *ladies* must take responsibility for prostitutes; they must seek them out and help them, or they who have had an opportunity for 'more light' are on a lower moral level than the prostitutes. Other pariahs needing help are pregnant slaves, over-worked seamstresses and laundrywomen. She applauds Lydia Maria Child for coming to aid of a woman who was charged with stabbing her seducer. Moreover, Fuller envisioned collective action by a sisterhood. In the American controversy over Texas, she thought of organising a meeting of women to express their moral convictions and take a stand in opposition to the annexation of another slave state. Not only must women join together for social action and to help each other, but they must learn to help themselves. They must develop self-trust and self-reliance.

To encourage self-confidence in women, she assembled a catalogue of famous women 'to show that no age was left entirely without a witness of the equality of the sexes in function, duty and hope' (Fuller, *Woman*, 1845, p 172). To affirm the power of woman, Fuller combed world literature for examples to illustrate her belief. She cited historical personages: Aspasia from Greece, Emily Plater from Poland, Queens Elizabeth and Catharine, Lady Godiva and Madame du Pompadour. She searched religious literature and appropriated Hagar, Mary, and Eve from the Bible; Sita from the *Ramayana*; Isis from Egyptian myth; and Ceres and Proserpine from Greek myth. She analysed literature for strong and noble female characters. She extolled Edmund Spenser's Britomart as an ideal woman, who was virtuous, strong, and independent. Her search led her beyond patriarchial Hebrew-Christian society for the prototype Earth Mother, a powerful Sibylline priestess whose intuition served as a medium to the divine. Although in Greece, 'even victory wore a female form', she used Cassandra as an example of a woman whose psychic powers were wasted. Ultimately, her quest was for the feminine principle. From her vast research Fuller found many role models for young women to emulate or to lament, as she evoked a chorus of women, historical, fictional, mythic, to attest to life's possibilities.

After assembling women from all time and civilisations to serve as witnesses to the genius women possess, in an autobiographical vignette, thinly disguised as the story of Miranda, Fuller linked her experience and life with that of her catalogue of women. She had begun *Woman in the Nineteenth Century* by using the conventional editorial 'we', but after 15 pages, she changed to 'I'. Later, she alternated between both pronouns, but towards the end of her peroration, she reverted to 'I' and at the end to 'us'. Throughout her work, she referred to the experiences of women she knew. What she has done, then, is to use her spiritual autobiography as a link from the famous women she cited to the lives of all women. Looking into her own soul, she saw reflected the frustrated aspirations of other women: 'What concerns me now is, that my life be a beautiful, powerful, in a word, a complete life in its kind. Had I but one more moment to l:ve, I must wish the same.' Then she prophesied 'the glories of that destiny; faint, but not to be mistaken streaks of the future day' (p 163).

With psychological acumen, Fuller understood the human heart. She believed that 'sex, like rank, wealth, beauty, or talent, is but an accident of birth'. She came to realise the androgynous nature of sexuality, that 'there is no wholly masculine man, no purely feminine woman'. She once observed to Emerson that a woman may be in love with a woman, a man with a man. She calls for an end to sexual stereotyping: 'But Penelope is no more meant for a baker or weaver solely, than Ulysses for a cattle-herd' (p 33). In England she noted with pleasure that men were cooks in the Reform Club and that she hoped to see the day when they would also do the washing. To support her view that girls who so wish should be allowed to use carpenters' tools, she cites socialist visionary Charles Fourier's utopian theories of attractive industry and sexual equality as paving the way for the new order that is to rise from love rather than strife. Children whose tastes are indulged are cheerful, whereas those who are thwarted grow sullen. Her call for an end to job segregation culminates in her most famous suggestion, that all positions should be open to women, even that of a sea captain.

She also understood that an impoverished spirit could be as destructive as an impoverished body. She described her own gloomy days full of dull people and domestic duties as 'rye-bread days'. Speaking of the Greek hell, she noted that all of the punishments of Tartarus meted out to a Tantalus or a Sisyphus involved baffled effort. Captivated by a painting in a Scottish castle, she noticed 'the face of a girl full of the most pathetic sensibility, and with no restraint of convention upon her ardent, gentle expression'. Fuller's comment was: 'She died young'. In Italy, she gave a chilling account of a woman taking her vows to be a nun.

It is no surprise that Fuller should call for emotional as well as financial independence for women. A woman should live *first* for God, instead of making an imperfect man her god. Love should mean no more to a woman than to a man: 'It is a vulgar error that love, *a* love to woman is her whole existence; she also is born for Truth and

Love in their universal energy' (p 177).

Woman in the Nineteenth Century is a public declaration that women must rely on themselves and free themselves from their dependence on men. A call for action, it is the feminist manifesto: 'We would have every arbitrary barrier thrown down' (p 26). Written in eloquent language befitting the high seriousness of its subject, *Woman in the Nineteenth Century* ultimately becomes a message to both women and men to discover within themselves their spirituality and permit it to grow. Men who are exploiters suffer with those they oppress. When the obstacle of the self is overcome, the world correspondingly reflects the transformed individual. Ultimately, the book transcends the issue of woman's rights and becomes a philosophic message on the inter-dependence of all people.

Margaret Fuller's manifesto had effect. Three years after its publication, a small group met in Seneca Falls, New York, to draft a declaration of independence for women, A Declaration of Sentiments. This was the nucleus of the organised feminist movement that fought for the next 72 years for American women to gain the right to vote. And yet, despite testimony from early feminist leaders as to Fuller's greatness, that she had vindicated a 'woman's right to think', and that, had she lived, they had hoped to have had her at the head of their organisation, Fuller's genius is still not widely acclaimed even by feminists today.

Her decline in influence began after the Civil War, a period when women had hoped to be enfranchised along with the liberated slaves they had worked to free. Instead of giving women the vote, the United States legislatures passed a Constitutional Amendment which for the first time appended the word *male* as a requirement for the ballot. Accordingly, there was a new mood of disillusionment and militancy among feminists. As Julia Ward Howe observed, Fuller's treatise was still valid, but thinkers of her day had little of her confidence in the existence of souls.

In addition to a general feeling that Transcendental optimism was not in accordance with reality, a specific defamation of Fuller was already in progress. As the 'traitors' in *1984* with unacceptable views were erased from history by Big Brother's 'Thought Police', so, too, have many outspoken women 'disappeared'. The distortion of Fuller's reputation after her death could easily be compared to the fate of other women who are ambitious, unorthodox, and a threat to the patriarchy.

The American feminists Ednah Dow Cheney and Caroline Healey Dall linked Fuller with the first American feminist, Anne

Hutchinson. Born in England in 1591, Anne Marbury Hutchinson emigrated to the New England Colonies. An Antinomian, Hutchinson held meetings (Conversations) for women in her home, and she soon came into conflict with the Puritan authorities. In 1637, she was put on trial, and, as Governor John Winthrop recorded in his Journal: 'Mr Cotton pronounced the sentence of admonition with great solemnity, and with such zeal and detestation of her errors and pride of spirit.' Some months later she was examined again. At first refusing to recant her views, she later capitulated. Still, the church authorities were not content: she was excommunicated and banished to the wilderness, and was later killed by Indians. One of the 'proofs' of her guilt was that Anne Hutchinson gave birth in exile to a 'monster', a deformed baby. Both Cheney and Dall, who attended Fuller's Conversations, made the connection between Fuller's teaching and Hutchinson's.

In erasing a woman from history, the traditional first step is to discredit her for her sexuality (or lack of it), as in the case of Wollstonecraft (see pp 40*ff*). Enemies of female emancipation used Wollstonecraft's sexual non-conformity to attack her cause. With freedom for women associated with promiscuity, young women seeking to win husbands avoided its 'contamination'. Initially, Fuller had been treated in reviews of *Woman in the Nineteenth Century* more kindly than one might have expected. She was not attacked in the American press as the 'whore of Babylon', as was the radical feminist lecturer, Fanny Wright, but snide comments were made about Fuller for being 'an old maid'. She was castigated in the *Broadway Journal* for writing on the subject of marriage (sex), which 'no virtuous woman can treat justly'. After her relationship with Ossoli became known, a chorus of detractors attacked her as 'a fallen woman'.

After her death, her friends wrote a memorial memoir, which had as damaging an impact on Fuller's reputation as had William Godwin's on Mary Wollstonecraft. In the *Memoirs of Margaret Fuller Ossoli*, compiled and written by Ralph Waldo Emerson, William Henry Channing, and James Freeman Clarke, Fuller is discredited, not because of the scandal of her liaison with Ossoli but because of the purported arrogance of her personality, her lack of beauty, and the poor quality of her writing. Emerson who claimed 'her pen was a non-conductor', even went so far as to say she was content with the role society assigned to women, which is, of course, a lie, and reflected his own wishful thinking. The chief architect of the distortion of Fuller's reputation, Emerson, probably was at one time 'in love' with her. In the *Memoirs* he ostensibly was trying to mitigate the scandal surrounding Fuller's belated announcement from Italy that she had a husband and a one-year old son. Hence, unlike Godwin who tried to 'explain' his wife's unconventional behaviour, the editors bowdlerised the radical and sexual side of Fuller, and presented a schizophrenic image of her, one that was both a virtuous 'true woman' and a charismatic but arrogant woman, who had, as Emerson expressed it, 'a mountainous ME'. Their portrait of an irrational, unhappy, sickly woman emerged as a feminist archetype – a witch who could not write, but who charmed by women's traditional weapon, her tongue. Fuller's writing began to go out of print, but the *Memoirs* continued to sell well. Although she had her sympathisers as well as detractors, subsequent biographers were hard-pressed to disagree with the long-lived Emerson, who came to wear the mantle of a secular seer. Biographers could not ignore the *Memoirs*, and therefore had either to undertake an arduous elucidation of its distortion, or to apologise for Fuller's conduct. The *Memoirs* became a judgmental nemesis.

Not only did Fuller's friends damage her by indirection; her enemies attacked her openly. James Russell Lowell in retaliation for her unflattering review wrote satirical verse on her egotism. Just as Fuller in her *Woman in the Nineteenth Century* had merged Eve with Britomart with George Sand, so too, was she transformed into a fictional character. Nathaniel Hawthorne protrayed her most notably in *The Blithedale Romance* as Zenobia, a fallen woman who, disappointed in love, drowns herself.[3] Hawthorne's rancour was carried into the next generation by his son. In 1884, Julian Hawthorne printed his late father's journal, in which the famous writer called Fuller's husband 'half an idiot' and Margaret a coarse woman whose life was 'ridiculous' rather than tragic. 'With a defective and evil nature,' she fell 'as the weakest of her sisters.'

In the twentieth century, Perry Miller, who possessed impressive credentials in the American academic establishment, gave the Harvard imprimatur to the denigration of Fuller, citing the *Memoirs* as the indispensable source book. Current scholars know it is no longer acceptable to castigate a woman openly for her sexuality, but are still intolerant of an assertive and aggressive woman. Three contemporary scholars who carry on the tradition of Miller despite their access to informed feminist criticism are Joel Myerson, Larzer Ziff and Gay Wilson Allen. Although Myerson has done an excellent job of compiling two Fuller bibliographies, in his introduction to a collection of Fuller's essays (1978), he still seems compelled to repeat Emerson's statement that she showed 'the presence of a rather mountainous ME'. Moreover, he draws a cause-and-effect relationship between her 'physical shortcomings' and Fuller's concentration 'on cultivating her mental powers', implying that, had she been beautiful, she would not have been interested in competing with men as an intellectual equal. In *The New England Transcendentalists and the Dial* (1980) Myerson reiterates the credo of 'Fuller — The Capital I', and, even more damagingly for a man with access to feminist criticism, comments: 'Only after her romance with Ossoli, who accepted her purely as a woman, did she successfully integrate the various facets of her personality' (p 235). Although Fuller was phenomenally popular with women, and Horace Greeley noted that women of all ranks, including chambermaids and seamstresses, confided in her, and Caroline Sturgis suggested that the members of her coterie loved her, Myerson wrote that both women and men disliked her. In another current study, *Literary Democracy* (1981), Larzer Ziff reiterates the *Memoirs*, emphasising that Fuller was a better speaker than a writer and a woman who turned to literature because she had no better outlet for her talents, until she found a lover in Italy and turned revolutionary. Also, in a new biography of Emerson, Gay Wilson Allen at last recognises Fuller's sexuality, but translates Emerson's timidity into 'Margaret's failure to seduce' Emerson. Although Allen notes that after Fuller's death, Emerson 'could not get Margaret out of his mind', and that he commented on her in eight separate pages of his journal, he does not reach the obvious conclusion that the Concord sage who invited Fuller to meet him in Paris had loved her longer than she did him.[4]

This is not to suggest that Fuller was not for a time greatly interested in Emerson, or that she was not egotistic. Of course she was egotistic, as any writer or thinker who has new ideas must be. What is being suggested is that many contemporary scholars are unable to apply the same criteria to a woman they evaluate that they apply to a man.

In the very necessary reassessment of Margaret Fuller, one must first explode the academic myth of objectivity. Study of Fuller's life suggests that precisely what befell her befalls other women who aspire to greater heights than the male power structure wishes them to reach. Considered especially dangerous are those women who encourage other women to revolt. Radical women can be simply excommunicated as were Anne Hutchinson and Anne Johnson; or they can be violated by contumely and distortion as were Wollstonecraft and Fuller. As any other revolutionary who demands sexual and social equality, Fuller is dangerous to those who benefit from exploitation. Such women are attacked for being ugly, arrogant, ridiculous, and sexually unorthodox or inadequate, as are the leaders of the feminist movement today. If it is asserted often enough that a woman cannot write, she will have few readers. People may still read *about* her, but they will not consider what she, herself, has to say.

An acquaintance with Margaret Fuller through her writing brings both female and male readers the contagion of hope and the courage to keep fighting for principle and truth in relationships of the heart and of the mind.

Notes

1 *Memoirs of Margaret Fuller Ossoli* 1852, ed Ralph Waldo Emerson, William Henry Channing and James Freeman Clarke, Phillips, Sampson & Co, Boston, 1:91. Hedge knew Fuller well whereas Larzer Ziff in *Literary Democracy*, 1981, (Viking, New York), p 158, dismisses Hedge's description as 'gallantry'.
2 Elizabeth Peabody made a partial record of a few conversations.
3 Interestingly enough, Evert A. Duyckinck, editor of *The Literary World*, upon first meeting Hawthorne's wife wrote she 'resembles Margaret Fuller in appearance though more robust than she was'. Edwin Haviland Miller, *Melville*, Braziller, New York, 1975, p 30.
4 Gay Wilson Allen, *Waldo Emerson*, Viking, New York, 1981, p 336.

Select Bibliography of Margaret Fuller

Conversations With Goethe in the Last Years of his Life, Translated From the German of Eckerman (translation), Hilliard, Gray & Co, Boston, 1839.
Correspondence of Fräulein Günderode and Bettina von Arnim (translation), E.P. Peabody, Boston, 1842.
Summer on the Lakes in 1843, Charles C. Little and James Brown, Boston, 1844.
Woman in the Nineteenth Century, Greeley and McElrath, New York, 1845.
Papers on Literature and Art, Wiley and Putnam, New York, 1846.
At Home and Abroad, ed Arthur Buckminster Fuller, Crosby, Nichols & Co, Boston, 1856
Life Without and Life Within, ed Arthur Buckminster Fuller, Brown, Taggard and Chase, Boston, 1860.
Love-Letters of Margaret Fuller, 1845–1846, intro by Julia Ward Howe, D. Appleton & Co, New York, 1903.

Barbara Bodichon:
Integrity in Diversity
(1827–1891)

Jacquie Matthews*

Feminist, law reformer, painter, publicist, friend of
George Eliot, illegitimate cousin of Florence Nightingale, educationalist, co-founder of Girton College, worker for women's suffrage,
married to an eccentric revolutionary French doctor, Barbara Leigh
Smith Bodichon has all but disappeared from the history of the
nineteenth century which her life spanned.

Eldest of the five children of Anne Longden and Benjamin Leigh
Smith, Barbara was seven when her mother died. Her grandfather
was William Smith, Radical MP for Norwich from 1784 to 1830 –
Jacobin, Unitarian Dissenter, lieutenant of Wilberforce in the anti-
slavery movement, art patron and reformer. Her father, Benjamin,
was elected to the same seat in 1837. Their London house was a centre
for radical, even Chartist-sympathising politicians, visiting American
abolitionists like Elizabeth Cady Stanton and Lucretia Mott, and
political refugees from Europe. The children were not sent off to the
nursery but encouraged to watch and listen. Bessie Parkes, great-
granddaughter of Joseph Priestley, became her life-long friend,
companion on an unchaperoned tour of Europe, co-founder of the
English Women's Journal. Harriet Martineau and W. J. Fox were
frequent visitors.

The children attended the Westminster Infant School, a 'Ragged
School', founded and financed by Benjamin, where James Buchanan
from Robert Owen's famous New Lanark school, taught and practised ideas of harmony, co-operation and experience of the physical
world. Much time was spent outdoors on the family farm at Scalands
near Hastings. They explored Europe and Britain in a horse omnibus.

*I should like to thank Hester Burton, Dr Alicia Percival, John Crabbe,
Phillida Bunkle, and the staff of the Fawcett Library, Girton College Library,
and Victoria University Library, for the generous help they have given me.

Benjamin was very unauthoritarian – Bessie Parkes's first memory of the family was his kneeling to tie Barbara's shoelace. He also held the unusual opinion that daughters should have an equal provision with sons, so when Barbara turned 21 he gave her an independent income of £300 a year.

In 1854 she published *A Brief Summary in Plain Language of the Most Important Laws Concerning Women*, opened an outsiders' school and began building for herself and with her own money a simple country cottage at Scalands. In 1855 she drafted a petition asking for legislation to give married women control of their earnings and property. This led to the growth of the 'Langham Place Circle' of feminist activities.

In late 1856 Barbara visited Algeria where she met Eugene Bodichon, a 46-year-old doctor, long-time resident of Algeria and former left-wing deputy of the 1848–49 Republic. She published *Women and Work* just before their marriage in London on 2 July 1857. They went for what Mrs Gaskell rather tartly called 'their honey-year' (actually seven months) to America. The account of it appears in *An American Diary* (ed Reed, 1972) which is partly journal, partly letters home. They travelled through most of the slave States, spending six weeks in New Orleans before visiting Washington DC, New York, Philadelphia, Toronto, Montreal and finally Boston. This journey was very important for her intellectual development and brought the Langham Place Circle more closely into the international women's movement.

Over the next years she spent most winters with Eugene in Algeria where she wrote, painted and travelled. In spring and autumn she taught in her school, read papers at Social Science Congresses, worked for the *English Women's Journal* and the Employment and Emigration Societies, studied with Corot, held exhibitions. Eugene joined her for the summer at Scalands. They had no children. After her father's death in 1860 she had a personal income of £1,000 a year.

Her three main involvements of the sixties and seventies – the promotion of education for girls at the lower and middle levels, women's suffrage and higher education, in particular the foundation of Girton College – were all in association with Emily Davies. Her friendship with George Eliot grew closer.

An attack of haemoplegia in 1878 left her partially paralysed and restricted her travels. Dr Bodichon was also in poor health, visiting England for the last time in 1881. At Scalands she continued to receive friends and held night classes for local young people until her death in 1891.

The bare bones of her biography suggest a surprising even a suspiciously wide range of activity. Dr Alicia Percival, in an unpublished study of the Langham Place set, sums her up as 'amateur, advanced'. But there is integrity in her diversity; she is many-sided but whole. With what Bessie Parkes describes as 'the sunshine of her vigorous intellect and her warm heart', Barbara is a tough and shining thread in the mid-century women's network.

Her fundamental ideas show up early as feminist, radical and comprehensive. 1848 is the year of revolution in Europe and Barbara turns twenty-one. She reads John Stuart Mill's *Political Economy*, just published, and in January 1849 writes an analysis of it, regretting that Mill 'touching so often on unsettled questions of the greatest importance and interest, has not gone away from Political Economy and . . . given us his valuable opinion on them'. She speaks of the 'injustice of men's laws to women and the absurdity of the present laws of marriage and divorce'.

> Philosophers and reformers have generally been afraid to say anything about the unjust laws both of society and country which crush women.

> There never was a tyranny so deeply felt yet borne so silently, that is the worst of it. . .

> But now I hope there are some who will brave ridicule for the sake of justice to half the people in the world. (Unpublished notes in Leigh Smith Papers, Girton College Library)

Even given her radical family, her Owenist education, her Aunt Julia, friend of American Women's Rights advocates, her reading of Wollstonecraft and Martineau, it is still striking to find this young Victorian girl looking so boldly and lucidly at philosophers, institutions and herself, and planning remedies. Why, with her income and favourable conditions, did she speak of tyranny?

It is likely that she had realised the contradiction between what her life was and what it might have been. Benjamin Leigh Smith, the man and father, was generous, unorthodox and permissive but she knew her case was exceptional. As an illegitimate girl child she could have expected emotional and material destitution under the patriarchal laws and institutions of her England. By law, she could inherit nothing, not even her surname. Marian Evans (George Eliot) refers to the Leigh Smiths as the 'Taboo'd family' (Eliot, *Letters*, 1955, Vol II, p 45) and Mrs Gaskell speaks of Barbara being 'in consequence of her birth a strong fighter against the established opinions of the world' (Gaskell, *Letters*, 1955, p 606). She must have known from her mother's sister Dorothy that Anne had been a 'ravishingly pretty milliner's apprentice of seventeen' (Mrs Belloc Lowndes in an unpublished letter) to her father's middle-class forty, and that she had died of consumption after bearing five children in seven years (not that holy wedlock protected mothers from that fate, as Charlotte Brontë could have told her). It was unclear whether Benjamin had Godwinian views or simply preferred not to marry his young mistress, but for her mother, and later for Barbara, emotional and financial security depended entirely on the continuing goodwill of one man. They had privileges but no rights. While appearing to renounce his patriarchal authority, Benjamin's choice not to marry made his power more absolute and more arbitrary. The conflict for Barbara must have been great – how to reconcile the love and admiration for her generous radical father with the memory of the 'poor little mother' and the laws which crush women. I believe that she found that reconciliation in her feminism.

Certainly it is early and deep. One of her first memories is Buchanan reading an Arabian Nights tale, the 'story of Perizade, the Princess who did not mind the black stones when she was bent on getting the living water . . . has made an impression on my whole life. Wasn't I glad she got to the top of the hill! Wasn't I glad she could do it though her brothers failed!' (Burton, 1949, p 8). The awareness of women was a consistent theme in her whole intellectual development. When she reads Mayhew it is the working women that interest her most and how their situation differs from that of men workers. When she summarises Mill for a Journal article she refers to the student as 'she' and takes her examples from familiar life. When she visits America she wants to know particularly how slavery affects women, what the social position and future are for black and coloured women living with white men. She is fascinated to hear Theodore Parker preach.

> He prayed to the Creator, the infinite Mother of us all (always using Mother instead of Father in this prayer). It was the prayer of all I ever heard in my life which was the truest to my individual soul. (Reed, 1972, p 158)

She believes that solidarity and mutual support are women's source of strength:

> The feelings that others rely on me has given me most strength of all things. If one leans on one side and one on another it gives

strength to what is weaker than either. (Letter to Hilary Bonham-Carter, quoted Burton, 1949, p 182)

She exchanges that kind of love and support with women friends throughout her life. She has a very close relationship with her two more unorthodox aunts, Julia Smith and Dorothy Longden, the one encouraging her work for women's rights and education and the other her radical and Chartist sympathies.

She was aware of the reality of women's lives behind the facade of male literary and artistic brotherhoods. When D. G. Rossetti brought Elizabeth Siddal to Scalands, Barbara saw the strain and sickness of the exhausted milliner and exploited model behind the languorous image of Millais' 'Ophelia' or Rossetti's 'Beatrice'. Barbara was concerned about Elizabeth's illness and wanted her to go to Florence Nightingale's recently established clinic for 'ladies of small means' in Harley Street.

Barbara stands out from her contemporaries in not defining the world and other women, in terms of men. Mrs Gaskell writes, 'I wish I could help taking to men so much more than to women' (Gaskell, 1955, p 808) and George Eliot says in almost identical words, 'I wish I could throw myself heartily into the love of other women besides you and Cara – but somehow the male friends always eclipse the female – pardon the word' (Gaskell, 1955, Vol II, p 38). Barbara rejected those feelings and that language; for her, female friends often eclipsed the male. In 1856 she founded the Society for Female Artists and clearly considered all three words positive.

She cut through accepted male formulations of what is intellectually important, practically possible, and appropriate for women. I have noticed the word 'theory' used only once about Barbara's ideas and that was in a letter from George Eliot about Barbara's friend, Dr Elizabeth Blackwell, the first woman doctor to practise in England, having qualified in Geneva (New York) and Paris.

Mr Lewes lunched the other day with Toynbee the great aurist (ear specialist) who said that she (Dr Blackwell) had been to his place to look over his apparatus and that there was more judgment and knowledge in her remarks than in any professional visitors he remembered. That will please both your friendship and your theory won't it? (Gaskell, 1955, Vol III, p 59)

Barbara has not been considered a theorist because theories are usually housed in vast tomes of authoritative and often turgid prose. Hers are clothed in a few pamphlets, in articles in the *English*

Women's Journal, in working papers read to a Social Science Congress, in diaries and letters to friends, all written with an immediate purpose. Her theories were worked out in framing a petition, starting a school, painting a picture, addressing a meeting, co-operating with a group of friends to run a press campaign, living a commuter marriage. She integrated a whole range of experience into linked projects directed towards social change, rather than engaged in abstract analysis.

Between her January 1849 comments on Mill and the 1854 publication of the *Brief Summary*, Barbara had herself become the person who would 'brave ridicule for the sake of common justice to half the people of the world'. That 'she was aroused by the Caroline Norton case' – the usual explanation for her movement – is an absurdly inadequate one for this momentous development, and underestimates the importance of her intellectual growth in those crucial five years.

Barbara attended the new socially mixed, non-conformist, female-administered Bedford College, rather than Queen's which had Royal Patronage, upper-class support and a 'Christian Socialist' man principal, F. D. Maurice. At Bedford there were lectures from London University Professors on Law and Political Economy as well as an art studio. There was also striking evidence before her that girls' random and restricted education left them ill-equipped to pursue higher studies. The Quaker principal Elizabeth Reid and councillor Aunt Julia were forced to set up remedial classes.

Barbara's intellectual and political circle was wide. She read the 1851 *Westminster Review* 'Article on the Enfranchisement of Women', and believed that its author was Harriet Taylor not J. S. Mill. Evidence suggests that she was already in touch with an international network of politically aware and active women. The *Westminster Review* article concludes with mention of the Sheffield Women's Political Association. Its secretary, Ann Knight, had supported Jeanne Deroin, still in Paris in 1849, in her fight against the exclusion of women from revolutionary political clubs and meetings. In turn, Jeanne Deroin addressed the 1851 Ohio Women's Rights Convention in a letter written from St Lazare prison. In 1853 and 1854 Jeanne Deroin was in exile in London publishing a small *Almanach des Femmes*; articles on the American Women's Convention, clothing reform, the death penalty, Saint-Simonian Women, women artists (Hatty Hosmer and Rosa Bonheur), and musicians, women doctors (Elizabeth Blackwell), mental asylums, infanticide, child-care, vegetarianism and temperance, anticipate the scope and format of the *English Women's Journal* founded four years later. Barbara certainly used Deroin's *Cours de Droit Social* when comparing French and English laws concerning women.

The 1854 *Brief Summary in Plain Language of the Most Important Laws Concerning Women* set out to rectify Mill's omission of a critical consideration of 'the laws concerning women' and especially the 'Contract of Marriage'. Barbara explains that in the almost total submergence of married women's legal identity under Common Law, a woman's body belongs to her husband and that he could enforce his right by writ of habeas corpus; that money earned by a married woman belongs absolutely to her husband; that without consent a married woman, or even a betrothed one, might not dispose of any property; and that when a wife's property is stolen, the property is described as his. The legal custody of children belongs to the father: 'During the lifetime of a sane father, the mother has no rights over her children . . . and the father may take them from her and dispose of them as he sees fit.'

Barbara noted that these were the provisions of the Common Law. The rich, through the Courts of Equity, could make property settlements 'to secure a wife and her children against the power of the husband' but the earnings of the working-class wife or the married middle-class writer or actress were quite unprotected.

It was a factual summary; the style was concise, careful and dispassionate, but it was not an academic legal exercise. The summary was 'brief' and 'in plain language' because she wanted it to be accessible and effective. Its publication was swiftly reinforced by two moves. The first was an appeal to the male legal establishment. Barbara arranged for it to be put before the Law Amendment Society. The second move was that of a radical feminist. She called a meeting of women and drew up a petition (the full text was published in the *Law Amendment Society's Journal*, 1855–56, Vol 1). They decided to circulate the petition with requests for signatures and additional meetings. Even more important than this incipient political organisation was that they asked for evidence of the hardship caused by the law.

The petition addresses itself to women of all classes. The question

> . . . must be recognised by all as of practical importance because of the numbers of women employed in manufacturing as sempstresses, laundresses, charwomen, and in other multifarious occupations.

The census of 1851 revealed interesting facts about working women whose earnings were the legal property of their husbands.

The petition shows Barbara's wide-ranging awareness of women's oppression, including marital violence. It is concerned with the vulnerability of all women under the law,

> . . . for the robbery by a man of his wife's hard earnings there is no redress; against the selfishness of a drunken father, who wrings from a mother her children's daily bread, there is no appeal. She may work from morning till night to see the produce of her labour wrested from her, and wasted in a gin palace; and such cases are within the knowledge of everyone.

Barbara's sense of justice is then expressed in a clause declaring that a husband should not be responsible for unlimited debts incurred by his wife, nor necessarily for the entire maintenance of his family. Barbara ends the petition strongly,

> . . . it is time that legal protection be thrown over the produce of their (women's) labour and that in entering the state of marriage, they no longer pass from freedom into the condition of a slave, all whose earnings belong to his master and not to himself.

The importance of this petition, which went round England in 1855–56 and by 1857 had collected 60,000 signatures, has been underestimated by historians. The very words of the title of the 1857 Married Women's Property Bill based on it falsely suggest privilege and inheritance.

The petition carried 26,000 women's signatures when it was presented to Parliament in March 1856. The London sheets alone showed 3,000 signatures including those of Elizabeth Barrett Browning, Harriet Martineau, Jane Carlyle, Marian Evans (later to be George Eliot), Maria Rye, Elizabeth Gaskell and Geraldine Jewsbury. It may be said that all the subsequent Married Women's Property Acts were based on Barbara's petition and *Brief Summary* and all the provisions therein were not finally passed till 1893.

The petition had other momentous results. The evidence invited by the Blandford Square Collective flooded in. The case histories and statistics and data collected, and the new enthusiasts recruited from the provinces were to provide the basis for the nascent feminist movement. The *English Women's Journal* was founded with the help of Barbara's money and Bessie Parkes as editor, but it was the contacts established by the petition which provided the readership. Within one year of its etablishment the *Journal* approached the circulation of the old-established *Westminster Review*.

The *Journal* was an important step towards public organisation. 1856 saw the Society of Female Artists founded and 1857 the new National Association for the Promotion of Social Sciences under the chairmanship of Lord Brougham. Isa Craig, one of the petition activists, was appointed Assistant Secretary. The appointment of a woman was considered 'surprising and revolutionary'. The Association provided important access to a public platform for feminists. Drawing on the empirical data generated by the petition, women read papers on a huge range of immediate issues, education, working conditions, employment, and social problems. The *Journal* published many of them.

Other important initiatives quickly followed: new rooms at 19 Langham Place and an employment bureau established by Barbara which later grew (under Jessie Boucherett) into the Society for Promoting the Employment of Women; Emily Faithfull began the Victoria Printing Press, and Jessie a remedial school in arithmetic and accounting; Maria Rye started a law engrossing office for copying legal documents, before she turned to promoting the emigration of women. They broke other barriers. A petition was got up to get women admitted to Royal Academy schools. When it was agreed to open the local swimming baths to ladies if they could muster 30 patrons, 30 young women downed tools and went off swimming on Wednesday afternoons.

All these projects and activities sprang more or less directly from a petition which did not carry Barbara's name, but those of Anna Jameson and Mary Howitt, whose position as older women writers made them more appropriate petitioners. Thinker, initiator, and organiser, Barbara seldom seemed concerned with who got the credit.

The years from 1851–54 were also the incubation period for Barbara's educational theories. Reading widely in education – Owen, Pestalozzi, Swedenborg, and probably Froebel – she re-evaluated her own radical education. She and Elizabeth Whitehead (later Malleson) visited many schools, among them the Utilitarian Birkbeck schools where they found the teaching efficient but the aims and attitudes too moralistic, prescriptive and unimaginative.

In 1854 they opened the Portman Hall School in hired rooms in a socially mixed neighbourhood off Edgeware Road. A fair slice of Barbara's £300 a year went to rent and salaries and equipment.

The school was co-educational, cost sixpence a week and forbade corporal punishment. There Garibaldi's son, a Jewish tailor's daughter, Elizabeth Whitehead's younger sisters, and pupils from families of 'advanced free thought' and Irish Catholicism, were singing, drawing, having lessons in physiology and health, doing gymnastics, visiting the Museum or going on expeditions on Saturdays. Miranda Hill was advised against joining the staff by the Rev F. D. Maurice because of the absence of all religious teaching.

That Barbara's ideas on education were not confined to a little philanthropic pottering in 'her' school can best be judged by her paper read in the 1860 meeting of the Social Science Association in Glasgow, and published in the November issue of the *English Woman's Journal.* Under the innocuous title 'Middle Class Schools for Girls' she presents a devastating critique of the cramped, conformist day schools taught by dispirited, despotic and often ignorant teachers. The purpose of these schools was largely to support the social pretentions of those 'too rich or too genteel' to go to the National Schools.

After a scathing attack she moves on to concrete proposals for financing new schools. One passage anticipates Virginia Woolf:

> The self-supporting principle is very admirable . . . but why should it be especially applied to girls? Magnificent colleges and schools, costing thousands and thousands of pounds, rich endowments all over England, have been bestowed by past generations as gifts to the boys of the higher and middle class. . . Neither Christ Church, Eton, nor Oxford are supposed to degrade those who are educated by them, yet they are in a good measure charities! (EWJ, Nov 1860, p 172)

To begin with she thinks some rich young English women should use the time and knowledge on their hands to form 'a sort of joint stock company' to start schools. They should associate themselves with one of the colleges like Queen's and become certificated. They should publish monthly reports and involve parents. Schools should be open to inspection. They could be made to pay expenses, exclusive of salaries, of one shilling per child per week.

She advocates opening to teachers and pupils of such schools the University Local Examinations. She has looked over the Cambridge Examinations for 1859–60 and finds they would need no modification if women were included among the candidates. She concludes with suggestions for a curriculum and teaching methods.

> Real knowledge develops not only the observation but the imagination and the poetical faculties . . . the apparatus and the museum are essential to good teaching. To acquire a string of names by heart, with no ideas or with wrong ideas attached to

those names, does not increase a child's real knowledge. . .
Schoolmistresses expect girls . . . to learn hard tasks in natural
science without witnessing experiments or handling specimens. . .
Professor Brodie would not teach chemistry to young men unless
he could show them substances and solutions, yet children are
expected to learn, and are punished for not learning, on a system
too stupid, too obsolete, to be applied to young men. (EWJ, Nov
1860, pp 174–5)

Barbara Stephen in *Emily Davies and Girton College* (1927, p 129)
describes this paper, so far ahead of its time, as remarkable for its
anticipation of the principal measures afterwards taken to improve
girls' education.

Barbara's approach was always comprehensive and eclectic. She
saw that women's legal, political, educational and economic disabilities were inextricably linked and must be tackled together. It was
useless providing employment possibilities without improved education or education without work. Without economic power and
access to the press the vote would be difficult to achieve and would
carry little weight.

The crucial importance of economic independence for women is
emphasised in *Women and Work* (1857) which combines new knowledge and insights from her work with the petition and from her new
acquaintance with Algeria and Eugene Bodichon. She insists that
paid work for women is both normal and desirable. She recognises
that industrialisation has created changes. 'The work of our ances-
tresses is taken away from us; we must find fresh work' (1857, p 9).

Women want work both for the health of their minds and their
bodies. They want it often because they must eat and because they
have children and others dependent on them – for all the reasons
that men want work. (1857, p 50)

She explicitly considers women in different classes and situations –
those that are exploited and those that are idle:

. . . in London 50,000 females are working (for) under sixpence
per day and above 100,000 (for) under one shilling a day. (1857,
p 46)

Working women, she says,

. . . are placed at a great disadvantage in the market of work
because they are not skilled labourers and are therefore badly
paid. They rarely have any training. (1857, p 51)

This makes them a pool of cheap labour but the answer is not to exclude them from paid work and labour organisation, but to train them and pay them the same wages as men. She expresses the germ of the idea that women's work is judged inferior and is badly paid *because they are women*, not only or necessarily because they are unskilled.

So long as nearly every remunerative employment is engrossed by men only, so long must the wretchedness and slavery of women remain what it is. (1857, p 46)

She faces squarely the prejudice against 'ladies' working for money: philanthropy is no more than a temporary palliative for idleness in upper- and middle-class women.

Of course we may give our labour, our work, our money where we think right; but it is as well to exchange them sometimes for money, to be sure we are as valuable as we think. Most of the work of the world must be done for money. . . To insist on work for love of Christ only is a profound and mischievous mistake. (1857, pp 48–49)

In these classes philanthropy is nevertheless preferable to the cultivation of vapid 'accomplishments'. *Women and Work* is full of anger on behalf of the hundreds of thousands of humiliated and frustrated women wasting their lives in trivial pursuits and duties which 'weaken their intellects and hearts' waiting for the 'good match' which for many of them, will never come. Even when these middle-class girls did marry it was late. In 1881 to every 1,000 married women between the ages of 20–25 in Kensington there were 5,401 unmarried ones, whereas in Bethnal Green the comparable figure was 1,085. (Census of England and Wales, 1901, quoted in Staars, 1909, p 326). She is speaking about and to the daughters and sisters of the educated and powerful man, as Virginia Woolf was to do 75 years later, and there is a similar sense of rage at the waste.

As a remedy she proposes a wide variety of work in every sphere – in hospitals and schools; in medicine and the church, in arts and manufacturing. 'I believe more than one-half the women who go into the Catholic Church join her because she gives work to her children' (1857, p 9).

She raises the economic question of paid and unpaid women's work.

Women who act as housekeepers, nurses and instructors of their children often do as much for the support of the household as their husbands; and it is unfair for men to speak of supporting a wife and children when such is the case. (1857, p 12)

This is very different from seeing marriage and even waiting for marriage as women's only proper task. 'We ardently desire that women *should not make love their profession.* Fathers have no right to cast the burden of support of their daughters on other men. It lowers the dignity of women and tends to prostitution, whether legal or in the streets' (1857, p 10). She blames mothers for saying 'you must marry some day. Women were made for men. Your use is to bear children, to keep your home comfortable for your husband' (1857, p 8). She rejects the ideology of domesticity at a time it is reaching its middle-class, mid-century peak. Although 43 out of 100 women above the age of twenty are unmarried (1857, p 10), marriage and motherhood are the *only* acceptable careers. A *Saturday Review* of the time is brutal but frank:

> Married life is a woman's profession and to this life her training, that of dependence, is modelled. Of course by not getting a husband, or by losing him, she may find she is without resources. All that can be said of her is, she has failed in her business, and no social reform can prevent such failures. (quoted in Burton, 1949, p 22)

Although Barbara never explicitly propounded a theory of love and marriage, she says women must have work if they are to form equal unions (1857, p 12).

> If women were in active life mixing much with men, the common attraction of sex merely would not be so much felt, but rather the attractions of natures especially adapted to each other. (1857, p 10)

Sexual stereotypes inhibit real relationships between women and men:

> To think a woman is more feminine because she is frivolous, ignorant, weak and sickly is absurd; the larger-natured a woman is, the more decidedly feminine she will be; the stronger she is, the more strongly feminine. You do not call a lioness unfeminine, though she is different in size and strength from the domestic cat, or mouse. (1857, p 18)

Charlotte Brontë had created such a character in Shirley, called her a panther, but left her tamed and diminished at the end of the novel.

Barbara wanted to remain a lioness and be loved.

D. G. Rossetti describes her to his sister Christina in 1854:

> If you were only like Miss Barbara Smith, a young lady I meet at the Howitts, blessed with large rations of tin (money), fat, enthusiasm and golden hair, who thinks nothing of climbing up a mountain in breeches, or wading through a stream in none, in the sacred name of pigment: (i.e. in pursuit of painting) (Doughty and Wahl, 1965, Vol I, p 163)

Others describe her as tall and 'radiantly beautiful'. Rossetti liked 'tin' and some of his 'stunners' were buxom, so perhaps it was the enthusiasm, energy and activity which he found disconcerting. He needed passivity and weakness to bolster his masculinity.

Not all men found her threatening. Carlyle's German secretary is said to have proposed to her and the egregiously vain but charming John Chapman, owner-editor of the *Westminster Review*, tried to persuade her to set up a free union with him.

He had earlier attempted to introduce Marian Evans (George Eliot) into the ménage à trois where he lived with his wife Susannah, and mistress Elizabeth. The Chapman episode is an example of the particular problems love or marriage present for the feminist intellectual (witness Wollstonecraft and Imlay). Chapman wrote her a series of extraordinary letters in the summer of 1855 alternating inquiries about her finances with ill-phrased sentimentalities. He offered her hair locks and medical advice about her menstrual cycle. He declared that:

> the strongest reason with me (for our union) is a consideration of your health and the conviction of the reinvigorating effects on your system of a fulfilment of love's physical desires. (Quoted Redd, 1972, p 35).

He proposed to rub her with wet and dry towels till she was of a rosy hue and health would soon return to her 'if your simple possession of me did not itself suffice to bring it' as he concluded modestly. He hopes she will finance the completion of his medical studies. He chides her for bad handwriting. He offers her the Arts section of the *Westminster Review*:

> You would soon get into the habit of dashing that off without consuming much time . . . It is much easier to write articles than to get them inserted. (quoted Reed, p 35)

Barbara's replies have not survived but Chapman's letters show her mounting reluctance to pursue the relationship. There is no denial of pain. This is the moment, she said to a friend, that she must cut out of her nature 'the strong necessity of loving' and that she did not wish to be 'in the power of any man' (Burton, 1949, p 80). The letters break off at the end of September 1855.

It is revealing to see how a recent editor/biographer, Joseph W. Reed Junior and his five male research assistants, handle the episode in the introductoin to *An American Diary*. He quotes Chapman's letters in extenso. He presumes a consummated liaison although the letters suggest the contrary. He invents a denouement.

> Pater says no . . . The correspondence breaks off and Barbara is trundled off with her sisters by her brother Ben to Algeria and into the arms, as it turns out, of Eugene Bodichon. (Reed, 1972, p 87)

The perfect put-down of the feminist woman intellectual. It is instructive to recall what was really happening in the time span covered by that sentence. The correspondence finished in September 1855. Barbara did not go to Algeria until October 1856. The intervening year was immensely significant and productive – it saw the framing and circulation of the Petition, the public meeting of the Law Amendment Society, the formation of the Society of Female Artists. Barbara began writing *Women and Work* and found a new intimacy with Marian Evans which allowed them to discuss their Chapman experiences. Her own engrossing work and Chapman's fatuity surely did more to end the relationship than her father's supposed opposition.

With Eugene Bodichon it was very different – there is a sense of equality, complementarity and exchange. They were both outsiders, both strong-minded. Doctor, explorer, anthropologist, naturalist, writer, Bodichon had come to Algeria in the mid-thirties, probably with a Saint-Simonian group. Some of Barbara's family and friends found him disconcerting with his bad English, eccentric dress and revolutionary ideas. In America he was frequently taken for 'coloured'.

They were both interested in medicine and the links between mental and physical health. They had both studied phrenology which was largely an attempt to find in the physiology of the brain a materialist explanation for human behaviour, rather than looking to the doctrine of original sin; it was closely linked with the progressive medicine of Broussais in France. They were both keen on the natural sciences and were early ecologists, engaging in a vast eucalyptus-planting project which Eugene believed would extend oases and hinder malaria (Barbara described it in 'Australian Forests and African Deserts', *Pall Mall Gazette*, 1868).

There were some areas of conflict. In the *American Diary* Barbara admires the exquisite children of mixed unions and we sense her wish to endorse Eugene's theory that one human family will be created through miscegenation. But in practice she finds it less idyllic; she learns that mulatto children are often sold by their white fathers or white half-brothers. She is sceptical about Eugene's later enthusiasm for spiritualism. But it was a remarkably equal union, apparently free of prescribed spheres and sex-roles.

When Barbara spoke in the 1855 petition of a woman passing on marriage into the conditon of a slave, she was not using the analogy casually. Wollstonecraft had used it, and so had William Thompson/ Anna Wheeler in their *Appeal of One Half of the Human Race . . .* (1825). They spoke of the law marking women with 'the brand of inferiority . . . indelible like the skin of the Black' (1825, p 165). Sheila Rowbotham writes that 'the general connection between the English anti-slavery movement and subsequent feminist organisation remains unexplored' (1974, p 48).

In Barbara's case it must have dated back to the 1840 London World Anti-Slavery Convention and her family links with the American abolitonist-women's rights groups. She had strengthened it through Elizabeth Blackwell, whose brothers were to marry two feminist abolitionists – Lucy Stone and Antoinette Brown. In America just after her arrival, she speaks of Lucy Stone and Oberlin College. After a discussion with a group of Southern defenders of slavery she reveals the importance of the connection in her personal philosophy.

> To live in the belief of a vital falsehood poisons all the springs of life . . . I feel in England how incapable men and women are of judging rightly on any point when they hold false opinions concerning the rights of one half of the human race. (Reed, 1972, p 63)

She believes that great questions like slavery and women's rights are 'woven into everyday life'.

> Every hour of the day brings up occasion of action involving them . . . It is less perverting to the mind to hold the most monstrously absurd doctrines of religious faith than to believe a man has a right to breed slaves (and) to sell his own children . . . (or) to believe that men have rights over women . . . Every day men acting on this false belief destroy their perception of justice and blunt their

> moral nature . . . Slavery is a greater injustice but it is allied to the
> injustice to women so closely that I cannot see one without think-
> ing of the other . . . (Reed, 1972, p 63)

Barbara here emphasises the moral choices in practical daily life. She
extends her concern into areas either ignored by traditional male
historians, philosophers and theorists or else treated as trivial. The
double day of working-class (and now middle-class) women, and the
economy of housework and childrearing have only recently been
treated seriously by feminist sociologists and economists.

When Barbara married Eugene Bodichon in 1857 she gave her
profession as artist on their marriage certificate. Painting for her was
not a genteel accomplishment. She wrote to Elizabeth Whitehead, 'I
should like to give all I had to schools and earn my own living by
painting.' The £10,000 she left to Girton was from her paintings and
her savings – any inherited money went back to the family.

Art was as much a part of her childhood as anti-slavery and radical
politics. Her grandfather William Smith was a friend and patron of
Opie who in turn was friend and painter of Mary Wollstonecraft. She
went with him as a child to see Turner at work in his studio; Barbara's
skies and masses of moving water sometimes recall Turner. She
contributed to the pre-Raphaelite circulating Folio and was one of
Corot's rare pupils. Throughout even her most militant years she
painted. In 1866, between two papers on Women's Suffrage and
during an intense press campaign, she held a one-woman exhibition
at the Dudley gallery and contributed to another. She exhibited
publicly more than 200 paintings which sold readily. Whether she was
working outdoors at Scalands or in her Algerian studio or in a clearing
in an American forest she worked long hours, often from 8 am to 3 pm
without a break.

Her work as an artist has recently been assessed by John Crabbe in
an article in *Apollo* (May 1981). He speaks of

> her simple blend of three strands . . . British water colour tradi-
> tions, the Barbizon school's love of the open air and Corot's belief
> that a painter . . . must eschew doctrines and interpret nature with
> entire simplicity and according to personal sentiment. (Crabbe,
> 1981, p 311)

Her individual creativity as a woman artist is essential to her sense
of identity, to her ability to contract an equal union with Eugene and
to her equal friendship with George Eliot. Recognition for her painting is important to her; in this alone she speaks of finding praise

delicious. Her art and her early deep feminism seem the bases from which she takes off into particular projects of education or law reform or woman's suffrage; they nourish her and permit her to accept a set-back, then move on again.

She uses the word 'God' more often in her published pamphlets than in her diary and personal correspondence; she is sceptical about the existence of a disembodied soul. As a Radical Unitarian she stood well apart from the Church of England either Anglo-Catholic or Evangelical. She found Quaker beliefs and practices congenial. In America she was impressed by the vitality of the Black churches and by the role played by religious groups in the Anti-slavery movement. Her comments on Catholicism, too, show that for her, 'standing face to face with God' was not a private contemplative affair, but a public and social responsibility and one that women must assume.

> Never, since the world began, have women stood face to face with God. Individual women have done so, but not women in general. They are beginning to do so now. (1857, p 7)

For her, radicalism and feminism are very closely linked; in her Petition and in education she showed herself very radical for her time and class. This is confirmed by comments in *An American Diary* (Reed, 1972) on the democratising effect of public school education, on the self-respect given to new immigrants by the right to vote, and on the absence of an inherited hierarchy, at least in the non-slave states.

She shares Eugene's views that anarchism is preferable to despotism. 'I wish Orsini had rid the world of one tyrant' she says of the 1858 assassination attempt on Napoleon III. Speaking of the 1789 Revolution and 'The Terror', she says that the rich have had more opportunity to tell their story; 'When the poor can buy books the other side has a chance of being written' (Unpublished Britanny diary, Girton College Library).

She considers the question of the economic responsiblity of manufacturer, employer and customer in the maintenance of slavery and wage-slavery. Speaking of the need to support the North in the American Civil War she acknowledges Manchester's dependence on the South's cotton but says, 'We can't expect the slave owner to give up his slaves when we rush with our money to buy the produce of this stolen labour.' Nor is ignorance any excuse if we buy lucifer matches when there is clear evidence that their manufacture is causing phossy-jaw in the girls making them. Her radicalism resembles her feminism – it speaks of the moral choices of daily life – 'We had never been taught to think of applying our consciences to this sort of everyday work of buying and selling' (EWJ, 1863, Vol XII: LXXI, pp 394–400)

One of the public responsibilities of women should be the exercise of the vote. Already in the *Brief Summary* in 1854 she mentions disenfranchisement as one of women's legal disabilities as a class. Speaking as early as 1858 of her meeting with Lucretia Mott in Philadelphia she says:

> She seemed absolutely to chuckle with glee to hear that we hold all that she and the Friends advocate and only wait to claim the suffrage because it would be useless to try for it now . . . (Reed, 1972, p 141)

She was a prime mover for suffrage in the sixties. She worked on the committee to elect J. S. Mill as MP for Westminster in 1865. He acknowledged that his success, a gratifying surprise to Helen Taylor and himself, was largely due to 'minorities' like women and working men who could not themselves vote.

Barbara judged that an immediate attempt should be made to include women in the proposed fight for an extended suffrage. She prepared a paper for the Kensington Society, a women's discussion group which included not only members of the Langham Place circle of the fifties but also Mrs Manning, Miss Buss and Miss Beale, Sophia Jex-Blake, Elizabeth Garrett, Frances Power Cobbe and Helen Taylor. Emily Davies, the secretary, found the paper capital but wanted it toned down. 'It does not quite do to call the arguments on the other side "foolish". Nor to speak of "outlawry". . . Nothing so irritates men as to attribute tyranny to them' (Stephen, 1927, p 109). The whole story is there. If changes are to be effected through Parliament and other male-dominated institutions, Barbara is asked not to antagonise men. She reads her paper and despite three 'opposition' papers the meeting carries a resolution in favour of Women's Suffrage. Barbara wants to form a committee immediately. Emily panics, partly because she feels it may jeopardise the negotiations on education on which they are engaged. 'If wild people get upon it (such a committee) who would insist on jumping like kangaroos . . . they would do harm.' Barbara persisted. She went to see Mill whose approval overrode Emily's fears. A Women's Suffrage Committee was formed and Mill agreed that if they could collect 100 signatures on a petition he would put it to the house. Barbara invited Helen Taylor to draft the petition but it was left to her to do. It is regrettable that in histories like *Emily Davies and Girton College* (Barbara Stephen) or *The Cause* (Ray Strachey), Helen Taylor's role is barely mentioned. It is even more so that Mill was to give the whole credit to Helen.

> The time appeared to my daughter, Miss Helen Taylor, to have come for forming a Society for the extension of the suffrage to women. The existence of the Society is due to my daughter's initiative; its constitution was planned entirely by her . . . though delicate health and superabundant occupation made her decline to be a member of the Executive Committee. . . (Mill, 1924, p 214)

In fact the movement was planned between Barbara, Helen, Emily and others and letters passed almost daily (see the Mill-Taylor collection in the British Library of Political and Economic Science). Barbara excelled in beginnings. She was never a one-issue woman, but combined a radical vision of the future with a realistic assessment of what was possible in the here and now. The petition was so judiciously worded that it neither specifically included or excluded married women from a proposed extension of the franchise to qualified women. This petition in the name of Barbara L. S. Bodichon and others was quickly signed by 1,500 women over the age of 21, including Harriet Martineau, Josephine Butler and Mary Somerville, the scientific writer who was to give her name to Somerville College. It was presented by Mill to the House in June 1866.

An intensive press campaign followed in which the Committee wrote letters and articles for insertion into papers and journals. They had 500 out of a possible 900 on their mailing list. At the October 1866 Social Science Congress in Manchester Barbara read the paper on women's suffrage that many journals had refused to print. It was especially significant. Lydia Becker said it marked 'an era in (her) intellectual life' and she went off to found a Manchester Committee. Tens of thousands of copies were printed as pamphlets. Its title was simply 'Reasons for the Enfranchisement of Women'.

In it she mentions first 'the general ground that under a representative government any class which is not represented is likely to be neglected' (p 3). She notes that this is indeed the case, giving the examples of education and the administration of charities where 'the same tendency prevails to postpone the claims of women to those of men' (p 4). The exclusion from the franchise

> casts a slur on the value of their opinions, and I may remark in passing that what is treated as of no value is apt to grow valueless. (1866, p 6)

She continues:

> Among all the reasons for giving women the vote, the one which
> appears to me the strongest is that of the influence it might be
> expected to have in increasing public spirit. . . As it is, women of
> the middle class occupy themselves but little with anything beyond
> the immediate family circle. They do not consider it any concern of
> theirs if poor men and women are ill-nursed in work-house in-
> firmaries, and poor children ill-taught in work-house schools. If
> the roads are bad, the drains neglected, the water poisoned they
> think it is men's business, not theirs, to look after such things. It is
> this belief – so narrowing and so deadening in its influence – that
> the exercise of the franchise would tend to dissipate (1866, pp 6–7)

She points to women who despite the lack of validation and dis-
couragement are in fact working, often voluntarily, in the fields of
education, the relief of the destitute and public health, which are
among Parliament's chief preoccupations; the disenfranchised include
Harriet Martineau, Florence Nightingale and Mary Carpenter: 'We
cannot but desire to add them to our electors' (1866, p 10).

In his address to the House proposing an amendment to the 1867
Representation of the People Bill which would 'leave out the word
"man" in order to insert the word "person"', Mill often appears to
take up Barbara's very words, not only those of the 'Reasons for the
Enfranchisement' but of the earlier 1855 petition.

The amendment was defeated in the House by 196 to 73, which was
a creditable though disappointing result. Barbara made a very
accurate assessment and forecast when she said to Emily Davies,
'You will go up and vote upon crutches and I shall come out of my
grave and vote in my winding sheet'. She had seen the strength of the
feelings and interests opposed to Women's Suffrage. George Lewes
had written an article opposing it, George Eliot was hesitant, and
they were her close personal friends. Queen Victoria had not yet
spoken of 'this mad wicked folly of "Women's Rights"' (quoted in
Martin, 1908, pp 69–70).

But this was the tone and level of argument used against them. The
campaign and its consequences nevertheless helped achieve the
extension of the municipal franchise to women ratepayers in 1869 and
the right of women to serve on School Boards elected under the 1870
Education Act.

Her realism then led her to concentrate on higher education for
women in which she was also engaged with Emily Davies. Her belief
that women should control their own education dated back to

Bedford College, her own school and the ideas expressed in 'Middle Class Schools for Girls'. She put into the project tremendous energy, money and support for Emily whose ideas were dominant in the day-to-day negotiations and administration. Throughout Emily's dealings with Barbara, despite her respect for Barbara's tact and inspiration, despite her gratitude for her donations and fund-raising efforts, despite her constant search for support and advice (there are 327 letters from Emily to Barbara in one carton in the Girton Library), she fears that Barbara may be too extreme. It is wiser not to have her on the founding committee. Later at Hitchin House and the new Girton College, she sees Barbara as too inclined to favour the students against her authority and to judge that they should partici- pate in decisions; too unwilling to submit to the double bind of strictly conforming to the most rigid and obsolete of Cambridge academic programmes for male students and at the same time being more ladylike than the girls in the drawing rooms at home. Barbara's comment in a letter to Helen Taylor sums up her clear insight into her own role.

> Tho' ever since my own brother went to Cambridge I have always intended to aim at the establishment of a college where women could have the same education as men if they wished it, I certainly would not have carried out the plan as Miss Davies has done. I am not strong enough or orthodox enough. (Stephen, 1927, p 200)

Barbara had wanted the college in Cambridge itself. Emily's choice prevailed and the first college for the university education of women was opened in 1869 with five students in a large house at Hitchin at a great enough distance from Cambridge to protect the students from the dissipations and dangers of male undergraduate life, and to allay the fears of their parents. Barbara was to supply warmth, colour, understanding, pictures of unorthodoxy to relieve the somewhat grim requirements of academic and moral excellence which Emily imposed. She also supplied encouragement for the natural sciences and laboratory work. Without Barbara's visits and invitations to the students, without her existence as a role model, Girton would have been a colder experiment. George Eliot even so had to go in by the back drive as she was not really Mrs Lewes. When Barbara said to the first students 'you must make your own laws' she was already inviting an independent spirit that Emily found unacceptable. She later wrote,

> I think Madam Bodichon goes too much by the temporary opinions and tastes and requirements of the existing generation of

students. . . She asks 'Are they satisfied?' when I think the question should have been 'Is it satisfactory?' (Stephen, 1927, p 295)

Emily nevertheless called Barbara in when there was friction – in one case over dressing in men's clothes for a play-reading. Barbara did 'talk' to them but her elation at their independent response pierces Emily's shocked letter on the subject.

Mrs Bodichon had her talk with the students last night, and reported that in all her experience she had never met such a spirit of revolt, and such self-confidence. She thought she had made no impression at all. . . (Stephen, 1927, p 244)

The controversy over the injurious effects of study, especially higher education, on the health of young women engaged her deeply. Study makes unfit mothers, says Dr Maudsley, quoting Clarke (see *The Nineteenth Century Woman*, Delamont and Duffin, 1978, p 103). If energy was used in the brain it was not available for the essential uterus and ovaries. Barbara's concern that Girton students should have healthy food, fresh air and gymnastics arose partly from her own experience. 'How terrible it must be not to have animal spirits,' she said as a young woman. At 40 she taught Professor Sylvester how to leap over a five-barred gate. She asserted that it was not study that injured health but heavy cramping clothes, overheated rooms and lack of real outdoor life.

She is concerned that taboos inhibit proper discussion of women's health. She and Louisa Lumsden, one of the first Girton students, exchanged letters on this. Louisa deplores the difficulty Mrs Anderson (Dr Elizabeth Garrett Anderson) will have answering the medical arguments 'without treading on people's sense of delicacy and modern refinement'. Barbara sees the social need for women doctors to counter this pernicious regulation of women 'for their own good'.

The 30 years of friendship between Barbara and George Eliot was crucial to the intellectual and emotional development of both women but can be mentioned only briefly here. It was to Barbara that Marian Evans turned when deciding whether to go to live with George Lewes and Barbara who said she would stand by her whatever the decision. It was through Barbara that Eliot found that male friends do not always eclipse the female.

Barbara's literary sensitivity was proved early. She knew Marian Evans as editor, translator and essayist. When George Eliot published *Adam Bede* only Lewes knew the identity of the author. But

Barbara instantly recognised the 'great big head and heart' of Marian Evans and wrote from Algeria in a rush of excitement. Her delight was not only in recognition, but in the success of Marian Evans the outlaw, another 'taboo'd' woman.

> I can't tell you, my dear George Eliot how enchanted I am . . . 1st that a woman should write a wise and *humorous* book which should take a place by Thackeray.
> 2nd that you whom they spit at should do it!
> I am so enchanted, so glad with the good and bad of me! both glad – angel and devil both triumph. (Eliot, 1955, Vol III, p 56)

In the friendship Barbara is the leader, the giver, the energiser. Despite Eliot's enormous erudition and imaginative genius, Barbara is bolder in thought and action, less easily impressed by 'great names'. Eliot, like Emily Davies, is uneasy at Barbara's direct questioning of male notables such as Ruskin; she finds excuses for a speech of Carlyle's which Barbara has termed odious. Barbara is culturally more open, at ease in France, Algeria, and America. It is she who lends Eliot the poetry of Blake and Donne. Eliot begs for more letters, more visits. 'You will come to me like the morning sunlight and make me a little less of a flaccid cabbage plant.' (Eliot, 1955, Vol IV, p 84)

There is a striking example of their different views on marriage and women's financial and psychological dependence. When Ellen Allen, teacher at the Portman Hall School, is about to marry although Eliot mentions Ellen Allen's hesitation before this 'splendid match' and that the groom 'last, not quite least . . . settled £150 a year on his future mother-in-law', she sees it simply as 'a very charming fairy-tale' (Eliot 1955, Vol IV, p 92). However, Barbara writes '. . . I *hope* it will be good, but he is a Roman Catholic and very *dévot*; and already bullies her and calls her a pagan!' (Allingham, 1911, p 80).

That Ellen Allen might have a more rewarding life teaching in the Portman Hall School (Barbara is desolated by her departure) than married to a rich sperm-oil merchant with bullying tendencies is inconceivable to George Eliot.

Eliot never imagined a woman character with Barbara's strength, diversity and autonomy. Barbara is the physical model for Eliot's Romola with her reddish-gold hair, her tall dignity, her 'expression of proud tenacity and latent impetuousness'. Romola, as heroine, is an idealised embodiment of women's intellectual power and piety, and also of women's friendship. But Eliot's 'real' women are shown as relative creatures either nurturing and supportive of men, or manipulative and destructive of them.

Barbara's generous sensitivity to her friend's needs was shown when George Eliot married Johnny Cross, 20 years her junior, 18 months after Lewes' death. She wrote:

> My dear I hope and think you will be happy. . . You see I know all love is so different that I do not see it unnatural to love in new ways. . . (Eliot, 1955, p 273)

Barbara's life and ideas are not outmoded. In speaking of her father's 'clear sight and strange tact' she describes her own attitudes and methods:

> A conviction was to him an action and if he felt sure a thing was right he must instantly do it . . . he worked always to get the good work done, not obstinately to do it himself. (Quoted Burton, 1949, p 67)

She displayed the same concern to move from theory into collective action; the same indifference to adulation. With her core identity as a working artist and feminist she showed great resilience in meeting particular setbacks. This is also a mark of her realism; the vote and legal reform are important but they are not a panacea for the oppression of women which springs from a deeper level.

Barbara clearly defies the dominant male voice and assumptions, sometimes with words on paper, but more often through her own life. She reads Ruskin and hears, 'Her intellect is not for invention or creation, but for sweet ordering and arrangement'. She does not argue, but holds a one-woman exhibition at the Dudley or French Gallery. She is told women must be wise 'not for self-development, but for self-renunciation' and she plans schools for girls which will develop women teachers and girl pupils at the same time. She observes that girls' physical experience of the world and of people is reduced by 'protecting them from all danger and temptation' and on that basis opposes Ruskin and the ideology of sentimental womanhood (Ruskin, 1905, Vol XVIII, pp 121–122). She rejects what Rousseau proposed for Sophie and chooses instead economic independence, intellectual autonomy, art as a profession, and participation in public life.

Barbara early challenged Comte and Herbert Spencer whose ideas on social evolution postulate a growing differentiation between male and female physiology and roles. These ideas were welcomed as proving that differentiation is 'natural', not socially imposed. They confirm women's moral superiority in the private sphere but justify her exclusion from participation in the political and public sphere. Spencer argues for example that it would be unjust to give women political rights as long as the responsibilities of war fall only on men. Barbara had already answered that argument in *An American Diary*:

> Women perform as great service to the state in bringing citizens into the world as men do in preserving their lives. (Reed, 1972, pp 61–62)

She believes that childbearing no more incapacitates them from voting and taking part in governmental concerns than does 'the duty of men to fight, to go to sea, to go to distant parts to defend the state'. It is wrong that women 'make and educate for ten years all the citizens in the state and they receive no rights for these services'. (Reed, 1972, p 62).

Barbara often makes the link between authority, hierarchy and language. She recognises the importance of names. When criticised for calling herself 'Barbara Smith Bodichon' she replies:

> I do not think there is any law to oblige a women to bear the name of her husband at all. . . I have earned the right to Barbara Smith. (Reed, 1972, p 134)

She chafes under Emily's admonitions to phrase her thoughts in a way which will not offend men. Silence and accepting others' 'naming' is almost intolerable. Visiting Eugene's conservative Catholic aristocratic relatives in Brittany in 1860 she writes that she:

> Would have exploded if (she) had stayed much longer, like the Great Eastern having all its safety valves turned down . . . think of Garibaldi being called 'monster' and Cavour 'right-hand of Satan!' (Quoted Burton, 1949, p 133)

She thus recognises the role played by language in creating as well as expressing reality.

She is essentially self-educated and her range is impressive. She moves from law to educational theory, from prison administration to afforestation, expressing herself with an unpretentious directness and a particular aim. She makes quick political and economic assessments despite her lack of formal training. She calculates very accurately the likely effect of the sewing machine and later the typewriter on women's employment. Her comments on educational methods, her distrust of institutions and systems, and rote-learning divorced from concrete experience, are still apposite. The connections she makes are those that are essential in Women's Studies courses today. She sees *relationships* and *connections*, having what we now call an 'interdisciplinary approach'.

It is often forgotten that she and Emily Davies and other pioneers of University Education for women had themselves no experience of sitting examinations, living in a resident college, meeting formal academic requirements. She saw that the most urgent need of women students was confidence in their own abilities and potential, taking responsibility for themselves, taking part in creating a new environment and new values. It was very difficult offering support to students without opposing or undermining Emily Davies. She did it by being herself a pioneer of a new life style. Speaking of a visit to Scalands one of the original Girton five wrote later:

> That visit was a revelation to me. It showed me a new way of life, the charm of simple surroundings. The living room with open hearth, wood fire and round table spread for a meal beside the open cottage door was entirely different from anything I had ever seen . . . she was a forerunner in the revolt against the Victorian worship of smug, stuffy pretentious comfort. (Quoted *Stephen*, 1927, p 48)

Indeed D. G. Rossetti found it altogether too Spartan: 'Barbara does not indulge in bell-pulls, hardly in servants to summon thereby – so I have brought me own' (Doughty and Wahl, 1965, Vol III, p 819).

In Sara Delamont's article in *The Nineteenth Century Woman* she says:

> the educational pioneers created two new female roles, the celibate career woman and the wife who was an intellectual partner to her husband, an articulate companion who could swap Greek epigrams or scientific formulae . . . both needed a houseful of servants to live out their new life styles. (1978, p 184)

Barbara managed to be artist, feminist-reformer, wife and friend and at the same time largely dispensed with bell-pulls, in a way that a 'Bohemian' male artist found intolerable!

Her voice seems so fresh because she consciously shakes off class and national constrictions, seeing herself as an outsider. Just before her marriage she wrote to Aunt Longden:

> I am one of the cracked people of the world and I like to herd with . . . queer Americans, democrats, socialists, artists, poor devils or angels; and am never happy in an English genteel family life. I try to do it like other people, but I long always to be off on some wild

adventure, or to lecture on a tub in St. Giles, or go to see the
Mormons, or ride off into the interior on horseback alone and
leave the world for a month. . . I want to see what sort of a world
this God's world is. (Quoted Burton, 1949, p 92)

It is clear from *An American Diary* that she chose to meet marginal
people – the mulatto family next door, immigrant workers, slave
mothers. She does not perceive the poor as inherently inclined to
sloth and vice, nor believe that workers should be educated to be
docile and diligent. She does not wish to impose on them the values of
'an English genteel family life'.

With Girton students she was particularly close to those who came
from outside the English upper middle-class. Hertha Marks* from a
poor Polish-Jewish immigrant family, and later brilliant physicist
friend of Marie Curie, was like an adoptive daughter. Hertha's
daughter, Barbara, became Labour MP for Hendon North. Barbara's
grief at not having a child is somehow softened for us by this warm
example of non-biological mothering and passing on a tradition of
being a woman citizen.

She lived her feminism out in all its contradictions and complexity,
holding her work as an artist, her political campaigns, and her
marriage all in a fine balance. Barbara's very diversity, integration
and balance seem disturbing and threatening to her recent male
biographer/editor. Professor Reed says she is a 'prickly personality
. . . who is determined to matter in as many ways and in as many
places as her considerable energies and talents and her limited time
will permit' (p 28). He speculates that Dr Bodichon was obliged to
dramatise himself by wearing a burnous, bringing Arab friends to a
London party, walking 'without a hat and with a jackal' (Wm.
Rossetti) because 'in the presence of Barbara he needed a little
attention called to himself' (p 31). Despite all the evidence that
Barbara felt her unorthodoxy and her irregular birth to be a possible
liability to the causes she espoused, and often effaced herself for that
reason, he writes, 'Barbara would have been content to have had her
illegitimacy bandied about as long as she could be assured that her
great-grandmother would disapprove' (Reed, 1972, pp 46–47).

His hostility and inconsistency recall the *Saturday Review* article
entitled 'Bloomerania' reviewing Barbara's *Women and Work* (1857)
and Bessie Parkes's *Remarks on the Education of Girls* (1856). In one
breath they are dismissed as 'pretty Fanny's talk . . . fatally deficient

---

* Editor's note: later Hertha Ayrton and worthy of much more attention:
Hertha Ayrton named her daughter 'Barbara Bodichon'.

in the power of close consecutive thought', with the next asking 'Is there a plague of Egypt worse than strong-minded women?' Professor Reed can no more accept Barbara than does the *Saturday Review* (quoted Stephen, 1927, p 50). He gleefully quotes D. G. Rossetti's description of her (see p 103), and one might guess that Reed the male had the upper hand over Reed the scholar at this moment, as he goes on to say that Barbara lent the Scalands cottage to Rossetti 'in the spring of 1870 when Elizabeth Siddall was in poor health' (p 44). Very poor indeed: she had died from an overdose of laudanum in 1862.

One might even guess that the male literary establishment still finds Barbara's voice threatening and regrets that Chapman divulged that it was easier to write an article than to get it published! (See also Lynne Spender, 1983).

Historians, both Liberal and Marxist, have ignored the radical dimensions of Barbara's ideas and life. Liberal history has focused on the thoughts and actions of the most powerful elites – political, economic, intellectual, literary, artistic – and *male*. Barbara challenged all of them in a consciously feminist way. Her illegitimacy further menaced patriarchal power. Chaste wives and legitimate children were the safeguard of the male line and inherited property. Neither Barbara nor her father are once mentioned in Sir Edward Cook's two-volume biography of Florence Nightingale, the cousin-heroine. The Langham Place women, with their headquarters in a district of prostitution and double standards, all represented a threat but Barbara embodied it most fully, and has consequently been the most buried, the most ignored.

'The unjust laws both of society and country which crush women' that she spent the fifties attacking are only once mentioned in G. M. Trevelyan's *Illustrated English Social History* (1964). They are patronisingly dismissed in a 'witty' footnote.

> Before the married women's Property Acts of the late Victorian period, a woman's property became her husband's at marriage. The law was in curious contrast to the words of the marriage service when the man was made to say 'with all my worldly goods I thee endow'. It was really the other way round. (Trevelyan, 1964, p 51)

The tone recalls that of the *Saturday Review* at the time (1857) which classed the Bill with those opposing live-bait fishing and the sale of dirty books. Ridicule masked the real fear expressed by the Attorney-General when he opposed it. It would involve 'a material change in the social and political institutions of the nation and would place women in a strong-minded and independent position'. That it passed its second reading by 120 votes to 65 attests to the impact of Barbara's *Brief Summary* and petition. But it had to be killed. A Divorce Bill was brought down from the House of Lords. Provisions to protect the most injured wives were hastily incorporated into it and the Bill was passed. This was overtly to 'prevent a greater evil', namely passing the Bill based on Barbara's petition which threatened to 'place the whole marriage law on a different footing and give a wife all the distinct rights of citizenship' (3 Hansard, 1857, CXLV, p 800). The inserted palliative provisions were drawn from the Hon. Caroline Norton's letter of 1855 to the Queen where she insists, 'I never pretended to the wild and ridiculous doctrine of equality' (Holcombe, 1977, p 12). The ploy is now familiar – the man's woman appealing to pity is played against the feminist asking for justice. Caroline Norton's name appears in the history books and Barbara's is written out.

The same trivialisation and omission occur in the history of girls' education. Trevelyan deals with it in another pithy summary:

> In the middle years of the century the secondary education of girls was very ill provided for. They were sacrificed to pay for the expensive education of their brothers. (Trevelyan, 1964, Vol 4, p 106)

The very observation made by Barbara at the 1860 Social Science Congress. For her it is a gross injustice and the basis of her work in the sixties. For Trevelyan it is a casual post-script to eight pages devoted to a really important topic – Boys' Public Schools. J. S. Mill is often credited with 'discovering' that educational endowments intended for both sexes had been used for boys only. In fact in 1866 he asked another man to confirm what women educationists had been proclaiming since 1860. If Barbara is mentioned at all in the history of education it is for the money she gave to Girton. No word of her rage at *The Times*'s comments on its proposed foundation:

> The virtues of home must be learnt at home and a girl's proper University, at the age when her brothers go to College, is to be found in her own family. (Quoted Burton, 1949, p 169)

This vivid radical educationist is turned into the conventional financial benefactress of an academic institution, safely embalmed as a majestic Victorian mummy.

The liberal male historian also spirits Barbara out of the history of Women's Suffrage. I open the Pelican *History of England* Vol 8 by

David Thomson (1950): 'The demand for extension of the vote to women was nineteenth century in origin. John Stuart Mill had come to favour it' (p 187). Or, if you prefer Trevelyan, 'The professional and social emancipation of women went forward on the lines advocated in Mill's *Subjection of Women*' (1964, Vol 4, p 171). Women's lives are banished to the edges of the world; every now and then an illustrious man holds out a hand to the poor creatures writhing in outer darkness. The part played by women in Mill's election is ignored. So are the extremely efficient press campaign of the Women's Suffrage Committee, and Barbara's paper to the October 1866 Social Science Congress, widely reported and re-printed, which together opened up public debate on the question. To suggest that the first important public statement was made by Mill in the Commons in 1867 is a serious oversight considering the work of the Women's Committee and all the links going back to Ann Knight, Jeanne Deroin, Lucretia Mott, Elizabeth Cady Stanton and Chartist women. These distortions and omissions must not be perpetuated or allowed to pass.

Marxist and Labour history has also been predominantly man-made. E. P. Thompson speaks of rescuing the working classes 'from the enormous condescension of posterity' (1968, p 12). Women, especially if middle-class, have now to be rescued from the enormous condescension of Marxist as well as Liberal male historians. Engels, Marx and Proudhon speak as males (see Marx and Engels, 1975, Vol IV, p 438). They perceive women as part of the world that revolutionary men are going to transform, rather than as agents of social change themselves. Later Marxist historians have tended to follow this path, sometimes in the face of all evidence. If Harold Laski could see Harriet Taylor as a 'really soft cushion' for J. S. Mill, any misreading is possible! (Howe, 1953, p 676).

Marx is quite unaware of the Langham Place collective. The Marx family were living in Kentish Town from 1856–1864 when Barbara's Portman Hall school was charging sixpence a week (to Garibaldi's son among others) for experimental, secular mixed-class co-education. Jenny and Laura Marx were attending the South Hampstead College for Ladies which had fees of £8 a term with languages, drawing and music extra. A 'Confessions' paper filled in by Eleanor Marx as a child suggests she would have found Barbara's school more congenial. She lists her favourite hero as Garibaldi and her pet hate at 'Eve's Examiner'. The latter was one of the outmoded catechisms of questions and answers on history, geography and the Scriptures set for rote-learning and blasted by Barbara in her 1860 paper on Middle

Class Education for Girls (Kapp, 1972, Vol II, pp 32–56).

In suffrage and labour history, historians have continued to dismiss Barbara as a feminist bourgeois lady with no understanding of working men and women. Historians of the women's movement have not placed her clearly enough in a historical tradition which is more radical, and has wider international affiliations than they have supposed. Conflicts in the later suffrage movement have been projected backwards on to the 1850s and 1860s and are distorting their history. Certainly on 19 November 1893 *Justice* did speak of 'fine-lady suffragettes of the Mrs Henry Fawcett type' and Eleanor Marx did have her amendment to enfranchise adult women overwhelmingly defeated by a Women's Suffrage meeting. But in the 1870s both Barbara and Eleanor Marx were working to elect women like Elizabeth Garrett Anderson and Mrs Westlake to the London School Board.

By this time Engels approved so much of women's entry into public office that he cast all his seven votes for Mrs Westlake. He wrote to a German woman friend:

> When we take power, not only will women vote, but they will be voted for and make speeches, which last has already come to pass on the School Boards. . . Moreover the ladies . . . distinguish themselves by talking very little and working very hard, each of them doing on average as much as three men. (Kapp, 1972, Vol II, p 183)

Indeed, there is a marked change in Engels's ideas between *Conditions of the English Working Classes* (1845) and *The Origins of the Family* (1884) where he comments that women's emancipation is impossible as long as they are excluded from socially productive work. Not that he really questions that domestic work will be done by women, or explores the political economy of housework.

Barbara is only one of the members of the early feminist collective to have been suppressed and forgotten. The activity of the period before the women's movement was consolidated into political organisations has been seriously underestimated. At this time of development, both in England and America, the impetus depended upon the vision and energy of particular vivid and vigorous individuals and was shaped by their connections. Awareness of this activity is easily lost because the story is in scattered personal records, not in institutional documents. The network that supported the movement at this vital formative stage has to be painstakingly reconstructed from sources often considered peripheral. The continuity of the movement is in the lives of its activists. The feminist impulse is sustained by their personal interaction. Their lives and range of action overlapped in many ways. They do not fit rigid political and class categories. The fact that the educated man's daughter and the proletarian wife do not have the same status or economic interests as their father or husband makes the imposition of rigid categories even more unrewarding. Bessie Parkes, Jessie Boucherett, Isa Craig, together with the Journals and organisations they worked in, deserve reassessment by historians of all persuasions.

Barbara's is a particularly flagrant case. We should not be cheated of this woman whose 'immense largeness of sympathy and independence of mind showed itself in the least little thing', who 'lived from the 1st of January to the 31st of December in a perpetual whirl of business, study and pleasure' (J. J. Piper, 1906, p 191).

She made few claims for herself. In a letter to Hilary Bonham-Carter she speaks of second-best expedients, of building 'a sort of rough wooden scaffold bridge of life where one day I hope to see a perfect arch' (Quoted Burton, 1949, p 183). But with her clear sight and strange tact I believe she found new ways of living and loving which speak very directly to women today.

Select Bibliography of Barbara Bodichon

1854   *A Brief Summary, in Plain Language, of the Most Important Laws Concerning Women.*
   3rd Edition, Trubner & Co, London, 1869.
1857   *Women and Work*, English Edition, Bosworth and Harrison, London.
   American Edition, intro Catharine M. Sedgwick, C. S. Francis & Co, New York, 1859.
1858   'Algeria Considered as Winter Residence for the English', (Dr Bodichon partly translated by BLSB?) London.
   'Slavery in America' By B (Dr and Madame Bodichon) *English Women's Journal*, October 1858.
   'An American School' *English Women's Journal*, November 1858.
1860   'Slave Preaching' *English Women's Journal*, March 1860.
   'Algiers : First Impressions' By BLSB *English Women's Journal*, September 1860.
   'Middle Class Schools for Girls' (Social Science Association) *English Women's Journal*, November 1860.
1861   'Slavery in the South' *English Women's Journal*, October, November and December 1861.
1862   'Painted Glass Windows executed by the Carmelite Nuns of Le Mans' *English Women's Journal*, January 1862.

1863   'Of those who are the property of others, and of the great power that holds others as property' *English Women's Journal*, February 1863.

'Cleopatra's Daughter, St Marciana, Mama Marabout, and other Algerian Women' *English Women's Journal*, February 1863.

1863 or 4   'Accomplices, Vol XII' *English Women's Journal*, p 394–400).

1866   'Reasons for the Enfranchisement of Women' (Social Science Association, London).

1866   *Objections to the Enfranchisement of Women Considered*, J. Bale, printer, London.

1868   'Australian Forests and African Deserts', *Pall Mall Gazette*.

1869   *Reasons For and Against the Enfranchisement of Women*, College Pamphlets, London. V.463.

1872   2nd Edition, McCorquodale & Co, London (National Society for Women's Suffrage).

1972   *An American Diary 1857–58*, ed Joseph W. Reed Jr, Routledge and Kegan Paul, London.

Some letters of Barbara Bodichon have been published in Haight, 1955, *Letters of George Eliot*; Allingham and Williams, 1911, *Letters to William Allingham*; and in Sharp, 1926, *Hertha Ayrton: A Memoir*.

Copies of letters which constitute a diary of her visit to Brittany in 1861 are among the Barbara Leigh Smith papers in Girton College Library. Others are held by the Yale University Library. Her articles and letters in the *English Women's Journal* and *The English Women's Review* may be consulted most easily in the Fawcett Library.

The Barbara Leigh Smith Papers in Girton College Library contain a partial catalogue of her paintings, some sketches, miscellaneous correspondence, the Brittany journal in the form of letters (unpublished), an abstract of Mill's 'Political Economy' with comments and diverse papers.

Lucy Stone:
Radical Beginnings
(1818–1893)

Leslie Wheeler

In an unsuccessful effort to prevent the National American Woman Suffrage Association from passing a resolution repudiating Elizabeth Cady Stanton's *The Woman's Bible* in 1896, Susan B. Anthony said, 'Suppose . . . when Lucy Stone did not take the name of her husband . . . we had passed resolutions against a woman's not taking her husband's name. Thank God! we had the strength not to do it' (Stanton *et al*, IV, HWS, pp 263–4). Evident from Anthony's statement is the fact that Stone's action in not taking her husband's name was considered as radical an attack upon a sexist institution as was Stanton's *The Woman's Bible*. Yet while *The Woman's Bible* appeared toward the end of a lifetime of militant agitation, Stone's action in keeping her name occurred relatively early in her career, and marked the outermost limits of her feminist protest.

Born on 13 August 1818, the eighth of nine children in a Massachusetts farm family, Stone's early life was characterised by a growing awareness of the roots of woman's oppression, and by a personal struggle to overcome the obstacles that lay in her path because of her sex. Her parents followed the traditional pattern of authoritarian husband and submissive wife. Although the family was prosperous enough, her father's tight control of the purse placed her mother in the humiliating position of having to beg for even the smallest amounts of money. Sparing with cash, her father did give her mother one thing: too many children. By the time Stone was born, her mother was already an old woman, worn out by years of hard work, the births of nine children, and the rearing of those who survived. Stone herself sought a way out of the degrading dependency of her mother's situation through education. Because her father refused to give her money to go to college like her brothers, she spent nine years alternately teaching in the district schools and studying at one of several secondary institutions. During this period she read Sarah Grimké's *Letters on the Equality of the Sexes*, and wrote to a brother that they served 'to confirm the resolutions I had made before to call no man master,' (Stone to Francis Stone, 31 August 1838, BFP).

By 1843, when she was 25, Stone had managed to save enough money to afford the cost of a single term at Oberlin College in Ohio, the first institution of higher learning in the country to open its doors to both women and blacks. Earlier, Stone had been fired by the example of such female anti-slavery agents as the Grimké sisters and Abby Kelley Foster, who were among the first American women to speak in public before mixed or 'promiscuous' audiences, and now she began to prepare for a similar calling herself, practising debating in secret, because the college authorities, for all their liberalism in other areas, did not approve of women speaking in public. Graduating from Oberlin in 1847, she delivered her first public address – a woman's rights speech – from the pulpit of her brother's church in Gardner, Massachusetts. A year later, she was hired as an agent of the American Anti-Slavery Society, and commenced a career that brought her some fame and a great deal of notoriety. The intensity of her convictions combined with a low, musical voice served to make her one of the foremost women speakers of her day. But as a lecturer on the unpopular subjects of abolition and woman's rights, she aroused tremendous hostility: people tore down the posters advertising her talks, burned pepper in the auditoriums where she spoke, and pelted her with prayer books and other missiles.

Nevertheless, Stone valued her hard-won independence, and probably would never have married if she had not had such an ardent and persistent suitor in the person of Henry Blackwell. Seven years her junior, he was an English-born businessman, abolitionist, and feminist, whose five remarkable sisters, including Elizabeth Blackwell, the first woman physician in America, predisposed him to admire strong-minded women. After a two-year courtship, Stone was finally won over by Blackwell's promise of an equalitarian union, and the couple married on 1 May 1855. At the time of their wedding they registered a public protest against the unjust marriage laws of the period, and somewhat later, Stone announced her intention of retaining her maiden name.

During the first two years of her marriage, Stone continued to pursue her lecturing career, but with the birth of her first and only child in 1857, she found it increasingly difficult to carry on with public agitation, and gradually gave it up altogether to devote herself to the rearing of her daughter. She did not return to public life until after the Civil War, when she emerged as a leader of the more conservative wing of the woman suffrage movement. Breaking with Stanton and Anthony over the question of which should come first – negro or woman suffrage – she and her husband helped to found the American Woman Suffrage Association in 1869, and a year later, established a weekly suffrage newspaper, *The Woman's Journal*, which had an uninterrupted existence of 47 years, first under their editorship and then under that of their daughter. Active in suffrage work until the end, Stone died of cancer in 1893 at the age of seventy-five.

Although less radical and outspoken in her later years, the broad thrust of Stone's early woman's rights stance placed her at the vanguard of the movement before the War. Dressed in bloomers, she travelled from town to town lecturing on woman's 'Social and Industrial, Legal and Political, Moral and Religious Disabilities'. Along with other pre-war feminists, she rejected the doctrine of separate spheres for men and women. 'Too much has already been said and written about woman's sphere,' Stone said in an 1854 speech. 'Leave women, then, to find their sphere' (Stanton *et al* HWS, I, p 165). Stone believed that women would be able to find their appropriate sphere if they were given equal educational opportunities with men, and by equal education she meant coeducation. She was among the backers of Central College in McGrawville, New York, a reformist institution founded in 1851, which admitted blacks and women on an equal basis with white males; and looked forward to the day when such bastions of male power and privilege as Harvard and Yale would open their doors to women (Stanton *et al*, HWS, I, p 631). In keeping with her belief in coeducation, she sent her daughter to the Chauncy Hall School in Boston, a former boys' school that had recently begun to admit girls, and later to Boston University, where her daughter was one of two women in a class of 26 men.

While hailing education as a means of woman's advancement, Stone cast a highly critical eye on institutions like the church which seemed bent on keeping women subjugated. 'I wonder if you know how dreadfully I feel about your studying that old musty theology,' she wrote to a close friend who was planning to become a minister. Religion, she maintained, had not only 'outgrown' its usefulness, but had also 'hitherto bemoaned *women* into *nothingness* (Stone to Antoinette Brown Blackwell, c. 1850, BFP). Stone's own questioning of the teachings of Christianity had begun when, as a small child, she had come upon the words in the Bible: 'Thy desire shall be to thy husband and he shall rule over thee.' Repelled by this injunction to subservience, but unwilling to dismiss the Bible completely, she decided that this and other anti-woman passages might be the result of mistranslation, and determined to go to college to learn Hebrew and Greek so that she would be able to read the Bible in its original form, and see for herself what it said about women. Her revolt against religious orthodoxy was further fuelled by the repressive stands of her own Congregational Church in refusing to recognise women as voting members of the congregation, and in denouncing the Grimké sisters for speaking in public. Thus it was not surprising that the perfectionism of Garrison and his abolitionists, with its glorification of the individual conscience and scathing critique of corrupt religious institutions, had a strong appeal for her. Nor, that when she was finally expelled from her own church for conduct 'inconsistent with her covenant engagements', she quietly embraced the more liberal faith of Unitarianism.

As a lecturer skilled in Biblical exegesis, Stone argued that 'Just as the people have outgrown the injunction of Paul in regard to [obeying] a king, so have the wives his direction to submit themselves to their husbands'; and rested her case for woman's rights on the golden rule, asserting that 'whatever in the Bible is contradictory to it, never came from God' (Stanton *et al*,HWS, I, pp 650–1). Yet she stopped well short of the type of all-out indictment of the Bible as a sexist document that Stanton made with *The Woman's Bible*. Even during her most militant phase, she was never completely comfortable with the stridency of Garrison's attacks on the clergy and the Bible, and later played down the anti-religious nature of feminism in *The Woman's Journal*. To have persisted in attacking the authority of the church as Stanton did would have alienated the large numbers of church women who after 1875 swelled the ranks of the Woman's Christian Temperance Union, and whose support of woman suffrage was crucial. It also would have gone against the grain of her own increasing tendency to look for social justice through the implementation of Christian morality by government. For along with other late nineteenth-century reformers, Stone found an antidote to the unrestrained individualism of the Gilded Age in the ethical socialism of Edward Bellamy's novel, *Looking Backward*.

Similarly, the vociferous quality of Stone's original attack on conventional marriage as an instrument of woman's oppression tended to become muted in the face of a growing desire to avoid the divisiveness of public confrontation. At the First National Woman's Rights Convention held in Worcester, Massachusetts in 1850 Stone spoke out against the system under which a woman became the exclusive property of her husband when she married. 'All that is left of a married woman to be marked on her gravestone is that she was the wife of somebody who had owned her,' she said (quoted in Stannard, 1977, p 95); and drawing upon abolitionist rhetoric, she condemned marriage as little better than 'chattel slavery' in her woman's rights speeches (cf Stone to Henry Blackwell, 26 April 1854, BFP). Indeed, the major thrust of her public attack on traditional marriage was directed against its economic aspects. When her younger sister married in 1845, Stone advised her of her belief that 'wives have a *right* in common with their husbands to the "purse" ' (Stone to Sarah Stone, 1845, BFP); and some 30 years later, she wrote in *The Woman's Journal*: 'Of all the little foxes that help destroy the domestic vines . . . the worst is that which makes it necessary for the wife to *ask* her husband for money to supply the daily recurring family necessities and her own,' thus fuelling her 'sense of humiliation, degradation, and separation' (WJ, 7 September 1872). She was active in the campaign for liberalised married women's property legislation; and when she and Blackwell married, they publicly repudiated the laws which gave the husband control of his wife's property and earnings, engaging instead to hold property separately, and to share the earnings derived from the exercise of their respective professions. Their correspondence over the 30-odd years of their marriage shows how vital the issue of financial or 'pecuniary' independence remained for Stone. For example, at a low-point in her marriage when she had given up lecturing to devote herself to the nurture of her daughter, she wrote, 'It is is more important to me than you have ever known that I should have the income of my property' (Stone to Blackwell, 9 August 1864, BFP); and on the occasion of their thirty-eighth wedding anniversary, she announced, 'After this *always*, I shall like to have my rent, interest, &c put in my bank . . . I never liked having it put in your bank but as I have said, you did so much for women that I allowed it' (Stone to Blackwell, 1 May 1893).

Central to the goal of economic autonomy was the issue of woman's right to work outside the home. Together with most nineteenth-century feminists, Stone believed that a woman's primary responsibility was to her home and family, but at the same time protested against her relegation to the purely domestic sphere, and sought to demonstrate in her own life that a woman could successfully combine marriage and motherhood with a career outside the home. She continued to travel and lecture after her marriage, and tried to do so after her daughter was born, but gradually came to the conclusion 'that for these years I can only be a mother – no trivial thing either' (Stone to

Antoinette Brown Blackwell, February 1859,BFP). Nevertheless, she expected to resume her profession after the childbearing and child-rearing years were over. In making this difficult transition from the private back into the public realm, Stone was particularly fortunate in having a husband who encouraged her to the extent of temporarily putting aside his business interests to join her on the lecture platform, and who later helped her carve out a career as a newspaper editor, which, in her view, was more 'consistent with . . . home life' and the 'proper care' of her family than that of an itinerant agitator (Stone to Antoinette Brown Blackwell, 31 October 1869, BFP).

But for all her insistence on the importance of remunerative employment for women, Stone's essentially middle-class outlook prevented her from having much sympathy with the problems of blue-collar working women. A victim herself of wage discrimination when as a teacher she was paid substantially less than her male counterparts, she called for equal pay for equal work in her early woman's rights speeches. But after the Civil War, when Stanton and Anthony tried, unsuccessfully as it turned out, to forge an alliance with working-class women, Stone kept clear of their efforts; and against a backdrop of increasing industrial violence, was outspoken in her condemnation of labour unions and strikes.

However, the problem was not simply one of woman's economic dependence; there was also the question of her sexual bondage, and as Stone and other pre-war feminists examined the institution of marriage, they decided that its major abuse lay here. Having witnessed the physical and emotional toll that too many pregnancies had taken on her mother, Stone felt that couples should both limit the number of children they had and space their births through the exercise of masculine self-restraint. But her call for male continence did not imply a purely passive role for women in the matter of birth control; rather Stone believed that a woman must have the right to her own body – that is, the right to refuse sex with her husband – and privately, she stressed the paramount importance of this right: 'It is clear to me that the question underlies this whole movement and all our little skirmishing for better laws, and the right to vote, will yet be swallowed up, in the real question, viz. has woman, as wife, a right to herself? It is very little to me to have the right to vote, to own property &c if I may not keep my body, and its uses, in my absolute right. Not one woman in a thousand can do that now, & so long as she suffers this bondage, all other rights will not help her to her true position' (Stone to Antoinette Brown Blackwell, May 1856, BFP).

Stone's belief in the need for birth control reflected a concern for woman's health, but it also went hand-in-hand with a repressive attitude toward sexuality in general. In the post Civil War era, she supported Anthony Comstock, campaigned for such social purity measures as raising the age of consent in sexual relations, and condemned Grove Cleveland as a 'male prostitute' for having fathered an illegitimate child during his bachelor days (Stone to Cornelia C. Hussey, 28 November 1884, BFP).

Regarding the touchy question of divorce, in her early woman's rights speeches Stone advocated this option in cases of drunkenness, and privately confessed her belief in divorce as a means of ending a loveless marriage, 'that a true love may grow up in the soul of the injured one from the full enjoyment of which no legal bond had a right to keep her' (Stone to Anna Parsons, 8 July 1853, BFP). But she displayed an increased reluctance to have both divorce and the broader marriage question discussed at woman's rights conventions. In July of 1856 she advised Anthony to use her 'own judgment about the time & place to discuss the marriage question', adding, 'But when it is done, it seems to me, we must not call it "woman's rights" for the simple reason that it concerns men, just as much'; and later when Stanton announced her intention of discussing marriage and divorce at the annual convention of 1860, Stone begged her to call a separate convention to discuss these issues, and when Stanton refused, continued to express her misgivings: 'It is a great grave topic that one shudders to grapple, but its hour is coming . . . God touch your lips if you speak on it' (Stone to Stanton, 15 April 1860, BFP).

The marriage question happened to be one upon which Stone herself was particularly vulnerable, because of her refusal to take her husband's name. To Stone, a woman's loss of her name in marriage was a symbol of the totality of her subjugation, and having already protested the legal specifics of her oppression at the time of her wedding, she decided to challenge this pernicious custom as well. In so doing her aim was to elevate marriage, not destroy it, but the general public could not be expected to appreciate this, and Stone found herself attacked on two fronts: by conservative defenders of the status quo, who saw in her action an attempt to undermine the institutions of marrige and family; and by many – though not all – of her feminist friends, who feared that by using a different name from her husband she would be deemed free lover, and would thereby discredit the entire woman's movement. Stone was never officially censured for her action, but when, in July of 1856, she instructed Anthony to leave the Blackwell off her name in the announcement of a forthcoming convention and sign her 'Lucy Stone (only)', Anthony quietly refused to comply. When Stone saw how her name appeared, she poured out her hurt in a letter to Anthony. 'At first it made me faint and sick until a flood of tears relieved me . . . Oh Susan it seems to me, that it has wrought a wrong on me that it will take many years to wear out' (Stone to Anthony, 2 September 1856, BFP).

The wound went deep: although Stone persisted in the use of her name, she did not publicly campaign for this right, nor did she further challenge the patriarchal system of nomenclature by giving her daughter her surname. Instead her daughter bore her father's surname and her mother's name as a middle name.

When Stone was next heard from, it was in the cause of suffrage. In 1857, invoking the principle of no taxation without representation, she refused to pay the property taxes on her home, while women were denied the vote.

After the Civil War suffrage became the chief focus of Stone's energies, at the expense of other issues like marriage and divorce. Henry Blackwell spoke for his wife when he wrote in *The Woman's Journal*; 'Some insist upon dragging in their peculiar views on theology, temperance, marriage, race, dress, finance, labour and capital. No one can estimate the danger . . . the cause of woman's enfranchisement has already sustained by the failure of its advocates to limit themselves to the main question' (WJ, 8 January 1870). Nevertheless, Stone's use of her maiden name remained an issue in private, if not in public. Since most judges, lawyers, and other bureaucrats refused to accept her name, she was forced to sign legal documents as 'Lucy Stone, wife of Henry Blackwell'; and she also used this form in signing hotel registers when she and her husband travelled together, for as late as 1867 (during the Kansas campaign) people still accused them of being free lovers because of their different last names. Then, in 1879, the question of Stone's right to her name suddenly burst out into the open when the state of Massachusetts passed a law giving women the right to vote for members of the school committee, and the board of registrars in Boston, where Stone lived, decided not to allow her to vote unless she used her husband's name. Stone protested in letters to the board, but although the case made the news in Boston and New York papers, Stone did not speak out on it in *The Woman's Journal*, nor did she take it to court. She was well aware that public opinion remained set against a married woman's using any name other than her husband's and she had no desire to jeopardise the cause of suffrage by linking it with yet another highly unpopular cause.

Thus, Stone's later career was marked by an increasing silence on many of the issues – especially her right to her name – upon which she had taken bold stands in her early years. As she grew older, she became more conservative, and after the notoriety of her youth, seemed glad to wrap herself in the mantle of respectability. If it was difficult for a man to remain true to his radical principles, how much more so was it for a woman; and Stone was not the only female rebel who, succumbing to internal as well as external pressures, withdrew from the heat of controversy in her later years. One thinks of Victoria Woodhull, the once daring free lover settled comfortably in London as the wife of a wealthy English banker. Never as radical a thinker, nor as controversial a figure as 'The Woodhull', Stone's transformation was much less dramatic: she continued to protest the injustices of a sexist society, but the scope of her attack was less broad than it had been in her earlier years. Absent from Stone's later speeches is the kind of ringing assertion of individual sovereignty that characterised Stanton's famous address, 'The Solitude of Self'. Perhaps the best summary of her mature views is to be found in an exchange she had with her daughter not long before she died. The two were speaking of a woman whose husband had turned out to be very unsatisfactory, and Stone said, 'But I do believe that a woman's truest place is in a home, with a husband and with children, and with large freedom, pecuniary freedom, personal freedom, and the right to vote' (Alice Stone Blackwell, unpublished reminiscences, BFP).

As contemporary feminists, we may not agree with Stone's glorification of home and family – an attitude she shared with many nineteenth-century advocates of woman's rights – but we can certainly appreciate her efforts to inject a greater degree of equality into the institution of marriage, and to demonstrate that a woman was perfectly capable of combining marriage and motherhood with a career outside of the home. We can also admire the assertion – quiet though it was – of a woman's right to an individual identity that she made when she chose to go through life as 'Lucy Stone (only)'.

Lucy Stone's ideas about women's liberation – and how to achieve it – are in many respects linked with contemporary ideas: 'In education, in marriage, in religion, in everything disappointment is the lot of women,' Stone proclaimed in what was perhaps the most famous of her early woman's rights speeches; and she vowed that 'It shall be the business of my life to deepen that disappointment in every woman's heart until she bows down to it no longer' (Stanton *et al*, HWS, I, 165). While the first statement gives an indication of the scope of her feminist critique of society, the second reveals her initial strategy for effecting change.

Stone's personal sense of disappointment and frustration as a woman led her to seek the education traditionally reserved for men, to break with orthodox religion because it counselled silent submission and self-sacrifice for women, and to assert herself in the public realm as an anti-slavery lecturer. Garrisonian abolitionism provided her with both a theory and practice of social change. The Garrisonians based their appeal for an immediate and unconditional end to slavery on the moral equality of the races. Similarly abolitionist feminists like Stone argued for woman's emancipation on the grounds of the common humanity of men and women. Stone pointed to the golden rule as set forth in the Bible, and also drew upon the 'natural rights' ideology of the American Revolution. Central to this ideology was the notion of 'self ownership', or the individual's right to 'life, liberty, and the pursuit of happiness', which Stone (and others besides her) saw in terms of individual growth and development. 'I have a bright ideal for the Future when wrong will be subdued,' she wrote Henry Blackwell during their courtship, 'that each man and each woman may give to his intellectual, moral, and physical nature the fullest development [*sic*]' (Stone to Blackwell, 21 June 1853, BFP).

Confined as they were to a narrowly domestic sphere, women, in Stone's view, were prevented from developing to their highest capacities. Hence, she rejected the notion of separate spheres for men and women, and put forward a series of demands on behalf of her sex for education, admission to the professions, property rights, and finally the right to vote.

As both an abolitionist and a feminist, Stone saw her primary function as the agitation of public sentiment. Before social change could be embodied in specific legal and institutional reforms, a revolution in people's ways of thinking must be effected. 'The Anti-Slavery and Woman's Rights Revolutions do not differ, in their philosophy from that of all other Revolutions,' Stone wrote. '*They* have ever been made successful, simply by a *change* in the *ideas*, and *feelings*, of those who are the object, and the cause, of the revolution', (Stone to Blackwell, 27 July 1853, BFP). For Stone and most other woman's rights activists of her generation, suffrage came to represent both the means and end of this revolution. The vote, she believed, would bring about a concrete improvement in woman's legal status, while at the same time, educating the popular mind to the principle of sexual equality. Specifically, the vote would impel women out of the private sphere of home and family, and into the public realm, where men would have to accept them as equals.

Thus Stone and other suffragists fell into the trap of seeking a political solution for what was essentially an economic problem. That they did so was not surprising considering their generation's optimistic faith in the efficacy of the political process. But in their eagerness to share in the fruits of Jacksonian democracy, Stone and her co-workers turned their backs on the roots of woman's oppression within the family. Stone was certainly aware that marriage cast women into economic and sexual bondage; and she hoped to remedy the former through legislation giving women control of their property, and the latter, through birth control or the assertion of a woman's right to her body. However, her adherence to the prevailing ideology of domesticity, with its glorification of homemaking and parenting as the functions for which women were most naturally suited, prevented her from advocating a radical reorganisation of labour within the family. Unhappy as she was during the years of her own domestic confinement (Stone suffered from raging headaches and periods of extreme depression, and at one point toward the end of the Civil War, seemed on the brink of total breakdown [for a fuller treatment of the causes contributing to this near breakdown, see *Loving Warriors*, pp 188–89]), it did not occur to her to demand that her husband share the domestic responsibilities, while she, in turn, assumed part of the burden of breadwinning. Thus, although financial independence had been an important goal for Stone before her marriage, and immediately afterward, she failed to develop the theoretical framework that would have enabled her to continue to work and be self-supporting after she became a mother. The conservatism of her later years reflected not so much a change in her ideas as an inability to carry her original insights to their logical conclusion. But if Stone fell sort of the type of thoroughgoing analysis of the economic sources of sexual inequality that would later be made by such feminists as Charlotte Perkins Gilman, she, nevertheless, made an important beginning in her recognition and articulation of the problem, and in the personal declaration of independence, financial and otherwise, that she made when she kept her name.

Given her prominence in her own time and the contribution she made to women's cause in theory and in practice, the question arises as to why Stone disappeared, for in the women's history of the nineteenth century, she has most definitely been eclipsed by Stanton and Anthony for example, and there has been surprisingly little research undertaken on her. The most commonly quoted explanation for her disappearance is that she didn't write the book, the 'official' guide to the times – that is, the *History of Woman Suffrage*: because of this, her ideas and activities were not so well documented as those of Stanton and Anthony. There is some plausibility in this. Since Stone usually spoke extemporaneously, not many of her speeches have survived. A few are quoted in *History of Woman Suffrage*, there are copies of a few more in the Blackwell Family Papers, and accounts of others appear in periodicals like *The Liberator*. But for an overview of her ideas and analyses, one has to plough through old files of *The Woman's Journal*, so the written record of Stone's intellectual expression is neither that impressive, nor that accessible.

But this isn't the only reason for her disappearance. It seems that women who have made public protests about women's position, have historically been discredited, with one of the most popular means being to question their morality (as in the case of Mary Wollstonecraft, Frances Wright, etc). Stone obviously suffered from this kind of attack when she and her husband were accused of being free lovers, and this is probably the reason she played down the name issue in her later years. So in this case, the strategy worked: the immorality charge contributed to her silencing during her own lifetime as well as possibly deflecting interest away from further study of her.

If Stone is remembered at all today, it is because she kept her name: the dictionary contains the epithet 'Lucy Stoner' and the definition is 'a person who advocates the retention of the maiden name by married women'. But the term is not a positive one and so while Lucy Stone has been remembered because she kept her name, it is a sort of crank: little or no attempt is made to deal seriously with the feminist ideology which led her to make this radical and unpopular decision.

Lucy Stone does not occupy a prominent or even a visible position in the current history curriculum (in a recent high school text she is mentioned twice and both entries are inaccurate). There is as much chance today as there was when I studied history, of passing through courses on nineteenth century America without ever coming across Lucy Stone. And perhaps because of her more conservative stand in later life, young feminist scholars do not find her attractive and so there has been little reclamation of her – which is a pity, for she was magnificent in her early days and does not deserve disappearance.

Select Bibliography of Lucy Stone

The two standard biographies are: Alice Stone Blackwell's *Lucy Stone, Pioneer of Woman's Rights* (1930), and Elinor Rice Hays' *Morning Star, A Biography of Lucy Stone* (1961). An in-depth discussion of Stone's use of her maiden name is to be found in Una Stannard's *Mrs Man* (1977). Extracts of some of Stone's speeches appear in the first four volumes of Elizabeth C. Stanton *et al, History of Woman Suffrage* (1881–1922). *The Woman's Journal* (1870–93) contains many editorials by Stone. The bulk of her correspondence is in the Blackwell Family Papers, (BFP), Library of Congress, with other letters to be found in the Schlesinger Library, in the Blackwell, Olympia Brown, and Anna Howard Shaw papers. A selection of 221 letters exchanged between Stone and her husband, but also including letters to other suffragists, appears in Leslie Wheeler, ed, *Loving Warriors*, Dial Press, New York, 1981.

Matilda Joslyn Gage:
Active Intellectual
(1826–1898)

Lynne Spender

Woman herself must judge of woman . . . man as man is still as obtuse of yore . . . He yet fails to see in her a factor of life whose influence for good or evil has ever been in direct ratio with her freedom. He does not yet discern her equal right with himself to impress her own opinions on the world. He still interprets governments and religions as requiring from her an unquestioning obedience to laws she had no share in making . . . man has assumed the right to think for woman. (1893; 1980, p 239)

So wrote Matilda Joslyn Gage in 1893. Her comments, however, could be mistaken for the concluding statements from a contemporary women's studies course. They are comments based on ideas and connections which many of us in the current women's movement have erroneously thought that we had generated.

It is both stimulating and sobering to discover that Matilda Joslyn Gage developed a similar, radical critique of the 'Patriarchate', as she called it, 100 years ago. It is stimulating when we realise that other women have for centuries recognised and challenged the values and assumptions on which patriarchy is based but it is sobering when we understand that it has all been said before – strongly and clearly – and that we didn't even know. We did not know because Matilda Joslyn Gage qualifies as one of those women whose disappearance from the records has been essential for the preservation of history – as it has been written.

It is ironical that Matilda Joslyn Gage who spent much of her energy reclaiming women who had gone before and validating women's contributions to a strong intellectual tradition, should herself now be the subject of the same process. Contemporary feminists such as Mary Daly, Sally Roesch Wagner and Dale Spender (1982 b) have 'rediscovered' Matilda Joslyn Gage and emerging from their work comes a picture of an amazing woman – a 'radical theoretician', an historian, an activist, a writer of both scholarly and popular material. Referred to as the third person of the 'triumverate' (Wagner, 1980, p xv) which also included Elizabeth Cady Stanton and Susan B. Anthony, Matilda Joslyn Gage appears as a woman whose ideas, theories and actions place her as one of the most far-sighted (both forward and backward-looking) and clear-sighted of the women who have stood apart from and dared to challenge the society in which they lived.

Information about her life and work is difficult to find – in part as both Mary Daly (1980) and Sally Roesch Wagner explain, because personal recognition was not one of her priorities. Also it seems that much of her work and especially her more radical critiques of male authority, particularly as expressed in relation to the church, has been deliberately excluded from mention and thus from further study. Women as critical and as credible as Matilda Joslyn Gage pose a threat to the establishment; their influence must be erased.

Even so, we do know that from the early 1850s in New York and when still a young woman, Matilda Joslyn Gage was actively committed to social reform (Wagner, p xvi). What seems so amazing today is that she did not merely write about social reform from a theoretical framework and from the safety of her living-room. Instead, at a time when public roles for women were far from acceptable, she was what we today call a 'grass-roots activist' (Wagner, p xvi). She wrote, petitioned, organised and addressed audiences on the major issues of social reform in the late nineteenth century. She opened her house in Fayetville, New York, as a 'station' on the underground railway used to help slaves escape to Canada. She was actively involved in the temperance movement which must not be considered, as is often the case, as an attempt to impose moral purity on society but as one of the few ways available to women to limit the violent and abusive behaviour of thousands of men whose drinking frequently resulted in the poverty and assault of women and children.

Elizabeth Cady Stanton makes reference to Matilda Joslyn Gage's first public speech on women's rights at the third Women's Rights Convention in Syracuse in 1852 in *History of Woman Suffrage*, (Vol I, p 528): Gage did not personally know any of the leaders of the movement and unsupported, rose and gave her speech which so impressed Lucretia Mott that she insisted it be printed and circulated as part of the movement literature (Wagner, p xv). The speech (reprinted in part in Tenner, 1971) demonstrates Matilda Joslyn

Gage's ability to reconceptualise society and the issues that affected women. In it, Gage challenged the notion that women must struggle to prove their worth in order to be granted the vote. Her archivist activity on women in history showed that women had already proven their worth in the areas of science, government, literature and the arts; her approach focused attention on the fact that the issue of womens rights did not centre around women's worthiness and their ability to show themselves 'responsible' in male terms but around men's reluctance to allow women freedom and responsibility for their own lives. It was male power and privilege that Gage wanted transformed.

In questioning male authority to dictate women's lives and women's knowledge, Matilda Joslyn Gage questioned the whole fabric of nineteenth-century American society. In the year that the United States celebrated its national centennial, Matilda Joslyn Gage wrote:

> Liberty to-day is . . . but the heritage of one half of the people, and the centennial will be but the celebraton of the independence of one-half the nation. The men alone of this country live in a republic, the women enter the second hundred years of national life as political slaves. (quoted in Wagner, 1980, p xix)

Her work in libraries and her research in reviving the lives and work of other women led to new understandings about history, to a sense of women reclaiming a positive past; Stanton said of Gage that 'She always had a knack of rummaging through old libraries, bringing more startling facts to life than any other woman I ever knew' (Wagner, p xxvi). She wasn't just 'lucky' in finding this information, it represented years of patient, hard work and a creative intellectual capacity to conceptualise what she was looking for. Her view of history was not one which represented a pattern of systematic progress in which the 'right' time had come for women to stand up and claim the vote. The right time had been and gone, according to Gage, and women had to take back from men what was rightfully theirs, not prove to men that they were capable of conducting themselves in ways of which men would approve. Gage formulated new strategies for women's total liberation. 'Woman is showing her innate wisdom in daring to question the infallibility of man, his laws, and his interpretation of her place in creation,' said Gage. And, 'Woman will gain nothing by a compromising attitude . . . it has become one of woman's first duties, one of her greatest responsibilities, to call public attention to . . false doctrines and false teachings in regard to the origin, condition and subjection of woman' (Gage, 1980, p 245).

If it were not for Sally Roesch Wagner's introduction to Gage's book *Woman, Church and State*, it would be possible to construct a picture of Matilda Joslyn Gage as a serious-minded, committed and intense woman. Certainly, Elizabeth Cady Stanton's comments about her in the *History of Woman Suffrage* could be construed to provide an image of eccentricity, and it would be easy to see her vulnerability to an assessment as the humourless, man-hating stereotype into which mould so many feminists have been cast. Fortunately though, Wagner draws attention to several of Gage's involvements with the public world where she demonstrated superb self-control and a delightful sense of humour. One such incident took place shortly after the Syracuse convention and was carried on in the Syracuse local press, as Wagner says, much to the joy of local readers. A Congregational minister denounced the women's movement in a sermon, condemning the bloomer attire of some of the women on the grounds that the Bible and God's will forbade women to adopt men's clothing. Matilda Joslyn Gage responded in the press by noting that the good reverend himself was guilty of similar biblical offence by his failure to wear a robe trimmed with bells and a bonnet of fine linen. Further, she reprimanded men for attempting to 'acquire feminine resemblance' (Wagner, p xvi) by shaving, when nature's law and that of Moses forbade it. Wagner refers to Gage 'teasing' the good reverend, whose argument that women should be in subjection to their husbands did not seem so weighty after Gage pointed out that the order of creation actually indicated that inferior creatures were first made – and woman created last of all.

Matilda Joslyn Gage's view of society, which allowed her to reconstruct society without placing men and men's laws at its centre and without acknowledging men's title to authority, enabled her time and time again to throw men's arguments back upon themselves. When the United States Supreme Court ruled that the US 'had no voters in the States of its own creation' (Wagner, p xix), Gage quickly prepared a response which established that the US had already created eight classes of voters and revealed again that it was not women who did not qualify to vote, but male decisions and male control which deliberately prevented them from doing so.

When in 1872, Susan B. Anthony was arrested and faced trial for voting 'illegally', it was Matilda Joslyn Gage, the activist, who sat beside her throughout the trial; it was Matilda Joslyn Gage, the strategist and theoretician, who turned the arguments around and who 16 times delivered the speech 'The United States on Trial, Not

Susan B. Anthony'. The speech was based on the premise that governments could not 'grant' those rights which existed along with human existence and that the legal issue was the US withholding those natural rights from certain people. Later, and again using men's own laws to demonstrate that male intention was the deliberate exclusion of women from full personhood, Gage prepared a petition to Congress which demanded for her the same relief of political disabilities that had been granted to convicted criminals who had regained the right to vote. The bill introduced into Congress did not pass but it did attract attention, and as Wagner points out (p xxi) must have 'set people thinking that even while male felons could regain the right to vote, any woman who voted was a criminal'.

While for over 40 years, Matilda Joslyn Gage applied her remarkably independent analysis and strategies to the cause of woman suffrage, she did not at any stage believe that suffrage was the fundamental issue involved in women's subjection. Nor did she for a moment think that women's lives would change radically after they received the vote. Her vision and understanding was far more broadranging than this; her speeches, her research and her writing indicate that she had grasped a century ago what some of us are only today beginning to see – that woman's subjection is the basis on which the dominance of men – and their institutions – is predicated. Only when men's actions and their obstructive and destructive motives are exposed will women achieve their rightful place. As Mary Daly says, Matilda Joslyn Gage recognised the enemy – and named him (1980, p vii).

From 1878–1881 Matilda Joslyn Gage edited and published *The National Citizen and Ballot Box*, a newspaper which was the official paper of the National Women's Suffrage association. The issues raised in the paper show how closely attuned Gage's concerns were with those that we are concerned with today. They also show how comprehensive and compelling was Matilda Joslyn Gage's understanding of women's oppression.

As far as Gage was concerned women's suffrage was only a symptom of a society whose illness lay in the basic social, political and economic structures that men had established to suit their own interests. Consequently she saw prostitution, marriage customs, rape, custody rights as an integral part of the problem that had to be challenged and articles appeared in the *National Citizen and Ballot Box* which explored all of these issues from a feminist perspective. Information and studies on collectives and co-operative life-styles were featured as was Gage's 'particular brand of feminist humour'

(Wagner, p xxv) Her constant awareness that society was not arranged on some arbitrary and inevitable basis but on the needs and interests of men, provided an overall and convincing framework for connections to be made between women's subjection and men's positions of privilege.

Dealing with women's unpaid labour in the home, Gage made the specific connection between it and the advantages that immediately accrued to men. As Dale Spender (1982 (b)) says, Gage was aware that because men own women's labour, the harder women work, the richer men get. Certainly Gage explained and exposed time and time again, that through the rationale provided by the church and the state, men had placed themselves in positions to 'steal' the fruits of women's labour.

But it was not only the fruits of physical labour that Gage saw arranged to pass to men. She also asserted that men had appropriated women's creative and intellectual labour. In her pamphlets *Woman as Inventor* and *Who Planned the Tennessee Campaign of 1861?*, as well as in her other work, Gage presented the information which revealed that men had deliberately arranged that credit for achievement be denied to women. Through their ownership of women's labour and effort, men were easily able to use them at their will and for their own benefit.

A century before we rediscovered the male rationale at the roots of witch burning and other systematic practices of violence against women, Matilda Joslyn Gage had made these connections. At a time when many women who had been associated with the original radical demand for suffrage had become increasingly complacent about the implications of male power, (and Elizabeth Cady Stanton was not one of them), Matilda Joslyn Gage was becoming more enraged and more outspoken in her claim that women and men constituted different interest groups, and that there was between them, a *conflict* of interest.

Again and again she stripped away the façade of male chivalry, protection, honour and respect and showed that these were nothing other than the trappings of a convenient rationale for constructing the belief that women are not workers; apart from denying the enormous contribution women made in terms of reproduction and in the home, this had the effect of denying living wages to working-class women (for after all, women did not work), and of enforcing 'idleness' on middle-class women (who also did not work).

It was not *one problem* that Gage set out to explain; she tackled the rules that were the basis of patriarchial society and which manifested themselves in a myriad of problems. Her fundamental premise – that men own the fruits of women's labour, emotional, psychological, intellectual and creative as well as physical – is as meaningful in explaining patriarchial structures today as it was in her own time. Her insistence that women must claim their own resources and use them in the interest of their own sex, instead of 'wasting' them by making them available to men to use in the interest of *their* own sex, is just as relevant and powerful today, as it was then.

To read Matilda Joslyn Gage today, is in many respects to be shocked; shocked that this perceptive and powerful analysis of society should have been formulated a century ago and not built upon, shocked that in the late 1960s we had to begin again without benefit of these valuable insights which she herself forged over a lifetime, but shocked too that a woman of the nineteenth century should have so clearly and uncompromisingly spoken out against men. We have been led to believe that nineteenth-century women were not capable of such fiery protest, such rage – and all based upon such scholarly arguments! Gage's anger was a response in part to the fact that she had been led to believe that no woman before her had been capable of such resistance. Our shock today, in seeing this, takes the form of a question – how many times does women's history have to repeat itself? For when Mary Ritter Beard came to similar conclusions to Gage, approximately 50 years after her, it was without any knowledge of Matilda Joslyn Gage or her work; when we began to come to our contemporary understandings it was without the knowledge of either of them.

In many respects Gage subtly reversed some of the existing theoretical arguments that related to women's position in society; it was not that women would be able to contribute to society only after they got the vote but that they had contributed to society in the past, and men had denied their contribution. It was not that civilisation was evolving to a higher state and that the next step would be to make women full human beings, but that women had been full, creative human beings in the past and men had robbed them of their resources. And it was not that the church or the state *caused* the subjection of women but that the particular organisation of church and state had been devised by men in order to preserve their power; church and state had been built upon the subjection of women and could not therefore be looked to as agents for changing women's position in society.

Needless to say, at a time when societies like the Women's Christian Temperance Union were looking to the vote for women as a means of establishing a Christian community based on 'proper' moral values, Gage's insistence (along with that of Stanton) that organised religion was the enemy of women because it was controlled by men, did not endear her to some of the women (Susan B. Anthony among them it seems, see Sally Roesch Wagner), who were seeking an alliance with men in order to obtain the vote. It was a mark of her courage and determination that isolated – even ostracised – as she often was, she kept naming the problem as male power.

Gage's research and theory led her into work on ancient goddess religions, on prehistoric matriarchies, on the persecution of witches as a specifically misogynist practice which benefitted men and the church and all of it tied in to create a coherent and cogent feminist world view. Her uncovering of the practice of *marquette*, whereby feudal lords in Christian countries were permitted access for three days after marriage to the newly-wed women on their estates, along with her scathing criticism of the church in aiding, abetting and providing a system to ensure women's subordination, makes startling and credible ready today. In fact, the church and organised religion are the focal point for much of Gage's criticism and underlie the thesis in her major work, *Woman, Church and State* (1893). In the book, she says,

> The most stupendous system of organized robbery known has been that of the church towards woman, a robbery that has not only taken her self-respect but all rights of person; the fruits of her own industry; her opportunities of education; the exercise of her judgment, her own conscience, her own will (p 238) . . . The whole theory regarding woman, under Christianity, has been based upon the conception that she had no right to live for herself alone. Her duty to others has continuously been placed before her and her training has ever been that of self-sacrifice. (1893, 1980, p 239)

Insisting on the validity of women's own perceptions and exposing the myths that men have fabricated in an attempt to deny them, Matilda Joslyn Gage pointed, quite simply, to the falseness of men's claim that women are emotional. Using the combination of humour and observation uncluttered by social conditioning that characterised her analysis, Gage stated that it was men at their political conventions, sporting events and in war and rape, who totally let go of their emotional control in a way that women have never done. It is man, she said, who 'has exhibited the wildest passions – the most ungovernable frenzy'; it is man who 'has shown himself less controlled by reason than possible for woman under the most adverse circumstances' (1893, p 243). The argument about women's emotional temperament, does not and did not stand up to Matilda Joslyn Gage's clear scrutiny.

Right until the end of her life, Matilda Joslyn Gage retained her radical vision – and action, her humour and warmth, her active commitment to women. In spite of the huge disappointment she felt at the betrayal involved in the union of the American Woman Suffrage Union and the National Woman Suffrage Association (which she had been instrumental in forming), and at what she saw as Susan B. Anthony's compromise of women's total position in favour of gaining the vote, Gage went ahead and formed the Women's National Liberal Union – a far more radical association. She herself called its first convention her 'grandest and most courageous work' (Wagner, p xxxvii) and as with many courageous acts, hers had to be paid for. More conservative women in other organisations felt obliged to dissociate themselves from Gage; Susan B. Anthony felt obliged to edit most of Gage's contributions from the *History of Woman Suffrage*; society generally found it convenient to excise Matilda Joslyn Gage from history.

Thus it is today that Matilda Joslyn Gage – the woman and her work – has been all but lost to contemporary women. Her knowledge, analysis and predictions for the future, all remarkably in tune with those of modern feminists, have not formed part of our understandings of woman's position in society and woman's fight to regain her rightful place. Although her encouragement to women to be disloyal to the laws that they had no part in creating and which do not incorporate their understandings, places her in the same tradition as women like Virginia Woolf and Adrienne Rich, most of us have not been aware of her existence. Because she stood apart from society, named men as the enemy and refused to argue sweetly, choosing instead to fight boldly, Matilda Joslyn Gage has been lost as a model and *we* have lost much as a result. It is time this remarkable woman was reclaimed as she herself reclaimed so many women before her. She must not be lost again.

Josephine Butler:
From Sympathy to Theory
(1828–1906)

Jenny Uglow

Josephine Butler was born in Northumberland in 1828 into a county family with strong radical and non-conformist sympathies. In 1850 she met George Butler, then a lecturer at Durham University, and after their marriage in 1852 they lived in Oxford and Cheltenham. In 1864 they moved to Liverpool, where Josephine began rescue work with prostitutes, and was drawn by Anne Clough into the educational struggle, acting as president of the North of England Council for the Higher Education of Women from 1868–1873. In 1869 she was persuaded to take the leadership of the Ladies National Association in the campaign against the state regulation of prostitution under the Contagious Diseases Acts. A magnetic personality, she proved a superb politician combining moving oratory with a shrewd sense of tactics. She not only led the British campaign until repeal of the Acts in 1886 but also became involved in similar movements on the continent and in India. Although she largely inspired W. T. Stead to stir up public concern about the White Slave Trade and the low age of consent in the 1880s, she drew back from the moral purity movements of the turn of the century. She died in 1906.

Personal Liberty
Josephine Butler made two great contributions to late nineteenth-century feminism. She shifted the grounds of the debate about women's subordination from the liberal analysis in terms of legal and civil rights which lay behind the arguments of Mill, Martineau and campaigners for educational and professional opportunity (Davis, Bodichon, Jex-Blake), to a more radical and comprehensive view of women's oppression within a total economic, political and sexual power relationship. Second, during her leadership of the Ladies National Association she developed theories and methods of feminist

attack which anticipated and influenced the campaigns of later activists.

Yet it becomes clear, from the mass of pamphlets, articles, addresses, letters and books which she produced during 40 years of public life from 1866–1906 that she was not an accomplished abstract theorist (within the 'classification scheme' we have inherited); indeed there are ambivalences, even irreconcileable threads, which run through her presentation of women's situation and potential role.[1] Her metier was persuasion rather than definition; she was an expressive polemicist with a good grasp of argument, whose apprehension of overall structures was derived first from intense emotional identification with the plight of individuals, and second from testing her observations against a set of largely unquestioned principles based on a mixture of libertarian ideals, *laissez faire* economics and 'vital' Christianity.

Butler's appeal to personal liberty is constantly backed by reference to the Gospels, 'it seems to me impossible for anyone candidly to study Christ's whole life and works without seeing that the principle of the perfect equality of all human beings was advanced by him as the basis of social philosophy' (1869, p 63) and she argues that all his acts towards women were gestures of 'Liberation', whether from legal, social, emotional or mental oppression. Her notion of Christian equality was inseparable from a belief in the value of economic and political self-determination, and this was to lead her into some paradoxical situations. For example she opposed protective factory legislation in the 1870s partly on the grounds that the demands did not come from women themselves, and she later supported Irish demands for self-government while defending British actions in South Africa as an attack against Boer racism. On the whole, however, her adherence to a personal rights philosophy was to save her from the exessively custodial moral attitudes of some of her followers.

The Liberal/Evangelical Temperament

These mingled strands in her thought derived less from an intellectual tradition in the sense of authors and authorities, although her reading was wide and detailed, than from her background and social milieu.[2] Her ideas were formed largely through conversation and debate, and personal contact with members of reform groups, from the liberal aristocracy of her childhood in Northumberland, to her later friendships with Italian Republicans, American abolitionists, Christian Socialists and finally with the women's rights campaigners active in the Social Science Asociation and the 'Langham Place Group' in the

1860s, especially Anne Clough and Jessie Boucherett.

Josephine grew up conscious of a strong network of supportive women, including her remarkable aunt, the early feminist Margaretta Grey, her mother Hannah, whose Moravian views coloured her own unconventional Anglicanism, and her beloved sister Hattie through whose Swiss husband, Meuricoffre, she developed links with European reform movements. A dominant influence was her father John Grey, a fierce supporter of his cousin, the Whig Prime Minister Lord Grey at the time of the 1832 Reform Bill, an anti-slavery advocate and influential agricultural reformer, who encouraged his seven children to read, question and discuss social and political matters. Her husband, George Butler, was an equally unusual man, a radical educationalist, who supported and campaigned with his wife although his career, family finances and health undoubtedly suffered as a result. Josephine herself acknowledged the confidence she gained from the men in her own life: 'It seems strange that I should have been engaged in taking up the cudgels against men, when my father, brothers, husband and sons have all been so good' (1894, quoted in Walkowitz, 1980, p 121).

After spending five years in Oxford (1852–7) where Josephine fumed against 'the exaggeration of the purely masculine judgement' (1893, 1909, p 23) in academic society, her ill health precipitated a move to Cheltenham, where George was Vice-Principal of Cheltenham College. There they met agreement for their support for Garibaldi, but found themselves ostracised for their identification with the Northern cause in the American Civil War, an experience Josephine later reviewed philosophically, 'It was a good training in swimming against the tide . . . the feeling of isolation on a subject of such tragic interest was often painful; but the discipline was useful; for it was our lot again more emphatically in the future to have to accept and endure this position for conscience sake' (1893, 1909, pp 45–6).

In 1864 after the accidental death of their five-year-old daughter Eva, George accepted the Principalship of Liverpool College. Josephine has left moving descriptions of her grief and of the loneliness of her early days in Liverpool and frankly acknowledges that her involvement with the women of the workhouse with its 'oakum sheds' and Bridewell, was begun largely as therapy. But the sense of 'sisterhood', which she gradually developed into a philosophy of solidarity, undoubtedly derived strength from being based not on philanthropic distance but on a shared experience of suffering, and she proceeded from identification with private misery to a sense of social outrage.

The sheer visibility of deprivation also provided her with a dramatic outer symbol of women's inner alienation and her description achieves an almost mystical intensity:

> It was a strange sound, that united wail – continuous, pitiful, strong – like a great sigh or murmur of vague desire and hope, issuing from the heart of despair, piercing the gloom and murky atmosphere of that vaulted room and reaching to the heart of God. (1867, 1909, p 60)[3]

The stylistic movement, common to all her writing, from description, logical argument, and practical proposals to a poetic symbolism which transcends the political 'reality' is in a tradition of feminist theoretical writing which stretches from Mary Wollstonecraft to Adrienne Rich. But it is also an effective polemical mode, and perhaps it is worth pausing to suggest the ways in which Josephine Butler's strengths as an activist affected, possibly hindered, her development of a conventionally coherent theory.

Activist Strengths: Analytical Weaknesses
First she was constitutionally incapable of separating theory from practice. For her understanding implied action; once convinced of an injustice her interest was in achieving change rather than understanding the reasons for its existence. Initially this was expressed on a personal level only. Thus her resentment of the hypocrisy of silence which cloaked discussion of sexual conduct at Oxford led from fruitless vocal protests to horrified senior members of the University, to the visible protest of her taking as servant a Newgate inmate convicted of the infanticide of her illegitimate child. In Liverpool her experience of the Bridewell was followed by her sheltering of destitute women in her own home, then 'when this became inconvenient' to the purchase of a nearby property as a 'House of Rest'. Her views on employment and training needs resulted in the creation of an Industrial Home (which later supplied all the envelopes for the CD Acts repeal campaign!). By the late 1860s her realisation of the scope of the problem, backed by her theoretical rejection of the attitudes behind 'medieval' individual philanthropy, prompted her commitment to action on a public plane, a commitment expressed first in the fight for women's education as president of the North of England Council for the Higher Education of Women, 1868–73, and then in her acceptance of the leadership of the Ladies National Association for the Repeal of the Contagious Diseases Acts from 1869–1886. The Acts were introduced and gradually extended in 1864, 1866 and 1869,

as a measure intended to control the spread of venereal disease in the army and navy. In designated garrison towns and ports ('subjected districts') they led to the establishment of a special police force who could identify women as 'common prostitutes'. The women then either agreed to submit voluntarily to regular medical examination, or if they refused, could be brought before a magistrate and forced to undergo compulsory examination, with possible incarceration in a local lock hospital or even imprisonment. The burden of proving innocence rested upon the women.

Butler agreed to head the LNA opposition in 1869 at the request of her friend Elizabeth Wolstoneholme, but even when she published her first statements on women's issues, the pamphlet on *The Education and Employment of Women* (1868) and the Introduction to the collection of essays in *Women's Work and Women's Culture* (1869), she was already involved in campaigns with specific targets. Under such conditions description can become a weapon, rather than a neutral mode of exposition, and one has to distinguish between attitudes which may be tactically expedient in winning the support of different constituencies at different times, and fundamental beliefs. The campaign context is partially responsible for apparent contradictions in Butler's attitude to women's special role, to marriage and to prostitution. She clarified her views best in debate and her position does tend to alter depending on her opponent. One of the most detailed and clearest statements of her early position is contained in a long vehement letter to the positivist Frederic Harrison who denied the right of women to employment. This private attack lacks the conciliatory tone of her first public utterances, 'Why are women paid less than men? This too is the act of men, not of God, and can therefore be altered.'[4]

Usually, however, she presented herself not as a debater but as a spiritual campaigner and her reliance on principle, rather than arguments based on logic or on the basis of empirical evidence, was an undoubted campaign strength. It enabled her to hold firm in her opposition to the 1871 Commission: 'We hold that the practical working of an Act, which is vicious in principle, is not fit subject for an enquiry, and therefore we do not require your verdict any more than if it were to tell us whether there is a God or not' (Royal Commission, 1871) and to reject compromise legislation such as 'Bruce's Bill' in 1872.[5] But it did hinder the development of a consistent analysis, especially when reliance on principle became increasingly bolstered by the rhetoric of faith, a feature illustrated by her assertion in 1888 that for 20 years she 'had often thought of this saying, that "God and one woman make a majority".'[6] It is extraordinary (but typical of Butler's 'blind spots') that such an intelligent observer of hypocrisy should have remained so uncritical of the paternalistic aspects of the Christian religion, reserving her attack only for its institutions; but she does remain content in any crisis, simply to appeal to 'God' or to the example of Christ.

Butler was quite aware of the outrage her support of prostitutes would arouse in respectable readers of the *Saturday Post,* and of the power of the vested interests she was attacking. Her fear was justified; the LNA were vilified as a 'shrieking sisterhood', and she was personally assaulted, threatened and harassed. On one occasion her clothes were smeared with excrement, on another bales of hay were set on fire beneath the meeting place, and yet again she was physically attacked by a band of men while the Metropolitan police (whose duty it was to enforce regulation), looked on calmly. She persevered, partly because she felt a sense of divine mission, and partly because she expected this response, having identified from the start the fundamental challenge she was presenting. 'If doubt were gone, and I felt sure he means me to rise in revolt and rebellion (for that it must be) against men, even against our rulers, then I would do it with zeal, however repulsive to others may seem the task' (1869 manuscript book, 1909). The history of the campaign and the arguments, affiliations and political manoeuverings of regulationists and repealers have been exhaustively analysed in recent years.[7] It is not my intention to recap the history, but, viewing Josephine Butler as a thinker on women's position, to suggest some of the ways in which the campaign led her to develop the principles already defined in her early essays, to sharpen her focus on particular issues and to develop a theory of feminist action.

Women's Subordination: the Politics and Economics of Sex
In the Introduction to *Women's Work and Women's Culture* (1869, (a)) Butler quotes with approval Bastiat's definition of 'Spoliation' as a fact of social life which finds its prime expression in the division of domestic labour: 'Repair to the hut of the savage hunter or to the tent of the Nomad Shepherd and what spectacle meets your eyes? The wife, lank, pale, disfigured, affrighted, prematurely old, bears the whole burden of dometic cares, while the man lounges in idleness' (1869, (a), p xiii). But this hint of a conspiracy has already been disclaimed, perhaps too defensively, as Butler protests that she does not 'charge any living being with a conscious and wilful participation in any existing social wrong. The evils of society to which public

attention is now awakened may be said to be in a great measure the result of accident, and of the halting and unequal progress of society' (1869, (a) p ix). Thus, although she attempts to explain women's subordination, her thinking reveals its contradictory quality, for on the one hand she describes oppression as a function of patriarchy and on the other she identifies it as a function of a materialist society in which all relations are expressed in economic terms.

Women are presented as the victims of a 'transition period' characterised by the development of new methods of production; 'stranded' as traditional occupations have disappeared. Yet greater numbers of women need to support themselves (the 1861 census gave 3½ million women working for subsistence, 2½ million unmarried). Opportunities are still further reduced by male attempts to block new avenues to women by creating apprenticeship schemes and professional qualifications for which they are ineligible (the 'conscious and wilful participation' becomes increasingly acknowledged). The result of economic pressures is to put all women in the position of 'cringing for a piece of bread'; expressed by destitution and prostitution among the poor, and the 'scramble for husbands' among the better off.

Sharpened by her Liverpool experiences Butler's sense of the relationship between class and sexual exploitation is much stronger than that of most contemporary feminists, and it was to become a significant feature of the repeal campaign. Within each class, she implies, women are a 'lower' group, so that the lowest caste, on whom the whole pyramid of exploitation is based, must be the destitute women: '*There is no analogy whatever among men, however certain classes of men may be, to the wholesale destruction which goes on from year to year among women,*' (her italics, 1869, (a), p xvi). Her insistence upon the plight of women as an aspect of economic exploitation allowed her to appeal to working-class supporters both on the basis of their experience, and of a sense of having common (although not clearly defined) enemies in the aristocracy, the exploiters of sweated labour, and the centralised state which threatened their personal freedom. In Edinburgh in 1871 she explicitly linked the Contagious Diseases Acts to other 'stringent, punitive and arbitrary' legislation affecting the urban poor which not only eroded customary freedoms but 'tends to the steady increase of the criminal class by the rapid creation of new crimes and new offences, followed by new pains and penalties' (1871, p 4).

The effect of being 'stranded' by the industrial wave upon middle-class women was not so much the loss of livelihood as the loss of identity provided by traditional roles. 'Their work is taken out of their hands; their place – they know not what it is' (1869, (a), p xxiii). Because of this, marriage becomes raised to the status of a 'feminine profession' which involves abject dependency disguised as 'petty helplessness'. It required only a step from her vivid denunciation of mercenary marriage to the analogy between bourgeois marriage and prostitution made explicit by some of her followers.

Not only does she inveigh against the elevated value of marriage but, more interestingly, against the internalisation of these values by women. 'I cannot believe it is every woman's duty to marry, in this age of the world. There is abundance of work to be done which needs men and women detached from domestic ties; our unmarried women will be the greatest blessing to the community when they cease to be soured by disappointment or driven by destitution to despair' (1869, (a), p xxxv). Under such circumstances, when dependency is shored up not only by legal, educational and employment restrictions, but by a prevailing atmosphere of acclaim for the very qualities which made women weak, any suggestion of free choice was nonsensical.

The Contagious Diseases Acts came to symbolise the complication of economic and sexual power relations. Her analysis of prostitution remained an economic one 'for this is not a question of natural vice nearly so much as one of political and social economy' (Letter to Harrison, 1868), and she held steadfastly to the view that prostitutes, whether they had 'fallen' as a result of seduction or material deprivation, were the victims not perpetrators of an offence, a point made in the original Ladies Protest (drawn up by Harriet Martineau, and signed by 124 prominent women) in the *Daily News*, December 1869. In this connection she even questioned the role of female penitents in rescue work, holding that it was men who should feel remorse,[8] and she totally refuted the idea that prostitutes were hardened exploiters of male weakness reflected in Acton's famous distinction that 'there is no comparison to be made between prostitutes and the men who consort with them – with the one sex the offence is committed as a matter of gain; with the other it is an irregular indulgence of a natural impulse' (Royal Commission, 1971).

The insistence on the prostitute as victim was tactically important. As Judith Walkowitz (1980) points out, repealers consistently underestimated factors like the large working-class element in the prostitute's clientele, the strength of the female subculture within which they worked, and the degree of commercial power they did exert. Butler was uncomfortable when faced with a woman who held a sheerly entrepreneurial view of the sale of sexual services. She dealt with this first by falling back on her personal rights philosophy – if a woman chose to sell herself she should be free to do so unmolested by police and unjust laws – and second, by seeing this 'hardened' attitude as representing internalisation of male values and therefore actually a feature of the male conspiracy, just as the internalisation of the myth of the Angel in the House ensured the continuation of bourgeois domestic slavery.

In many of her speeches and pamphlets the assertion that prostitutes are victims and vehicles, rather than instigators of pollution, is used to highlight emphasis on the prevailing double standard of sexual morality. She does not enter openly into the debate about male and female sexuality nor does she introduce the topic of the confinement of sexuality within marriage, and this is an undoubted weakness as it means she does not address herself to the issue of women's sexual rights and freedom of expression; nor does she entirely heal the breach between the 'pure' middle-class wife and the sexually active prostitute. She does, however, argue that they are separated not by a predisposition to 'sin' but by material circumstances, and are forced apart by the 'logical necessity' of the double standard whereby 'One group of women is set aside, so to speak, to minister to the irregularities of the excusable man. That section is doomed to death, hurled to despair, while another section of womanhood is kept strictly and almost forcibly guarded in domestic purity' (1885, (a)). From the very beginning she expressed disgust at Lecky's notion of the prostitute as scapegoat for men's sins ('the supreme type of vice, she is ultimately the most efficient guardian of virtue', W. Lecky, 1869) as a travesty of Christian teaching (1869, (a)).

Commentators have pointed to her good relationship with George as evidence of sexual harmony, and she showed no fear of dealing with the topic of internal examinations or venereal disease but she did remain very reticent on the subject of sexual appetite and of unconventional sexual liaisons.[9] This is the one area where, as the succeeding section which examines her relation to social purity movements makes clear, all her impetus was towards control rather than liberation. What she does concentrate on is the social construction of sexual drives; the fact that once one had accepted the male sexual urge as imperative, and positively harmful if checked, this, in a male-run society, turned women into a means of sexual release which could (indeed should) be bought and sold without guilt. If one accepted that women, on the other hand, were not possessed of an innate appetite and thus once they became sexually active, even if 'used' to the benefit of men, they somehow denied their essential feminity, then they could be portrayed as transgressing their social role. They became 'degraded' and called down upon themselves disapproval and revulsion, embodied under the Contagious Diseases Act by a whole series of punitive legal and medical measures. Prostitution represented a visible assertion of this 'unnatural' sexuality on a grand scale and public discussion of it was tinged with fear and hostility, as in this *Westminster Review* article of 1850: 'If the passions of women were ready, strong and spontaneous, in a degree even remotely approaching the form they assume in the coarser sex, there can be little doubt in that sexual irregularities would reach a height, of which, at present, we have happily no conception' (ed Keith Nield, 1973).

Butler objected, not to the premise, but to the fact that this led as it does today to women being punished for satisfying a male demand.[10] The hypocrisy was further compounded, in her view, by a set of laws designed to protect men from the consequences of their actions, which effectively sanctioned prostitution while condemning prostitutes and which helped to create 'professional' groups of women who became cut off from the communities which had previously supported them. She even argued that sexual hypocrisy meant that women could now be punished for infection which was actually the result of male homosexuality in the army and navy.

State regulation of prostitution is therefore represented by her as the institutional embodiment of prevailing ignorance and hypocrisy about sexuality, as the crystallisation of the double standard and as the expression of men's hatred and fear of women which takes the form of creating an outcast group who can be presented as polluting and threatening society. The actual operation of the Contagious Diseases Act helped Butler to define this misogynistic strain as revealed in institutional form still further. It revealed openly what she had suggested but resisted saying in her 1869 essay, that the control of women by men was no less total than that of a slave by its master. Every aspect of autonomy was denied, a point she made when repeating the complaint of a woman from the subjected districts in Kent;

> It is men, only men, from the first to the last, that we have to do with! To please a man I did wrong at first, then I was flung about from man to man. Men police lay hands on us. By men we are examined, handled, doctored and messed on with. In the hospital it is a man again who makes prayers and reads the Bible for us. We are up before magistrates who are men, and we never get out of the hands of men. (*Shield*, 9 May 1870)

Much of the repeal literature concentrated on sensational tales of the entrapment of innocent women, or on the horrors of the examination which was presented as a hostile voyeuristic assault, an 'instrumental rape' with the speculum, the 'steel penis'. This was linked specifically by Butler to other gynaecological and obstetric practices which seemed designed for the humiliation of women and which often represented a male takeover of traditional women's healing and caring roles, an extension of control through 'forcible doctoring' described by a campaigner as the 'medical lust of handling and dominating women'.[11] Her final analysis is startlingly radical; she describes a vicious circle – the security of men's physical strength and the desire for sexual control over women's bodies underpins a complex legal, economic, political and ideological structure – the result of the pressures of these structures is that women are driven to employ sexual submission as a means of economic survival, by selling themselves either in marriage or on the streets.

Arguments for Change: Equal but Distinct

Butler argues for emancipation on two fronts, that the present inequitable treatment of women demands redress on straightforward egalitarian, civil-rights grounds, and that greater freedom will bring positive social benefits through releasing women's 'special qualities'. Both arguments are present in the introduction to *Women's Work and Culture,* and both echo through the campaign pamphlets and the long series of journals with which she was associated. Taking a stand on personal rights she demands the recognition of women as independent and not defined solely by their relation to male kin; if they are to enjoy equal status as citizens it follows that they must have unrestricted access to education, employment and the ownership of property and equal political and legal representation. In this respect her position is not very different from that of Mill with whom she corresponded and whose *On the Subjection of Women,* originally written in 1861, appeared just before her book in 1869, clearly rather to her chagrin.

Her demand for equal rights is evident in her support of the campaign for women's higher education, her support for the Married Women's Property Bill, and in her insistence on the importance of the struggle for the vote. She was one of the signatories of the petition presented by Mill in 1866, and she repeatedly emphasised the need for the vote, even expressing her fear that the repeal campaign might indeed be diverting energy from this goal. In 1893, in a letter sent to a WCTU meeting in London she still repeated, 'My friends we must have the suffrage. It is our right, and it is a cruel and confirmed injustice to withold it from us' (1893, 1909, p172).

A fundamental complaint against the CD Acts was that they deprived half the population of their legal safeguards, and represented an extreme example of the unequal treatment of men and women before the law. This is the basic argument of *An Appeal to the People of England* (1871) and of *The Constitution Violated* (1871) in which she identified the police power of summary arrest and examination as a violation of Magna Carta itself.

She never lost her insistence on equity and looked back on her crusade as one for both 'purer morals and for juster laws'. But it is in relation to her first claim, as a campaigner for purer morals, that Josephine Butler is often remembered and she was certainly typical of her era in arguing from an accepted view of women as guardians of domestic virtue to the extension of this 'special influence' which would come if women were involved in public life. By taking this stance one could argue for public involvement without denying the sanctity of the family.

Butler does seem to have held some idea of 'essential' feminine qualities, but she does not relate these specifically to biological bases; she grants the paternal instinct (although tinged with ideas of possession) as much power as maternal love.

In *Women's Work and Women's Culture* the most she seems to acknowledge is that women have certain ordering powers based on a long tradition of care for individuals, which leads to the creation of a sense of 'home', and that this individual care, while wholly inadequate as a basis for philanthropy, could be harnessed to social good, in alleviating the 'wholesale' impersonal nature of 'masculine' institutions, and in constantly reminding people of the basis of love and respect on which relations between individuals should be conducted. This is very different, as she points out, from arguing that women's sphere should actually be *in* the home, a view which she presents as a cruel irony. She does reiterate the fact of her own happy family life, but this is a political tactic to gain credibility and to ward off the accusations of being embittered and ignorant which were flung at all campaigning feminists. When arguing for the role of women in public life she finds it expedient to emphasise their tenderness, just as later, in relation to suffage, she realised it was tactically better to avoid emotionalism, 'for I long ago rejected the old ideas of this "division of labour" that "men must work and women must weep" ' (1883, 1909, p 176). In her campaign writing her use of 'separate sphere' ideology is equally affected by tactical considerations as Judith Walkowitz detects when considering her identification with the concept of motherhood, and the presentation of her campaign as one which would save 'daughters': 'Butler's defense of motherhood was a political device, aimed at subverting and superseding patri-archal authority: it gave mothers, not fathers, the right to control sexual access to the daughters. In this way Butler sanctioned an authority relationship between older middle-class women and young working women that, although caring and protective, was also hier-archical and custodial. At other times, however, she approached prostitutes on a more egalitarian basis, as sisters, albeit "fallen" ones, whose individual rights deserved to be respected' (Walkowitz, 1980, p 117).

There is no doubt that Butler did believe in the collective power of women to alter social habits for the better and to justify this she relied less on observation or theory than on a sense of divine mission. 'Women are called to be a great power in the future . . . God has prepared in us, in the women of the world, a force for all future causes which are great and just. We shall not stop, our efforts will not cease when this particular struggle is at an end' (1883, 1909, pp 181–2). The two strands, egalitarian and custodial, intertwine throughout the campaign literature and meet in the demand for an equal moral standard. Here it is quite clear, although she was horrified by the proposal of Edmondson in 1875 that legislation should be introduced to make fornication illegal,[12] that Butler was not advocating equal sexual liberty for women, but equal restraint for men. Linda Gordon has summed up neatly the ambivalence which underlay the moral reform movements in both England and America: 'Liberal in its commitment to legal equality and to a single standard but conser-vative in the desire to enforce traditional . . . moral values on the whole society' (Gordon, 1974, p 111). But the memory of the social purity wave of the 1880s and 90s has tended to make people overestimate the coercive side of Butler's thinking on personal morality.

Certainly the protective emphasis increased during the 1880s when she became more involved in the attack on the White Slave Trade and therefore concerned with juvenile and child sexuality. Here the custodial role was traditional and at first Butler saw nothing but good in the raising of the age of consent to 16 and in the legal sanctions to be imposed on brothel keepers. Indeed she was one of the early committee members of the Social Purity Alliance, and had whole-heartedly supported their 'consecrated rebellion against the rule of materialism and sensuality' (1879, p 5) in two important pamphlets, *The House Before the Dawn* and *Social Purity,* but she resigned when she felt the repressive element in the movement. She later dissociated herself entirely from any pressure to institutionalise individual behaviour. 'Since the beginning of our crusade I had been convinced in my conscience and understanding of the folly, and even wickedness, of all systems of *outward repression* of private immorality, for which men and women are accountable to God and their own souls, but not to the *State*' (1896, 1909, p 174). As guardians of standards of morality women had to awaken, educate and change the consciousness of the population, claiming their own individual rights but continuing to respect those of others; this is the knife edge on which all liberal and feminist campaigns relating to private behaviour have tried to perform their almost impossible balancing act.

Theories of Social and Feminist Activism
The urgency of Josephine Butler's desire for equality and for application of the moral power of women was enhanced by her theory of history and her appreciation of processes of social change. Her Christianity was far from rigidly deterministic; but she did see social and political history as representing a perpetual battle of good and evil, which she frequently describes through the rhetoric of God and the Devil, the forces of heaven and the powers of hell. (Even Frederic Harrison's views on women's employment in 1868 are described as 'Satanic'). The capacity of men to achieve liberation through love, along the lines she indicated in her reading of the Gospels were continually tested by circumstance. Since she believed that one's concern must always be with the weak and oppressed, as she felt Christ's was, it was not possible to take a simple progressivist view of history. Her concentration was on the victims rather than the survivors of social evolution.

Butler manages (though rather uncomfortably) to fit a theological sense of design onto a definition of change through social, even genetic, evolution. Her vision of the misery of exploited labour encompasses the 'ever accumulating weight of crime and misery which is passed on as a family heritage, and even the physical type degraded for successive generations, till finally our Prisons, Penitentiaries and Workhouses are crowded to overflowing with worthless, inhuman, unwholesome weeds, low browed apes in whom intelligence is all but extinguished and love has perished, and the instinct of hunger and the lowest animal instincts remain' (1869, (a), p xxxvi). By the end of the century her fears had reached apocalyptic proportions, so that although her view of what determined consciousness remained primarily environmentalist, it became increasingly tinged with theories which supported eugenicism, and nationalism.

However confused and unpalatable her theory of historical development may seem it did have important implications for developing feminist ideas of how change should be effected. First she insists that to break a cycle of social deprivation the oppressed class must be made aware of their situation and must seize the right to self expression and self-determination. 'It is only when the slave begins to move, to complain, to give signs of life and resistance, either by his own voice, or by the voice of one like himself speaking for him, that the struggle to freedom truly begins' (1875, 1909, p 151). This is why it was essential for 'womanhood' to take a separate stand to avenge the generations of sexually exploited women whose situation was formally sanctioned by the CD Acts. Furthermore, she says, individual protest will be powerless unless it encompasses a sense of the unity of that oppressed group from which it springs. The loyalty of the LNA leaders to each other was backed by a sense of cross-class solidarity with the women they fought for, which persisted despite the tension between egalitarian/custodial approaches that we have noted. Butler made this quite explicit: 'Moreover womanhood is *solidaire*. We cannot successfully elevate the standard of public opinion in this matter of justice to women, and of equality of all in its finest sense, if we are content that a practical, hideous, calculated, manufactured and legally maintained degradation of a portion of womanhood is allowed to go on before the eyes of all' (1900, 1909, p 285). She also maintained the importance of international solidarity in campaigns for educational and political rights as in the fight against state regulated prostitution.

Her understanding of the importance of a separate but collective voice is expressed in her tactics, which combined separate organisation with women speaking at mixed meetings and refusing to be excluded from the general campaign. Her fear of monolithic organisational structures under 'male experts' which could obscure fundamental crusading purposes, and her sense of urgency, prompted her to push the LNA into participating in by-elections, lobbying and other militant activities in the face of widespread public hostility.

Butler also confronted the problem of linking a single-issue campaign to wider educational purposes. For while she accepted the need for a fierce attack on existing abuses and called for 'revolt', 'rebellion', 'holy war' or 'Revolution', she felt that enduring change, whether for the worse, like the process of deterioration into 'unwholesome weeds', or for the better, must be gradual: 'Organic growth cannot be healthy except under conditions of freedom from constraint; from the pressure on the one hand, of the swaddling clothes of the past, in the shape of bad or outworn laws or customs, which must be torn off and put away before there can be any free growth; from the pressure, on the other, of too great an urgency' (1869, (a), p ix). And she also asserts, in her characteristic Christian rhetoric, that legislative or institutional change is meaningless, unless accompanied by a deep seated alteration in personal consciousness: '. . . for my part I have not an atom of faith in any reform, moral, social or political, which has not at its root a real repentance before God, a ruthless banishing from the heart and life by individuals of all that is opposed to justice, purity and holiness . . .' (1885, (a), p 11).

The style of this quotation marks the century gap which lies between us and Josephine Butler, and assessing her influence has always presented problems for those who seek to trace a unified, coherent development of feminist argument. Her courageous and charismatic leadership of the women's campaign against the Contagious Diseases Acts is accorded a rather sideways glance in histories of the movements.[13] Acclaimed for its assault on the double standard of sexual morality, it is presented nonetheless as a diversion from the main drive towards suffrage. Elsewhere Butler is claimed as a fore-runner by libertarian groups and by social purity campaigners; her rhetoric is echoed by radical feminists and by upholders of 'family influence'; she is a patriot and an internationalist; her attitude to the working class is described as egalitarian and as custodial. She is at once the hero of militant separatists and a 'forgotten saint'. Indeed, her unresolved conflicts, which have led to such a contradictory inheritance, prefigure many later feminist dilemmas. If one feels that a liberal demand for equality is simply claiming the right to mimic men, how does one assert women's 'special qualities' without colluding in oppressive domestic myths? If one feels that the prime act of women's subordination is that of heterosexual exploitation how does one break the circle? Does one attack the economic and political forms of oppression or concentrate on, or even withdraw from, personal heterosexual relationships? How does one attack prostitution as an embodiment of male contempt for women and yet support The Programme for the Reform of the Law on Soliciting (PROS) in fighting for the prostitute's right to legal safeguards and public acceptance? How does one campaign against pornography or the commoditisation of sex without slipping into repressive attitudes towards varied erotic and sexual expression? How does one maintain solidarity with all women without denying their difficult, even antagonistic relations within the class struggle? Perhaps Josephine

Butler's chief virtue as a theorist is that not only did she define the contour lines of the sexual/political battleground, but she also uncovered so many of the minefields which lie in wait on our own side.

Notes

1   The complete list of Josephine Butler's writings amounts to over 90 works, ranging from short addresses and open letters to long pamphlets and books. She also contributed to periodicals such as *The Shield* and later edited *The Dawn* and *The Storm-Bell* herself as a vehicle for her ideas. The attached bibliography lists a few key works; a nearly comprehensive list can be found in app III, *Josephine E. Butler: An Autobiographical Memoir* ed L. Johnson 1909. The Fawcett Library, City of London Polytechnic has a collection of her pamphlets and a large and well catalogued collection of letters.

2   No satisfactory full-length biography exists despite the wealth of material available. Autobiographical material is contained in the memoirs of her father and husband, in *Personal Reminiscences of a Great Crusade* (1896) and in the *Autobiographical Memoir*, ed Johnson. Recent works on the Repeal Campaign relate her background to that of other members of the LNA and suffrage movements: see especially P. McHugh *Prostitution and Victorian Social Reform* (1980), pp 18–26, 169–176 and J. R. Walkowitz *Prostitution and Victorian Society* (1980), pp 113–136.

3   Several letters describing her work in vivid detail were copied into a notebook by her neice Fanny Leopold. This notebook is now in the Fawcett Library.

4   See Letters to Albert Rutson 7 May 1858 and Frederic Harrison 9 May 1868. Fawcett Library Collection.

5   The Royal Commission upon the Administration and Operation of the CD Acts 1866–69, took evidence in 1871. Initially the LNA refused to acknowledge it although Butler did later give evidence. She led the opposition to the Bill introduced in 1872 by H. A. Bruce which would have repealed the Acts but extended regulation through wider application of other statutes (Vagrancy Act, 1824; Poor Law Amendment Act 1867). For a clear chronological account see McHugh (1980) Ch 3.

6   'Women and Politics', Speech to the Portsmouth's Womens Liberal Association, 11 April 1888. I am indebted to David Doughan of the Fawcett Library for this reference.

7   See especially Sigsworth, E. M. and Wyke, T. J. 'A Study of Victorian Prostitution and Venereal Disease' in *Suffer and Be Still – Women in the Victorian Age,* ed M. Vicinus 1972, pp 77–99; Glen Petrie *A Singular Iniquity: The Campaigns of Josephine Butler* (1971); Paul McHugh (1980); Judith Walkowitz (1980) and Keith Nield, ed *Prostitution in the*

Victorian Age 1973. The last two works, despite different emphases, both draw attention to class and gender tensions as reflected in the campaign's organisation and tactics.

8 *Paper on the Moral Reclaimability of Prostitutes,* 1876.

9 For example her correspondence in 1875 reveals a quite extraordinarily ambivalent attitude to Elizabeth Wolstenholme's liaison with Ben Elmy. She never defines her personal view, but shelters behind effect on the 'Cause' of adverse publicity. Fawcett Library Collection.

10 A succinct modern attack on the double standard, which echoes Butler's polemical style quite uncannily, is Susan Brownmiller's speech in the New York Legislature in 1971. Speaking in the context of rumours of impending state regulation, she attacks the 'legislation of sexual slavery', and, like Butler, emphasises the inextricability of economic, political and sexual oppression. Included in *Radical Feminism,* ed A. Koedt, Quadrangle, New York, 1973.

11 See Craigie Hall Address, 1871, and letter from Josephine Butler to Joseph Edwardson 28 March 1872, quoted in Paul McHugh (1980), p 25. Walkowitz (1980) draws attention to campaign literature on medical examinations; eg J. J. Garth Wilkinson *The Forcible Introspection of Women* (1870), and to Mary Hume-Rothery's *Women and Doctors: Or Medical Despotism in England* (1871).

12 The proposal was contained in a letter from Joseph Edmondson to H. J. Wilson, 9 August 1875, and contains the splendid statement, 'We should have to define the difference between rape, adultery, bastardy and fornication, but this would present no serious difficulty.' Butler's view as passed on by James Stuart, 4 September 1875, was that this was impractical, and 'unChristian.' Fawcett Library Collection.

13 See for example R. Strachey, *The Cause: A Short history of the Women's Movement,* Ch 10; J. Kamm *Rapiers and Battleaxes,* Ch 6; and M. Ramelson, *The Petticoat Rebellion,* Chs 10 and 11, which concentrates more on the popular base of the campaigns.

Select Bibliography of Josephine Butler

The Education and Employment of Women, Macmillan, London, 1868.

Women's Work and Women's Culture, Macmillan, London, 1869, (a).

Memoir of John Grey of Dilston, Edmonston, Edinburgh, 1869, (b).

An Appeal to the People of England on the Recognition and Superintendence of Prostitution by Governments: By an English Mother, Banks, Nottingham, 1870.

On the Moral Reclaimability of Prostitutes, National Assoc, London, 1870.

Sursum Corda: Annual Address to the Ladies National Association, 1871.

Address in Craigie Hall Edinburgh, Ireland, Manchester, 1871.

Vox Populi, Brakell, Liverpool, 1871.

The Constitution Violated, Edmonston, Edinburgh, 1871.

The New Era, Brakell, Liverpool, 1872.
The Hour Before the Dawn: An Appeal to Men, Trubner, London, 1876.
Social Purity, Morgan Y. Scott, London, 1879.
A Woman's Appeal to the Electors, Dyer, London, 1885.
The Principles of the Abolitionists, Dyer, London, 1885.
Recollections of George Butler, Arrowsmith, Bristol, 1892.
Personal Reminiscences of a Great Crusade, Marshall,London, 1896.
An Autobiographical Memoir, ed G. and L. Johnson, Arrowsmith, Bristol, 3rd Edition, 1909.

See also her contributions to:
The Shield, National Association, London, 1870–1886.
The Dawn, Burfoot, London, Quarterly, 1888–1896.
The Storm-Bell, Burfoot, London, Monthly, 1898–1900.
and *Correspondence* in the Josephine Butler Collection, Fawcett Library, City of London Polytechnic.

Hedwig Dohm:
Passionate Theorist
(1833–1919)

Renate Duelli-Klein

As long as it is said man will *and woman* shall, *we live in a state governed by* might *and not by* right *(1876).* [1]

When some months ago I decided to have a closer look at Hedwig Dohm I had only a vague recollection of who she was. What made me consider her as a 'lost' nineteenth-century feminist theorist were some rather faint memories of how amazed and delighted I was when in 1976 I read about her in the opening chapter of Marielouise Janssen-Jurreit's *Sexismus* in which she describes Hedwig Dohm as a radical feminist, ahead of her time, outrageous and irreverent, one who flatly denied men's alleged natural superiority to women and who asked for women's full access to education in order that they may be economically independent of men. [2] I also remembered that Hedwig Dohm is credited with being the first woman in Germany to seek the vote at a time – in 1873 and again in 1876 – when this demand was still seen as 'premature' even within the German women's movement. And, indicative of my own male-oriented socialisation, from reading *Sexismus* I could remember that she lived to be very old and became known as the gentle, lovable and benevolent tiny great-grandmother 'Urmiemchen', as described by her grand-daughter Katia Mann (Thomas Mann's wife), whose views were diametrically opposed to Dohm's feminism (Mann, 1974, p 13). I vaguely recalled having read a couple of recent articles on her in *Emma* (one of the German feminist journals), and she had been mentioned in the first *Frauenkalender* (women's diary) of the contemporary women's movement, published by Alice Schwarzer in 1975, as one of our most radical sisters – then and now.

After rediscovering Hedwig Dohm the more I read by her and about her the more I want to know! Her radical attacks on man-made assumptions about women's nature, expose and ridicule the illogicality of masculinist views, and I am impressed with the breadth of her knowledge of women's position worldwide and her understanding of the 'woman question' as the problem of men, or, to put it differently, that it is power which is the problem, not women! And I love the combination of passion, intellect, irony, humour, common sense and knowledge – wisdom – that inspires her ingenious and sharp argumentation whether she argues *against men* or *for women* which for me is feminist theory at its best. But this is not all. I am equally fascinated by the 'other selves' of Hedwig Dohm: her own views about herself as she expresses them in recollections from her life, and Hedwig Dohm as the writer of novels on and for women in which her heroines are caught in the painful struggle between the 'old' and the 'new' world for women. These are the dimensions of this extraordinary woman that I have come to admire greatly.

Hedwig Dohm lived in Berlin and was a most prolific writer producing a wealth of theoretical treatises, pamphlets, articles, and book reviews, as well as plays (comedies) and a considerable amount of fiction – novels and short stories – all of them related to her quest for ending women's oppression. Significantly, a large part of her work, published in feminist, socialist as well as mainstream journals, consisted of forceful replies to attacks on feminists, and her presentation (like that of her opponents) is strikingly similar to modern feminist (and anti-feminist) debates.

Women are at the centre of her life and work, or, in her own words: 'Everything I write is for the sake of women' (1896, 1980, p 89). And her writing is based on women's experiences: her own, her friends', those of women from other social groups, from other cultures and from earlier times in history. Based on her own painful experiences of being restricted by the mores and customs of her times she says:

> Whatever I write about women is what I have experienced at the very deepest level of my soul. Self-experienced truths are beyond scrutiny . . . The pain I suffered from being a prisoner who knows about the sunshine outside, kindled my ideas for the liberation of women. (1912, 1980, p 78)

Also in words that have not lost their contemporary relevance:

> I do not have to ask anyone what the right thing is to do within the women's movement. I know. If a tile drops on your head you know instantly that the roof is defective. You don't need an investigation first. (1896, 1980, p 122)

But at the same time she is wary of being prescriptive, of creating new dogmas for women. She respects the fact that women have different needs and interests. What she sees as the overall aim for women's emancipation is to grant all women material and psychological independence to free them from men's domination and enable them to move beyond the limiting and debilitating bonds of man-made womanhood to become autonomous human beings in their own right. She acknowledges that there are different roads to this goal and thus she cautions:

> Never would I think of wanting within the women's movement anything other than the right to free self-determination for women . . . To command women: 'this you must do, that you must not, I open this door for you but I close that one' – what an arbitrary act! (1903, p 29)

Hedwig Dohm's Life

Born in Berlin in 1833 as the eleventh of 18 children – 16 survived – eight of whom were brothers, Hedwig Dohm was the sensitive, frightened 'cuckoo' in the nest and she almost went under in that huge Jewish bourgeois family. Boisterousness abounded, and intellectual stimuli as well as space for her dreams were few. Her father, a tobacco-merchant, was either away or silent, and her mother, pregnant most of the time, overworked and irritable, had little understanding for Hedwig's sensitivity. She managed the family with German perfection and rigour including frequent beatings, which were to induce in Hedwig a thorough contempt and horror of physical punishment and violence for the rest of her life, and contributed to deeply unhappy memories about her relationship with her mother.

After failed attempts to gain her mother's love, Hedwig retreated even further into her dream world, oscillating between identifying with Cinderella and taking delight in the dreams of fame and glory which would be bestowed upon her when she became Europe's most famous poet. And of course, there was also the prince on the white horse whose riches she would use to eradicate all poverty on earth – upon which, the deed done, she would generously forgive her mother for all the distress she had caused her!

These childhood experiences marked her life for ever and she explicitly talked about them in one of her novels *Schicksale einer Seele* (Destinies of a Soul, 1899). Elsewhere, she asked, 'Why have mothers the right to cause so much suffering to their children?' (1912, 1980, p 77) – a painful question that made her become an ardent advocate for children's rights, in particular daughters' rights, starting, however, from the firm premise that it must be every woman's individual *right to choose* whether to give birth, and to how many children.

Hedwig loved school, except, as she recalled it, it was always too easy. At 15, however, having completed elementary school, the time of education was meant to be over for Hedwig Dohm – or rather Hedwig Schleh, as she was called then. She was to stay home and do domestic duties, while her brothers, lazy as they were and un-interested in any kind of learning, were forced to continue their education. When after one-and-a-half years of misery embroidering ugly flowers, waiting for something to happen, she finally succeeded in convincing her parents to let her attend a teachers' training college, she was dismayed by the preposterous quality of the education she received. She describes it as the dreary learning by heart of geo-graphy, botany and historical facts and figures – but, most of all, psalms and religious verses. Quite categorically she later states:

> Was it we women who organised further education for girls, was it we who made up the curriculum? As for me, I decline any respon-sibility for orthographical or grammatical mistakes I might make in this essay. I refuse to take the blame. I say: 'it is men's fault'. Each incorrect punctuation is their doing, for each mistake may they be humiliated by society's contempt. In my childhood I went to the best possible school that existed, and it was the worst possible. (1873, p 40)

Small wonder, then, that at 19, when 'the prince of her dreams' appeared, she left her little-loved home before she had finished her teacher training. She married Ernst Dohm, 14 years her senior, humourist and editor of the satirical journal *Kladderadatsch*, who for a short period in his life, had also been a clergyman. Dohm had quite a reputation for his sharp, spirited tongue and his heart on the 'left side' which often brought him into conflict with the police who guarded the ideas of the ultra-conservative, rigid and Catholic Prussian state. In addition, according to Janssen-Jurreit (1976, p 20), he seems to have had certain problems with managing money as well as a passion for gambling.

Little is known about this relationship for while she wrote about her childhood and adolescence and also talked about these periods to her grandchildren, Hedda Korsch (1980), and Katia Mann (1974), she is silent on the topic of her marriage, and strangely enough, she who intersperses almost all of her writings with personal experiences does not follow this practice in a specific essay on marriage 'Von der alten und der neuen Ehe' (On Marriage – Old and New Style, 1902).

Still, we do learn a few things about her marriage: Ernst Dohm sewed on his own buttons (1903, p 47) and at times he was ashamed of Hedwig's ignorance, for which she angrily disclaims responsibility and comments: 'Isn't it ridiculous that men are ashamed of their wives' ignorance for which they themselves are intellectually responsible' (1873, p 40). However, most importantly, she tells us that during her five pregnancies (she had four daughters, and a son who died early) she went through hell:

> I suffered martyrdom which made me have suicidal thoughts . . .
> It was worst when I had nothing to do and thus I started translating
> Spanish poetry into German . . . And these were the only bear-
> able hours in the day, when I, full of exciting mental activity,
> forgot myself and my suffering and was searching for the best
> word, the best rhyme. (1897, 1980, p 141)

Outrageous words for a well-situated middle-class woman to say – in fact for any woman – in her time! Yet that irreverence *vis à vis* prevalent values and standards is precisely what characterises much of Hedwig Dohm's writings: she does not mind going against the conventional wisdom of her time which she unmasks as 'principles made and relevant for men only' (1873, p 171).

However, despite the nightmare of her pregnancies, she later obviously enjoyed her role as a mother and reared her four daughters with all the love and tenderness (and education) she herself had lacked in her own childhood. And while 'dutifully' assuming her role as mistress of the house, she clearly used the circumstances of her marriage to improve her own education.

Her biographer, Adele Schreiber-Krieger, writes in 1914 (p 19):

> . . . from the petty bourgeois narrowness of her family home she
> moved into the centre of the spiritual and political debates of
> liberal circles in Berlin, got to know some of the most extra-
> ordinary personalities of her time and became the 'Hausfrau' of a
> home which came to be famous as a meeting point for a selected
> group of people.

However, being the 'Hausfrau' certainly wasn't a role that Hedwig Dohm found very satisfying and fulfilling. She herself said more than once in her writings how burdensome and boring she thought those duties to be, which, given the middle-class nature of her household meant mainly supervision: giving orders to the cook, the nanny and organising the lives of the family members. Thus, although she participated in the *jours fixes* when the Dohms' held their open house for Berlin's intellectual élite, she did not seem to have greatly enjoyed being the 'mistress of the house' and is remembered as a quiet listener and observer rather than the centre of attention. We can only guess how many times after these events she sat up all night at her desk either reading or putting on paper all those ideas and thoughts that the evening's discussions may have sparked off, and thus laying the foundation for her later writings.

The breadth of her reading was to be reflected in all her writings: she discusses the position of women referring to oriental customs and Hindu rites, women's roles throughout pre-historic times, Greece and Rome – including an interesting appraisal and defence of Sappho's poetry, which was being judged as the product of 'an elderly blue-stocking' (1874, in Campbell 1896, p 60) – the Middle-Ages, the Renaissance, etc as well as events of her time in many different countries. She quotes from the work of Caroline Schlegel, Bettine von Arnim, Mme. de Staël, George Eliot, George Sand and many other feminists, but also incorporates thoughts on women by Fontaine, Thackeray, Flaubert, Heine, as well as by socialists such as Bebel and Lassalle. The many references throughout her work to publications by American and English feminists (to Harriet Taylor ('Mrs Mill'), Harriet Martineau, Elizabeth Cady Stanton, Susan B. Anthony, the English Suffragettes, to name only a few) reveal an enormous knowledge of past and contemporary feminist activities in a considerable number of countries. And she also read Kant, Rousseau, Nietzsche, Stirner and Schopenhauer and discussed both their philosophies of liberation and their misogynist assessments of women in her theoretical as well as her fictional work (in particular in *Die Antifeministen* (The Antifeminists, 1902) and her novel *Christa Ruland* (1902)), and unhesitatingly poked fun at the supposed infallibility of the logic and philosophical depth of learned men. Thus she ends her essay on Nietzsche's anti-feminism (1902, p 33) with:

> Well, then, I know that great spirits too have a range of experiences that does not go beyond the width of their five fingers. Outside this realm they stop thinking and what starts is their enormous empty space and their stupidity. *Also sprach Zarathustra* (Thus spoke Zarathustra).

When she started writing, (1865–69), it was not yet on a feminist topic but was an historical account of the development of the Spanish national literature (*Die Spanische Nationalliteratur in ihrer geschicht-lichen Entwicklung*), following a six months' stay in Spain. A few more years were yet to elapse before she started her feminist writings. In 1872, when she was 39, her oldest daughter 19 and the three others in their teenage years, she wrote her first feminist pamphlet, a 100-page treatise full of mockery of the clergy's abysmal, dogmatic treatment of women (*Was die Pastoren von den Frauen denken*, What Clergymen Think of Women). This was quickly followed in 1873 by a more than 200-page work on the dogmatism, hypocrisy and bigotry that accompanied the oppression of women in the family (*Der Jesuitismus im Hausstande*). In it she vehemently attacked men's double-standard whereby women are hailed as having 'natural' talents as housewives and mothers, yet at the same time men impose their rules and regulations, reducing women to lesser beings for the good of one sex only: men. It is in this book that she makes her demand for women's suffrage (p 166) which she is soon – in 1876 – to elaborate in a special theoretical treatise: *Der Frauen Natur und Recht, Eigenschaften und Stimmrecht der Frauen* (Women's Nature and Privilege). But in between, in 1874, she published yet another book: *Die Wissenschaftliche Emanzipation der Frau* (The Scientific Emancipation of Women), in which she discussed and refuted new theories by 'learned men' – anatomists, physiologists and doctors – on women's inferior nature.

After this outburst of publications – silence. However, she *did* continue to write: plays, in fact comedies, published in 1876. And then, in 1883, Ernst Dohm died; as far as I know she did not write about his death and we can only speculate as to the extent this event changed her life in terms of material as well as psychological circumstances.

In 1890 she published a collection of short novels after which in quick succession followed four novels and a collection of novellas. In 1902, she turned back to non-fiction and published a book of essays on Antifeminists (*Die Antifeministen*) in which she identified four types of male experts on women. But no matter which category males belonged to, argued Dohm as she developed her ideas about men, they were without authority to arbitrate on women's 'true nature'.

This was not the only attack Dohm made on misogyny and its adherents (there had been the spirited and witty attack on Nietzsche): she also attacked a medico, Möbius, who had written a widely acclaimed pamphlet on the imbecility of women – scientifically proven, of course! But she recognised that it was not only men who showed contempt for women – and were misogynist – but that some women (for understandable reasons) displayed the same feeling. In a chapter in *The Antifeminists*, 'Woman against Woman', Dohm analyses the anti-women theses of three members of her own sex, and argues that some women, especially 'successful' ones, can collude with men and become social males – taking on, uncritically, the value system espoused by men. It is a position which she vehemently rejects for herself ('The absolutely last thing I ever wanted to be was – a man', 1902, p 136), but one she can understand women adopting from necessity – the necessity of economic survival. With her usual clarity in exposing shallow reasoning and logical flaws in arguments, Hedwig Dohm accuses these three prominent women of accepting without question men's yardsticks for measuring women's worth. This is especially true regarding women's biological functions. It is only *young* women who are accorded an (albeit second class) place in men's society. Drawing from her own experience of growing older, she pursued the topic of aging and agism. Having already written in 1874 that, 'Strangely, women are blamed for growing older' (1977, p 64), a large part of *Die Mütter* (1903) – a comprehensive and very 'modern' treatise on questions in education – is devoted to older women and she passionately urges women, especially older women, to enjoy life, to do things on their own and for their own pleasure, reassuring them of their right to autonomy. 70 years old herself, she says:

> Listen, old woman, what another old woman tells you: make an effort. Have the courage to live. Don't think for a moment about your age. Age is an enemy – fight it. Do what gives you pleasure . . . If you like it and if it is comfortable, have your white hair floating free. Join the learners . . . There are no herbs against death but there are many herbs against the early death of woman. The most effective is unconditional emancipation for women and with it the salvation from that brutal myth that her right of existence is based on her sexuality only. (1903, p 220–23)

Hedwig Dohm herself followed her own guidelines on old age. According to accounts from her relatives, and tributes to her eightieth birthday, in 1913, she remained active and relatively healthy, she travelled with her grandchildren, enjoyed her great-grandchildren and continued to write, for example, a number of articles for the *Socialistische Monatshefte* in 1912. One of her articles is entitled 'Das Recht der Ungeborenen' (The Rights of the Unborn Child) which might suggest at the outset a stand against birth control or abortion. But this is not the case and it is a mark of how 'names' can be appropriated that her plea for the rights of the unborn child is a plea for the state to guarantee the child and the mother a decent, humane and materially secure life. These are the *rights* she demands.

That the state was not enthusiastic in its support of women did not escape her attention and this recognition led her to devise strategies for procuring change: one of them was to urge women to practise civil disobedience, 'Each woman who is subjugated to laws made by others without her consent has a right to refuse to pay taxes' (1876, 1977, pp 209–10).

Unfortunately, after having spent a life time thinking and writing about the possibilities and the realities of a better world, Hedwig Dohm's last years were overshadowed by war and led to her demoralisation, and yet still further resistance. She was dismayed by what she saw as the betrayal of many women's groups who traded their feminism for chauvinism in the interest of men, as she saw the war and the euphoria leading up to it as barbaric, and felt deeply hurt by women's participation in men's wars.

Her Ideas

Fundamental to all that Hedwig Dohm wrote was her feminist framework, that is, a commitment to women and an awareness of the contradictions within society, and within each individual. She was not afraid to show this commitment to women, nor to reveal the different facets of her understandings. While in her theoretical writing she was the 'pushy' straightforward feminist who could not have cared less about exposing men's ridiculous (because male-centred) behaviour and ideas, in her *fiction* she allowed herself to become vulnerable; to expose her doubts, pains, and disillusionment about having to live in a male-dominated society, which did not take women seriously nor let them explore possibilities to become persons in their own right. Thus in her novels all the female characters are torn between the old (oppressive) and the new (liberated) roles for women and feelings of despair abound; only a few of her heroines make the transition to liberation: most die – either of a broken heart, or else they commit suicide.[3]

In many respects Hedwig Dohm demonstrates that she is both oppressed *and* powerful, both rational *and* emotional, both confined *and* unlimited, and for me this constitutes part of the attraction – and relevance – of her work today.

Throughout her life Hedwig Dohm addressed what she saw as the three aspects of women's plight – sexual, material and psychological oppression. She used her pen to rail against the injustices of sexual slavery, against women having nothing to trade but their bodies, against women being confined to the role of 'mothers of the race' which implied that, once they were older and no longer useful as breeders 'their right to exist ceases too' (1903, p 204). Thus she warns, 'One day, women will be totally fed up with having babies if they are told over and over again that this is all they should expect of life' (1903, p 34). And, on many occasions, she disputes the notion of the 'maternal instinct' and derides the idea that every woman, simply because of her female body, should be by nature a gifted mother and educator of her children – an outrageous thing to say in her time!

She was equally aware of the grim realities of economic oppression and exposed the inadequacies and hypocrisies of men's myths about women: if bourgeois women were too frail to be admitted to the 'hard' work done by men in well paid jobs, then working-class women were not too frail to undertake the most menial and laborious work that was beneath men. Yet were not both groups *women*? Her question was:

> How is it possible that this absurd talk about a woman's sphere is still heard in the face of those millions of women who earn their bread by the sweat of their brows in fields and factories, in streets and mines, behind the counter and in the office? (1876, in Campbell 1896, p 126)

and elsewhere she writes:

> The important point in the sexual division of labour is not the right of women but the advantage of men . . . Intellectual labour and the work that pays well is for men: the one that pays badly is for women. (1977, p 11)

And then, there is women's psychological exploitation: 'Women are educated into dependence' (1874, 1977, p 23) says Dohm, they are trained so thoroughly in the belief that men must think for them 'that finally they give up thinking' (1874, 1977, p 61). And once women have given up thinking for themselves the possibility of resistance is limited and they collude with men in their own oppression.

If the psychology of women's oppression required further examination, argued Dohm, so too did the psychology of male dominance. 'Men', she comments, 'derive their rights over women from their power over them' (1876, in Campbell 1896, p 143). This is possible because we live in a world in which women are controlled by man-made laws: '. . . they make a law of nature to their own taste. It is ridiculous' (1876, in Campbell 1896, p 131). And these laws, she argues, are always geared towards men's interest ('Good God, why should each thing be judged according to what advantage men get out of it?' 1873, p 114). Thus, when discussing men's alleged sexual instinct which renders them brutal towards women and which in turn, as they say, necessitates precautions to protect women she states: 'Naive conclusions to draw from man's brutality! Because man is a brute, woman has to be locked up so that she will remain unharmed . . .' (1902, p 37).

Hedwig Dohm is never taken in by male pretention! She mocks the sheer irrational impertinence of men's claims that they are the thinkers, the rightful enclosure makers. She even mocks their pretentions to justice – for, so her thinking goes, if they were indeed 'just' they would respond to women's demands. They cannot be relied upon to be either just or rational, she argues, for while they persist in thinking of themselves as the centre of the universe, as the norm, their sense of justice and their capacity for reason is severely reduced. Over and over again Dohm emphasises that women do not need men to direct their lives.

Inherent in all her theoretical writing is the absolute confidence that women themselves are best equipped to be the active architects of their own lives and she uncompromisingly and radically denies men the right to affix their values and standards to women. (This is not the case in her fiction, where she allows herself to express her sadness that in her own lifetime the chances of seeing women's liberation seemed remote.) But it is this outspoken belief in 'the new women's' abilities to make their own way towards their self-determined liberation and to reconceptualise the nature of human relationships, taking *women's needs* into account, that distinguishes Hedwig Dohm from many of her contemporaries.

For example, while on many occasions in her writing she makes her plea for women's access to men's education, being an ardent supporter of 'Knowledge is Power' (the title of an article she wrote in 1913), she does *not* uncritically accept men's education as 'good', but suggests that once women have access to it they will examine it in the light of their own needs and transform it to meet those needs. Moreover, says Dohm, of its own, access to education is not enough: why should women seek education within the present framework, when they are later prevented from applying their skills? Is it, she asks bitingly, 'to be hungry, to commit suicide, to become prostitutes?' (1874, 1977, p 28).

Linked with her demand for education is that of the vote: but both are only pre-requisites for women's independence and not an end in themselves. That women should have the right to vote is not even open to debate she says:

> I can admit nothing which others do not admit in me. There is no freedom if not for women. If a woman has no authority why should man? If every woman has a lawful tyrant, then have I no sympathy for the tyranny some men must endure from their own sex. The thing which makes the right of women to the suffrage so difficult is its supreme simplicity. (1876, in Campbell 1896, p 147)

For many of her contemporaries, who thought that women were not yet ready for the vote, that they first had to prove themselves knowledgeable, Dohm went too far in her demands. This does not appear to have caused her to modify them in any way, and she vehemently rejects as demeaning the assumption that an average women's 'natural' intelligence does not equal that of an average man.

Hedwig Dohm, however, is not without her contradictions. While holding pacifist convictions she nonetheless urged women to organise and make the presence of their power known to men:

> Why don't you get to know your strength, why don't you get enraged, my gentle sisters, why not, even when an honourable gentleman declares that 'woman has only duties but no rights'? Who denies you your rights? Man. Can he do this? Yes, he makes the laws. Well then, take away the monopoly of law-making from him – do it, even if you might have to use the suffragettes' tactics. (1909, 1977, p 216)

Earlier, she had written:

> And do not forget one thing: demands *minus* the power to enforce them mean little. Despotism has always been limited only by the growing power of the oppressed . . . How will you get power? By the concentration of all female forces who are willing to fight for the political rights of women . . . (1876, p 184)

But while she occasionally advocated militancy as a means, it was not one she ever elected to use for herself: Hedwig Dohm, the woman with the brilliant mind and the tremendous sense of logic, wit, irony humour, passion and anger, the woman asserting women's right to self-determination more radically than any of her contemporaries, did not once in her life make a public speech, or assume official responsibilities as an active member of one of the existing women's groups. The power and autonomy she chose were those of the pen; she was superb in her ability to plant and nurture the idea of women's right to autonomy and to encourage women to resist and refute the ideas of men.

Assessing Hedwig Dohm: Then and Now

Not surprisingly, Hedwig Dohm met with much ridicule and scorn in her own time, and in a sense this is a measure of her influence and power. Perhaps even worse than scorn though is dismissal, and, as Mary Wollstonecraft found before Hedwig Dohm (and many have found since), many women have been neutralised because they were not taken seriously. Dale Spender (1982, (b)) has provided example after example of women who have been removed from the realm of serious intellectual consideration, and this pattern of erasure applies also to Hedwig Dohm. Rather than the radical and brilliant nature of her writing, it was her physical appearance that was likely to be the focus for comment: that she was tiny, timid, lovable, sweet – and goodhearted – are comments which occur in every assessment of her that I have encountered. No doubt such patronising remarks undermine her image as a serious thinker. Even one of her admirers, her biographer, Adele Schreiber-Krieger, goes so far as to say that Hedwig Dohm deserves special praise because in spite of the radical nature of her writing she 'did not forfeit any of the charm and softness of her personality, her idealism and her faith as well as her imperturbable sense of justice and her mildness' (1914, p 94).

The fact that she fought with her pen and not from a public platform also becomes a convenient way of devaluing her force: she was too shy to address a crowd we are informed. Schreiber-Krieger writes: 'When meeting her in person, she was of such enormous modesty, or indeed timidity, that she never could bring herself to speak out what her pen communicated so brilliantly to the public' (1914, p 46). Thus Hedwig Dohm's *ideas* are pushed aside. Or if her writing is discussed it is labelled 'polemic'. Never is she called a *theorist* but, for instance, 'our pamphleteer', which reduces her to some sort of a local celebrity, a crazy woman whom one need not really take seriously (1874, 1977, p 2). The distinction between 'theory' and 'polemic', and the subtle devaluation of women it implies, is part of the pattern of women's oppression under patriarchy. It relies on male definitions of *theory* which were (and are) resistant to any inclusion of personal experience drawn from everyday 'real' life. It is thus not surprising that Hedwig Dohm's work, which is full of accounts of and reflections on personal experience, was called 'polemic' and 'anecdotal' and did not meet the androcentric criteria of 'theory' as 'based on general, objective principles, independent of the facts, phenomena, etc explained' (Concise Oxford Dictionary 1979, p 1201).

In the context which contemporary feminists have contructed it is relatively easy to define Hedwig Dohm – whose commitment was to women – as a theorist: and it is relatively easy to see that her ideas were no less aimed at the transformation of society than were the militant activities of the suffragettes; in other words her writing was not only theoretical but at the same time highly political. However, not only was she not accepted as a theorist she was also dismissed as 'apolitical' – and this not only by anti-feminists – and seen by many as an individualist who might have achieved a sense of liberation for herself but as for ending the oppression of women in general, her work was of little importance. However, to deny her political and intellectual contribution is to persist in the belief system that facilitated Dohm's disappearance and which may well jeopardise much of our current work and assist it to meet a similar fate.

In my view, one of the contributing causes to Dohm's erasure from history was the fact that she did not conveniently fit any one category: there was no group that aspired to claim her for itself and thus continue to discuss her ideas after her death: the socialist wing of the women's movement found her suspiciously bourgeois; the radical wing was not at ease with her solitary life style and the liberal wing found her too radical for their reformist ideals. And of course there were her novels with those less-than-strong and decisive women who were torn between the 'old' and 'new' world: she was something of an embarrassment to a dogmatic 'right on' feminist who could not cope with a sister's open admission to moments of self-doubt and scepticism.

And today? While Alice Schwarzer in 1975 and especially Marielouise Janssen-Jurreit in 1976, must be given credit for reminding us of Hedwig Dohm's existence and the radical and irreverent nature of her writing, it is somewhat astonishing that, since then, not much more has been written on her. If she is mentioned in accounts of first-wave feminism in Germany, it is usually in relation to her early demand for women's suffrage rather than for her much more radical work. However, some of her books have been reprinted,[4] and two papers have been recently published: an overview article by Elisabeth Plessen (1981) and an essay in English (with German quotes) by Ruth-Ellen Boetcher-Joeres (1980), which is to my knowledge the first attempt to compare parts of Dohm's non-fictional *and* fictional work (see note 3).[5]

But how is she represented? Certainly *not* as a theorist but again as a polemicist. Thus, although Janssen-Jurreit states that:

> If Hedwig Dohm had not written her radical pamphlets, the testimony of the German women's movement – compared to the political statements by American, English and French women of her time – would be little more than a poor collection of provincial literature for 'höhere Töchter' (daughters from good families), (1976, p 13)

she also says that Dohm's pamphlets 'are masterpieces of a literary form little valued today: polemics' (1976, p 12). And Boetcher-Joeres concurs, calling Dohm's non-fiction 'polemic work', 'social writings', 'social tracts' and comments that 'Hedwig Dohm seems destined to be remembered as a polemicist' (1980, pp 256–57).

While I would certainly not want to deny that some of Hedwig Dohm's statements are brilliant in their satirical succinctness, for me it is the passionate *interaction* of irony, humour *and* intellect which is the essence of her theories about women, oppression and resistance: her 'polemics' lend the spice to her theories! However, the question remains why this is not acknowledged and all I can suggest is that because she deliberately does not keep a distance between her 'public', well thought-out, clear ideas and her 'private' qualms, doubts, admission of contradictions and open questions, as expressed in her novels and in some writings about her own life, she does not fit the category of 'theorist' – not even for feminists! However, if, as Stanley and Wise have said (1981), feminist theory is about 'what feminists spend our lives doing', then Hedwig Dohm's work, combining 'life' experiences and 'book' knowledge, communicates this synthesis and is feminist theory at its best. In particular, in reflections on her own life and in her fiction, the 'other' Hedwig Dohm speaks up: the one who does not shy away from making herself vulnerable. She has doubts about herself, her intellectual capabilities, and qualifications, her stamina to carry her ideas through to action, and about 'the world' (men's world to be precise), which has created women who, like herself and the characters in her novels, are caught between two worlds: the 'old' where women are dependent and in chains but 'taken care of', and the 'new', where women are self-determined, autonomous – but at the same time scared, insecure and possibly alone and lonely. Thus in *Kindheitserinnerungen einer alten Berlinerin* (Recollections of My Youth in Berlin, 1912) she writes:

> It is the most serious misfortune for a person to be born in the wrong time in the wrong place in the wrong family . . . unfortu-

nate circumstances, but the misfortune of having a weak character was even more in my way when it came to filling in gaps in my knowledge . . . Therefore I was to remain a dilettante . . . a spiritual teenager . . . Those who indulge in brooding over their dreams are people who will never get deeds done. Revolutionaries in their thoughts who daringly and courageously shake the world's foundation – bloodless cowards in reality who dare not move a pebble – as I am one. (1912, 1980, pp 71–72, 75, 78)

Going back to the question of how today's feminists assess Hedwig Dohm, I daresay that acknowledging contradictions and valuing them positively seems to present problems: we still need to create 'heroines' who, sturdy as rocks and unshaken in their beliefs, fight for their ideas. Thus when reclaiming Hedwig Dohm as one of our 'most radical foremothers' we – and I include myself – happily quote her most outrageous statements but omit those pieces in her writing where she voices her insecurities, because as Plessen for example admits (1981, p 140), they do not 'fit' with our one-dimensional ideas about the strong and tough and irreverent woman, Hedwig Dohm. This reluctance, not only to face and discuss contradictions, but on the contrary to use them in an affirmative way to 'upgrade' a person's work by giving credit to the complexity of her nature, may account for the fact that Hedwig Dohm's life, her fiction and her theoretical writings are rarely discussed together. Thus, while Boetcher-Joeres says:

Hedwig Dohm's writings, both polemical and fictional, complement each other in their philosophy of feminist thought although it should be clear by now that their methods are different. (1980, p 276)

The point I want to make is different. For me, in her theoretical writing, the *feminist* Hedwig Dohm allows us to look at one of her selves, and in her novels she shows us the *writer* Hedwig Dohm, both of which interact reciprocally with each other, *and* with her *third* self: the *woman* Hedwig Dohm.

While Boetcher-Joeres stays clear of explicitly bringing in Hedwig Dohm's 'private' self as an active part of both her fictional and non-fictional work, I, in turn, think that it is precisely this third self that simultaneously creates and is part of her theories and her practice.

I think that the dismissal of Hedwig Dohm as a theorist (and of many other women who refuse to let themselves be compartmentalised!) should make us think about our own adherence to either/or thinking, belief in authority, and deference to man-made 'standards', about our lack of irreverence and willingness to take risks. For me, Hedwig Dohm embodies both the oppression *and* the resistance of women and she expresses the tension, the pain and the joy of that experience in a very powerful way. The following words then represent a call to rebel, to act, and to celebrate the power women possess, and they are as important today as 80 years ago:

> More pride, you women! How is it possible that you do not rebel against the *contempt* with which you are met . . . More pride, you women! The proud person may arouse disdain but not contempt. It is only on those who submit to the yoke that the would-be masters can put their foot. (1902, pp 164–65)

Notes

1   Hedwig Dohm 'The Rights of Women's Suffrage' in *Women's Nature and Privilege*, 1896, p 143 translated by Constance Campbell from *Der Frauen Natur and Recht: Zwei Abhandlungen über Eigenschaften und Stimmrecht der Frauen* (1876). These translations as well as her biography by Adele Schreiber-Krieger (1914) can be found at the Fawcett Library, Old Castle Street, London, to the staff of which I owe a lot of thanks for their kind help. Most of her essays and novels are available at the Zentralbibliothek and the Museumsgesellschaft in Zürich, Switzerland, and Berta Rahm from the Ala Publishing House in Zürich kindly shared some additional information about Hedwig Dohm's life with me.
      As far as I know Constance Campbell's translation of three essays by Hedwig Dohm 20 years after they were originally published remains the only translation of her work into English. The third article in *Women's Nature and Privilege* is called 'The Scientific Emancipation of Women' (*Die Wissenschaftliche Emanzipation der Frau*, 1874), I indicate the quotes I use from her translation by marking them 'in Campbell, 1896'. In all the other quotes the translations are mine.
2   Marielouise Janssen-Jurreit *Sexismus. Über die Abtreibung der Frauenfrage*, 1976, Carl Hauser Verlag, München is now available in a shortened and reworked English version: *Sexism. The Male Monopoly on History and Thought*, 1982, Pluto Press, London.
3   Lack of space prevents me from a discussion of her novels which are full of autobiographical notes and which shed a lot of light on her theoretical work. This is particularly true of her trilogy *Schicksale einer Seele* (Destinies of a Soul, 1899), *Sibilla Dalmar* (1897) and *Christa Ruland* (1902), the heroines of which all live in middle-class conformity with husbands and have few economic problems but try to break out of

the narrowness of their boring existence by means of either 'learned men' who acquaint them with new liberating philosophies, or strong female friends who live as independent single women, artists or scientists. However, these 'new' women oscillate between happiness and despair. Ruth-Ellen Boetcher-Joeres (1980), in a highly interesting article, is the first writer to compare this trilogy with Dohm's theoretical work; in particular with *The Antifeminists* which Dohm wrote at the same time (1902).

4   Bertha Rahm, the editor/owner of a small independent publishing house in Zürich, Switzerland, (Ala Verlag), is to be given credit for reprinting two of Dohm's original works (*Was die Pastoren von den Frauen denken*, 1872, 1977; *Die wissenschaftliche Emanzipation der Frau*, 1874, 1977) and assembling a collection of Dohm's own work, responses from her adversaries, her daughters and grand-daughters' writings, as well as excerpts from tributes to Dohm's eightieth birthday and obituaries: *Erinnerungen* (Recollections), 1980. Another small publishing house in Frankfurt has reprinted *Die Antifeministen* (1902, 1976) and one of Dohm's novels: *Wie Frauen Werden – Werde, die Du bist* (How women are made to be women – Become who you are), 1894, 1976, Verlag Arudtstrasse, Frankfurt/Main. And Gisela Brinker-Gabler, the editor of the series *Die Frau in der Gesellschaft – frühe Texte* (Woman in society – early texts), Fischer Taschenbuchverlag, Frankfurt, has reprinted original texts by Hedwig Dohm, eg in the volume *Frauen gegen den Krieg* (Woman Against War, 1980), and in other volumes in *her* series (eg *Zur Psychologie der Frau*).

5   Herrad Schenk (1979) also discusses her categorisation of anti-feminists (1902) and Ruth Esther Geiger and Sigrid Weigel (1981), make a few references to her as a woman 'ahead of her time' in questions of women's unconditional participation in all spheres of human society (p 59).

Select Bibliography of Hedwig Dohm

Was die Pastoren von den Frauen denken, Schlingmann, Berlin, 1872; Ala, Zurich 1977.

Der Jesuitismus im Hausstande, ein Beitrag zur Frauenfrage, Wedekind und Schwieger, Berlin, 1873.

Die Wissenschaftliche Emanzipation de Frau, Wedekind und Schwieger, Berlin, 1874; Ala, Zurich, 1977.

Der Frauen Natur und Recht, Wedekind und Schwieger, Berlin, 1876.

Wie Frauen werden – Werde die Du bist, Novellen Schoftländer, Breslau, 1894; Verlag Arndstrasse, Frankfurt, a/March, 1977.

'Selbstanzeige des Romans Sibilla Dalmar' (1896), in *Erinnerungen*, Berta Rahm, ed Ala-Verlag, Zürich, 1980, pp 89–91.

'Die Ritter der Mater Dolorosa' (1897) in *Erinnerungen*, Berta Rahm, ed, Ala-Verlag, Zürich, 1980, pp 54–78.

Sibilla Dalmar, Roman, S. Fischer Verlag, Berlin, 1897.

Schicksale einer Seele, Roman, S. Fischer Verlag, Berlin, 1899.

Christa Ruland, Roman, S. Fischer Verlag, Berlin, 1902.

'Von der alten und der neuen Ehe' in *Die Antifeministen*, Ferdinand Dümmlers Verlage-buchhandlung, Berlin, 1902, pp 138–67.

Die Antifeministen, Ein Buch der Verteidigung Ferdinand Dümmler, Verlag, Berlin 1902; Verlag Arndstrasse, Frankfurt a/Main, 1976.

Die Mütter, Beitrag zur Erziehungsfrage, S. Fischer Verlag, Berlin, 1903.

'Kindheitserinnerungen einer alten Berlinerin' (1912) in *Erinnerungen*, Berta Rahm, ed, Ala Verlag, Zurich, 1980, pp 45–78.

'Das Recht des Ungebnorenen' in *Sozialistische Monatshefte*, Bd.2, pp 746–49.

'Wissen ist Macht' in *Voss'che Zeitung*, 1913.

Millicent Garrett Fawcett: Duty and Determination
(1847–1929)

Ann Oakley

Her memorial in Westminster Abbey describes her as having 'won citizenship for women'; her obituaries call her 'the Mother of Women's Suffrage' (*Oxford Mail*, 5 August 1929) and 'a great reformer' (*Manchester Guardian*, 6 August 1929); it is certainly part of that amputated history of women most of us encounter during our formal education, that British women owe their enfranchisement to some unanswerable combination of Millicent Fawcett's sweet reason and the Pankhursts' window-smashing activities.

There is no doubt that by far the greatest part of Millicent Fawcett's life and energy *was* devoted to the cause of the vote. But for 61 of her 82 years she worked for an objective – the enfranchisement of women – that she herself always believed would be achieved eventually because of widespread social change rather than because of the activities of a single political movement – or, indeed, her own (or anybody else's) as an individual. In 1886, 16 years after her first public speech on the subject, and 32 years before women obtained the vote on equal terms with men, she wrote:

> Women's suffrage will not come, when it does come, as an isolated phenomenon, it will come as a necessary corollary of the other changes which have been gradually and steadily modifying . . . the social history of our country. (quoted in Rover, 1967, p 2)

She compared progress towards the vote with 'the gradual triumph of Christianity' (letter, quoted Strachey, 1931, p 240), and with 'the movement of a glacier . . . like a glacier . . . ceaseless and irresistible' (Strachey, 1931, p 321). Denial of the importance of her own role as leader of this 'ceaseless and irresistible' movement was a motif of her speeches and writings throughout her life; 'I am always troubled' she once wrote 'by the knowledge that I get so much more praise than I deserve' (Strachey, 1931, p 317). In her introduction to the 1891 edition of Mary Wollstonecraft's *Vindication of the Rights of Woman* she stated (partly, no doubt, in order to console herself that such a morally questionable figure as Mary Wollstonecraft should have been associated with the same cause as herself), 'There is no truer or more consolatory observation concerning the great movements of thought which change the social history of the world than that no individual is indispensable to their growth' (p 2).

So, the two largest unanswered questions about Millicent Fawcett have to concern what the vote meant to her (why was it important?) and how she managed to pursue with such apparently unfailing determination and optimism a goal that took so long to reach and which she did not see as within her power to win anyway. The paradox of the second question provokes two possible answers. Either Millicent Fawcett's relation to the enfranchisement of women must have been akin to the irrational fervour of a religious crusade (God/ good will triumph in the end and I believe in him/her), or there must have existed in her character strong qualities of dogged persistence and an unrevolutionary lack of imagination. Both answers appear, in some measure, to carry some weight.

Millicent Fawcett was born Millicent Garrett, either the seventh or eighth child of Newson Garrett, an East Anglian shipowner, and his wife,[1] an intensely religious woman who worshipped her husband and was a domestic superwoman, organising her large household of ten children with such methodicalness as would have qualified her, according to Millicent, for a role in big business. Millicent was fond of saying that she was born in the year of the Irish famine and the repeal of the Corn Laws (1847), and that the following year saw the downfall of half the old autocratic governments in Europe. In her autobiography, *What I Remember* (1924), her mother is scarcely mentioned, but the close relationship that existed between her and her father gets a good deal of attention, and it was undoubtedly very important in moulding her outlook on life. Through her father, the political events of the day and their importance were communicated to her. She recalled at the age of six holding her father's hand while he persuaded men to volunteer for the navy at the start of the Crimean War; and some time later him 'coming in at breakfast-time with a newspaper in his hand, looking gay and handsome, and calling out to all his little brood, "Heads up, shoulders down; Sebastopol is taken"' (Fawcett, 1924, p 10).

Important events in the emancipation of women had a habit of happening on Millicent's birthdays: Queen's College, the first institution for the higher education of women, opened on her first birthday in 1848; on her ninth in 1856 came the first petition for the removal of the disqualification to the holding of property by married women; on her eighteenth in 1865 her sister Elizabeth (later Elizabeth Garrett Anderson) qualified as the first woman doctor; and on her seventy-first birthday in 1918 the Representation of the People Bill, giving women their first right to the franchise, became law. She claimed to have been a woman suffragist 'from my cradle', a deeply held sentiment which was reflected in her biography of one of the historical figures she most admired, Joan of Arc: 'Someone in the crowd called out to ask if she were not afraid. Her reply was "I was born for this"' (Fawcett, 1905, p 16). The apocryphal story of how Millicent first explicitly appropriated the fight for the vote as her own is recounted by Ray Strachey in *The Cause* (1928, 1978). It tells how she, her sister Elizabeth and Emily Davies, Elizabeth's friend and pioneer of women's education, were sitting together one night in the Garretts' house in Aldeburgh.

> After going over all the great causes they saw about them, and in particular the women's cause, to which they were burning to devote their lives, Emily summed the matter up. 'Well, Elizabeth,' she said, 'it's quite clear what has to be done. I must devote myself to securing higher education, while you open the medical profession to women. After these things are done,' she added, 'we must see about getting the vote.' And then she turned to the little girl who was still sitting quietly on her stool and said, 'You are younger than we are, Millie, so you must attend to that'. (Strachey, 1928, 1978, p 101)

Growing up in such a household taught Millicent the lesson that there was nothing odd about the ambition to improve the lot of women; such an ambition was, in fact, expected of her. In particular it was expected of her by her father, who was also instrumental in encouraging her sister Elizabeth, through a series of vicissitudes, to enter the medical profession. A streak of feminism ran through the extended family: her sister Agnes and her cousin Rhoda trained as home-decorators, an occupation as unfeminine at the time as that of doctoring; various women in the family supported Josephine Butler's campaign against the 1866 and 1868 Contagious Diseases Acts, and allianced themselves with one branch or another of the suffrage movement. It was her sister Louie who took Millicent to one of J. S. Mill's election meetings in 1865 – the first public occasion on which women's suffrage was brought before the English electors as a practical question. Mill's example, personality and convictions 'kindled tenfold' Millicent's own nascent enthusiasms.

Girls in the Garrett household were encouraged to non-domestic achievement, but they were also expected to marry. This Millicent did at the age of 20. The man she married was a blind 33-year-old Cambridge academic and liberal politician, Henry Fawcett, best known for his career as Postmaster-General in Gladstone's 1880 Government (a position in which he made substantial improvement in the employment conditions of women post office workers). The proposed marriage created a rift between Millicent and her sister Elizabeth – not the only one they were to experience; Elizabeth opposed the marriage, and Millicent's biographer, her lifelong friend Ray Strachey, does not say why. However, according to Josephine Kamm (1966), Elizabeth herself had been invited to marry Henry Fawcett some years earlier, and remained especially fond of him (p 133).* Such complications in Millicent's life are hard to uncover, partly because, in commissioning Ray Strachey to be her official biographer, Millicent almost certainly made clear that there were a number of things she wished to be omitted; and partly because with absolutely proper Victorian reserve, she herself was not given to committing her feelings to paper or, indeed, indulging in them publicly at all.

Millicent was quite obviously devoted to her husband. For some years she acted as his secretary, a function that served her own advantage as well, in that it marked what she called the beginning of her true political education; '. . . naturally I had to read and write for my husband. I grappled with newspapers and blue books, and learned more or less to convey their import to him. He took care that I should hear important debates in the House of Commons. . .' (1924, p 64). But, most significant from the point of view of Millicent's own development as a public figure, was not the marriage but the sub- sequent death of her husband in 1884 at the early age of 51 when Millicent herself was 37. It was after this that she took up in earnest her work for women's suffrage (the parallel with her competitor- collaborator Emmeline Pankhurst is striking; Emmeline was widowed in 1898 at the age of 40.)

Millicent's only child Philippa was 16 when her father died. There is every reason to believe that Millicent was a devoted mother according to the fashion of the time (she knitted baby clothes and attended to Philippa's early education herself), but by the age of 16 it was evident that Philippa herself was a help rather than a hindrance to the noble

---

* Editor's note: Josephine Kamm does tend to make much of 'romance'.

cause her mother had chosen to pursue. In 1887 she went to Newnham College, Cambridge, the college that was founded in her parents' drawing room when she was only old enough 'to toddle about in her white frock and blue sash among the guests' (1924, p 73). In 1890 Philippa Fawcett was placed first in the mathematical tripos – far above that honour oddly entitled 'senior wrangler' which could only be awarded to a man. This was a most significant 'first' for women as a class, proving, as the *Westminster Gazette* put it, 'their intellectual . . . sinew . . . sheer mental strength and staying power' (9 June 1890) – qualities which had hitherto been regarded as entirely foreign to women. So far as her mother was concerned, Philippa did not sustain this early brilliance. She was unmoved by any of her mother's suggestions as to appropriate careers – as an astronomer, physicist, lighthouse designer or engineer. Instead she returned to Newnham to teach mathematics, until her mother dug her out of this rut by applying on Philippa's behalf for an assistantship to the Director of Education in the London County Council, a job never held before by a woman. Philippa got the job, and stayed with the LCC until her retirement in 1934, during which time she did manage to achieve the appropriate goal of establishing equal pay for men and women in that employment.

It is too simple to say that, having got marriage and motherhood behind her, Millicent could turn her energies outwards to the world. After Henry's death, she did have more time on her hands to pursue political activities of her own, yet she had never really regarded women as being in need of confinement to the home. It was under her husband's auspices that she first began her career as a political writer and campaigner. Her first article, on lectures for women in Cambridge, was published in 1868, and she gave her £7 fee towards J. S. Mill's election expenses. In 1870 she completed *Political Economy for Beginners*, which was immediately successful and went rapidly through ten editions, and two years later she wrote with her husband a volume called *Essays and Lectures on Social and Political Subjects*. In the year of her marriage she joined the newly formed London Women's Suffrage Committee and it was at the second public meeting of this committee that she made her first speech. In 1870, in Brighton, her husband's constituency, she took the platform again (a vote of thanks was passed to her husband for 'allowing his wife to lecture').

Another measure of the degree to which Millicent had already become a public figure before her husband's death, and before her best known suffrage work, was the fate of another of her enterprises, novel-writing. In 1874 a fall from a horse kept her at home for six months and during this period she wrote her novel *Janet Doncaster*, the heroine of the title bearing a marked resemblance to herself, and the whole adding up to a tract against the evils of alcoholism. The book did well, but Millicent suspected that its success was due merely to her own reputation. To test her suspicion, and with characteristic determination and shrewdness, she wrote a second novel, published it under a pseudonym, and watched it fall completely flat.

It was in the 1870s that Millicent Fawcett emerged as the leader of the women's suffrage movement. One of the members of that first committee wrote to Millicent years later: 'I sometimes tell my children how when you first came to our Women's Suffrage Committee . . . you looked like a schoolgirl rather than a married woman, and how you listened to opinions and suggestions as they fell from different members, and would then throw in your own counsel, which always seemed the right thing for us to adopt' (quoted in Strachey, 1931, pp 43–44). In the same year that widowhood released Millicent for a wider public role, she was offered the post of Mistress of Girton, which she refused on the grounds that she was incapable of 'thinking about any subject but one' (quoted in Strachey, 1931, 106–107).

Although nothing during her early adult years dissuaded Millicent from a belief in the rightness of the fight for women's suffrage, in her autobiography she notes that a number of seemingly trivial episodes etched on her conscience the truly appalling situation of women. One day she was in the waiting room at Ipswich station, between two clergymen's wives who were engaged in lace-making for the benefit of their respective parish schools. ' "What do you find sells best?" said No. 1 to No. 2, who instantly replied, "Oh! Things that are really useful, such as butterflies for the hair!" ' (Fawcett, 1924, p 117). On another occasion, she had her purse stolen. The thief was apprehended and charged, and on the charge sheet Millicent saw that the alleged offence was described as 'stealing from the person of Millicent Fawcett a purse containing £1 18s 6d, the property of Henry Fawcett'. 'I felt as if I had been charged with theft myself,' she commented (Fawcett, 1924, p 62).

The suffrage question was relatively quiescent from 1870 to 1884, when it re-emerged with Gladstone's Reform Bill. One particular change since 1870 necessitated a reappraisal on the part of the suffragists of their strategy, which had hitherto been to argue for the enfranchisement of single women only. Since the basis of the franchise at that time was a property qualification, this was the only plausible case to argue before the Married Women's Property Act came into force in 1882. Millicent herself had contended this: 'We find in practice,' she wrote to her cousin Edmund Garrett as late as 1885, 'that where there are ten men who favour single women having votes there is only one who is in favour of married women having it: this is what makes the women's suffrage workers as a body rather keep back on the claim on the part of married women. Half a loaf is better than no bread. . .'[2] The Married Women's Property Act enabled married women to hold property in their own right, and therefore made it possible in theory for the franchise to be claimed on their behalf as well. Millicent decided in due course to back this claim. Gladstone's refusal to consider the women's suffrage amendment when the Reform Bill came before the House had deeply angered her, and indeed his decision fuelled a growing sense of disillusionment among members of the suffrage movement with the ability of the British party political system to deliver the goods – a disillusionment that was in no way altered by the events of the succeeding 30 years. The passage in 1883 of the Corrupt Practices Act, which outlawed paid canvassing at elections, created further difficulties for the suffrage movement, difficulties through which Millicent again steered it on a straight course. Following the 1883 Act, women's usefulness as unpaid canvassers was obvious; the Liberal party even issued printed instructions directing its agents to 'make all possible use of every available woman in your locality' (Fawcett, n.d., p 32); but Millicent saw clearly that women would not (at least at that stage) win the vote by alliancing themselves as unpaid political handmaidens to men.

Lydia Becker, who had co-ordinated the work of the women's suffrage societies from their inception, died in 1890. Millicent took over the leadership of the organisation, in 1897 renamed the National Union of Women's Suffrage Societies (NUWSS), and she maintained that position until 1919. Those years were years of drama for women, for Britain and for the world. Yet the outstanding impression one gains from surveying Millicent Fawcett's life was that it was marked by monotony and by great tranquillity of spirit, and by no detectable change or development in her moral philosophy or political attitudes. The central question of her life, why she espoused the cause of women's suffrage with such steadfast determination, is partly answered by the biographical circumstances of her childhood; yet it also has to be seen as part of the general view on political affairs and human values to which she held throughout her life.

Without the complication of women's suffrage, Millicent Fawcett would have been a staunch liberal supporter. She followed the philosophical individualism of her mentor and her husband's friend, J. S. Mill, and took the view that a sound and sane society can only rest on the foundation of self-help. Accordingly, she eschewed the demand for free education: 'On moral grounds there are many reasons for believing that its influence would be pernicious,' she wrote, 'many a father may have overcome the temptations of a public house, through the ambition to give education to his children' (Fawcett and Fawcett, 1872, pp 64–65). Free education would raise the birth- and alcoholism-rates. Poverty, she contended, does not call for such remedies as cheap food or lowered taxes, but for the imposition by the State on parents of their full responsibility for maintaining themselves and their children. To this end she disagreed profoundly with Eleanor Rathbone on the matter of mothers' pensions and family allowances, which she saw as the ruin of family life, and a nail in the coffin of Britain's greatness rather than as the road to women's economic freedom. Indeed, it was on this issue that she found herself finally alone, and eventually renounced her personal membership of the NUWSS altogether.

Millicent Fawcett may have put the vote first, but she seems to have had a limited view of women's role. Writing on 'The Electoral Disabilities of Women' in 1872, she said: '. . . surely the wife and mother of a family ought to be something more than a housekeeper or a nurse – how will she be able to minister to the mental wants of her husband and children if she makes the care of their physical comfort the only object of her life?' (Fawcett and Fawcett, 1872, p 245). In a speech she made in Manchester she asserted that 'We want the electoral franchise not because we are angels oppressed by the wickedness of "the base wretch man" but because we want women to have the ennobling influence of national responsibility brought into their lives.'[3] And, looking back in 1920 in her book *The Woman's Victory – and After*, she reminded the reader that the 50-year struggle had not been fought for women but for the benefit of the entire community: 'this is what we meant when we called our paper the Common Cause. . . It was the cause of men, women and children. We believe that men cannot be truly free so long as women are held in political subjection' (p 157).

She always recognised that her work for women's suffrage was simply one aspect of a many-sided movement – the three main other sides were education, morals and employment. On these aspects too she contended that women's emancipation was principally for the good of society as a whole. Discussing the Report of the Schools Inquiry Commission referring to Girls' Education (the Taunton

Commission, 1864) she observed that 'Women cannot really be good wives and mothers if charming accomplishments and domestic tasks are to be considered their highest virtues. . . The likelihood of a girl becoming a mother ought to be to her parents one of the strongest inducements to cultivate her mind in such a manner as to bring out its utmost strength, for upon every mother devolves the most important educational duties; from her . . . are derived the child's first notions of duty, of right and wrong, of happiness, of a supreme Being, of immortality . . . how vastly important for national welfare it is that mothers of children should be persons of large, liberal and cultured minds. Such women as the one Wordsworth speaks of:

> The reason firm, the temperate will,
> Endurance, foresight, strength and skill;
> A perfect woman, nobly planned
> To warn, to comfort and command.'
> (Fawcett and Fawcett, 1872, pp 200–203)

She said that people with inferior and ill-developed capacities were no good as wives, either.

This most traditional line of reasoning was no doubt partly a response to the atmosphere and attitudes of the time. The objection that educating or enfranchising women would destroy the family had to be met with the answer that, on the contrary, educated and enfranchised women were just what the family needed. In her speeches, Millicent Fawcett displayed what was obviously a talent for anticipating and countering in a highly spirited and often amusing way the common objections to women's emancipation. For example:

It was sometimes put forward as an argument that home was the best place for a woman. She did not object to that argument, in fact she heartily concurred in it – but, on the other hand, if they accepted this view, home was surely the best place for a man also. (Laughter)

On the constitutional unseriousness of women, she observed that:

She once heard a couple of gentlemen discussing the respective merits of the candidates for a North Country borough, and one of them strongly recommended a gentleman on the ground that his brother's dog had won the Waterloo Cup. (Loud laughter)[4]

This was all splendid fighting stuff, but delivered in tones and in words which never suggested any antagonism towards men as a class. Millicent Fawcett seemed always able to maintain a belief in the inherent goodness of men towards women. There are occasional undertones of disapproval, as in a letter she wrote in 1892 to a colleague supporting the inclusion of women on Hospital Boards:

> Don't you remember . . . what the old waiting maid in *Felix Holt* says: 'It mayn't be good luck to be a woman. But one begins with it from a baby; one gets used to it. And I shouldn't like to be a man – to cough so loud, and stand straddling about on a wet day, and be so wasteful with meat and drink.' (Letter, quoted in Strachey, 1931, p 163)

And in her book *Women's Suffrage*, she was quite clear what the basic problem was: 'However benevolent men may be in their intentions,' she observed, 'they cannot know what women want and what suits the necessities of women's lives as well as women know these things themselves' (p 57).

An intrinsic element in Millicent Fawcett's campaign for the emancipation of women was an improvement of their moral status, an issue to which the question of men's moral habits was directly relevant. Millicent entirely approved of Josephine Butler's crusade for the repeal of the Contagious Diseases Acts, and although at the time (the 1870s) she took a firm decision not to express her support in public lest the cause of women's suffrage be damaged, she undertook to write with E. M. Turner a biography of Josephine Butler for the centenary of her birth. (The book was written when Millicent herself was 80.) In this she called Josephine Butler 'the most distinguished Englishwoman of the nineteenth century' and could find no fault with her apart from 'the one with which Mary Magdalene was also charged when she broke the precious box of spikenards over the Saviour's feet. Mrs Butler was recklessly generous to those whom the perverseness of men's laws and also of men's lawlessness had brought very low in the world's esteem' (Fawcett and Turner, 1927, p 151). In particular she filled the coffin of a young prostitute she had befriended with camellias. Millicent's response to this was to cite Judas, 'to what purpose this waste?' and to ask what camellias cost in March in Liverpool.

The moral values that motivated Millicent Fawcett are the least accessible side of her character. However, there are a few pointers. One is the very obvious distaste with which she viewed, in her introduction to the *Vindication*, the personal side of Mary Wollstonecraft's life (although she did feel herself able to argue that Mary Wollstonecraft 'in her writings, as well as in her life, with its sorrows and errors, is the essential womanly woman. . .' p 23).

Another clue is a letter from Thomas Hardy in reply to one of hers (not surviving) in which she apparently expressed an appreciation of his novel *Tess of the D'Urbervilles*.

> With regard to your idea of a short story showing how the trifling with the physical element in love leads to corruption; I do not see that much more can be done by fiction in that direction than has been done already. . . The other day I read a story entitled 'The Wages of Sin' by Lucas Malet, expecting to find something of the sort therein. But the wages are that the young man falls over a cliff, and the young woman dies of consumption – not very consequent, as I told the author.[5]

But the oddest (least known and certainly least understood) episode in Millicent Fawcett's life concerns a one-woman campaign she launched in 1894 against an MP, Henry Cust, who was at the time standing for the Conservative candidature in the constituency of North Manchester. She had heard ('on good authority') that the previous summer Cust had seduced a Miss Nina Welby, 'a young girl of good Lincolnshire family' who subsequently became pregnant. Cust deserted her and offered marriage to someone else. Nina Welby wrote Cust an imploring letter which he 'showed to other men at the country house where he was staying, with odious remarks intended to be facetious'.[6] Millicent sent these details to the Honorary Secretary of the Women's Liberal Unionist Association in Manchester, because she considered that Cust's conduct threatened the sanctity of marriage and the family and that such a man ought not to be in a position of public responsibility. When no action was taken, Millicent persevered, indeed seems to have gone to extraordinary lengths to persecute Cust. Cust had given up his candidature, and had married Miss Welby (who had lost her baby and began pleading with Millicent to leave her husband alone). By the spring of 1895, Millicent's friends were beseeching her to stop, telling her that they had heard people say that a woman who was behaving as she was behaving did not deserve the suffrage (and that they themselves would withdraw their own support for women's suffrage).

This was perhaps the only exception to the rule of Millicent's utterly single-minded and lifelong devotion to the suffrage cause. The ennobling of women by the vote was for Millicent itself almost a moral, rather than political, objective – although she was also keen to point out that a whole host of other freedoms were not likely to be obtained without this fundamental human right.

Such feminism as there was in Millicent Fawcett's thinking tended to be overruled by another set of values – those to do with defence of, and love for, her country. Millicent was a nationalist and an imperialist. She was a 'worshipper at the inner shrine, the holy of holies, all that England stands for to her children, and to the world' (Letter quoted in Strachey, 1931, p 301).

Admiration for English institutions has to be seen as the most potent determining factor in Millicent's ability to campaign for the vote *in a constitutional manner* over a period of many years. 'We have a peculiar skill for inserting the graft of new ideas into the stem of old institutions,' she wrote in a women's suffrage speech of 1899,

> . . . this has given a continuity to our political history which has frequently received the tribute of respect and admiration from foreign observers. It has enabled us to achieve progress without revolution, to avoid all breaks with our past, while stretching forward to the new ideas and new life of the future. It is because an extension of the parliamentary franchise to women householders is in distinct accord with these national traditions that I urge its acceptance on you. . . All that we need to obtain this goal are the commonplace English qualities of courage, patience and tenacity; if we have these, we shall make way with the task we have in hand. . .[7]

It consequently probably came as no surprise to her that, as she often pointed out, it took a mere two years less to obtain the vote for women than it took for men to win household suffrage for themselves (and they started with the advantage of already having 2 million voters).

Again, there was nothing out of line about Millicent's nationalism. Many of her colleagues on the suffrage committees were strong nationalists, and Blake's poem 'Jerusalem' was the suffrage hymn, although it lacked a suitable musical setting until Millicent and a friend, Kathleen Lyttleton, asked Sir Hubert Parry to compose one for the celebration of the suffrage victory in 1918 (this is the setting that is used today). But Millicent was more inclined to put her country first than many other suffragists. In 1901 she became a member of an all-women commission selected by the Government to investigate conditions in the Boer War concentration camps in South Africa. The overall function of this commission and certainly Millicent's own part in it was seen in some quarters as 'whitewashing' i.e. implicitly approving of the concentration camp system and of the political principle and practice of persecuting the Boer people. The eventual report produced by the commission restricts itself almost entirely to a discussion of the living conditions of the camps and the steps necessary to ameliorate them. Yet it definitely does not indicate any sympathy on the part of commission members with the world-view of the camp inmates; the inmates were, for example, blamed for the high death rates obtaining in the camps, the cause of which was said 'to be found in their extraordinary notions regarding the treatment of disease. Bathing the person is not, in health, commonly practised . . . in illness they regard the washing of the patient as next door to a miracle.'[8]

Millicent's nationalism also made her a primary instigator of the move, adopted by the NUWSS at the outbreak of the First World War, entirely to suspend the suffrage campaign for the duration of the war, and carry out such work as was necessary to relieve war distress and sustain 'the vital forces of the nation'. Her message to her followers was clear:. 'Women, your country needs you. . . Let us show ourselves worthy of citizenship, whether our claim to it be recognised or not' (Strachey, 1931, p 276). She called it the 'supreme sacrifice' and there are signs that she was truly depressed at what the war might mean – indefinite postponement for women's freedom. Nevertheless, her attitude to pacificism in the case of international war was curiously at odds with her attitude to militancy in the intranational war of women to obtain the vote. Many leaders of the NUWSS wanted women to do more than sustain the vital forces of the nation while men got on with the war; they wanted an international women's peace movement. Millicent was very strongly opposed to this, believing that national loyalties had to be put first (accordingly, she was also very much against conscientious objectors). In 1915 there was an internal struggle for leadership within the NUWSS between Millicent and the pacificists: Millicent won. This was the second period of great personal difficulty she had met during her allegiance to the suffrage cause. The first occurred with the emergence of the militant campaign orchestrated by the Pankhursts some years earlier.

There is little direct evidence available as to what Millicent Fawcett thought of the Pankhursts or they of her. Sylvia Pankhurst's account of the movement contains a number of asides pertaining to her view of Millicent's character and contribution to the cause: 'always strictly temperate in her observations' (Pankhurst, 1931, 1977, p 523), 'a trim, prim little figure' (p 182), she recalls the abrupt change of attitude on Millicent's part that occurred between 1906 and 1907. In 1906 Millicent gave a banquet at the Savoy hotel for the first suffragette prisoners. 'Some comment was made on the fact that the invitation was not extended to me,' Sylvia could not refrain from observing. 'The reason given was that though I had gone to prison on the same day my sentence had been shorter. It was clear, however, that the name Pankhurst savoured a shade too strongly of militancy for the non-militants, even in that expansive moment' (p 239). A year later the expansive moments were no longer in evidence, and Millicent was issuing statements explicitly opposing the strategy of the militants.

Yet she remained, to some degree, ambivalent in private, and the public front she turned to militancy was, like so much else in her life, a decision taken on the basis of political expediency. In 1909 she wrote to her friend Lady Frances Balfour, of the militants' activities: 'The physical courage of it all is intensely moving. I don't feel it is the right thing and yet the spectacle of so much self-sacrifice moves people to activity who would otherwise sit still and do nothing till the suffrage dropped into their mouths like a ripe fruit. . . .'[9] When Lloyd George argued that the Government could not possibly support women's franchise while the militant campaign continued, she responded that it was not within her power to stop it, but only within his: if he gave women the vote the militancy would stop. He replied by repeating the same point, namely that militancy was losing the suffrage campaign support. Millicent then drew his attention to a recent case in his own constituency when his supporters savaged the Conservative Club and were let off by the magistrate on the grounds 'that allowance must be made for political excitement'. 'Why,' asked Millicent, 'is allowance made for political excitement in the case of men who can and do express their feelings at the ballot-box, but no allowance is made in the case of women when they are excited by political injustice and are driven to express their indignation by acts of violence? Of course there was no answer to this inquiry,' she added uncompromisingly, 'but Mr Lloyd George deftly turned the subject and said he wished to introduce me to his wife' (Fawcett, 1924, p 195).

But, so far as the militant campaign was concerned, Millicent could not, she said, in the end support a *revolutionary* movement, nor was she able (she noted, somewhat contradictorily) in good faith to support a movement that was ruled 'autocratically at first by a small group of four persons, and latterly by one person only' (1924, p 185). There is a nice anecdote which expresses the conflict between her desire for unity and the distaste she felt for violent tactics: ' "Why can't we all be united?" a militant suffragist once asked her. "Yes," she replied breezily, "shall we all break windows, or shall we all not break windows? The Gadarene herd was very united" ' (*Daily Telegraph*, 6 August 1929).

In setting herself as leader of the constitutional movement up against the alternative of militancy, Millicent constantly needed to remind herself of, and draw courage from, a quotation from Morley's life of Gladstone: 'No reformer is fit for his (*sic*) task who suffers himself to be frightened off by the excesses of an extreme wing' (Strachey, 1931, p 212).

These conflicts did depress Millicent a good deal, not least because they were associated with a division of opinion and action within her own family. From 1908–11 her sister Elizabeth supported the militants and at over 70 took part in one of the raids on Parliament. It is a measure of the solid upper-class standing of the suffragists (not to mention some of the militant suffragettes as well) that in the face of Millicent's distress at the danger Elizabeth might be in, a promise was secured behind the scenes from the Home Secretary by Millicent's friend Lady Frances Balfour that Elizabeth would not be arrested. However, the internal dissension in the family could not be dissipated so easily; Elizabeth's daughter, Dr Louisa Garrett Anderson, continued to support the militants and was herself arrested in 1912, thus providing Millicent with a continuing uncomfortable prod to her conscience: people whom she loved, trusted and respected could, and did, hold very different opinions to her own on matters which were literally those of life and death.

Temperamentally, Millicent Fawcett was a different person in private from her public image. Although, like Joan of Arc 'born' to, or for, her particular struggle, she detested most of the activities this struggle foisted upon her. She disliked public functions and speech-making terrified her. 'No one knows how speaking takes it out of me,' she wrote in 1884. 'Before that last [meeting] . . . I was downright ill, but I know I don't show it, and I believe people think I rather like making speeches' (Strachey, 1931, p 100). (She is reported to have welcomed the vote when it eventually came precisely because she would not have to make any more speeches.) Her speeches were always prepared personally in extensive handwritten notes, and in the same vein she refused ever to employ a secretary, or have a telephone installed in her home. He friend Ray Strachey recalls the elaborate process of speech preparation:

> It was her habit, when she had an important speech to make, first to work over it at her desk, taking notes and arranging her ideas, and then to sit down somewhere else with a piece of needlework in her hands and go over it again carefully in her head. In that way, she said, she stitched the outlines firmly into her mind, so that

there was no danger of losing them. (Strachey, 1931, p 229)

The effect of these carefully prepared products, however much anxiety they engendered in the speaker, was 'clear, logical, self-possessed, and pre-eminently "ladylike". . .' (Strachey, 1931, p 46). She was not, according to those who heard her, especially eloquent, not did she appeal to the emotions. Indeed, she was said to be obsessively afraid of showing emotion, and maintained a rigid self-control in the face of all personal and professional disasters. When asked to sign a petition for women's suffrage which stated that she 'passionately desired' it, she responded with '*Must* I be passionate?' Then: 'Oh, very well' (Rover, 1967, p 58). It was probably this very lack of passion that accounted for her appeal as the very model of the kind of woman who proved that women would use the vote well. Her physical appearance aided this impression. Very small, with a lovely complexion and a lot of shiny brown hair, she was undoubtedly an attractive example of femininity, and was always beautifully dressed, usually in a dark silk gown with a large lace collar. *Time and Tide* argued that her unemotional style of argument ideally suited her to the pioneer role, but worked, particularly, because 'she looked nice, dressed becomingly, was married to a heroic blind politician and was to him the perfect wife. . .' (16 August 1929). 'If only for her triumph as a wife,' added the *Northern Mail*, 'Millicent Fawcett's career was an inspiration' (5 August 1929). Such lack of deviation from the accepted path for women was no accident. It was Millicent's self-consciously chosen direction. 'She meant to spell revolution without the "r"', she wrote of Emily Davies, writing at the same time about herself: 'She did not want any violence either of speech or action. She remained always the quiet, demure little rector's daughter, and she meant to bring about all the changes she advocated by processes as gradual and unceasing as the progress of a child from infancy to manhood (*sic*)' (Fawcett, 1924, p 40).

People *liked* Millicent, and they were particularly drawn by her sense of humour. 'I think it quite delightful,' she wrote to a friend in 1929, 'that now everyone takes the woman voter as if she had existed from the time of Adam and Eve'.[10] In 1887, when asked by an American lady, who took the view that women professionals must be incompetent (and unsexed) by definition, whether she knew of any woman doctor at whose hands she would be willing to undergo an operation, Millicent replied, 'Yes there's one woman doctor by whom I would rather have my head cut off than by anyone else' (Strachey, 1931, p 138).

The series of events that finally led up to the Representation of the People Act 1918 has been described in detail elsewhere.[11] Before the war brought about a suspension of the campaign, Millicent had experienced a difficult time with an issue on which she had always felt strongly – namely that the best chance for women's suffrage was to be secured by supporting individual MPs who espoused the cause, rather than by attempting to secure the backing of one party as a whole. The defeat of the 1913 Reform Bill led her to reverse this opinion and to pledge the loyalty of the NUWSS to the only party – the Labour party – which had declared a relatively unequivocal demand for female suffrage. It may well be that on this matter Millicent's judgement was erroneous and that, had the policy been adopted earlier by the NUWSS, the vote would have been won sooner than it was. But that, of course, raises the question of how it was that in the end the Government of the day saw fit to enfranchise women after more than half a century of broken pledges and Parliamentary disappointments. The *Manchester Guardian* in its obituary presented what was then and is still now a balanced view of the case:

> There were three stages in the emancipation of women. The first was the long campaign of propaganda and organisation, at the centre of which, patient, unwearying and always hopeful, stood Dame Millicent. The second was the campaign of the militants, which, since it depended on sensation, brought to the movement the enthusiastic attention of the popular press and made it a live political issue. The third was the war. Had there been no militancy and no war, the emancipation of women would still have come, although more slowly. But without the faithful preparation of the ground over many years by Dame Millicent Fawcett and her colleagues neither militancy nor the war could have produced the crop. (6 August 1929)

Or, in the words of the *Daily Telegraph*:

> The names of the militants who broke windows, chained themselves to pillars, or went on hungerstrike in goal, are sometimes quoted by the unthinking as the leaders to victory, but in reality it was the woman of sweet reasonableness, womanly manner, quiet dress, and cultured style who did more than any other in the cause of emancipation. (6 August 1929)

Her 'sweet reasonableness' was the quality which has condemned Millicent Fawcett to the reputation of having won citizenship for women, and has detracted from a proper consideration of other factors, individuals and organisations that were essential to this goal. Yet whatever the answer to the question of how the vote was won (and it is not likely to be a simple one), Millicent Fawcett must surely be admired for her early and public adoption of a cause that was at the time both marginal and sensational; for her refusal ever seriously to be distracted from the central ambition of enfranchising women; and for her adamant insistence on not being the cult figure public opinion inclined to make her, especially in the years after the 1918 Act (a mark of which was her conversion into a Dame Grand Cross of the British Empire in 1924).

Millicent Fawcett retired from active political work in 1919. When asked, in that year, why she would not stand for Parliament, she said she had 73 reasons: 72 were her age, and the seventy-third that she did not want to. Nancy Astor, the first woman MP, said she felt almost ashamed to take that place instead of Millicent Fawcett. However, retirement did not mean the end of Millicent's work for sex equality; between 1919 and 1929 she continued to participate in the affairs of the London and National Society for Women's Service and in particular helped to secure the opening of the legal profession to women. At the age of 74 with her sister Agnes she visited Palestine for the first time, returning on three further occasions, becoming quite involved in the work of the British Administration there, and recording some of her reflections on the subject in a book (1926). It was in Jerusalem that she heard of the final victory in 1928, when the basis of women's enfranchisement became the same as that of men. 'It is almost exactly sixty-one years ago since I heard John Stuart Mill introduce his suffrage amendment to the Reform Bill on May 20, 1867 . . . I have had extraordinary good luck in having seen the struggle from the beginning,' she said (Strachey, 1931, p 349).

In that year she was still busy writing, and in 1929, her eighty-third year, she and Agnes set off to see the Far East. On 18 August 1929 she was guest of honour at a public luncheon given by the National Union of Societies for Equal Citizenship (as the NUWSS was suitably re-titled) to celebrate the first woman Cabinet minister and the return to Parliament of 14 women MPs. Three days later she went to bed with a cold, and died of double pneumonia two weeks later with her sister, daughter and old friend Dr Jane Walker by her side. At her memorial service in Westminster Abbey some months later, the Dean read the passage from Ecclesiastes 'Let us now praise famous men (*sic*)' – and of course they sang 'Jerusalem'. The woman with whom she did not always agree, and to whom she handed over the Presidency of the NUWSS, Eleanor Rathbone, said of her that practical wisdom was her outstanding feature:

> It was this quality which looked out of her grave clear eyes with the lids slightly drooping at the outer corners, and the humorous twinkle in them, which was like the gleam of sunshine on a dark pool. . . She saw the end from the beginning and the unity which transcended all our differences.' (*Manchester Guardian*, 8 August 1929)

Notes

1 Born Louise Dunnell; neither the Strachey biography nor Millicent's autobiography name her.
2 Letter from Millicent Garrett Fawcett (MGF) to Edmund Garrett, 21 February 1885; Fawcett Library Collection (FLC).
3 M. G. Fawcett, 'Women's Suffrage', speech delivered to the Women's Debating Society, The Owen's College, Manchester, 13 February 1899.
4 M. G. Fawcett, 'Women's Suffrage', address delivered at the Junior Constitutional Club, Piccadilly, London, 1897, McCorquodale and Co, pp 6–7.
5 Letter from Thomas Hardy to MGF, 14 April 1892, FLC.
6 Statement made by MGF to A. J. Balfour, 19 March 1894, Fawcett Library Archives (FLA).
7 M. G. Fawcett, 'Women's Suffrage', Manchester Speech, 1899.
8 Concentration Camps Commission *Report on the Concentration Camps in South Africa by the Committee of Ladies Appointed by the Secretary of State for War*, 1902, HMSO, London, p 16.
9 Letter from MGF to Lady Frances Balfour, 30 June 1909, FLC.
10 Letter, MGF to 'Miss Ward', 18 June 1929, FLC.
11 A good short summary is contained in M. Pugh, *Women's Suffrage in Britain 1867–1929*, Historical Association Pamphlet, 1980, London.

Charlotte Perkins Gilman: The Personal is Political
(1860–1935)

Ann J. Lane

For all of us, in one way or another, our work is an extension of us, of our personalities. Sometimes that connection is subtle, tenuous, hidden. With Charlotte Perkins Gilman the body of her work came almost directly out of her personal struggles. We cannot comprehend the scope, the power or the limitations of her ideas without a close understanding of her life. In a sense she studied history and sociology, economics and ethics, in order to understand where she came from, why her parents were the way they were, why her life took the form it did – and ultimately how to learn to control her destiny and to manage her life.

She was born Charlotte Anna Perkins on 3 July 1860, in Hartford, Connecticut. She was raised by her mother, Mary A. Fitch, because her father left his wife and children soon after Charlotte's birth and thereafter provided little support, emotional or financial, to his family, which included, in addition to Charlotte, a son, Thomas. Charlotte's mother, as a young girl growing into womanhood, was blessed with all the assets for success, matrimonial success, which was the measurement for young women, for she was beautiful, wealthy, musically gifted and, her daughter later said, 'femininely attractive in the highest degree'. Yet Charlotte described her mother's life as 'one of the most painfully thwarted I have ever known', and it became the model for Charlotte of precisely the kind of life women must learn to reject. Mary Fitch began her adolescence in much the same way *her* mother had, as a great success in being courted and wooed, even as a schoolgirl. But unlike her mother, she did not marry until she was almost 30, staving off marriage with one broken engagement after another. Finally, after a broken engagement to her distant cousin Frederick Beecher Perkins was mended, the couple married. Frederick Perkins, at his end, married Mary Fitch only after his first chosen love was rejected as unsuitable by his mother. It was not an auspicious beginning for the couple.

With marriage, Mary Perkins began the re-enactment of a woman's story through most of time, one pregnancy after another, three in three years; and then Frederick Perkins left home. Mary Perkins was prepared to be, had every reason to expect to be, a wife, supported and taken care of by a loyal husband, a woman who would devote her life to rearing children and heading a household, a role her mother had filled, a role provided for her by the world in which she grew. After years of attention and adoration from male admirers, Mary Perkins suddenly found herself an abandoned wife, with two infants, and no way to earn her living. A woman whose only place was in the home found herself without a home of her own, living tenuously and painfully in the homes of others as a poor relation.

If marriage was the only acceptable career for women, as Mary Perkins was raised to believe, then rejection by a husband spelled failure at life's work. Psychologically unable to turn against her rejecting husband, Mary Perkins took the blame on herself and turned her anger inward and onto her children, although the embittered mother justified and rationalised her rejecting behaviour. Said Charlotte in her autobiography:

> Having suffered . . . for lack of a husband's love, she heroically determined that her baby daughter should not so suffer if she could help it. Her method was to deny the child all expression of affection as far as possible, so that she should not be used to it or long for it.

In later years Mary Perkins admitted to her adult daughter: 'I used to put away your little hand from my cheek when you were a nursing baby.' Little Charlotte, having already lost a father, was left with a rejecting mother, and so grew up in a cold and punishing home. Mary Perkins turned the loss of a husband and a home with its status and sense of place into a form of maternal self-sacrifice, and she was determined to exact indebtedness from her children for her loss. Half victim, half accomplice, she accepted the world's definition of herself as a failed and abandoned woman.

As for her father's role in her life, Charlotte wrote: 'My childhood had no father.' As a young girl and then a young woman, she made frequent overtures to him, but he always remained a remote and ungiving figure in her life.

Frederick Beecher Perkins, her father, was the grandson of the noted theologican, Lyman Beecher, which made Charlotte's great aunt the famous Harriet Beecher Stowe, author of *Uncle Tom's Cabin*. The Beecher family was probably the most famous family in America, and the Beecher name was a hard yardstick by which the less gifted or less driven members of the clan could measure themselves. Frederick, the oldest of four children born to Mary, daughter of Lyman Beecher, did not fare well. The tensions he suffered as a Beecher, as a failed Beecher, seem never to have been satisfactorily resolved. He saw himself as a man of letters, but he never achieved much success in that work. A man of some literary and intellectual gifts, inspired with bursts of passion for justice and reform, he was, ultimately, unable to put his strengths together in a well-ordered and satisfying life.

From the age of 16 to 21 Charlotte lived, for the first time in her life, in one home for an extended period of time, primarily with her mother alone, and it was during this time that she took upon herself a new mode of living that included health and dress reform and a commitment to reading and learning, studying painting and art. In her autobiography, Charlotte designates this critical period in her life with the title: 'Girlhood – if Any'. It is during this time that she began a conscious search for self-definition. During these years Charlotte struggled, with a good deal of success, to alter her personality and strengthen her body in preparation, she articulated, for some important work she was destined to do, although its exact nature was still uncertain. She declared herself free of her mother's power on her twenty-first birthday. To her father she wrote: 'Do you know – I think I should have liked you very much – as a casual acquaintance. Yours truly, C. A. Perkins.'

The overriding problem Charlotte struggled with during the next period was what to do with her life. Her struggle for identity and self-awareness took place in a context defined by the nineteenth-century's notions of masculine and feminine, appropriate male and female behaviour. She saw herself as having to choose between the masculine route, which meant career and a life with women, or the feminine route, the traditional one of husband and children. She wanted to use her mind and her gifts but she had never been systematically trained. Some women of her generation, such as Jane Addams, were able to break through the barriers of their social constrictions, but they tended to be upper middle-class women who were educated in ways Charlotte was not and who, as a consequence, established friendships, developed skills, saw role models after whom to pattern themselves, and who chose to live within the support and security of largely female worlds. This was the first generation of college-educated women in America and these college connections were crucial for these women. Charlotte was excluded from this community by virtue of her poverty and absence of education.

The summer she was 21 she wrote extensively of her inner struggles to her closest friend, Martha Luther. After several agonising months she determined never to marry, not 'to devote one's life to private pursuit', but rather to be a 'person, cultivate public work, public career, and relinquish traditional roles that come with femaleness'. The decision was not easy to reach or easy to sustain. Her strength seemed to reside in Martha's unflagging loyalty and support. But Martha soon married and left her, betraying the trust Charlotte had placed in their lasting, unencumbered friendship.

In January 1882, not long after Martha's 'desertion', Charlotte met Charles Walter Stetson, an extremely handsome local artist. Within days he proposed marriage, and she refused. For the next two years, while Walter pursued and Charlotte resisted, she struggled again with the dialogue she had had with Martha. 'I knew of course', she wrote to Walter, 'that the time would come when I must choose between two lives, but never did I dream that it would come so soon, and that the struggle would be so terrible.' Ultimately, with grave reservations, she married. (Years later Charlotte Gilman wrote many fictional pieces that describe the disastrous marriage that flows from a woman accepting a man's proposal, flattered at the attention and the pleasure of being desired, but *responding* to *his* ardour and passion, not *hers*.)

The fears and self-doubts that persisted during the courtship led into despondency and depression in marriage. When a child, Katherine Beecher, was born the following year, beginning the re-enactment, Charlotte Stetson became so seriously depressed, so unable to function at the simplest chores as wife and mother, that she was persuaded by her husband to consult the internationally famous Philadelphia neurologist, Silas Weir Mitchell, a specialist in women's nervous diseases.

His treatment, which he called the Rest Cure, required extended bed rest and near total inactivity and isolation for months. The infantilising regime had two goals. First, subject to such severely enforced isolation and inactivity, the patient was, in Mitchell's words, 'surfeited with it and welcomed a firm order to do the things she once felt she could not do' – that is, return with unquestioning acceptance to the busy life of wife and mother. Second, she was introduced to the 'moral medication' of the physician, so that she would come to trust and depend on him for moral guidance. Enforced rest, enforced passivity, acceptance of the commands of male authority, Mitchell's treatment was an extreme version of the cultural norms that operated outside his sanitorium. Neither better nor worse than the prevailing wisdom of his day concerning the needs of women, Mitchell could not imagine a woman like Charlotte Stetson and therefore he could not treat her. A few years before he met Charlotte Stetson he described hysteria 'among women of the upper classes . . . caused by unhappy love affairs, losses of money, and the daily fret and weariness of lives, which passing out of maidenhood, lack those distinct purposes and aims which, in the lives of men, are like the steadying influences of the fly-wheel in an engine.' That a woman might have a 'distinct purpose' the same as 'in the lives of men' was apparently beyond his comprehension, and so in good conscience he could prescribe to Charlotte, as he pronounced her cured and sent her home:

> Live as domestic a life as possible. Have your child with you all the time . . . Lie down an hour after each meal. Have but two hours intellectual life a day. And never touch pen, brush or pencil as long as you live.

And the consequences?

> I went home, followed those directions rigidly for months, and came perilously near to losing my mind.

'I made a rag baby,' said Charlotte years later, 'hung it on a doorknob and played with it. I would crawl into remote closets and under beds – to hide from the grinding pressure of that profound distress.'

Calling upon some inner sense of survival, she rejected both husband and physician and fled to the house of the Channings, friends in Pasadena, California, whose daughter, Grace Ellery Channing, was Charlotte's dearest friend. Walter and Charlotte Stetson were divorced some time later. He immediately remarried – Grace Ellery Channing – and the three, remaining cordial thereafter, were jointly involved in the rearing of Katherine, although Katherine was raised in those early years after the divorce by Walter and Grace.

For a time in California, while the divorce was pending (there was no way in those days of being granted a divorce for incompatibility), Charlotte supported herself and her daughter (as well as her mother, who stayed with her until her death by cancer in 1892), by running a boardinghouse. In this difficult period Charlotte Stetson, who months before had been unable to cook a meal, launched her career as a writer and lecturer.

Her first major piece of work was the chilling short story, 'The Yellow Wallpaper', an intensely personal examination of her private nightmare. It is a study of a young mother's descent into madness, driven there by a well-meaning but insidious husband-doctor who follows S. Weir Mitchell's Rest Cure. In Charlotte's later fiction there is always a happy ending because the leading character breaks out of conventional moulds to shape her own life. Only in 'The Yellow Wallpaper' does the protagonist permit others to determine her life, and she goes mad.

Charlotte Stetson, an untrained, uneducated women, herself but a short step away from the edge of sanity, audaciously urged women to follow her recommendations for cure in direct violation of Mitchell's well-known treatment, and she boldly and vividly described the inevitable hideous, irreversible dangers to those who do not defy and resist. Years later she wrote that Mitchell's instructions brought 'me so near the borderline of utter mental ruin that I could see over'. She cast aside his orders and resumed work – 'Work, the normal life of every human being; work, which is joy and growth and service, without which one is a pauper and a parasite.'

The following year Charlotte Stetson published a book of verse called *In This Our World*. In 1894 she and Helen Campbell, a renowned reformer, co-edited *The Impress, A Journal of the Pacific Coast Women's Association*. She was a contributing editor to *The American Fabian*, along with Henry Demarest Lloyd, Edward Bellamy and William Dean Howells. Bellamy's novel, *Looking Backward*, pictured the world in the year 2000 under a form of utopian socialism, which he called Nationalism, and inspired the formation of thousands of Nationalist clubs whose goal was to implement the ideas espoused in the book. Charlotte Stetson was drawn to the ideas of Bellamy and the Nationalist movement, and she soon became a regular lecturer in their circles. She began to earn a living on the lecture circuit addressing audiences concerned with issues of woman suffrage, trade unions and socialism. She spoke to women's clubs and men's clubs, to labour unions and suffrage groups, to church congregations and to Nationalist clubs.

It was at this point that Charlotte and Walter Stetson agreed that their child should live with her father and his new wife, whom the child knew and loved. Charlotte Stetson, by this time moderately well known, particularly in California, was vigorously attacked in the press for 'abandoning her child' and for being an 'unnatural mother'. 'The Unnatural Mother' was the title of a short story Charlotte wrote in 1916. In it the mother is condemned as unnatural because she is willing to sacrifice her child's life in order to save an entire community. Ironically, the child in the story survives, the town inhabitants survive and only she and her husband perish. Even after death she is condemned as unnatural because, said one, 'a mother's duty is to her own child . . . the Lord never gave them other children to care for'.

Charlotte had already affronted public opinion by divorcing a man for no apparent cause and, even worse, continuing a warm friendship with his new wife. Unforgivable, however, was her placing her career above her reponsibilities as a mother. She was so unnerved by the assaults that she literally gave up her own home. From 1895 to 1900 she led a nomadic existence, ceaselessly lecturing and writing, forging for herself a role as ideologue and propagandist, a humanist-at-large. She created a kind of self-imposed exile, reproducing the marginality of her early life.

Out of this rootless environment came her most famous book, *Women and Economics*, published in 1898. It was soon translated into seven languages and won her international recognition. In 1900 came *Concerning Children*. In 1903, *The Home: Its Work and Influence*. In 1904, *Human Work*. From 1909 to 1916 she edited and wrote all the copy for *The Forerunner*, a monthly magazine. Beginning in 1909 with 'no capital except a mental one', and ending when she decided she had said what she wanted to, the monthly journal contained editorials, criticism, comments and observation, book reviews, essays, poetry and fiction that dealt with a whole range of subjects from venereal disease to noise pollution, but the overriding commitments were to the rights of women and to socialism. Writing in the years when the woman's movement and the socialist movement were each trying to win mass support, she sought to unite them by demonstrating their essential and necessary interdependence. Each year two books were serialised in *The Forerunner*; the full seven year run equalled in pages twenty-eight full-length books. In 1911 she published *Man-Made World*; in 1923, *His Religion and Hers: A Study of the Faith of Our Fathers and the Work of Our Mothers*. In 1935, shortly after her death, her autobiography, *The Living of Charlotte Perkins Gilman*, appeared.

In the Spring of 1900, after a long and complicated courtship, carried out essentially through letters, she married George Houghton Gilman, her first cousin, also a descendant of Lyman Beecher. If Charlotte Stetson withheld her deepest fears and anxieties from her husband Walter, then Charlotte Gilman withheld almost nothing from her husband, Houghton. In the years before the marriage finally took place, Charlotte, travelling and lecturing, wrote letters almost daily to him, their average length some 15 handwritten pages. She revealed much in that extraordinary collection of self-exploring correspondence. Not since she wrote 'The Yellow Wallpaper' had she plumbed her emotions so deeply. To Houghton she expressed her fears, her passions, her doubts, her anxieties, her triumphs and her nagging feelings of excessive dependence. Houghton Gilman could have no doubt about his wife's commitment to her career, her recurring anguish and concern about her sanity, her doubts about her abilities as a mother, her worries about their forthcoming marriage, her determination to reach self-realisation through her work; her need for his stability, love and strength, and her resolve to conquer, or at least learn to co-exist with, her devastating and terrifying depressions that she suffered throughout her life.

They lived very happily for more than three decades, until Houghton Gilman died suddenly in 1934. Although a Wall Street lawyer, Houghton was not a man driven by ambition or the desire to achieve material successes. He was a caring, nurturing, comforting, gentle partner for Charlotte. By the time of her husband's death, Charlotte Gilman knew she had inoperable cancer. After he died, she moved back to Pasadena, near her daughter, who lived there until her death in 1977. Grace Channing Stetson, also a widow, joined her there, thus reuniting the women of the family.

Grace Channing was the woman, Charlotte said, who in her earlier days 'pulled me out of living death, set me on my staggering feet, helped me to get work again, did more than I can say to make me live, and I love her, I think, as well as anyone on earth'. The relationship between these two evolved into a lifelong mutual dependency between two remarkable women who loved and respected each other and who chose to ignore the inevitable tensions in their difficult situation. Charlotte did not allow Grace's marriage to estrange them; on the contrary, she used the connection to create a deeper bond between them.

When Charlotte fled her home to take to the road she socialised the idea of home by taking on the community-as-home. In a similar way she socialised motherhood, by including Grace as second mother to her child. Many of the ideas that came to be later worked out in *Herland*, her feminist utopian fantasy, have their roots in this part of her life. Unable herself to sustain a private mother-daughter relationship, she would later create a world in which that relationship was socialised, all mothers caring for all children.

Shortly before her death, Charlotte, age 75, wrote to Grace, age 72, 'It's been an honour to be your friend, dear Grace. And I have loved you a long time – some 56 or 57 years isn't it?'

In 1935 Charlotte completed her autobiography, *The Living of*

Charlotte Perkins Gilman, made certain that the royalties, which unhappily were never to be substantial, would be a legacy to her daughter, and selected the cover for the book. She said good-bye to her family and friends, and with the chloroform she had long been accumulating, ended her life. The note she left appears in the last pages of her autobiography:

> No grief, pain, misfortune or 'broken heart' is excuse for cutting off one's life while any power of service remains. But when all usefulness is over, when one is assured of unavoidable and imminent death, it is the simplest of human rights to choose a quick and easy death in place of a slow and horrible one . . . I have preferred chloroform to cancer.

Charlotte Perkins Gilman had an enormous international reputation in her lifetime, although she is almost unknown in ours. Post First World War audiences found unappealing her double commitment to the rights of women and to socialism. Demand for her lectures and books declined markedly by 1920 and continued downward thereafter, until new interest, sparked by the contemporary woman's movement, rescued her from oblivion.

A serious critic of history and society whose intriguing ideas have never been examined systematically, she tried to create a cohesive, integrated body of thought that combined feminism and socialism. She struggled to define a humane social order built upon the values she identified most closely as the female values of life-giving and nurturing. She constructed a theoretical world view to explain human behaviour, past and present, and to project the outlines of her vision for the future. It was a theoretical structure that encompassed anthropology, history, philosophy, sociology and ethics. Her cosmic efforts were not always successful, but she did create a social analysis that is largely coherent internally and awesome in its proportions.

She came of age during a time of struggle over the ideas of Charles Darwin and their application to society. Darwin's theory of evolution did not directly apply to social theory, but intellectuals translated his ideas of natural selection into social language, and argued about their interpretation. One view, formulated by English theorist Herbert Spenser, and defended in the United States by William Graham Sumner, was that society's laws are irrevocably rooted in the evolutionary process, and that there is no way to interfere with the struggle for existence and the survival of the fittest. Lester Frank Ward, an American sociologist, rejected that interpretation of Social Darwinism, as it was called. He insisted that it was possible for humans, who, unlike other animals, possess a Mind and therefore a Culture, to shape the social laws under which they operate. Gilman early identified herself with the ideological camp of Ward in believing that human beings were the key to determining their own destinies and in using evolutionary theory as a weapon in the movement for social change. Convinced of the plasticity of human nature, she vehemently sought to destroy the moulds into which people, especially but not only, female people, were forced. Her specific contribution to this wing of Social Darwinist thought was her assertion that women, as a collective entity, could, if they so chose, be the moving force in the reorganisation of society.

Gilman's ideas matured at the turn of the century. Like most other intellectuals of her time, particularly those in the new social sciences, she struggled to create a theory and to envision a world that relied neither on class violence nor on uncontrolled individualism. Unlike other social scientists, most of whom were university-affiliated, she did not seek explanations for social problems or solutions to them from experts in these newly created disciplines.

The new social sciences that emerged in this period, for all the differences that separated sociology, anthropology, psychology and political science, had a common set of assumptions about society that distinguish them as a group. They all affirmed the primacy of culture over biology as a central force shaping human society and institutions. They believed in a social intelligence, dominated by trained, disinterested specialists who ostensibly would transcend politics, but who, in reality, shared a tacit commitment to the prevailing ideology. They relied primarily on descriptions of the inter-dependence of institutions and relations in society, which inevitably raised questions of how society functions but left untouched questions of why and for whom it operates the way it does or how it had evolved to that point; that is, the role of power was unexamined. By stressing the relationships among all social phenomena, implying that all are of relatively equal significance, these new social scientists in the United States obscured the reality of class, sex and race rule, and therefore made irrelevant any programme to alter that view.

Charlotte Gilman self-consciously dissociated herself from this intellectual environment. Her work, on the contrary, was an effort to devise and to carry out a strategy for change. Opposed as she was, temperamentally and ideologically, to violence or force, she also separated herself from Marx's revolutionary ideology. In her vision, the peaceful collective action of women replaced Marx's class struggle. Because women are nurturers of the young and bearers of the cultural values of love and co-operation, and because women have been excluded from the sources of power, Charlotte argued, they are in an ideal position to create an alternative social vision. By the early twentieth century, women also had decades of sophisticated collective action and a trained leadership, shaped by the struggle for suffrage and other of their rights.

Charlotte's politics were probably closer to that of the Fabians than to any other group. Indeed, during her frequent trips to England she spent time with G. B. Shaw, the Webbs and other leaders in the Fabian community. When H. G. Wells went to the United States in 1906 the only American he asked to meet was Charlotte Perkins Gilman. Still, it must be understood that Charlotte's socialism was never systematically explored or studied. She believed in co-operation and not competition, she believed that the genuine needs of the community should determine social policy, not profit. She supported, in general, most socialist demands, but ultimately she defined her own brand of socialism and feminism and sought to propagandise on its behalf through her individual work and not through participating in any socialist community or party or group with whose ideology and politics she could identify.

Describing herself as a humanist, not a feminist, she argued that since 'it is only in social relations that we are human . . . to be human, woman must share in the totality of humanity's common life.' Women, forced to lead restricted lives, retard all human progress. Growth of the organism, she said, the individual, or the social body, requires the use of all of our powers in four areas: physical, intellectual, spiritual and social. In each, women are denied their share of human activities.

Women's historic subordination she dated from the expropriation by men of the surplus that women produced in agriculture. It was, she said, in a line of argument closely resembling that set forth by Frederick Engels, the first form of subordination, and it became the model for subsequent exploitation. Beginning with recorded history, men appropriated women's work and, by forcing them to depend economically on male authority, demeaned them. By the nineteenth century it was assumed that one entire sex should function as the domestic servants of the other. What we call masculine traits are simply human traits, which have been denied to women and are thereby assumed to belong to men: traits such as courage, strength, creativity, generosity and integrity. To be 'virtuous', a woman needs but one 'virtue' – chastity. 'Women are not undeveloped men', she said, 'but the feminine half of humanity is undeveloped humans.'

At one time in human evolution, she asserted, the involuntary sacrifice of equality made by the female sex had been necessary for progress, because male traits of assertiveness, combat and display were essential for the growth of the social organism. Civilisation, however, now requires the restoration of the original male-female balance to include those female qualities of co-operation and nurturance.

The most important fact about the sexes, she said repeatedly, men and women, is the common humanity we share, not the differences that distinguish us. But women are denied autonomy and thus are not provided the environment in which to develop. Men, too, suffer from personalities distorted by their habits of dominance and power. A healthy social organism for both men and women, therefore, requires the autonomy of women. That autonomy can be achieved only by women's collective political action. Just as women have been socialised to accede to their own subordination, she suggested, so can they be moved to lead the struggle for a humanised-socialised world. She saw the first step toward resolving the world's predicament in the ideological sphere, and she saw herself engaged in a fierce struggle for the minds of women.

Charlotte Gilman's sociological and historical works analyse the past from her peculiar humanist-socialist perspective. (She was not a feminist, she said; rather, the world was masculinist and it was she who sought to introduce a truly humanist concept by integrating women to their rightful place.) *Women and Economics* has as its subtitle the subject matter of the book: *A Study of the Economic Relation Between Men and Women as a Factor in Social Evolution.* In it she explores the origin of the subordinate relationship and its function in the evolutionary process. Man, by supporting woman, has become her economic environment. Woman makes a living by marriage, not by the work she does but by the situation of the man she marries. As a result her female qualities dominate her human qualities, because it is the female traits through which she earns her living. We are the only species where the female's economic environment is the male, where the male, not nature, provides sustenance. The result is that women are, in her words, over-sexed. To use her illustration, one that demonstrates her wit, let us take the relative condition of a wild cow and a milch cow. The wild cow is a female, produces healthy calves, for whom she has sufficient milk. That is her female function. Otherwise she is more bovine than feminine. She is strong, nimble, able to fight and care for herself. Humans have artificially exaggerated the cow's milk-producing capacity. 'She has become a walking milk-machine, bred and tended to that express end, her value measured in quarts.' But the secretion of milk is a maternal function, a function of the sex not of the species. So, 'the cow is over-sexed'. Women too belong to an animal species with great power and strength. But women have been bred to market their feebleness, their docility, their weakness, and these qualities are called feminine. We speak of a 'feminine hand' or a 'feminine foot', by which we mean it is small and weak. We would not speak of a 'feminine paw' or a 'feminine hoof'. In reality, the hand is an organ of prehension as the foot is an organ of locomotion. They are not secondary sex characteristics, except insofar as society has defined women's weakness as feminine and then rewarded it. 'All the main avenues of life [are] marked "male" and the female [is] left to be a female and nothing else.'

'Women's economic profit comes through the power of sex-attraction', said Charlotte repeatedly, but when we confront this frankly 'in the open market of vice, we are sick with horror'. But when we see the same economic relationship made permanent, 'established by law, sanctioned and sanctified by religion, covered with flowers and incense and all accumulated sentiment, we think it innocent, lovely and right'. More pointedly: 'The transient trade we think evil. The bargain for life we think good.' But in both cases 'the female gets her food from the male by virtue of her sex-relationship to him.'

In her fiction, the hundreds of short stories and several novels, Charlotte Gilman suggests the kind of world we could have if we worked at it; the kinds of choices we could make, if we insisted on them; the kinds of relationships we could achieve, if we went ahead and demanded them. The fiction illustrates the human drama inherent in the history and sociology, for, as she said, 'Until we can see what we are, we cannot take steps to become what we should be.'

Charlotte's fiction is part of her ideological world view and therein lies its interest and its power. We read her novels and short stories today because the problems she addressed and the solutions she sought are, unhappily, as relevant to the present as they were to her time. Several themes appear persistently. Children are central to her fiction, and their needs are examined in a variety of ways. Children are best reared collectively. They are raised by women, but not ordinarily by their biological mothers. It is through the intelligent and lovingly planned socialisation of children that humane and democratic values are to be achieved and permanent change thereby sustained. Charlotte envisioned an ideal society in which the profit motive is removed from social life and where genuine community dominates, although she never challenged the value and supremacy of nuclear family or monogamous heterosexual marriage.

The prerequisite for genuine autonomy for all adults is economic independence, and all citizens leave their homes each day to do their 'world-work'. Children of all ages do their work as well, that is, they go to baby gardens (nursery schools) or school, and the family is reunited at the end of the day in a home that is a place of love and relaxation, not a place of work for any of its members. Household work is accomplished as all work is accomplished – as a public activity, as a form of work for those who choose it. Housecleaning and cooking, laundry and sewing, are social activities no different from shoemaking or coal mining or ship building. The distinction between women's work and men's work disappears, with the exception of child-rearing, as the category called women's work disappears. She recognised that the home was the primary location of inequality for women.

Charlotte used fiction as a device to offer an answer to a question that seemed to be posed in the form of 'But what if . . .?' What if she wants a family and a career, and her husband-to-be objects? What if her children are grown up and she is bored? What if her husband is abusive and she wants to leave him but does not know how? What if her vacuous life causes her to make impossible demands upon her caring husband? What if she does not have the patience to rear the child she loves? What if the work she desperately wants takes her away from her lover? What if her elderly mother is ill and she does not want to sacrifice years nursing her? The questions, in one form or another, came from Charlotte's own experience, either because she had herself come to a satisfactory resolution or, more often, because she had not and suffered the consequences, which she wished to spare subsequent generations. If there were not many models after which young women could fashion a new way of life, then Charlotte would create them in fiction.

'The Yellow Wallpaper' must have haunted her all her life because it answered the question: But what if she had not fled from her husband and renounced the most advanced psychiatric advice of her time? The risks were severe, but the alternative was worse, and she knew it. Rigidly enforced confinement and absolute passivity – elements significant in the lives of women of her time and carried to an extreme in S. Weir Mitchell's treatment – contributed strongly to the madness in her short story, and needed to be discarded, as she herself had discarded them, if women were to achieve sanity and strength. In 'The Yellow Wallpaper' we see what happens to our lives if we let others run them for us. In her other stories we learn what choices are really ours. Charlotte Gilman's life remains as a legacy of inspiration. Her daily living, her ideas, her writing, her lectures, are all of a piece. She drew upon the painful and debilitating elements in her own inner and outer life as a central focus of her work. By confronting her life through resolutions achieved in her work her ideas continue to have enormous significance and power for today.

All quotations are from Charlotte Perkins Gilman's autobiography, the Living of Charlotte Perkins Gilman, *1935.*

Emma Goldman:
'Anarchist Queen'
(1869–1940)

Alix Kates Shulman*

In the first decades of this century, Emma Goldman's name was a household word in the United States. She was known as the Queen of the Anarchists,[1] the Most Dangerous Woman in the World, Red Emma. During her 30-year American career as an anarchist agitator, free speech activist, birth control advocate, and, as a writer, editor, and speaker, leader of the anarchist movement, the notorious Goldman was widely feared as a promotor of free love and violence. This outspoken enemy of family and state served three prison sentences – for allegedly inciting workers to riot, for instructing a large audience in the use of contraceptives, and for conspiring to obstruct the draft – and was arrested so often that she never spoke in public without taking along a book to read in jail. But as with so many other accomplished women, upon her death her reputation began to change, her prodigious work was forgotten, her five books gradually went out of print. Her once formidable name, if remembered at all, was said with a smile, as if it were the punch line of some old joke about anarchism or feminism, both considered irrelevant anachronisms in most parts of the English-speaking world. Until somewhere toward the end of the 1960s Goldman's libertarian vision was derided as hopelessly utopian and laughably naive.

Then, in the late 1960s, things began to change. Old punch lines became new slogans. By the seventies Goldman was beginning to appear back in her old haunts, up to her old tricks. Once again she could be envisioned defending herself at a conspiracy trial, going underground for a while (alias E. G. Smith), leading women strikers to a May Day rally, thumbing her nose at a congressman, defending

* © Alix Kates Shulman, 1972, 1982, 1983. Parts of this essay appeared in *Socialist Review*, No. 61 (vol 12, No. 2) March–April 1982 and, in another version, in *Red Emma Speaks*, which is to be republished by Virago, 1982 under the title, *Dancing in the Revolution: Selected Writings and Speeches of Emma Goldman*.

homosexuality and free love. The legend of Goldman was revived, even if her work remained, for the most part, ignored.

Who, then, was this woman, whose life had once been described as 'the richest of any woman's of this century', and what was her work?

Emma Goldman was born into a Jewish family of changing fortunes in czarist Russia on 27 June 1869. Her childhood seems to have served her as an object lesson in the demoralising effects of capriciously exercised authority: young Emma's sensibilities were steadily assaulted by the spectacle of wives and children being beaten, peasants whipped, pregnant girls ostracised, Jews outcast, and even the poorest peasant shaken down by an endless stream of corrupt petty officials. And in her own family her despotic father, whom she remembered as 'the nightmare of my childhood' evidently singled her out as the special object of his frequent rages, ensuring that from the very beginning her development was, as she later summed it up, 'largely in revolt'.

At 13, with her academic aspirations dashed, Emma moved with her family from the remote village of Popelan to the St Petersburg ghetto. It was 1882, Czar Alexander had been assassinated less than a year before: it was the year Russia experienced one of its worse periods of political repression.

But St Petersburg was also a city of resistance, alive with libertarian and egalitarian ideals. Forced to take a factory job, Emma began eagerly devouring the forbidden novels and tracts and began to revere some of the young revolutionary women – such as Vera Zasulich who shot the police chief and Sophia Perovskaya who conspired against the czar – and to question the accepted values of the society in which she lived.

She questioned the restricted ghetto life of her family, and the authority of her father. When he tried to marry her off at 15 she was ready to do anything to prevent it. She pleaded with him, protesting that she wanted to study and travel instead of marrying. Her father, in a characteristic rage, grabbed her French grammar and threw it in the fire: 'Girls do not have to learn much', he screamed, only how to 'prepare minced fish, cut noodles fine, and give the man plenty of children!'

She fled with her sister to America in 1886 full of golden images and dreams. Like so many other immigrants from Eastern Europe she arrived seeking freedom and opportunity and found instead repression and squalor. Ghetto and factory life in Rochester, New York were not much different from what she had left behind under the czars: making overcoats for ten hours a day and $2.50 a week, she was lonely and defeated and soon married a fellow Russian immigrant. Almost immediately the marriage disintegrated.

Her response to repression in America was much the same as it had been in Russia, the difference being that whereas in Russia she had revered the revolutionaries, in America, particularly after reading about the executions of several Chicago anarchists, she determined to become one.

She divorced her husband and, aged 20, went to New York City to begin her radical life. Her only assets were a sewing machine with which to make her way, $5 (borrowed) and a passion to join the revolutionary anarchists whose scathing tracts she had read so avidly in Rochester.

Before her first winter in New York was out, she was living in a commune with several other young Russian-born anarchists, including her first great love, Alexander Berkman, with whom her entire life would be meshed. And after only six months she set off on her first independent speaking tour with the aim of 'making revolution'. With the success of that tour Goldman launched a career which would eventually make her one of the most charismatic and volatile speakers in the history of American oratory and a forceful political leader, seeking for the 'supreme deed' which she and her fellow anarchists believed would rouse the working masses to revolution. The brutally suppressed steelworkers' strike of 1892 in Homestead, Pennsylvania seemed to present the right opportunity. The nation's attention was focused on the violence at Homestead and Emma Goldman and her two comrades thought it provided the perfect moment for the violent deed of propaganda that would, according to their anarchist theories, arouse the people against their capitalist oppressors. As their Russian idols had assassinated the czar, they would assassinate the man responsible for the bloodshed at Homestead, the chairman of the company, Henry Clay Frick.

Goldman's tasks were to raise the money for the gun and afterward to explain the deed to the world. Berkman was to pull the trigger, sacrificing his own life in the process. Desperate to get the money to buy a gun, Goldman even tried whoring, but in the end she had to borrow the money. On 23 July 1892, Berkman aimed at the tycoon's head and shot him twice before being knocked to the ground by onlookers and carried off by the police. The chairman recovered quickly which rendered Berkman's crime punishable by a maximum of seven years, but the charges against him were compounded and he was sentenced to 72 years, of which he ultimately served 14.

And Emma Goldman's task of explaining the deed to the world?

Though she applied her considerable powers of oratory to the defence of their act, the world did not want to hear: few people understood their motives, much less approved their deed.

Emma Goldman's demonic legend was launched from this time. Her own trial and conviction the following year, for delivering a speech that allegedly incited the New York unemployed to riot (though no riot occurred) was, predictably, sensational news. To a reporter Emma Goldman prophesied her one-year sentence, 'not because my offence deserves it, but because I am an anarchist'. When she emerged from prison a year later, she found herself a notorious celebrity. 'Red Emma', she was called, enemy of God, law, marriage, the state. There was no one else like her in America.

Dedication to her vision kept Goldman travelling and speaking in the succeeding years, participating in each radical crisis as it came up. Generous and loyal almost to a fault she moved back and forth across the country collecting funds and supporters for every movement cause and financing herself by odd jobs so that she could avoid charging admission to the poor whom she so desperately wanted to reach. After two trips to Europe (1895 and 1899), during which she studied nursing, contraception, and mid-wifery in Vienna, lectured in London, and attended clandestine anarchist meetings in Paris, she began to build an international reputation in revolutionary circles.

But in 1901 her public organising came to an abrupt halt. President William McKinley was assassinated by a young man who claimed to be an anarchist, and as the most notorious anarchist in America, Goldman was immediately arrested as an accomplice – despite the fact that she was in no way connected with the deed and had even reached the conviction that such actions of terror could no longer be condoned. She was jailed, but released for lack of evidence; however there was such an avalanche of public wrath against anarchism that she was forced to go underground and it was several years before she could again appear in public under her own name.

In 1906 she returned to full public life as the publisher of a new radical monthly, *Mother Earth*, which would flourish for ten years. In 1910 she published her book *Anarchism and Other Essays*, which contained articles on anarchism, education, prisons, political violence, and five pieces on the oppression of women, always one of her major concerns. Despite her swing to print she continued to lecture, and, combative by nature, she presented the most provocative topics in the most dangerous places, thus feeding her legend. She talked of free love to puritans, atheism to churchmen, revolution to reformers; she denounced the ballot to suffragists, patriotism to soldiers and patriots. 'The more opposition I encountered,' she boasted, 'the more I was in my element.' With her libertarian vision always hovering just before her eyes, she was impatient of compromise and intolerant of any hint of equivocation.

Finally in 1917, her habit of opposition went too far. For setting up No-Conscription Leagues and organising anti-war rallies all over the East even after the United States had entered the war, she and Berkman were arrested and charged with 'conspiracy' to obstruct the draft, and they were deported to Russia. About to leave New York harbour, Goldman made a final statement to the American press: 'I consider it an honour to be the first political agitator deported from the United States.'

Goldman fully expected to find in Russia the revolution of her dreams and she was prepared to switch her enormous energies from opposing the institutions of society to supporting them. But almost from the beginning she found herself again in opposition, and her travels with Berkman, across Russia, were an experience of steady, agonising disillusionment. The two anarchists applied for passports to leave Russia. In 1921, 'desolate and denuded of dreams' they went into an exile that led them on a succession of temporary visas all over Europe. Eventually Berkman settled in France and Goldman in England where she earned a meagre living by writing and lecturing, either unheeded or hated by the left for criticising the Bolshevik regime. Not even the brief success of her lucid autobiography, *Living My Life*, could renew her reputation. But ever political, she continued to work and write, issuing early warnngs about fascism and even, when armed resistance to fascism broke out in Spain, rushing off to join the Spanish anarchists for whom she served as propaganda minister. She died of a stroke in 1940 in Canada, where she had gone to raise funds for the Spanish cause, still fighting at the age of seventy.

Attempting to separate Emma Goldman's ideas from her deeds is a futile task, for in her the two were inextricably linked. 'Revolution is but thought carried into action,' she wrote in her essay 'Anarchism'. She was critical of 'philosophical anarchists' and unlike many other radicals who, in the pages of leftist journals, argued endlessly over the niceties of 'correct' interpretation of events, Goldman showed at all times her determination to *do* something about them. As both an anarchist and feminist she always tried to make the revolution by inventing new ways to carry her thought into action.

Still, in her writings, as well as in some of her more imaginative actions, she did make important contributions to anarchist theory, most distinctively by her constant insistence that sexual oppression is as important as class oppression in causing human suffering, and limiting human freedom. In her analysis of society, she differed from most male anarchist intellectuals, who may have routinely acknowledged the 'Woman Question', but did not understand its pervasive and devastating effects and were themselves often blindly sexist in their dealings with women. One wonders if it is perhaps for this reason that even among anarchists Goldman is remembered hardly as a political thinker at all, despite her body of writings and her important intellectual services as an editor and lecturer. (It was she who, for example, spread the works of Ibsen and certain ideas of Freud among American audiences.) There is little doubt that since the resurgence of feminism in recent decades Goldman has returned to public consciousness as a colourful personality, but her distinctive contribution to social analysis – her expansive feminist brand of anarchism, her libertarian brand of feminism – has usually been overlooked or dismissed, both in her time and ours, even by feminists. Those who would dismiss her ideas have had ready reasons. That the movement to which she devoted her life was not the woman's movement but the anarchist movement, no less sexist than other male-dominated movements of her time, supplied motives for both anarchists and feminists to ignore her thought. Her own dismissal of the women's suffrage campaign and her bitter opposition to the social purity doctrines that inspired many feminist reformers, led her to reject for herself the label 'feminist', as it led some feminists to denounce her as 'an enemy of women's freedom' and 'a man's woman'. Nevertheless, I would like to argue that within the context of her life and work Emma Goldman was actually one of the most radical and advanced feminists of her era.

To understand Goldman's thought we must understand that feminism is not a monolith. There are and always have been different strands of feminist politics: economic issues, issues of sex and the family, legal and constitutional issues, woman-centredness; and these strands aggregate in different patterns of overlap and exclusion, depending on the time and place and the individuals who embrace them. In Emma Goldman's time there were diverse forms of feminism as there are today, with the sprawling women's movement including a myriad of tendencies, including bourgeois feminism, the women's trade union movement, reform feminism or what has been referred to as social feminism,[2] the women's club movement among others. There was the feminism that centred around social purity and there was radical feminism, a tendency surviving from an earlier time and which based its analysis of gender divisions on a radical critique of the family and often embraced the sexual radicalism of the birth control and 'free motherhood' movements.

Where did Emma Goldman's thought fit into this complex (and perhaps divisive) picture? First and most important it seems to me she was a sexual radical when it came to women. She recognised issues of sexuality and the family as absolutely basic to women's oppression. Not only economic factors, but socio-sexual issues like sexual repression, enforced childbearing, marriage, and the nature of the patriarchal family caused women's restricted life. While her contemporaries were stressing the legal and economic barriers to women's freedom, Emma Goldman was denouncing what she called the 'internal tyrants' that thwart and cripple women. Throughout her two volume autobiography runs the steady narrative of the injuries dealt her as a woman, by anarchists and others alike. She felt that almost every man she lived with tried in some way to inhibit her activities as unsuitable to her sex: they treated her – even her! – as, in her words, 'a mere female'. In speech after speech, essay after essay, she made clear that women's oppression was distinct from men's oppression[3], that some of the restrictions on women's liberty had different causes and consequences than the restrictions on men's liberty: women, she argued were oppressed precisely as *women*, in addition to whatever they suffered as citizens, workers or from poverty.

Professional women, 'emancipated' women, prostitutes and wives alike were all in Goldman's view victims of these forces. Even at the workplace she identified women's specific oppression as women and in the framework which we would now label sexual harassment she said, 'Nowhere is woman treated according to the merit of her work, but rather as a sex. It is therefore almost inevitable that she should pay for her right to exist, to keep a position in whatever line, with sexual favours' (1979, pp 164–65).

As an anarchist, naturally Goldman identified the state with its laws and the church with its morality as agents of women's oppression, but she never doubted that sexual and reproductive matters were at the very heart of women's position in society. To my mind, this uncomprising sexual radicalism, on which Emma Goldman acted repeatedly throughout her life, makes her an indisputable radical feminist, worthy of recognition. Her position went beyond the sexual radicalism of the bohemian women of her day who practised free love in Greenwich Village, for unlike them Emma Goldman was always political, trying to change the social structures that restricted women instead of simply changing her own life.

Emma Goldman's major anti-feminist stand, her detractors charge, was her opposition to women's suffrage. How shall we understand this? By her time the US suffrage movement was predominantly a middle-class movement, at least one great branch of which was deeply conservative, puritanical, even racist, going so far as to propose literacy tests to keep immigrants and other poor disenfranchised. For Emma Goldman, whose life had been spent in the struggle of workers and the poor, such a movement would have to be suspect. Further, as an anarchist who opposed government in all its forms, whether elected or not, who considered all government corrupt and the state the major agent of oppression, she thought the struggle for the vote a diversion from women's real struggle and opposed it.

To Goldman it was obvious that suffrage could not do what many believed it would do. It wouldn't change women's oppression and it certainly wouldn't bring a refining or purifying element into politics. 'To assume that [woman] would succeed in purifying something which is not susceptible of purification is to credit her with supernatural powers,' wrote Goldman (1969 p 198). At best, the vote would be irrelevant for women.

Like Matilda Joslyn Gage, Emma Goldman saw the suffrage movement – which had initially been radical but had become conservative with time and the entry of such women as Frances Willard – not as a movement of liberation but as a movement towards conformism. Many of the suffragists wanted the vote, argued Goldman, in order to make woman 'a better Christian and homemaker and citizen of the state – the very Gods that woman has served from time immemorial' (1969, p 197).

Goldman's prediction of how little benefit women would actually gain from the vote has turned out to be accurate, even to this day.

One of the main problems I see in Goldman's analysis is the credibility given to 'will' in much anarchist theory, so that a failure to change can be seen as a failure of individual will. Thus Emma Goldman sometimes seems to blame women, the victims, for their own oppression, and to attribute the absence of change in women's lives to the women themselves. Given the way Goldman changed her own life this short-sightedness is perhaps understandable.

Emma Goldman did not always identify with women in their struggles, especially middle-class women and especially wives (given her own great hostility to marriage). In her writings, as in her life, there is a peculiar mix of understanding and blame. To her the solution was in defiance and rebellion, in free love, free motherhood, without the sanction of church or state as she herself had lived. At times she almost seems to say if you suffer in marriage, then you shouldn't have married: leave your husband and be free. It was this unfeeling attitude that must have both shocked and angered many feminists, even other women anarchists. Even Voltairine de Cleyre, Goldman's anarchist comrade, responded angrily to the explanation of women's opression as a failure of will:

> It has often been said to me, by women with decent masters, who had no idea of the outrages practised on their less fortunate sisters, 'Why don't the wives leave?' Why don't you run when your feet are chained together? Why don't you raise your hands above your head when they are pinned fast to your sides? Why don't you spend thousands of dollars when you haven't a cent in your pocket? Why don't you go to the seashore or the mountains, you fools scorching with city heat? If there is one thing more than another in this whole accursed tissue of false society which makes me angry, it is the asinine stupidity which with the true phlegm of impenetrable dullness says, 'Why don't the women leave?' Will you tell me where they will go and what they shall do? When the state, the legislature/legislators, has given to itself, the politicians, the utter and absolute control of the opportunity to live; when through this precious monopoly, already the market of labour is so overstocked that workmen and workwomen are cutting each others' throats for the dear privilege of serving their lords; when . . . seeing and hearing these things reported every day, the proper prudes exclaim, 'why don't the women leave?' They simply beggar the language of contempt . . . There is no society for the prevention of cruelty to women. (1914, pp 351–52)[4]

If Emma Goldman was impatient with middle-class and married women she did identify strongly with the needs and desires of the working-class women she helped to organise. As a trade union organiser in the tradition of bread and roses, she insisted that women ought to earn enough money so that they might be more than mere drudges, so that they might have some pleasures in life – roses, books, occasional tickets to the theatre, and of course, romantic love. Even as a young revolutionary Goldman had demanded pleasures in life: when her male comrades disapproved of her love of dancing as a frivolity unworthy of a revolutionary, she grew incensed and retorted that a revolution without dancing was not worth fighting for.

Nor did Goldman have trouble identifying with the women she met in prison, with the ghetto women she counselled on birth control as a midwife, or with the despised prostitutes. With these victims, her understanding of their plight was large, her sympathy generous. That she could not so readily identify with middle-class wives, especially those who felt personally threatened by her views, was, I think, less a failure of her feminism, than it was a function of an ordinary failure of imagination.

Insofar as feminism is more than simply a movement to help women under capitalism get ahead, Goldman's anarchism worked for, and not against her feminism. Anarchism, by definition, and radical feminism as it has evolved, share many premises, for both are fundamentally anti-hierarchical and anti-authoritarian. Both operate through loose, voluntary social organisation from the bottom up, relying on collective activity by small groups: both favour direct action to promote change. As the anarcho-feminist Lynn Farrow wrote a few years ago, 'Feminism practises what anarchism preaches.'

Emma Goldman's vision of the world was one in which everyone would be free and she was prepared to fight for the realisation of this vision. Her main quarrel with her own contemporaries was, I think, that she steadfastly refused to see women as inherently better or worse than men. If male egotism, vanity and strength operated to enslave women, it was partly, she argued, because women idolised those qualities in men, creating a self-perpetuating system. In the tradition of a long line of women from Mary Astell and Mary Wollstonecraft through to Frances Wright, Harriet Taylor, Margaret Fuller, Elizabeth Cady Stanton and Matilda Joslyn Gage, Emma Goldman argued that when women changed their consciousness, broke that circle, and freed themselves from such ill-suited ideals, they might not only liberate themselves but might also 'incidentally' help men to become free. But it was up to women to make their own revolution.

Goldman's line here between blaming the victim and recognising the necessity for a new consciousness is thin but crucial. In one of her most frequently quoted remarks – which has often been invoked in the name of consciousness raising and even of the women's liberation movement itself – she insists on complexity and struggle:

True emancipation begins neither at the polls or in the courts. It begins in woman's soul. History tells us that every oppressed class gained true liberation from its masters through its own efforts. It is necessary that woman learn that lesson, that she realise that her freedom will reach as far as her power to achieve freedom reaches. (Goldman, 1979, p 142)

That women were no better than men meant to Emma Goldman that women should stop trying to change (or purify) men and should start taking responsibility for their own lives and their own struggle in the quest for self-determination, in the quest for 'being considered human'. This was the essence of Emma Goldman's vision.

As is customary with most strong public women, Emma Goldman's life and work have been alternately ignored, distorted, maligned. Her strong infusion of radical feminism into anarchist theory has not received the serious treatment it deserves. In fact, Goldman has even been unfairly claimed by some radicals to belong to the anti-feminist camp. This is a gross misrepresentation of her thought. The most frequently invoked popular image of her portrays her as a joke, somewhere between a wild libertine and a bomb-throwing fanatic – perverted distortions of her undoubted strengths, vision, tenacity, integrity. Such assessments not only devalue her work but push her toward the periphery of history where neglect and then obscurity can imperceptibly enclose her.

There is only one sure antidote to neglect and misrepresentation: it is of course to study the life and work first hand and form one's own judgments. In the case of Emma Goldman, such study can be richly rewarding, for she has left behind an engrossing record of a full and vivacious life. If you are attentive, you will hear her yourself stumping for free speech, rising to the defence of prostitutes, rousing workers to organise; you will admire her courtroom performance, see her booed without flinching; you will be able to cheer her as she thumbs her nose at a congressman.

Notes

1   See Elizabeth Sarah's chapter on Christabel Pankhurst for an analysis of the rise of the word *Queen* in relation to active and protesting women.
2   For further discussion of social feminism see Naomi Black's chapter on Virginia Woolf.
3   For further discussion see Dale Spender, 1982 (b): Margaret Stacey and Marion Price (1981) also discuss the way in which nothing else changed when women got the vote.
4   For further discussion of Voltairine de Cleyre see Margaret Marsh, 1981.

Olive Schreiner: New Women, Free Women, All Women
(1855–1920)

Liz Stanley

Ruth First was assassinated by letter bomb on 17 September 1982 in Maputo, Mozambique, supposedly by 'persons unknown' but almost certainly by the South African security services. Her life is an example to us, for it shows us that whatever divisions exist within feminism are as nothing compared with what binds and unites us.

Her writings, such as The Barrel of a Gun, 117 Days *and* The South African Connection, *provide an overview of African politics and political movements that marks her as a direct successor of Olive Schreiner. These two women, both properly claimed as feminists, both passionate socialists, both concerned to live, to practise, their convictions and not just to preach them, so clearly show the power, insightfulness and humanity of feminism in action. It is altogether fitting, then, that Olive Schreiner's most comprehensive biography should have been co-authored by Ruth First.*

Perhaps Ruth First's greatest gift to feminism and to the African liberation movements she was for so many years involved in, lies in her refusal to divide, to dichotomise, and her insistence on the unification of theory, research and experience. Feminism has preached this unity for many years now; Ruth First lived it. Living feminism isn't easy, but it is politically effective. And her death shows us in terrifying simplicity what is likely to be the consequence of effectiveness. Oppressors do not give up their power readily. They use any and every means to keep it, from letter bombs to lynchings to rapes to sexist stereotypes and assumptions; and we forget this at our peril.

Olive Schreiner was a woman who aroused, and indeed still arouses, powerful emotional reponses in other people. Sometimes these responses are negative, sometimes positive, and frequently are aroused in the same person at the same time. She was for a number of years the central figure in Havelock Ellis's life (1859–1939); yet she moved from house to house, from town to town and then from continent to continent in a bewildering and incomprehensible way. For Eleanor Marx (1855–98) she was a deeply and dearly loved passionate friend, the strongest person she knew and the person she most relied on to provide an outlet for her feelings about her lover Edward Aveling's sexual and other misdemeanours; yet she knew that Olive Schreiner despised male sexual incontinence and saw relationships such as theirs as a fundamental feature of women's oppression. Edward Carpenter (1844–1928) experienced her as merry, laughing and playful; yet recognised that beneath this there was an intensely determined personality marked by an ineradicable pessimism, a pessimism of tragic proportions because her feminist analysis uncovered so much to be pessimistic about. To Samuel 'Cron' Cronwright-Schreiner (1863–?), whom she married, she was a bewildering genius; but one who failed to write, publish or produce much material evidence of this because she strayed from the quiet room, sharpened pens and pencils, that he so carefully prepared for her,and his loving admonitions to write.

Such complicated reactions continue still. For Yvonne Kapp, Eleanor Marx's biographer, Olive Schreiner is an over-wrought neurotic who enveloped Eleanor Marx and reduced her to a sub-servient and emotionally-bound subject, and who reacted to the news of Eleanor's suicide with a prurient and unhealthy interest in the details of her death. Olive Schreiner's most recent biographers, Ruth First and Ann Scott,[1] point out her determination, energy and enthusiasm, her pioneering writings and her still insightful analyses; and yet connect these with a psychoanalytic interpretation of a damaged childhood leading to adult neurosis displayed in psycho-somatic illness. One earlier biographer, Marion Friedman, indeed sees her writings as the working-out of emotional problems by a woman damaged beyond repair by her childhood experiences.

That Olive Schreiner should arouse this curious and sometimes contradictory array of emotional feelings and responses is, however, not surprising. This is how we react and relate to real people in our everyday experience of them; and even a 100 years removed from her, and reached only through biographies, autobiographies, remi-niscences, letters and published works, Olive Schreiner appears absolutely and tremendously real. Her short and dumpy physical appearance, her frenetic manner of talking, her restless energy, her frequently sardonic comments on other people, on religion and on politics, all impress her on one's mind as a woman with an immensely vivid personality. She spoke her mind, and in all circumstances. Not for her the 'typically Victorian' deference to men – she argued, shouted them down, sneered at them, interrupted them and mocked them.

But there are additional reasons for such reactions to her. Olive Schreiner's life and her feminism are related in what are, to those of us involved in our own contemporary feminist movement, extraordinarily familiar ways. For Olive Schreiner, as much as for any feminist now, 'the personal is the political'. Olive Schreiner simply didn't recognise any hard and fast distinction between life and politics, between life and writing, or between politics and writing. What she wrote she tried her best to live. Frequently she failed, but her 'failure' was as interesting as any more ordinary 'success' would have been. Frequently hurt, even more frequently disappointed (usually by herself rather than by others), Olive Schreiner never considered removing herself from situations in which these disappointments were bound to occur. She believed that there was no alternative to trying to make life better for women, all women, no matter what the personal cost to herself.

The links between her writing and her life are important, so important that neither makes complete sense without a consideration of the other. Some of her writings were unpublished in her lifetime and remain unfinished. What is now published makes an impressive collection,[2] although one not easily understood and interpreted if viewed through the political frameworks, understandings and preoccupations of our time. To appreciate exactly how startling, how daring and how insightful she was we must resist temporal chauvinism and evaluate her only within her own time and among her own contemporaries. Doing this, my own conclusion is that her life and work are of immense significance within the social history of her time, and that even now there is a very great deal that we can learn from her.

Her socialism was not of the variety familiar to us now; it was rooted in an absolute conviction that 'socialism' meant living the new life, not waiting for someone or something else to bring it into existence through institutional and structural change. In this, of course, she was not on her own. Her political beliefs were given concrete expression through her association with a variety of socialist groups in London and elsewhere in the 1880s and the nexus of relationships which arose out of this, including and most importantly with Eleanor Marx, Edward Carpenter and Havelock Ellis. Her feminism was of the same variety. Her intellectual interpretation of 'the woman question' was that its origins were complex, that women's oppressive situation was most obviously experienced in relationships, and that both men and women were instrumental in this aspect of its perpetuation. Frequently harshly critical of men's behaviours and deeply bitter about their reactions to women's attempts to change their situation, nevertheless Olive Schreiner believed that much of the answer to the problem lay in the hearts, minds and behaviours of women themselves. That is, she believed that feminism was at least as much a matter of personal change consciously embarked upon as it was a matter of institutional or structural change. Olive Schreiner produced one of the most accurate and devastating analyses of racism in her account of its effects on white colonialists themselves. She also retained a patronising adherence to racist stereotypes and liberal pronouncements on questions of race in South Africa. However, this later changed to a position of uncompromising radicalism in which she must be seen as the person who produced the sharpest-eyed contemporary assessment of questions of race at a time when few other feminists or indeed few socialists in Britian did anything other than unquestioningly accept the existing relationship between Britain and its colonies.

Because of all these things I find Olive Schreiner the most fascinating theorist of the last feminist renaissance because she evades all simple assessments, neat categorisations and easy summings-up. She was undoubtedly contradictory, annoying, argumentative, domineering, infuriating, powerful, bitter, insightful – and absolutely her own woman. Therein lies her fascination; it also makes her a very difficult person indeed to write short introductory essays about!

Her Life: a Very Brief Chronology

Olive Schreiner was born on 24 March 1855 in the Cape Colony of South Africa, to missionary parents. At a very early age her humanistic interpretation of Christianity brought her into conflict with her family; and this later became a socialist and progressive freethinking. Between 1872 and 1873 she lived with a brother and sister at New Rush (later Kimberley) and began the writing that was to become her three novels, *Undine, The Story of an African Farm* and *From Man to Man.* Between 1874 and 1881 she was a governess in various places throughout the Cape Colony, continued working on the manuscripts begun at New Rush, and saved up money to pay for her trip to Britain. At this time she intended a medical career for herself.

She came to Britain in 1881 and remained until the end of 1889. Failing in her medical ambitions she was persuaded, if persuasion was necessary, that a literary career was what she was most suited to. By 1883 *The Story of An African Farm* had been published and had attracted a spectacular set of reviews. From its publication came not only some financial security but also some of the most important relationships she was to have.

Edward Aveling reviewed *The Story* in the socialist press and linked it to an explicitly socialist framework. It was probably through this that her original meeting with Eleanor Marx came about. Soon they were on the very closest terms, remained in frequent and loving contact until Olive Schreiner left England in 1889; and they probably corresponded as eagerly as ever until Eleanor's suicide in 1898.[3] In 1884 Havelock Ellis, casually coming across the book, wrote to express his critical yet empathetic admiration for it. After some correspondence they met and swiftly became each other's closest companion for the next few years, although they never became lovers in any conventional sense. Through Ellis she came into contact with the Progressive Association and the Fellowship of the New Life and struck up a lasting friendship with Edward Carpenter, soon to leave London for his own socialist new life at Millthorpe, near Sheffield. Out of her involvement in the Fellowship, and her constant reiteration there of what was known as 'Olive's subject' – women's oppression and women's liberation – came the foundation of the Men and Women's Club in 1885. Through this she became involved in a serious academic analysis of what for others was the 'women's situation'; but for her the 'problem of women' was then and always the 'problem of men' too. A key figure in the Club was Karl Pearson, later involved in the eugenics movement and a jingoistic supporter of empire, but at this time still a socialist radical. She embarked upon a piece of work which was to have been her magnum opus on women's situation, but which was destroyed later during the Boer War.[4] Her relationship with Pearson was intellectual only for him, more complexly involved for her. Its breakup in 1886 occasioned a breakdown for her, which she dealt with by leaving for South Africa in 1889.

There she arranged for Ellis to deal with the publication of her first book of allegories, *Dreams*, and was still completing some of those published after her death in *Stories, Dreams and Allegories*. She wrote, between 1890 and 1892, the essays later published as *Thoughts on South Africa*. She met, liked and politically despised Cecil Rhodes, who was equally impressed by her. She met Samuel Cronwright in 1892, just before returning to England again for a brief few months in 1893. On her return they married early in 1894. She gave birth to a baby in 1895; it lived only a few hours and she never got over its death.

In the period immediately before the Boer War Olive Schreiner wrote 'The Political Situation', a pamphlet which exposed the role of monopolistic capitalism in South Africa, and emphasised that political repression was a necessary and inevitable result of capitalistic exploitation.

She then wrote her extended anti-war allegory *Trooper Peter Halket of Mashonaland*, published early in 1887 and an immediate bestseller. This was followed up by *An English South African's View of the Situation*, which warns that any war would be a hard and difficult one. During the period of the Boer War, while living under strict martial law, she rewrote some of the destroyed text of her magnum opus on women, published in 1911 as *Woman and Labour,* and some additional allegories.

After the Boer War Olive Schreiner's relationship with Cronwright changed, so that they increasingly spent long periods living apart, apparently amicably and without any signs of regret on either part. By this time the 'flawed nature' of her genius had become apparent to him. Her earlier analysis of women's oppression as a condition of women's sexual, emotional and economic dependence on men, reasserted itself and she, quite simply, removed herself from the conditions of such dependence. In political terms she became increasingly preoccupied with the question of the South African franchise as the focus of attempts to challenge racism and sexism. She never saw this as an end in itself but instead saw political organisation around it as a means to gain political and agitational skills and to develop a more radical analysis.

In 1913 increasing ill-health led her to leave South Africa for England, en route for Italy for treatment. The outbreak of the First World War, however, meant that she spent its duration in England. Remaining close to Ellis and Carpenter during the period of the war, she was nevertheless appalled at what she saw as their hypocrisy and betrayal of political principles in departing from a pacificist stance which condemned all militarism. The only feminist she retained any respect for by the end of the war was Sylvia Pankhurst, for much the same reasons.

Early in 1920 Cronwright came to London, not long before her planned departure for South Africa. The outward appearances were maintained; inwardly the relationship was marked by all the conflicts which might be expected in a marriage between such a keen observer of male sexual oppressiveness as Olive Schreiner and such an insensitive man as Cronwright. Her plans remained unchanged by his arrival. Back in South Africa she sorted out her papers, arranged for a post mortem, completed the arrangements for her burial and waited for death. It came, quickly and obediently, and absolutely painlessly. She was found propped up in bed, her reading glasses still on, a book in her hands, and the candle burnt down, in the early morning of 11 December 1920.

Her Major Contributions to Feminist Theory
The bibliography of Olive Schreiner's works at the end of this essay shows the scope of these and hopefully gives some indication of how difficult it is to reduce down the main themes she dealt with. Necessity being the mother of invention, I have decided against reviewing each of the major forms she wrote in – her novels, her allegories, her essays, and *Woman and Labour* – in favour of a more eclectic approach. An additional reason is that Olive Schreiner herself most certainly wouldn't have thanked me for carving her work up into 'forms she wrote in'. She saw everything she did, whether live, write, speak, love or agitate, as absolutely political and totally interconnected. She simply failed to recognise boundaries in the way that people did then and do now. This is important to grasp and keep clearly in mind, because without grasping it her life becomes a series of failures, her writings unsatisfactory, her beliefs and attitudes inexplicable. It is the key to recognising her unique contribution to radical politics of her time, as a woman who overturned all the dichotomies, divisions, distinctions, which are the hallmark of sexist society of her time and ours.

'The Personal is the Political'
Olive Schreiner saw her life as a means of giving expression to her beliefs, beliefs which were also the foundation of her writings. For her, socialism wasn't a purely economic change achieved by institutional revolution but a way of living and conducting loving relationships with all manner of people. And her feminism wasn't a future utopia achieved through conventional revolutionary means but one brought into an existence beginning now, by women effecting many small and apparently insignificant changes in their lives.

She saw relationships as immensely political. For Olive Schreiner, they were the expression of the social structures of oppression within everyday life. In particular, she analysed marriage as a form of legalised prostitution in which the economic and emotional dependence of women on men was institutionalised and justified in a sexual form. She analysed prostitution outside of marriage in similar terms. She argued that women's oppression should be seen as *sexual* politics, because its essence lay in the sexual relationships of women to men. However, in her work we find no simple onslaught against men as the totally culpable causal factor in this oppression. She emphasised that this relationship is no simple one, because the bonds between women and men are often loving ones. She was also very aware that there are loving bonds enforced by women on themselves and other women, bonds which help to hide women's oppression from view, which cushion its impact, and which help to confine women even more than is necessary. Sexism, then, Olive Schreiner argued, influences and constrains all relationships, not just those between women and men.

Perhaps the key feature of her analysis is her emphasis on the absolute necessity for a holistic approach. For her there was an essential unity of 'the political' with all other aspects of life – it was not just institutions and not just relationships, but both. Both are to be analysed together; and both must be totally changed. She also discerned an essential unity between life and death, rejecting any sharp distinction between them or any idea that one should be seen as the antithesis of the other. Her ideas about death were complex. She saw death and other analagous states as involving an end to women's and all other oppressions; and saw the act of dying as a transition into a state of being which involved liberty, equality and freedom. But this was no Christian heaven or any conventional form of 'afterlife'; it was rather her interpretation of what 'unity' meant. She saw the trance-like states in which she wrote her allegories, and 'separatist' lives in which women removed themselves from all forms of dependence on men and used their energies in service for others, as analogous to death because they removed women from those relationships and structures crucial to women's oppression. She saw childhood in analagous terms too, because the interests of children are in fundamental opposition to the adult world of power, authority and punishment. This analysis too she attempted to integrate within her life and relationships, in particular by trying to establish child-like (not childish) relationships with men she loved. Doing so with Havelock Ellis has lent fuel to the flames of psychoanalytic ideas about her 'immaturity'. Doubtless Cronwright found it equally threatening.

This holistic approach is continued in Olive Schreiner's rejection of attempts to draw clear distinctions between her novels and allegories, and her 'political' writings. For her, all of her writings were political, because all of them deal with the same fundamental themes. These include women's oppression and the sufferings entailed within this; the relationship between women and men, and between women and women, in sexist society; and sexism as something which affects all aspects of life, including those not apparently connected. All of her writings deal with personal life in sexist society. This she took as not only her theme but also her approach to its analysis. This approach was what she called 'the method of life'. It involved her in confronting life as it truly is – as eventful, complex, contradictory, surprising and, except in a superficial and general sense, absolutely unpredictable. It was and is revolutionary, not only because it led her into working with experimental form and content of her allegories, but also because she applied the lessons learned there within her more conventionally analytic work. Olive Schreiner was never led into the seductive path of searching for one cause of women's oppression; nor was she ever led into locating blame for this oppression in any one section of the population nor any one facet of social behaviour. Olive Schreiner believed the problem was not a simple one; therefore it was unrealistic to expect there to be any simple answer to it.

New Life, New Women, Free Women
Lyndall in *The Story* glimpsed the possibility of a new life for women, and for herself in particular; and in that possibility lay her analysis of the conditions of the old. Relationships and the conditions under which they were conducted formed the key to both. In spite of this, Lyndall's rebellion is one doomed to failure, not because there was anything wrong with her analysis but because she is essentially alone. Rejecting dependence of any kind on men, there is nothing she can do with her passionate convictions, her insights and her over-whelming sense of unity within the universe. Olive Schreiner's analysis, in sharp distinction, placed her very firmly in company with all other women, as the allegories 'Three dreams in a desert' and 'I thought I stood' make clear with their message that liberation can't be achieved for one woman only.

'New women' was the phrase that Olive Schreiner used to describe women who had already effected some change away from sex-parasitism (battening on surplus produced by others) and who were working towards the possibility of a new life of equality. But the 'new life' she so conceptualised was in a sense achievable in the here and now, because she insisted that some of the facets of oppression can be changed, or such a change at least attempted. The important thing for her was the attempt, as the second dream in 'Three dreams' says, and not success narrowly defined. The attempt is a beginning, and beginnings make things easier for all women who come after. It is in this light, of course, that we should evaluate Olive Schreiner's own life and work. She attempted a very great deal indeed. That she didn't entirely succeed, and that aspects of her life can be seen as contradictory, her analysis partial and her insights not those of our own time, is neither surprising nor to be seen as constituting any kind of failure.

Free Women, All Women

One aspect of her writings, perhaps more than any other, demonstrates the contradictions just mentioned. This concerns race and racism or, as she would have phrased it, 'the Native Question'. Certainly her early essays on South Africa are almost uncritically laudatory of Boer society and explain away, as bound to change, its religious bigotry, narrow-minded inwardlooking, and its total lack of any consideration for black Africans as truly human. This should be remembered, but so should two other things. One is that her analysis changed, and changed rapidly over a comparatively short period of time, from patronising liberalism to support for revolutionary movements. It involved her in a determined stand against anti-Semitism, against the exploitation of all non-white peoples, and against the actions of South African feminists in excluding black women from their suffrage demands. The other is that over a period of time, from the writing of 'I thought I stood' in 1889, to the point where she left the Women's Enfranchisement League in 1910 or 1911 and angrily scrawled on its leaflet 'The women of the Cape Colony – *all* women of the Cape Colony', Olive Schreiner learned to practise the lesson she had earlier spelt out. This is that all women must stand together, for no woman can stand alone; and that unless all women are free no woman can be free. Let us hope that we learn it as well as she did.

Why the Current Neglect?

Before beginning work in order to write this essay I had read a great deal *about* Olive Schreiner in secondary sources of various kinds, including those by contemporaries such as Ellis and Carpenter. From these I gained the very definite feeling that she was an interesting woman who made a lasting impression on people around her and on the feminist and socialist politics of her time. Having now read a great deal *by* Olive Schreiner, I am struck by the great breadth and scope of her writings and the impact these made at the time of their original publication. Olive Schreiner was no mere friend of the political and literary great – in many ways she was foremost among them. Her work was immensely important because it reached such a wide audience. This includes not only the apparently straightforward novel *The Story* but also the allegories in *Dreams* and in *Dream Life and Real Life,* while the first edition of *Trooper Peter* sold out within weeks of its publication and *Woman and Labour* was seen as the most influential piece of feminist writing of its time.

It is quite clear, then, that Olive Schreiner was one of the most important and influential feminist writers of the late nineteenth and early twentieth centuries. She came to feminism and socialism through ideas about the 'new life', a political style in which rhetoric and personal life were seen as necessarily complementary. That is, Olive Schreiner lived her politics as well as wrote and spoke them. Moreover, her politics were such that there were few facets of life which escaped her attention – prostitution, the domestic details of Boer homestead life, international capital and racism, the domestic division of labour, women's sexual oppression, childhood and service to others, death and life, friendship and love between women. And as a thread running through all of these, is the insistence that social systems and institutions can and must be seen through 'the method of life', through examining the details of everyday life and the relationships therein. But Olive Schreiner is now almost completely unknown outside a small and limited circle; and even within this she is known primarily for *The Story.* This therefore seems all the more extraordinary when set against her contemporary significance.

Much of Olive Schreiner's now-published work wasn't published while she was alive. *Undine, From Man to Man, Stories, Dreams and Allegories* and the collected edition of *Thoughts on South Africa* were all published after her death, along with *The Letters of Olive Schreiner* and *The Life of Olive Schreiner.* Therefore it might be argued that its scope wasn't apparent until comparatively recently. However, in her lifetime *The Story, Dreams, Dream Life and Real Life, Trooper Peter* and *Woman and Labour* were all published, sold rapidly and went through numerous editions. The scope and importance of her work was absolutely apparent to her contemporaries and this suggested reason for its neglect must be seen as specious.

Olive Schreiner lived a largely peripatetic life, moving backwards and forwards between continents and within whatever area she was 'settled' in. It could be argued that some aspects of her analysis were derived from one context and applied inappropriately to another. The major evidence for this argument concerns *Women and Labour,* in which the charge of sex-parasitism was levelled at women at precisely a time when ever more European and American women were engaged in the labour force. It has been suggested, therefore, that sex-parasitism characterised only a very small number of women, principally middle-class and aristocratic women. The notion of sex-parasitism, the argument continues, is rather an analysis of the situation of white women other than Boer Women in South Africa. All white women existed in the state of sex-parasitism there at least until the 1940s, when Doris Lessing described precisely the same phenomenon in *A Proper Marriage* (1975). However, Olive Schreiner's introductory remarks in *Woman and Labour* make it absolutely clear and unmistakable, one might think, that she is very much aware of women's increasing participation in all sections of the labour force in Britain and elsewhere. What she is doing in *Woman and Labour,* as in her allegories, is to isolate key issues, ideas, phenomena, the better to analyse them and thus to become aware of their likely future consequences. Sex-parasitism she knew was a minority condition; its significance she believed was immense. This argument is thus one which can be sustained only by ignoring what she wrote about her work; and it too must be rejected.

Olive Schreiner's work has been described as quintessentially Victorian, a strange description when applied to a woman who in her time was seen as a radical, and a dangerous radical at that. Nevertheless, there are aspects of her style of writing which, superficially, lend credence to such an interpretation. Much of it is not only frankly polemical, it is also outspokenly didactic in character and deliberately and wholeheartedly preaches a message. This overt 'preaching' occurs in the allegories within the novels, with their fairly straightforward moral messages, but also within set-piece speeches given by various characters. Thus Lyndall's discourse on women's oppression to Em and to Waldo in *The Story*; and much of *From Man To Man* is made up of written discourses on similar themes by Rebekah. Another aspect of her style concerns the allegories, both those in the novels and also the collections and the novel-allegory *Trooper Peter.* These are often interpreted as religious in content and tone in an embarassingly naked way and thus as another form of preaching.

At least some aspects of Olive Schreiner's style must indeed seem problematic to people reared on a diet of materialism, particularly an interpretation of materialism which excludes from it dreams, parables, fantasies and the like. Her 'method of life' sees all aspects of the human condition as materially based, if 'materially' isn't interpreted in any narrow fashion. In this she is in good company of course, for the company includes Karl Marx and Eleanor Marx among others. In some ways her work prefigures that of Virginia Woolf; and a comparison of Schreiner's allegories with Woolf's *The Waves* (1931) throws light on both the radicalism of Olive Schreiner's writing and also the grounds on which it might be criticised. Like Woolf, Olive Schreiner too deals with the details of an inner world, and in the connections between an inner life and relationships with other people in everyday life. However, the style of radical politics which developed after the First World War was one which resolutely excluded all aspects of personal life from any definition of 'the political'. A consequence was that it wasn't only Olive Schreiner who went so completely out of fashion; it was also all of the other people concerned with 'new women' and the 'new life'. The new realism and materialism which replaced 'new life' politics is of course only now being seen as an integral feature of an anti-feminist backlash. As we come to re-evaluate the sexist component in this 'realism' which largely excludes women and all the realities of our daily lives, so we can now appreciate Olive Schreiner's contribution as being as remarkable as it undoubtedly was.

Following on from this, I've already pointed out that there was an unusually close relationship between Olive Schreiner's life and her work. A response to this is that there has been an equally unusual concentration on what are depicted as the problems, confusions, inadequacies and failures of her life. This I see as a key reason for the current underestimation of the scope of her work and its contemporary significance. Cronwright was first and foremost in giving voice to his perception of her inadequacies. Obviously Cronwright was no dispassionate observer, and had his own reasons for suggesting that inadequacy was her fundamental characteristic. He was but the first of many people to so portray her; Olive Schreiner has been unusually unfortunate in attracting a crop of commentators hooked on psychoanalytic frameworks of interpretation. These have focused on the ambivalent relationship between her and her parents, particularly her mother; they have pointed out the split between her intellectual attraction to men who were 'passive and effeminate' and her sexual attraction to men who were butch; they have seized eagerly on what they see as her confused and ambivalent sexuality, including what they see (and apparently disapprove of) as an unconscious lesbian attraction between her and Eleanor Marx; and all of these things have been wrapped up in a package referred to as 'Olive Schreiner's "asthmatic personality" '.

Many people have seen Olive Schreiner's work as the crutches of an emotional cripple. This must surely be belied by what we now know of her work and her life. She was a serious feminist and socialist. Within her contemporary setting this meant that she attempted to put her analysis and her ideals into practice. In trying to put feminism into practice in everyday life we become aware of the immense complexities involved in so doing. We become aware, as Olive Schreiner did, that 'oppression' can be behaviours done by people we love and respect. We become aware, as Olive Schreiner did, that 'oppression' is often to be found within us, our own thoughts and behaviours. We become aware, as Olive Schreiner did, that we are frequently attracted by things, behaviours and people which aren't politically right-on. And we also become aware, as Olive Schreiner surely did, that putting feminist beliefs into practice is, to say the least, difficult.

Edward Carpenter was right when he said that her complete feminism was Olive Schreiner's tragedy. Feminism brings with it too much understanding of suffering ever to make its proponents unreservedly happy. What Carpenter didn't add, and what most certainly needs adding, is that Olive Schreiner's feminism was also her crowning achievement because it made her aware of all human suffering. For her, awareness meant action; and so her feminism made her totally politically active in attempting to change all aspects of social life and relationships.

Notes

1   I owe a great debt to Ruth First's and Ann Scott's detailed and comprehensive biography of Olive Schreiner.
2   The published works of Olive Schreiner appear in a bibliographical note following this essay.
3   Letters sent to Eleanor Marx by Engels, Dollie Radford and Edward Aveling as well as those sent by Olive Schreiner were destroyed by Aveling after Eleanor Marx's death: Cronwright carried out a similar pruning of Olive Schreiner's letters upon her death.
4   The details of this are given in her introduction to *Woman and Labour*, 1911, 1979.

Select Bibliography of Olive Schreiner

Published works
The Story of an African Farm, Chapman and Hall, 1883; Donker, Johannesburg, 1975; Penguin, Harmondsworth, 1982.
Dreams Unwin, 1890.
Dream Life and Real Life, Unwin, 1893.
The political situation, Unwin, 1896.
Trooper Peter Halket of Mashonaland, Unwin, 1897; Donker, Johannesburg, 1974.
An English South African's View of the Situation, Hodder and Stoughton, 1899.
'A letter on the Jew', Liberman, 1906, *Letters*, app F.
Woman and Labour, Unwin, 1911, Virago, London, 1979.
Thoughts on South Africa, Unwin, 1923; Africana Book Society, Johannesburg, 1976.
Stories, Dreams and Allegories, Unwin, 1923.
From Man to Man, Unwin, 1926; Virago, London, 1982.
Undine, Benn 1929.

Other Sources

Edward Carpenter, *My Days and Dreams*, Allen and Unwin, London, 1916.
Samuel C. Cronwright-Schreiner (ed), *The Letters of Olive Schreiner*, Fisher Unwin, London, 1924.
Samuel C. Cronwright-Schreiner, *The Life of Olive Schreiner*, Haskell House, New York, 1924.
Havelock Ellis, *My Life*, Heinemann, London, 1940.
Ruth First and Ann Scott, *Olive Schreiner*, Andre Deutsch, London, 1980.
Marion Friedman, *Olive Schreiner: A Study in Latent Meanings*, Witwatersrand University Press, Johannesburg, 1955.
Phyllis Grosskurth, *Havelock Ellis*, Quartet, London, 1980.
Yvonne Kapp, *Eleanor Marx*, vol 1, Virago, London, 1972.
Yvonne Kapp, *Eleanor Marx*, vol 2, Virago, London, 1976.
Sheila Rowbotham and Jeffrey Weeks, *Socialism and the New Life*, Pluto, London, 1977.
Barbara Scott Winkler, 'Victorian Daughters: The Lives and Feminism of Charlotte Perkins Gilman and Olive Schreiner', *Michigan Occasional Papers in Women's Studies*, no. 13, 1980.

Vida Goldstein:
The Women's Candidate
(1869–1949)

Gaby Weiner

A woman without a master,
A government without a debt,
A home without a mortgage,
A party without a boss,
A people without a pauper,
A city without a slum.

So wrote Henry B. Blackwell in Vida Goldstein's notebook when she visited the United States in 1902. It aptly describes the political beliefs of one of the most important and yet most neglected of the Australian feminists, Vida Goldstein, who was influential both inside and outside government in the first decades of the twentieth century and who waged a constant war against social injustice and deprivation, particularly where it affected women and children.

Australian women gained the vote long before their American and European sisters, with whom they were in close contact and to whom they looked for leadership and inspiration. Suffrage was granted to women in South Australia in 1894, West Australia in 1899, New South Wales in 1902, Tasmania in 1903, Queensland in 1905, Victoria in 1908 and federally, in 1902. This compares favourably with the United States and Great Britain where all women did not gain the vote until 1920 and 1929 respectively.

There have been a number of social and political reasons given for the early adoption of female suffrage in Australia, many of which devalue the women and the work they did to obtain it: that since white Australian society was itself in the process of formation there were few established institutions which barred the way of the feminists; that the emigration of European radicals to the Southern hemisphere led to new ideas of social reform and democracy; that the limited objectives of the early Women's Movement i.e. moral reform and the vote, and the small scale of Australian society enabled reforms to take place without too great a struggle (Evans, 1979, p 62).

However, without the commitment and courage of feminists such as Vida Goldstein in fighting for a foothold in Australian political institutions, it is probable that progress would have long been delayed.

Vida Goldstein was born in 1869 at Portland, Victoria, in the same year that Henrietta Dugdale, a writer and early supporter of women's rights 'spoke and wrote on the question in Victoria, arousing the usual ridicule and calumny' (Goldstein, 1911, p 747). However, it was not until 1884 that the first suffrage society was formed, the Victorian Franchise League, with Henrietta Dugdale as its president.

Five years later a Labour member of the Legislative Assembly introduced the first Woman Suffrage Bill to the Victorian Parliament and though it was defeated, it received considerable support. In 1891 The Women's Christian Temperance Union and the now numerous suffrage leagues united to present a mammoth petition containing over 30,000 signatures to Parliament. Vida took part in the organisation of the petition and was thus initiated into the Victorian Women's Movement.

Her grandfather, Lieutenant-Colonel Jacob R. Goldstein, was the eldest son of a Polish Jew who had sought refuge in Ireland from the revolutionary upheavals in Europe. He married Mary Pulvercraft, and their son Jacob, who was born in Cork, left the Irish family home and emigrated to Portland in Victoria, in 1858, where he joined the Victorian Army. Ten years later Jacob married Isabella Hawkins, who came from a wealthy Scottish squatter family which had been one of the first to settle in Victoria. They had five children, the eldest of whom was Vida.

Two years after Vida's birth, the family moved from the South Coast to Warrnambool where the Goldsteins lived until 1877, when they settled permanently in Melbourne, the state capital. She was educated by an excellent and well qualified governess, Julia Sutherland, and then from the age of 15, at the Ladies Presbyterian College in East Melbourne, where she matriculated with honours. The college was also attended by Constance Stone, the first woman to practise as a doctor in Victoria.

At this time the Goldstein family belonged to the Scottish Presbyterian Church but its minister, the Reverend Charles Strong, was expelled after a dispute with his fellow church leaders and immediately founded the Australian Church, taking the Goldsteins with him. Vida held firm religious convictions throughout her life, and her faith to a great extent was moulded by the activities of Reverend Strong who, shocked by the conditions of the poor, persuaded Vida and her mother to take an active part in an anti-slum campaign.

The most important influence on Vida, at this time, however, was her mother Isabella who had a lifelong concern for social reform and women's equality at a time when women were openly abused for holding any political views whatsoever.

> Mrs Goldstein's heart was always warm to the sufferings of the poor, and she had a wide grasp of the social questions of her time. She soon realised that the ordinary charitable efforts were less than futile, and for this reason, allied herself with the more enlightened efforts of the Australian Church Social Movement, when attempts were made to remove poverty altogether rather than to give them doles and to leave them destitute. She was the heart and soul of the anti-sweating movement (against low pay for piece work), and the women workers owe much of their emancipation from their worst conditions to her. She was one of those who founded the crêches which have enabled many women and children to live respectably.
>
> Mrs Goldstein was one of the founders of the Queen Victoria Hospital for Women and Children, which had provided such an opportunity for medical women and was the first institution where women could be treated by members of their own sex. Mrs Goldstein, with Mrs Bear-Crawford, took the first steps required to secure women factory inspectors, women on the Benevolent Asylum Committee and women as members of School Board Committees. (Goldstein, *The Woman Voter*, 1916)

Even Vida's father, though he was opposed to female suffrage, strongly encouraged all three of his daughters to become economically independent and to hold their own opinions.

Vida's political involvement was brought to a temporary halt by the great financial crash of 1893 which, although not entirely impoverishing the Goldstein family, forced Vida and her sisters to look for paid employment. They decided to open a co-educational preparatory school at Ingleton, in East St Kilda, which was successful for several years and helped put the family finances on an equitable footing once more.

Another important influence on Vida's political life was Annette Bear (later Mrs Bear-Crawford) who was the daughter of a former member of the legislative council of Victoria and had recently been involved in the English Suffrage Movement. On her return to Victoria, Annette Bear had been responsible for organising the numerous suffrage societies and pressure groups for social reform into the United Council for Women's Suffrage (UCWS). The Council was a democratic and representative body and was remarkably successful in lobbying Parliament and in organising petitions and parliamentary support (especially in the Lower House).

In 1899 Annette Bear-Crawford died suddenly, leaving Vida Goldstein who had been a strong supporter and energetic co-worker, at the age of 30, as leader of the suffrage movement. Vida immediately closed down her school to pursue the women's cause with the principal idea that the conditions of women and children would not improve until women had the vote. In the same year Vida made her first public speech in Prahran Town Hall as leader of the UCWS and was eminently persuasive, according to contemporary newspaper reports, although women at that time rarely spoke in public.

A year later she founded the monthly paper, *The Australian Women's Sphere*, which she both owned and edited. The first issue, which appeared in September 1900, had eight pages and cost one penny. The paper was openly feminist in tone but also contained the usual ingredients of the traditional woman's paper. It was most successful however in giving information and publicity on existing social conditions and proposed reforms.

In 1901 Vida received and accepted an invitation from the American Women's Suffrage Association to attend the conference in the following year in Washington which was to found the International Woman's Suffrage Society. Vida went as the Australian representative to the first ever international gathering of leading suffragists, and there met many of the publicly known American feminists including Carrie Chapman Catt and Susan B. Anthony, as well as representatives from a number of other countries. She was appointed conference secretary and from her notebooks it can be seen that she found her experiences in America both stimulating and exciting.

She travelled from the East to the West Coast and back again and was particularly impressed by the scenery and the friendliness of the American people. She was, however, less complimentary about the American political institutions and particularly scathing on the party system, a criticism she was to incorporate in her own political programme back home.

The political inactivity of the better educated American men, is largely due to the power wielded by the political machine, by which, it seems to me, the Americans as a whole are completely hypnotised . . . it is as conservative as a country can well be.

A democratic form of government does not necessarily mean that the people rule. The people of England under a monarchial form of government enjoy more real political freedom than do the people of the Great American Republic, a fact almost entirely due to their complicatedly written and hidebound constitution, which has played directly into the hands of the moneyed and unscrupulous politicians. (Goldstein, 1902, pp 49–50)

On returning to Australia with an increased commitment to working for female suffrage within the existing political structure, Vida found the UCWS in some disarray. Because, in recent years, the sole function of the Council had been to present annually a suffrage bill to the Lower House where it was passed, and to the Upper House of the state legislature, where it failed, some of the younger feminists, unhappy at this impasse, broke away to form a more active and radical group. Vida joined them to found the Women's (Federal) Political Association which had as its two main aims the organisation of women in connection with Federal politics and the education of women in the principles of democratic government. Vida was elected first president of the WFPA, and though initially open to men, it effectively became a women's only party when the men deserted after the political decision was taken on non-alignment to any existing male party.

Following the establishment of the Women's Party, Vida was persuaded to stand as the Women's Candidate in the first Australian Federal Elections, which were to take place in 1903. The Federal Parliament had decided to follow the example of the states of South Australia, West Australia and New South Wales which had already enfranchised women, and it now granted the vote to all women in the federal sphere.

Vida decided on the radical step of directing her campaign almost entirely towards women voters and placing women's issues at the centre of her platform. She published her election manifesto in the October issue of the *Woman's Sphere* and as if it were not enough to be the first woman candidate in the British Empire ever to stand for Parliament, her candidacy was defiantly feminist.

In accepting the invitation of the Women's Federal Political Association to contest the Senate Election, I have undertaken anything but an easy task. I have to combat not only the prevailing prejudice amongst many of the electors to a woman taking part in the affairs of state, but also the opposition of some of my co-workers on, as it appears to me, the mistaken ground that the candidature of a woman at the present time is likely to injure the cause of the state suffrage of women.

Much as I regret this opposition of my friends, I determined to accept the invitation extended to me for the following reasons.

1   Because I believe that women should enter Parliament as representatives of the home, and to voice the opinions of women on important domestic and social affairs, which the increasing specialising of labour – educational, industrial and social – is bringing more and more into the political arena.

2   Because I believe that no matter how ready men may be to protect the interests of women and children, they cannot do it effectively, because they cannot see such matters from the woman's point of view. Before working men got into Parliament their interests were misunderstood, when they were not entirely neglected; in the same way the interests of women are misunderstood or neglected.

3   Because I believe the cause of state suffrage will be advanced by public attention being drawn to the absurdly anomalous position in which the women of Victoria are placed today, in having the vote for the National Parliament and not for the State Parliament. (Manifesto by Miss Vida Goldstein to the Electors of Victoria, 1903)

Though her campaign was directed at women and despite the fact that she had little hope of election on a non-party ticket, Vida polled 51,497 votes which even her opponents recognised as a considerable triumph. Much of her success was due to careful organisation and an undoubted talent for public speaking and the fact that many women knew the strength of her arguments. Not only were all her election meetings crowded to capacity but the publication of the polling returns revealed that the Women's Candidate always received more votes in those areas in which she had personally held meetings.

Vida obtained a degree of official support although her position on non-alignment dictated that most newspapers and political organisations were opposed to her candidacy. Support came firstly from most of the active suffragists in Victoria who felt that Vida's campaign would keep the issue of woman suffrage in the public consciousness. Women teachers also rallied to her support, particularly drawn by her advocacy of Equal Pay and Equal Opportunities for Promotion. Several local papers indicated sympathy for the Women's Candidate including the *Australian Punch* which commented:

> She (Vida) is the best known of all the members of her sex who have advocated the woman's cause and with three or four other candidates to vote for, a great number of male voters will spare a vote for the 'ladies' candidate. (*Australian Punch*, 1903)

Vida was delighted with the result, explaining in an article entitled 'The Australian Woman in Politics' several months after the election,

> I had against me the combined power of the morning and labour papers, deliberate misrepresentation by two of them, a considerable lack of the sinews of war, and the prejudice of sex. The successful candidates were either ex-Ministers of the Crown, or had the support of the press or wealthy organisations behind them. Yet I, with no daily paper to trumpet forth my claims, was close on the heels of the two 'Age' candidates . . .
>
> I have never for a moment regarded my candidature in any personal sense – I stood for the sake of a cause, the cause of women and children; I stood as a protest against the dictation of the Press, against the creation of the ticket system of voting, and I am proud to think that over fifty thousand people in Victoria supported me in what seemed at the outset a most unpopular crusade. My campaign proved beyond a doubt that I had the majority of the people who heard what I had to say with me, in regard to the desirability of women entering Parliament. (Goldstein, 1904, p 50).

Encouraged by her success in the polls, co-operatively with Dr Maloney and the Reverend Charles Strong (her earliest religious mentor), Vida inaugurated the Men's League for Woman's Suffrage, and this group working with the Women's Political Association, began to put pressure on the anti-suffrage Premier of Victoria, Sir Thomas Bent, to make woman suffrage a government measure. Success was finally achieved in 1908 when women were granted the vote in Victoria on an equal footing with men.

In 1905 Vida discontinued the paper which had carried her through the Senate campaign, *The Australian Women's Sphere*, in order to give more time to the woman's suffrage movement in Victoria. However, four years later she founded another paper, *The Woman Voter*, a weekly letter to the Women's Political Association, in time to support her second candidature to the Senate in 1910. She again stood as an independent but since women had by then received the vote in Victoria, she altered her manifesto to concentrate more specifically on federal marriage and divorce law reform and elective public posts. This time she was taken more seriously by the opposing parties and the campaign was more hotly contested.

Vida received over 2,000 votes more than in her earlier campaign but still failed to secure the seat. She stood as an independent in three more federal elections, for the House of Representatives in 1913, and for the Senate in 1914 and 1917; however she was never to regain the interest and support of her earlier campaigns.

Nevertheless, in her later attempts at gaining public office, Vida's appeal to the female electorate was as persuasive, practical and feminist as ever.

To the Women of Kooyong

1   Do you want your own views upon the questions of the day voiced in Parliament?

2   Do you want the interests of tens of thousands of women wage earners to be properly safeguarded?

3   Do you want the interests of women who are wives and mothers to be represented by a woman who understands them better than the best of men can do?

4   Do you want a representative who will voice your demand for an Equal Moral Standard for Men and Women, and that the highest?

5   Do you want the interests of wage-earning children and of deserted wives and children to be specially considered by Parliament from the woman's point of view?

6   Do you want a representative who will stand staunchly by women, who will never be too busy with other questions to consider their demands?

7   Do you want a representative who will put the honour of women and children before everything else, and protect them against the vicious and depraved, against the evils of the White Slave Traffic?

If you want these reforms, then you want *Women in Parliament*. (Election Pamphlet, WPA, 1914)

In 1911, Vida accepted an invitation from the English suffragette organisation, the Women's Social and Political Union (WSPU) to visit England and to join the English campaign. She received a great deal of attention on her arrival, contributed articles to the WSPU paper *Votes for Women* and spoke at numerous meetings on the advances that women's emancipation had brought to Australia.

While in London, Vida was also active in the establishment of the Australia and New Zealand Women Voters Association, to safeguard the interests of women under Imperial legislation and to promote the women's movement in all parts of the British Empire.

On her return to Australia, Vida continued to work on behalf of the Women's Political Association until war broke out in 1914. The Goldstein family bravely declared itself pacifist, and Vida took the chair of the newly formed Peace alliance. Despite accusations from the Press that she was pro-German, Vida also managed to persuade the WPA to adopt a pacifist policy.

Vida's political activity more or less ceased at the end of the war, although she remained in contact with the international women's movement until her death, at the age of 80, in 1949. Until then, she spent the rest of her time either travelling, to Europe and the United States, or in devotion to the practice of 'Christian Science'.

Vida Goldstein was a feminist with beliefs and principles which though formulated and articulated in the first decades of the twentieth century, have much to offer to the modern women's movement. Whilst she upheld the ideal of the family as the single most important social unit, she recognised the necessity for certain reforms to restructure the essentially patriarchal nature of family life. In common with other Australian feminists, she identified two of the most important tasks of the modern family as the socialisation of children and the control and confinement of sexuality. Both functions were in need of reform, reinterpretation and reconfirmation, and it was the responsibility of women, who held a definitive view on these subjects, to fight against inequality.

She believed that women were a superior moral force and that their entry into politics could only be beneficial.

> The labour cause in its widest sense is the cause of humanity, so is the woman's cause; but labour seeks to reach the goal mainly by material means; women, having due regard for the material, place a higher value on the spiritual. As we women of Australia proceed with our work of political education, studying the principles at the base of all legislation dealing with our social, domestic, industrial and international relations, we shall assuredly come to the point

when we shall see that it is righteousness alone that exalteth a nation. (Goldstein, 1904, p 50)

For Vida, as for many other feminists, the issue of free love was raised, for women who could be associated with that movement could readily be publicly discredited. Vida stated that she disapproved of those feminists in Europe and America who advocated free love and Anne Summers (1975) says of the issue that:

Vida Goldstein issued a formal repudiation against a rumour perpetrated during the first Federal Elections that she was in favour of free love. Although this was rarely stated, many feminists opposed artificial methods of contraception in favour of self-restraint. (Summers, 1975, p 365)

Whilst acknowledging the power and importance of the family, Vida and the WPA argued strongly for the right of women to be self-supporting, to gain social recognition of their individual worth, regardless of marital status, and to have the opportunity to express opinions and take action in government matters, particularly where they related to raising the status of women, children and the family.

Vida found, as do some feminists today, that the established party system did not offer a clear line of support for feminist politics. Consequently she preferred to articulate her political ideas in principally feminist terms, outside the main sphere of Australian political activity. She condemned the party system for manifesting a cynical disregard for the effective representation of women in the past, and believed that women would only become effective politically, if non-aligned. Non-party affiliation was a means by which principle would be restored to politics.

By adopting (a non-party) policy it is not to be supposed that we are a body of gelatinous creatures who have no definite views. We have all got decided views as to the merits of the various political parties – some of us are protectionists, some are free traders, some are single taxers, some are labourites, some are socialists, but we differ from those organised on party lines in one important particular. We believe that questions affecting honour, private and public integrity and principle, the stability of the home, the welfare of children, the present salvation of the criminal and the depraved, the moral, social and economic injustice imposed on women – we believe that all these questions are greater than party and that in nine cases out of ten, they are sacrificed to party interests. (Goldstein, *The Woman Voter*, 1909)

She was essentially a feminist socialist who believed in universal suffrage and the extension of democracy to include all public functions whether federal, state or municipal. Additionally, she fought for social and political reforms directed towards increasing the status and political power of the working class.

The name of Vida Goldstein is rarely to be seen in history books, either of a general nature or on women's achievements. This is despite the fact that she was one of the foremost of Australian women's leaders and the most influential and famous woman in the state of Victoria for the first decades of this century. She was an acknowledged social reformer who took a front seat in at least two major advances, i.e. the establishment of the Queen Victoria Hospital for Women and Children (where women could be treated by female doctors) and the Children's Court Act (1906) where she alone defeated the clause allowing the imprisonment of seven-year-old children. In addition, she was a radical political campaigner, the leader of the women's movement in the state of Victoria for 20 years, the owner and editor of two successful women's newspapers and the first woman ever to stand for parliamentary office in the British Empire.

Why this apparent neglect? There are a number of contributory factors which may or may not be associated with the traditional invisibility or low status of women or issues recognised as principally relating to women.

She remained unnoticed in general historical records for many years because her political activities were external to mainstream Australian political development. Although successful on her own terms, as Vida failed to secure public office, her name does not appear in official government records. She was a non-militant, preferring to work towards the achievement of her objectives within the existing political structure – she thus did not achieve the notoriety of, say, the Pankhursts, by presenting a threat to law and order.

A probable explanation for her non-inclusion in historical bibliographies of women's achievements is that, in recent years, much of the historical work on feminist analysis and politics has focused on European and American developments, and has given scant attention to feminist activities abroad, if they did not contribute directly to those two movements.*

It is opportune that Vida Goldstein's life and work now receives wider attention, as the issues with which she was concerned are central to the development of the modern women's movement: whether feminists should work within the existing system or work towards a radical alternative; and whether it is possible to achieve feminist political objectives within the established party structure or if the foundation of a Women's Party would be potentially more effective. Most importantly, she placed emphasis on the necessity for women to gain control over their lives and to protect their own interests, independent of men.

Select Bibliography of Vida Goldstein

Unpublished Documents:

Vida Goldstein's Notebooks 1, 2, 4 & 5 in the Fawcett Library Archives, City of London Polytechnic, Old Castle Street, London E1.

Newspaper and Journal Articles and Cuttings

1   Articles from the Australian papers, *Truth, Age, Argus*, etc (1902–4) – in Fawcett Library Archives
2   Goldstein V., 'The Australian Woman in Politics', *Review of Reviews*, 20 January 1904.
3   Goldstein V., *Woman Voter No 1*, August 1909.
4   Goldstein V., 'Before and Since Woman Suffrage', *Votes for Women*, Part 1, 18 August 1911, Part 2, 25 August 1911, Part 3, 1 September 1911.
5   Goldstein V., 'Mrs Goldstein', *The Woman Voter*, 20 January 1916.

Pamphlets

1   Goldstein V., *The Senate Election – Manifesto to the Electors of Victoria*, Melbourne, 1903.
2   Malcolm I. and Moor B., *Why Women Teachers Should Vote for Miss Goldstein*, Melbourne, 1903.
3   Goldstein V., *Parliament for Women*, Melbourne, 1914.

---

*Editor's Note: I would of course advance additional reasons for Goldstein's disappearance in a country where men completely dominate the political institutions they have created and where it is convenient to assert that women have no political contribution to make now, as they have had none to make in the past. Acknowledging the existence and the success of Vida Goldstein in the first years of the nation's formation is to invite questions about what has happened since that time – and the part men have played in that process does not portray them in a particularly flattering light, and is therefore, in terms of men's interest, best forgotten.

Christabel Pankhurst:
Reclaiming her Power
(1880–1958)

Elizabeth Sarah

Christabel Pankhurst was born on 22 September 1880 in Manchester, the eldest daughter of Emmeline Pankhurst with whom she later worked closely in the militant suffrage movement.

By contrast with countless feminists who have been ' "gas-lighted" for centuries' (Rich, 1979, p 190), whose ideas and experience have disappeared without trace, too insignificant or too threatening to be acknowledged by men in *their* record of 'man's' endeavours (history), Christabel Pankhurst is quite famous – or rather, given what is known about her – infamous.

Of course, Christabel Pankhurst is not the only feminist who has 'survived'. A (small) number of 'exceptional' women have been selected for the history books – their activities either neutralised into 'good works' for the benefit of *man*kind (Florence Nightingale is a good example) or morbidified – rendered unwomanly and patho-logical – to caution women of the dangers of resisting biological destiny. However, not only is the mythology of psychological dis-turbance and perversity particularly extreme in the case of Christabel, but feminists who have been engaged in recovering our feminist past during the last ten years (mainly socialist feminists) have generally endorsed the male verdict – despite their expressed commitment both to feminism and to challenging the individual personality focus of traditional history (Rowbotham, 1974; Liddington and Norris, 1978).

There is no doubt that the interests and priorities of feminist historians writing today have a lot to do with their 'judgement' of earlier feminists like Christabel Pankhurst. The question is, why have they been inclined to 'judge' at all, and what (feminist?) criteria have they used in making their assessments? Anyone doing research selects and interprets the available evidence on the basis of a particu-lar perspective – and we know from what perspective traditional male historians are working. But if the motivation of feminist historians in uncovering our feminist heritage is *not* to reclaim our foremothers from obscurity and malignment – what is it? Before going on to explore Christabel Pankhurst's contribution to feminism, it seems necessary to investigate how she has been portrayed by historians (traditional and feminist) – and why – in a little more detail.

Strange Bedfellows: The Verdict of Traditional Historians and Socialist Feminist Historians on Christabel Pankhurst
The Male Historian's Verdict:
In his book *Queen Christabel* (1977), David Mitchell presents his readers with a huge mass of 'facts' about Christabel Pankhurst. If length of text and number of sources used are anything to go by, he has done an extremely impressive piece of research. And no doubt, his own private collection of suffrage material contributed to making his task just a little easier.

What is a 'fact'? Basically, a fact is whatever those with the authority/power to create meaning choose to call 'a fact'. The 'truth' is political. However, some facts are less controversial than others. Christabel Pankhurst was born in Old Trafford, Manchester, she was the eldest daughter of Emmeline and Richard and she had two sisters – Sylvia and Adela – and two brothers – one of whom died young. For these 'facts' verification is unnecessary, and similarly, the facts concerning events and dates in the political life of Christabel *may* be equally unproblematic. On 10 October 1903, the Women's Social and Political Union was founded, at the initiative of Emmeline and Christabel, in Manchester. On 13 October 1905, the WSPU's Campaign of Militancy was inaugurated with the disruption of a major Liberal Party meeting at the Free Trade Hall in Manchester. Annie Kenney and Christabel took it in turns to ask one of the Liberal MP's on the platform, Sir Edward Grey, 'Will the Liberal Government give women the vote?' The action went according to plan and after a general commotion, the two women were arrested and opted to spend a few nights in prison rather than pay fines. On 18 November 1910, a deputation of suffragettes to the House of Commons met with extreme violence and hostility from East End police specially drafted to Parliament Square for the occasion and many women were sexually assaulted. The event is known as 'Black Friday'. These are just a few of the many 'facts', verified by all sources (both primary and secondary), concerning the history of Christabel Pankhurst, the WSPU and the suffragette movement in general. [1]

But historical studies of any period are not simply catalogues of 'all the facts'. If they were, the publications of different historians would duplicate one another. Although new books on the suffrage movement are often rationalised on the basis that they present new material that has previously not been explored, the reality is that, on the whole, each book presents a slightly different selection of the same evidence. Since historians have privileged access to information, they are in a position to select and order it in such a way as to guarantee that readers will reach the 'right' conclusions. And their mastery of the subject does not end there – historians may also rely on their authority as 'professionals' and the authority of the printed word to transform their personal biases into 'truth'. The historians' interpretation of the facts as well as the facts themselves become valid evidence. Indeed, it is almost impossible for readers to make a distinction between the two, since academic convention ensures that the opinions of historians are never made explicit. Opinions are always expressed within texts by reference to other 'authorities'. The rule is, if someone else has said it as well (published sources carry more weight of course), it must be true.

So, to return to *Queen* Christabel. The title of David Mitchell's book is in itself a rather obvious indication of what particular version of 'the truth' about Christabel Pankhurst is contained in its pages. The conventional perspective of historians has always been the examination of history in terms of the actions of 'great' people – notably kings and queens. Mitchell's analysis of Christabel Pankhurst is clearly part of this tradition. The picture Mitchell draws is not unlike that of a tyrannical king – Peter the Great or Henry VIII perhaps; Christabel is charismatic, autocratic, ruthless, vengeful, ambitious, self-seeking, single-minded, callous, rigid, compulsive. But Christabel is a woman – a queen – and herein lies the difference: her power over her 'subjects' (the suffragettes) is not something obvious and natural – a 'divine right' – it is abnormal, perverse: 'Christabel exulted in the witchery of the WSPU' (Mitchell, 1977, p 5). 'Witch' is the name men have given throughout the centuries to the women who have posed a threat to their power. It is a word which has been invested with evil and sinister meanings. Queen Christabel is Witch Christabel. This is the image of Christabel Pankhurst which Mitchell projects and every aspect of her political life as a feminist is interpreted through it. If we take a look at some of the 'unproblematic' facts referred to earlier, we may see the full implications of Mitchell's interpretation of Christabel Pankhurst. First, the Free Trade Hall event, 13 October 1905:

The oratory, the strategy, the tactics had all been rehearsed.

Christabel's contribution was determination to go to prison, trumpet her brief incarceration as a symbol of woman's estate, and so that the deed should have a wider popular appeal, take Annie Kenney, the rebel mill girl with her. . . The theatre chosen for this Pankhurst premiere was . . . the Free Trade Hall, where on 13 October, 1905 the Liberals were to hold a major meeting. (p 62)

In thousands of impatient feminists this *coldly calculated* manoeuvre released a warm, quasi-orgasmic gush of gratitude and heroine worship. (p 1, my emphasis)

The motives imputed to Christabel for all her 'deeds' as a feminist are those of self-aggrandisement and power. Readers are encouraged to see Christabel pursuing an endless series of 'coldly calculated manoeuvres' to promote her own interests – and simultaneously those of the WSPU, of which she was *the* leader. Even 'Black Friday' is interpreted in this manner:[2]

Black Friday had been tactically imperative for the WSPU. It earned some badly needed headlines in the much-maligned (but assiduously courted) man-manipulated press, produced three real martyrs, blooded some new samurai, and piled up a stock of moral indignation sufficient to keep the militant spirit alive through a further period of truce. (p 162)

But cold calculation was not all there was to 'Black Friday'. Given that sexual assault was a central part of the proceedings, Mitchell must champion the wisdom of his sex in agreeing that, external motives apart, some of the women wanted to be sexually abused:

Clothes were ripped, hands thrust into upper and middle-class bosoms and up expensive skirts. Hooligans, and occasionally policemen, fell gleefully upon prostrate forms from sheltered backgrounds. Wasn't this, they argued, what these women REALLY wanted? . . . Perhaps in some cases, and in a deeply unconscious way it was . . . (p 160).

Mitchell suggests that suffragette demonstrations provided 'a splendid excuse' for men 'to wage their own class – and sex – war' (p 160). No doubt 'in a deeply unconscious way', writing about Christabel Pankhurst has provided 'a splendid excuse' for Mitchell 'to wage' the 'sex war' on his own behalf.

Throughout *Queen Christabel*, Mitchell is determined to divest Christabel of every ounce of integrity – and it is not only specific cases of direct action which are under attack. Everything she did and said receives the same treatment. In 1912, arson, bombing and other *crimes* against property were adopted on a wide scale by the militants and the WSPU went 'underground'. To avoid arrest, Christabel escaped to Paris on 6 March 1912, and for six months (until 13 September when *Votes for Women*, at that time the official organ of the WSPU, made a public announcement), only a handful of people – her mother, her sister Sylvia, and Annie Kenney amongst them – knew of her whereabouts. Given the mystery surrounding Christabel's exile in Paris, it is not surprising that Mitchell should find in it a perfect opportunity to put the finishing touches to his exposé of the *Queen*:

> It was Christabel's fate for the honour of the Union – to sit, well-dressed and well-fed in a comfortable apartment, sending messages to amateur incendiaries and glorifying the women's revolution. (p 205)

And if familiarity with the position and manner of queens leaves readers less than shocked, Mitchell informs his audience that while she was in Paris Christabel socialised with the notorious 'Sapphic or androgynous circle of which . . . the boyishly slim lesbian pin-up Ida Rubinstein and two wealthy American expatriates, Natalie Barney and Romaine Brooks, were members' (p 207). Just in case readers are not very well acquainted with the ways of lesbians and how they come to be as they are, Mitchell adds:

> Natalie Barney . . . according to Cocteau seduced all the most attractive women in France. Romaine Brooks' lesbianism seems to have been rooted in incestuous feelings for a neurotic mother – an experience which one feels was not unknown to Christabel . . . (p 207)

Certain that readers will now add 'lesbian' to the long list of sinister character defects, Mitchell is confident of his success in discrediting Christabel's critique of male-dominated society. In 1913, Christabel wrote a series of articles on venereal disease which amounted to a sustained challenge to the organisation of sexuality in the interests of men and a cogent analysis of the relationship between male control of sexuality and the subjection of women in general. This is what Mitchell has to say about her work:

> The Pankhursts had deliberately set out to make news and by 1913 Christabel was a resourceful bravura journalist. In Paris, it was more than ever her raison d'être to purvey literary blood and thunder, thus justifying her privileges as an exile. The Moral

Crusade is a good example of her capacity for staying ahead of the feminist pack. (p 221)

> Well into her stride, aware too that the Moral Campaign was having a healthy effect upon the sales of the *Suffragette* – it appealed to ferocious spinsters of the type which had alarmed Sylvia, and long-suffering wives who relished a vicarious revenge – Christabel continued her series until 19 September. (p 226)

'Ferocious spinsters' and 'long-suffering wives' – these are the women who were devotees of Queen Christabel and the 'feminist pack' of 'frustrated samurai' (p 72) who 'heroine-worshipped' her (p 1). Clearly, it is not just Christabel Pankhurst whom Mitchell seeks to malign. After all, she would be an insignificant eccentric, certainly unworthy of the serious historian's attention if it were not for the feminist movement of which she was a part. And how better to discredit that movement – and the anger and determination of the thousands of women who were involved – than to depict Christabel Pankhurst as a ruthless despot, acting on her own initiative and for her own purposes, leading a 'pack' of maladjusted, sycophantic followers and providing 'vicarious' satisfaction for the equally maladjusted, though less frantically impulsive hangers-on?

It is difficult to take Mitchell's book seriously – it is so full of vitriol and contempt for women in general and Christabel Pankhurst in particular that it verges on the ridiculous. This is nowhere more clear than in his last chapter, entitled 'Bitch Power'. Here, Mitchell finally dispenses with the guise of 'professional historian' and becomes that great source of sociological and psychological wisdom – 'the man-in-the-street'. Focussing on radical feminism of the 1970s, he identifies the current women's liberation movement with the ideas and actions of the suffragette movement (actually, a useful comparison which I will return to later) in an attempt to discredit both:

> Millenial manifestos lurk around almost every radical feminist corner, though the formula has changed in detail. . . But the utopian sentiment is much the same as Christabel's. Nor is there any significant difference between Christabel's Great Scourge thesis and the *wilder* rantings of Kate Millett, Ti-Grace Atkinson, Germaine Greer or Martha Shelley. . . Some of Christabel's editorials came very near to the threat of Valerie Solanas of the Society for Cutting Up Men (SCUM) . . . and she also came close as she dared to Martha Shelley's claim that 'lesbianism is one road to freedom from the oppression by men. Lesbianism involves love

between women. Isn't love between equals healthier than sucking up to an oppressor?' (pp 318–20, my emphasis)

To make sure that he has driven his point squarely home, Mitchell goes on to compare the WSPU with the Baader-Meinhoff gang. There's nothing like playing on the anxieties of male readers concerning the erosion of their prerogative and disruption of the stable order of their world, to guarantee that any vestiges of sneaking admiration they may still have for those fearless female 'samurai' of yesteryear be firmly abandoned – and, of course, female readers are unlikely to be too favourably impressed by 'terrorists' either:

> The WSPU's private war of 1913–14 developed techniques which have had an influence beyond feminist circles. . . The history of the Baader-Meinhoff Gang, with Ulrike Meinhoff as a Mrs Pankhurst-cum-Christabel, provides a recent example of that nagging exploitation of the guilt-ridden liberal conscience. . . Like the WSPU, the Baader-Meinhoff leadership commanded a remarkably high degree of loyalty, seemed to release a deep-rooted need for romantic gesture of which . . . Christabel was such an accomplished impresario. Finally, the WSPU parrot-cries about man-made laws resemble the German ideological gangsters' sneers at democratic justice ('juridicial cretinism'). (pp 321–22)

Despite the obvious absurdity of 'Bitch Power', it is not possible simply to dismiss Mitchell's work as too silly to be threatening. In an important sense, of course, it isn't threatening; however vicious Mitchell may be, his words are powerless to stop today's feminists from taking what we want from the experience of the early feminist movement, and thinking and acting as we want now. However, as I pointed out earlier, Mitchell has the authority of the historian and of the published writer to back him up, and what is more, by a clever use of 'authorities' to support his assertions, he ensures that feminists past and present may be seen to agree with his verdict.* Throughout *Queen Christabel*, Mitchell quotes numerous feminists, non-militants and militants alike, to confirm his interpretation of Christabel Pankhurst. For example, Helena Swanwick (a non-militant): 'She gave me the impression of fitful and impulsive ambition, of quite ruthless love of domination' (p 4). (For what reasons and in what context, Helena Swanwick made this statement, we are not told.)

*Editor's note: It is also significant that until this article of Elizabeth Sarah's, David Mitchell's biography of Christabel Pankhurst was the only source readily available.

However, it is in his last chapter, 'Bitch Power', that Mitchell's use of the judgement of feminists becomes most problematic. We might smile a little at his reference to Arianna Stassinopoulos for the profound: 'Some degree of male dominance is necessary in sexual relationships' (p 319), but the use of Juliet Mitchell (author of *Women's Estate*, 1971) and, especially, Sheila Rowbotham (author of *Hidden From History: 300 Years of Women's Oppression and the Fight Against It*, 1974) is rather more unnerving:

> Sheila Rowbotham observes that 'the use of violent tactics progressively isolated the WSPU and changed the nature of the suffrage campaign from a mass organization to an elite corps trained in urban sabotage.' The WSPU, 'for all its militant flurry' was 'a pressure group – Emmeline and Christabel did not think in terms of building a mass organisation or of mobilising women worker's to strike, but of making ever more dramatic gestures. . . Once they had begun to adopt militant tactics, the choices closed in on them.' Feminist pride and bourgeois prejudice forbade them to accept alliance with other insurgents, so 'the only alternatives were to escalate attacks on property and to suffer more martyrdoms or to give in'. (Mitchell, p 318, quoting Rowbotham, 1974, p 88)

Unlike the general readership of *Queen Christabel*, feminists may not acknowledge Mitchell's authority to denounce the suffragettes, but the authority of other feminists to do so is less likely to be called into question. One wonders how comfortable Sheila Rowbotham and Juliet Mitchell are with the knowledge that their words have been put to anti-feminist uses by a traditional male historian? And the sad truth is that they haven't been mis-quoted. David Mitchell's motive for presenting a totally negative image of Christabel Pankhurst is quite easy to uncover. But what are the socialist feminists' reasons for condemning her?

Three Socialist Feminists on Christabel Pankhurst:
From the point of view of socialist feminist historians, Christabel Pankhurst was bourgeois, elitist and reactionary – and so too was the WSPU which she led. Christabel is judged according to socialist prescriptions for good radical/revolutionary conduct and found wanting.

To begin with, Christabel refused any alliance with the socialist movement, maintaining that socialist men were no better than conservatives and liberals as long as they failed to promote the interests of women. In socialist terms, the WSPU's policy of autonomy from all male political parties can only be seen as isolation:

> The suffragettes deliberately *isolated* themselves, cutting their last links with their supporters in the labour movement with the decision to attack Irish and Labour MPs as much as Liberals and Conservatives. (Rowbotham, 1974, p 86, my emphasis)

If the only political structure that counts is one of male political parties and groups, then separation is bound to look like isolation. But Rowbotham's failure to understand the suffragettes' reasons for deciding to work autonomously goes further than a preoccupation with the primacy of socialist politics – apparently they 'did not want to place any reliance on men, because it reminded them too poignantly of their *old* humiliation' and '(t)here was too a sexual *suspicion* of men' (p 84, my emphasis).

The idea that the only significance feminism could have as a radical social movement was by alliance with socialist theory and practice, permeates the socialist feminist account of Christabel Pankhurst and the WSPU. And autonomy is not the only problem. Since the model of agitation which was adopted by the WSPU was not a socialist one, it was therefore not democratic either – if the WSPU was not a 'mass organisation', it must have been an 'elite corps' (Rowbotham, p 88), whose activities and ideas were neither shared nor supported by the mass of women:

> They had no constituency; they represented no one but them-selves; they could speak for no mass movement and they could exert no pressure on trade unionists. (Liddington and Norris, 1978, pp 188–9)

Socialists have very definite ideas about what building a mass organis-ation involves. Socialist activists go down to the factory gates and mobilise the workers around the issues which concern them. Against this model, the WSPU must appear elitist; its members did not *tell* other women to become feminists, instead they took responsibility for their own actions and expected that other women, quite as capable of perceiving female oppression as they were, would do the same. The WSPU was not a mass organisation, but a mass organisation is not the same phenomenon as a mass movement. It does not follow that because the WSPU was not a mass organisation, that masses of women were not mobilised, much as feminists have been mobilised during the past decade, by the awareness, engendered by feminist debate, that it was possible to challenge male power.

Since, in socialist terms, the WSPU was not a mass organisation which 'tried to build up grass roots support' (Liddington and Norris, 1978, p 174) and was consequently not ruled from the bottom, then according to one line of reasoning it must have been ruled from the top (Rowbotham, 1974, p 87). There is no room within this framework for the notion of an organisation made up of women acting on their own initiative and committing themselves to militant feminist practice. Like David Mitchell, socialist feminist historians characterise the suffragettes as puppets in the hands of a ruthless leadership – they were not impelled to action by their own sense of urgency and determination to challenge male power at all (p 88). However, at the same time, Rowbotham acknowledges that: 'New tactics would seem to have been introduced on the initiative of individual women and then adopted by the WSPU' (p 86). Where does this fit in with the model of leadership from the top? The WSPU is simply beyond socialist analysis. In view of this it is hardly surprising that it is likened to a 'terrorist'-type of organisation – presumably of the Baader-Meinhoff variety. David Mitchell and Rowbotham are in agreement again: 'The tactics of illegality made secrecy and a para-military discipline in response to orders necessary' (Rowbotham, 1974, p 88). Although Rowbotham states that the suffragette movement 'was not a simple question of reactionary middle-class feminists versus enlightened working-class socialists' (p 79), there is no doubt that she identifies middle-class feminists with reaction and working-class socialists with enlightenment. The fact that after 1907, Christabel and the WSPU deliberately 'courted' middle-class women (Rowbotham, p 79), provides a splendid vindication of this analysis. Upper middle-class women are, of course, reactionary by definition, if you see power in simplistic class terms and forget that upper middle-class women, unlike their male counterparts, derive their class position from being the property of upper middle-class men.

It is not surprising that socialists like Rowbotham see the suffrage movement as providing a tenuous 'single issue' unity – 'uniting women of different political views' (p 82). It is inconceivable that there could be a fundamental identity of interest between middle-class and working-class women when class conflict is seen as the central dynamic in society:

> Some of the women went *further*. The state and laws were not only controlled and created by men in their own interests: they also represented the coercive power of a *class*. (Rowbotham, p 85, my emphasis)

Needless to say the women who 'went further' allied themselves to the socialist movement.

From a socialist perspective, the suffragette movement was 'undoubtedly mainly middle class' (Rowbotham, p 79), not only in terms of its personnel, but also in terms of its objectives:

> It is curious that at a time when increasing sections of the labour movement were becoming disillusioned with parliament, the women were ready to risk and suffer so much for the vote. (p 82)

> The women were using violence against property for a constitutional end. Parliament had blocked them so they were taking direct action – in order to be received within. (p 87)

For socialists, the only genuine form of radical social action is that which is directed at overthrowing the capitalist system and replacing it with socialism. Given this model, it is impossible for the suffragettes' behaviour to be viewed as anything other than reformist/reactionary. Rowbotham is baffled that the suffragettes 'were trying to shock and divide male ruling-class opinion' (p 87) and has no framework for understanding the challenge of feminists to the rule of men. Rather than fixing their hopes for sexual equality on a future man-made society (socialism),[3] the suffragettes were determined to confront male power as they found it organised within the existing society.

While Rowbotham maintains a consistent position of assessing Christabel Pankhurst and the WSPU by reference to strict socialist prescriptions for revolutionary activity, Liddington and Norris not only invoke socialist judgement, they also resort to a fairly anti-socialist personality analysis of Christabel. Although the apparent motivation of Liddington and Norris in writing *One Hand Tied Behind Us* (1978) was to show that the suffrage movement was not simply a middle-class phenomenon confined to London (p 11), they set out to prove this by rejecting the authenticity of the Pankhursts – particularly Christabel – not by including the militant suffragettes as part of a larger movement. The need for accounts of early feminism which look beyond the Pankhursts and their personalities is without question. But sadly, *One Hand Tied Behind Us* reinforces rather than challenges the traditional image of Christabel Pankhurst. Like David Mitchell, Liddington and Norris quote Helena Swanwick's judgement of Christabel, but more fully: 'she was unlike her sisters, *cynical* and *cold* at heart' (p 169, my emphasis). Two more unpleasant personality characteristics to be added to the list.

Liddington and Norris go to considerable lengths to analyse what happened within the WSPU and between the WSPU and other suffrage groups in terms of Christabel's autocratic personality and elitist manner. Above all, 'co-operation was not in Christabel's nature' (p 192), and this inability to co-operate was the main factor responsible for the splits and divisions in the suffragette movement, which, according to Liddington and Norris, 'seriously limited the effectiveness of the WSPU, the radical suffragists and the overall suffrage campaign' (p 192). Given their socialist perspective, it is impossible for Liddington and Norris to see the differences which emerged between groups of feminists in a positive light. Differences must always be about conflict and the domination of individuals and groups – they can never be seen as reflecting a variety of perceptions which are then expressed in a variety of ways. For socialists, there is only one right way of doing things – but Christabel took another view: 'All the women suffrage societies, with their different leaders and methods were united in aim' (Pankhurst, 1959, p 83).

It is quite apparent that a socialist framework is inadequate for understanding Christabel Pankhurst's contribution as a feminist and the nature of the WSPU. And this inadequacy is not compensated for by brief forays into the realm of 'personality'. Unlike the action of social classes which is very carefully theorised by socialists, the behaviour of individuals is shrouded in mystique and made to speak for itself – relying on the readers' history-book familiarity with kings and queens and tyrants to make sense of things. There is no doubt that Christabel Pankhurst had a powerful personality and that feminists need to think about the role of individual personality in feminist movements. For the moment, however, let us see how far a radical feminist perspective takes us in understanding the ideas and strategy of Christabel Pankhurst.

Christabel Pankhurst: Radical Feminist

None of the existing studies of Christabel Pankhurst and the WSPU examine the substance of Christabel's ideas as a feminist. The focus on her personality has been used either to discredit everything she did and said (David Mitchell, 1977) or to virtually ignore her ideas altogether (Liddington and Norris, 1978). Similarly, the emphasis placed in socialist analyses on the mode of organisation and activity adopted by the suffragettes interpreted from a socialist point of view, leaves the theories developed by the militant feminists and their own rationale for their actions totally out of account (Rowbotham, 1974; Liddington and Norris, 1978).

As Dale Spender argues (1982, (b)) women have always been

discouraged from seeing themselves as intellectual – as capable of generating ideas – and this has served to make some contemporary feminists wary of dealing with the realm of the intellectual which is then characterised as elitist and pretentious – quite fittingly the 'preserve' of men. But men do not have a sole claim to intellectual creation – any more than they own sexuality for example. Every aspect of society may have been moulded by male definitions and put to male uses, but this is not to say that women cannot and do not define and arrange reality differently. To confine ourselves to whatever minute areas of social life have been left uncontaminated by man-ipulation is hardly likely to effect the liberation of women from male domination. A far better strategy would be to say the emperor has no clothes and, to invest 'the intellectual' with new, feminist meaning. Feminists have already begun to do this with sexuality, claiming the right of women to define sexual expression for ourselves. Lesbian feminists in particular give the lie to the prevailing phallocentric definitions, demonstrating that sexuality need not be defined solely in terms of heterosexuality and reproduction.

But the relationship of contemporary feminism to intellectual endeavour is more ambiguous – unlike sexuality, women 'claim' intellectuality less easily. However, while intellectual activity is frequently rejected as the realm of men, the very act of defining ourselves as feminists involves the assertion of a whole range of women-centred ideas in direct contradiction to the male view of the world and of our place, as women, within it. What is more, today's feminists have not only been the source of new ideas about the way society is organised, we have also developed ideas that were expressed by feminists before us (often, without even realising it). In acknowledging that being a feminist is about asserting feminist ideas in the face of male ideology, we are forced not only to own our intellectual creativity, but also to examine the intellectual contribution of earlier feminists. That said, let us consider the ideas put forward by Christabel Pankhurst.

Man-made World and the Subjection of Women:
An important factor which has contributed to the distortion/invisibility of the ideas of the militant suffragettes has been the inability of historians to make sense of the struggle for the vote. To traditional male historians and socialist feminist historians alike, the movement for the vote was simply that, and they stand aghast and uncomprehending at the 'extremes' that women went to to achieve a fairly moderate constitutional end. By examining the suffragettes' actions

without reference to their ideas, historians are without adequate tools to understand the suffrage movement.

Among suffragists – militants and non-militants alike – the struggle for the vote was known as 'The Cause',[4] and this was not simply a form of shorthand. 'The Cause' summed up every aspect of women's subordination and the commitment to overcome it all. 'The Cause' was women's freedom and self-determination – the exclusion of women from the political franchise symbolised their utter subjection to the will of men:

> The vote is the symbol of freedom and equality. Any class which is denied the vote is branded as an inferior class. Women's disenfranchisement is to them a perpetual lesson in servility, and to men it teaches arrogance and injustice where their dealings with women are concerned. The inferiority of women is a hideous lie which has been enforced by law and woven into the British Constitution, and it is quite hopeless to expect reform between the relationship of the sexes until women are politically enfranchised. (Pankhurst, 1913, p 118)

From the point of view of the suffragists, if women had the vote, an important ideological battle would be won and the rationale for the maintenance of male power would be undermined. Moreover, the fight for the vote 'on the *same* terms as it is or may be granted to men' did not imply an acceptance of the existing class structure as was suggested by socialist critics at the time.[5] What these early feminists were doing was laying claim to sexual equality by challenging the power of men at its very basis – the belief that women could not participate in decision-making because sexual difference decreed that the two sexes could not be treated on the same terms. Christabel was well aware that the plea for universal suffrage, like the insistence on the necessity of a socialist revolution first (Pankhurst, *ILP News*, August 1903),[6] was being used as a delaying tactic by male politicians and was not an honest claim for complete democracy:

> Let it be as democratic as you like and the more votes the better, says the WSPU to Mr Asquith, PROVIDED you are not putting forward this suggestion for wrecking purposes – providing . . . in other words that you are not expecting us to assent to enfranchisement of women being postponed until, and being made conditional upon the enfranchisement of all men. (Pankhurst, 'Not If But When', *The Suffragette*, vol 3, no 89, 26 June 1914, p 180)

It is impossible to understand the campaign for the vote and the methods adopted by the suffragettes to achieve it, without exploring their ideas about the subordination of women. For the suffragettes in general, and for Christabel Pankhurst in particular, the subjection of women as a group, to men as a group, was the fundmental determinant of all other aspects of social life. This belief is nowhere argued more clearly than in the series of articles Christabel wrote for *The Suffragette* in 1913 on the issue of venereal disease, published later that year in one book with the general title: *The Great Scourge and How to End It.*

Taking as her starting point the widespread existence of venereal disease in society, Christabel sets out to show that 'The cause of sexual disease is the subjection of women' (p 13) and that the organisation of sexuality in a man-made world determines the nature of women's subordination:

> The Anti-Suffragists see in women sex and nothing more. Women they hold to be solely and simply females – a sub-human species useful so far as female, but not otherwise. These females they divide into two classes. Those belonging to the first class are expected to give birth to legitimate children. They are called 'wives'. The second class . . . are called 'prostitutes'. They are used for the physical satisfaction of men. . . In addition to the wives who are neither persons nor parents, and in addition to the prostitutes, there are other women who are described by the Anti-Suffragists as 'superfluous women'. Wives are needed . . . prostitutes are needed. For the rest of woman-kind the Anti-Suffragist sees no use at all. In fact, he has a peculiar fear and horror of them. (pp 136–67)

For Christabel, both wives and prostitutes are the victims of the organisation of sexuality in the interests of men, and they are kept in subjection both by man-made laws and through economic dependence:

> It should be noted that the man's instinctive endeavour is to keep the woman in a state of economic dependence. This desire to keep women in economic subjection to themselves – to have women, as it were, at their mercy – is at the root of men's opposition to the industrial and professional employment of women. If a woman can earn an adequate living by the work of her hand or brain, then it will be much harder to compel her to earn a living by selling her sex. (pp 43–4)

> The system under which a married woman must derive her livelihood from her husband – must eat out of his hand, as it were – is a

great bulwark of sex-subjection, and is a great reinforcement of prostitution. People are led to reason thus: a woman who is a wife is one who has made a permanent sex bargain for her maintenance; the woman who is not married must therefore make a temporary bargain of the same kind. (p 115)

Impelled to write about venereal disease in order to expose the extent to which women are infected by their husbands, Christabel's analysis ranges far beyond the incidence of sexual disease. The purpose of the series of articles is three-fold: to explain the existence of venereal disease in terms of the subjection of women to men in man-made society; to indicate the ways in which the relation between 'a master and his slave' (p 19) is maintained through economic dependence and man-made laws designed to protect the property rights of men (p 97); and to show how women may challenge their subordination and are doing so already. Christabel points out that one way that women can (and do) resist their subjection is through control of their own fertility:

The birth-rate is declining. Bishops, men, sociologists and others are bewailing the fact. Of course they blame the women. That men have done since Adam. They seem to forget that the question of how many children shall be born is one for women to decide. (p 96)

Women may have been defined by men as sex-servicers and mothers but:

What men, including eugenecists and social reformers of all kinds, must realise, is that: the power of maternity is something that women have in addition to their other powers. The power of maternity corresponds with the power of paternity and not to some other power or quality in men. (p 111)

Although men have made a concerted attempt to justify the subjection of women in terms of female inferiority and physical weakness and the role of women in child-bearing, Christabel points out that with the growing awareness of their subordination and an increasing confidence in their own powers and the possibility of living a fulfilled life independent of men, 'sacrifice yourself, sacrifice yourself' is a cry that is losing its 'hold over women' (p 100):

For generations women have been very silent. But they have thought the more, and the time has come to put their thoughts into words. It is now the turn of the men who have hitherto done all the talking to listen to what women have to say. (p 107)

Christabel indicates that it is because of their new-found awareness of the subordination of women in general that women are able to make individual choices about resisting the power of men over their lives – by not getting married and by not having children. Moreover, 'the more developed sense of comradeship among women' ensures 'that so long as there exists a huge class of slave women, the more fortunate women cannot live peaceably and contentedly as though all were well' (p 129). However, there is more to feminism than sisterly feeling and an awareness of alternative life-styles for women – the issue of political power is a crucial one:

> When women have political power, equal with that of men, they will not tolerate the exploitation of their sisters. . . Nor will they themselves submit to exploitation. They will secure such economic independence and prosperity as shall save them from the danger of being driven to live by the sale of their sex. (p 154)

It was in connection with her study of female sex slavery, that Christabel raised the slogan 'Votes for Women and Chastity for Men' (p iii). The power of women will check the power of men:

> Out of the present impasse in sex matters, there is only one way – chastity for men, guaranteed and confirmed by the greater independence that the vote will give to women. (p 133)

In *The Great Scourge and How to End It*, Christabel Pankhurst demonstrates in no uncertain terms that 'the relation between men and women has been that of an owner and his property – of a master and his slave' (p 19). One can't help agreeing with David Mitchell that indeed Christabel's thesis bears a striking resemblance to the writings of today's radical feminists! (Mitchell, 1977, p 319).

Of course, as pointed out earlier, Mitchell's purpose in making this comparison is to discredit the ideas of all radical feminists, Christabel included. Needless to say, it depends on your point of view.

The Enemy is *Male* Power:
One of the most controversial aspects of the practice of Christabel Pankhurst and the WSPU was the determination to treat *all* men as the enemies of women (including socialists) as long as they took no action to actively promote the interests of women. This flagrant disregard for the significance of the conflict of class interest between men is totally unacceptable to socialists who damn Christabel as middle-class and reactionary. The truth is, Christabel recognised the importance of class, but she viewed domination of women by men as more

fundamental. Given the primacy of the interests of men in all classes, it is not surprising that even socialism is male-defined:

> . . . a man-made socialism is not less dangerous to women than a man-made capitalism. So long as men have the monopoly of political power it will be impossible to restrain their impulse to keep women in economic dependence and so sexually subservient. (Pankhurst, 1913, p 45)

Christabel, like her parents, began her political life as a socialist (and a member of the Independent Labour Party). However as she became involved in feminism, Christabel found that while socialists were adamant that the interests of the working class could never be represented by the ruling class, many of them were convinced that the interests of women could be adequately represented by their husbands. But Christabel thought differently and what is more she observed that 'working men are just as unjust to women as are those of other classes' (*ILP News*, August 1903). Christabel reached the conclusion that the priorities of socialist men were no different from those of bourgeois men – both groups were preoccupied with protecting their own interests:

> One gathers that some day, when the socialists are in power and have nothing better to do, they will give women votes as a finishing touch to their arrangements, but for the present they profess no interest in the subject. (Pankhurst, *ILP News*, August 1903)

> It will be said, perhaps, that the interests of women will be safe in the hands of the men's Labour Party. Never in the history of the world have the interests of those without power to defend themselves been properly served by others. (Pankhurst, letter, *Clarion*, 13 March 1903, *Labour Leader*, 14 March 1903)

The odd mixture of astonishment and hostility with which Christabel's irreverence for socialism is treated by socialists today, is well-matched by the reaction of socialists in the early part of this century. Apart from conducting a war of propaganda which attempted to discredit the WSPU by characterising it as 'an organisation of rich women' (Pankhurst, 'Labour Members and Votes for Women', *The Suffragette*, vol 1 no 3, 2 November 1912, p 39), socialist men also resorted to physical force; 'in many instances', suffragettes who attempted to bring up the issue of votes for women at Labour meetings were 'roughly handled and violently ejected' (Pankhurst, *The Suffragette*, vol 1, no 21, 7 March 1913, p 232).

No wonder suffragettes found the distinction between 'classes' of men of academic interest only – there was after all little to distinguish between being treated violently at a Liberal Meeting or at a Labour Meeting – or by the police in Parliament Square . . . it was all violence and it all spoke of one thing – men's resistance to the demands of uppity women.

From the time she became active as a feminist, Christabel did not cease to make war on all the male political parties, although no doubt she expected most from Labour given their claims for equality, and least from the Conservatives. And there is plenty of evidence to suggest that the active promotion of women's interests on the part of Labour members in Parliament would have made a difference to the suffrage struggle:

> The Labour members of Parliament have betrayed the cause of working women. They have the power of life and death over the government, not only because of their actual voting strength in the House of Commons, but because the very fact of their opposition would destroy the government's prestige. In many divisions during the present session, the Labour Party have been solely responsible for saving the government from defeat. So lately as Tuesday night, the government owed their salvation entirely to the Labour members. 28 of them voted for the government. As the votes count 56 on a division, the government could, if the Labour members had been pursuing an anti-government policy in the interests of women have been defeated by 28. (Pankhurst, 'The Labour Members Betrayal of Women', *The Suffragette*, vol 1, no 17, 17 February 1913, p 253)

It is easy for socialist critics to make of Christabel's anti-Labour policy, a lack of understanding of the importance of wealth in society and a disregard for the lives of working women. They couldn't be more wrong. Like many radical feminists today, what Christabel objected to was a *male-defined* socialism in which the interests and lives of women were either left out of account altogether or assumed to be identical with those of men. Christabel recognised that an analysis of the homes in which working women toiled endlessly – often after their days' stint in the factory – and the excessive poverty of working women in relation to working men was conspicuously absent in socialist thinking:

> A fairer distribution of wealth is a necessity when thousands of mothers of families are breaking their hearts and wasting their

lives because they have too little to spend, while one man announces that he, and he alone, bought and owns the very heart of London.

But the problem is a bigger one than that and it cannot be solved in its entirety, except by a very thorough change in the conditions of women's lives . . .

Before the mass of people can be well fed and well tended, domestic industry must pass out of its present rudimentary state and co-operative housekeeping become the rule . . .

The apathy and even hostility of the enfranchised working men where co-operative housekeeping is concerned is a thing to marvel at, or would be so, did we not bear in mind that poverty is the women's burden rather than that of men. (Pankhurst, 'The Burden of Poverty', *The Suffragette*, vol 2, no 63, 26 December 1913, p 245)

Sisterhood is Powerful:
Christabel and the WSPU did not completely rule out the possibility that some men might support 'the cause' of women – indeed the efforts of sympathetic men in Parliament were carefully watched. However, men who wanted to promote the interests of women were urged to do so from the outside – they could not be part of a woman's movement.[7] The decision to organise autonomously as women was born, not only of an understanding of the nature of male-dominated political parties in which men's interests came first, but also of an awareness that women should work for themselves and that the experience of working together separately from men would reinforce women's collective identity:

The *Daily Herald* [Labour Party paper] can help us if it will by attacking the Government: firstly on account of the refusal to give votes to women, and secondly on account of the policy of coercion. Between the WSPU and the Daily Herald League and Movement there can be no connection. Ours is a Woman's Movement and the Herald League is primarily a Man's Movement, or at any rate a mixed movement. . . The great need of this time is for women to learn to stand and to act alone. . . No men, not even the best of men, ever view the suffrage question from quite the same standpoint as women. . . The women's rebellion has been in preparation for centuries. It is expressing something deeper and bigger than anything expressed by present day unrest among men. (Pankhurst, letters 7 and 11 August 1913. Quoted in Mitchell, pp 232–33)

Women must grow their own back-bone. It is helpful and IT IS GOOD FOR MEN THEMSELVES when they try to promote women's emancipation, but they have to do it from the outside, and the really important thing is that women are working for their own salvation . . . and are able to do it, even if not a living man takes any part in bringing it about. (*ibid*, Mitchell, p 233)

Is it surprising that radical feminists past and present are condemned by socialists? Christabel Pankhurst's position and that of radical feminists today is at complete odds with the central tenets of socialist belief – women and men cannot share an identity of interest in a male-dominated society; the oppression of women is more fundamental than the conflicts between different groups of men; women must work separately for their own liberation. And what is more, 'Ours is not a class Movement at all. We take in everybody. . . The bond is womanhood!' (*ibid*, Mitchell, p 233)

The commitment of Christabel Pankhurst and the suffragettes to the 'bond' of 'womanhood' was not simply theoretical. The WSPU was formed on 10 October 1903 by disenchanted members of the Independent Labour Party 'on an independent, non-party, non-class foundation' (Pankhurst, 1959, p 44) and attracted 'women of all three parties and women of no party' and united them as 'one independent force' (Pankhurst, 1959, p 69). Many women, who had previously had strong affiliations to particular political parties, abandoned them to join the WSPU when they became aware that their interests were totally subordinated in the men's parties (1959, p 74). All the women who committed themselves to an autonomous women's movement shared the understanding that only by working for themselves would male-dominated society be transformed into one which reflected the interests and power of women:

Social Justice will never be established until the men's point of view of which our present social system is the expression, is corrected by the women's point of view. Therefore women who come into the militant suffrage movement wearing the label of one or other of the men's political parties learn to discard these labels because they realise that what is needed for the regeneration of society is not the separation of women into various classes, different parties and divided camps but joint action for a common purpose – that is to say for the establishment in social practice of women's ideals. (Pankhurst, 'Independence', *The Suffragette*, vol 2, no 57, 14 November 1913, p 103)

An important aspect of women's independent organisation and the promotion of their own interests, was the establishment of independent feminist presses for the publication of journals, books and pamphlets. Not ony did women need their independent groups through which to develop their 'bonds' as women and to 'work for their own salvation', they also recognised the importance of reaching out to women not yet 'converted' to 'The Cause', and of informing the general public of their own point of view. To do these last two things, independent feminist presses were essential. Like newspapers today, the newspapers in the early part of the century either did their best to ignore the feminists, or did as much as they could to undermine them and ensure that they would not appeal to other women – an older version of the 'bra-burning-women's-libbers' formula. The suffragists – militants and non-militants alike – were determined not only to talk to each other, but to address women not yet actively involved (although non-militants tended to promote their image at the expense of the militants – reassuring readers that they were not like those awful militants).ⁿ That the feminist presses were successful in fulfilling their objectives is demonstrated by the sales of their publications. For example, during 1907, the WSPU 'effected a sale exclusive of leaflets of 80,000 books, pamphlets and other publications' (*Votes for Women*, vol 1, no 1, 1 October 1907, p 1). Similarly, in the first six months of circulation, sales of *Votes for Women* rose from 2,000 to 5,000 (vol 1, no 7, April 1908, p 97).

Christabel recognised that the independent political commitment of the women who established feminist presses was not enough to ensure that their papers would in fact be independent. If the venture was too expensive to be *financed* independently, women might find themselves constrained and controlled by the wishes of their financial backers:

The weekly press derives its great and growing value from the fact that it is, or can be, an INDEPENDENT press. The enormous cost of producing a daily paper means that the independence of such a paper is easily prejudiced. It is subject to the influence of advertisers; it is subject to the influence of persons with capital to supply; subsidies from the political parties are also a possible cause of disaster to the honour and liberty of daily papers.

The cost of running a weekly paper is infinitessimal compared to the cost of running a daily paper. Therefore it is very much easier for a weekly paper than for a daily paper to have a soul of its own.

(Pankhurst, 'An Independent Press', *The Suffragette*, vol 3, no 79, 17 April 1914, p 5)

Virtually free of the 'influence' of advertisers and backers, neither Christabel, nor the militants in general, had any intention of compromising their politics with the publication of newspapers directed at a less enlightened 'public' audience. It was because *The Suffragette* (edited by Christabel) for example, expressed the militant policy of the WSPU, that the government of the day attempted on a number of occasions to suppress it (Pankhurst, 'Raided by Police', *The Suffragette*, vol 1, no 29, 2 May 1913, p 493). As Christabel put it: 'The full militant story is to be found in *The Suffragette*, and there alone' (vol 3, no 79, 17 April 1914, p 5). All in all, Christabel was well aware of the importance of suffragettes being in charge of their own image:

> The WSPU must not only be strong; it must not only be independent; it must not only be uncompromising. It must also APPEAR to be strong, it must APPEAR to be independent, it must APPEAR to be uncompromising. (Pankhurst, 'The Inner Policy of the WSPU', *The Suffragette*, vol 2, no 68, 30 January 1914, p 353)

Christabel understood the extent to which 'the strength of women' ('The Strength of Women', *The Suffragette*, vol 2, no 61, 12 December 1913, p 200) was dependent upon 'the sisterhood of Women' ('The Sisterhood of Women', *Votes for Women*, vol 3, no 115, 20 May 1910, p 550), and she firmly believed that female solidarity could be achieved on a broad scale despite the ways in which women were divided from one another by male-dominated society:

> . . . the struggle to gain freedom for women, not for our own sake individually, but in order to win dignity and development for our own sex has given us something that history and classic literatures tells us women once possessed amongst themselves. It has given us back a sense of unity with a great race, womanhood: independent in its point of view, reliant upon its judgement, confident in its standards of value, strong in the consciousness of its ideals, and determined to reach its goal and attain its purpose . . .
> This consciousness of the solidarity of women is breaking down personal rivalries, destroying class distinctions, and doing away with numberless suspicions and jealousies that have been fostered by the lives which women have led for many past generations . . .
> In this movement especially we see women losing sight of all that divides them and remembering only the ties of common experience and common destiny which bind them together.

(Pankhurst, 'The Solidarity of Women', *Votes for Women*, vol 1, no 26, 3 September 1908, pp 424–5)

'Deeds Not Words':
According to Christabel, the WSPU had 'two great strengths . . . that it binds together women of different creeds . . . and classes' and 'that it is militant' ('Why the Union is Strong', *The Suffragette*, vol 1, no 11, 27 December 1912, p 160). An integral part of the suffragettes' recognition of 'sisterhood' was an awareness of the ability of women as a group to actively change the man-made society in which they lived. Certainly, there were thousands of committed suffragists who valued the 'bond' of 'womanhood' and were also firmly non-militant.[9] However, what separated the militants from the non-militants was a determination to challenge male power directly by unleashing the power of women. The motto of the WSPU was: 'Deeds Not Words':

> . . . to get the vote without having the vote was impossible by peaceful persuasion. To get the vote you had to HAVE the vote or find some substitute enabling you to compel those who would deny you the vote to yield. (Pankhurst, 1959, p 26).

For three generations women had been trying to get political power by asking nicely, and had got nowhere. A position of powerlessness is not one from which to bargain with the oppressor. Christabel realised that men would not give up their power unless they were forced to do so: 'Pressure upon the government is essential to victory' ('Militancy a Virtue', *The Suffragette*, vol 1, no 13, 10 January 1913, p 186). However, although she came to feel that passive resistance was inadequate, she had no intention of resorting to the sort of force which men rely on in their conflicts – the destruction of human lives:

> . . . warfare as developed by men has become a horror unspeak-able . . . a mechanical and soulless massacre of multitudes of soldiers. . . Not only soldiers though: non-combatants die too, some by enemy attack – others from famine and disease, the result of war. . . War is bad enough now. Men are making it worse. Aviation, which should be a link between nations, is to be used to make war more dreadful . . . any 'defended' place, however thickly populated, may have bombs rained down upon it from aeroplanes. . . War as it is and as it is going to be is the tragic result of the unnatural system of government by men only. ('How Men Fight', *The Suffragette*, vol 3, no 88, 19 June 1914, p 163)

The rationale for a 'war' on the male power structure – without 'bloodshed' – was that the most effective way to challenge the rule of men would be to undermine the principle supports of their power by disrupting male order and, later, attacking male property (Pankhurst, 'Women at War', *The Suffragette*, vol 1, no 2, 25 October 1912, p 20). The campaign of militancy which began with the disruption of the meetings of the men's political parties in 1905 continued until the outbreak of the First World War. Contrary to the expectations of the militants, the male power structure remained remarkably intransigent. Consequently, while some women continued to pursue the strategy of passive resistance, engaging in civil disobedience with a view to arrest (for example, the Women's Freedom League),[10] others felt compelled to adopt more extreme forms of militancy as milder forms failed to have the desired effect – women were excluded from men's political meetings and the police, wishing to avoid publicity and martyrdom, declined to arrest them on demonstrations (Rosen, 1974, p 116). The disruption of meetings, church services and restaurant meals, the establishment of Women's Parliaments (1907) and the organisation of public meetings, demonstrations and deputations, gave way to a nationwide campaign of violence against property which began with window-breaking in June 1908 and went on to include letter-burning, the destruction of golf-courses, bowling greens, cricket pavilions, race stands (and other arenas of male sport), and the burning down of railway stations and mansions.[11] One-off acts of militancy included an attack on the Crown Jewels (*The Suffragette*, vol 1, no 17, 7 February 1913, pp 260–1) and the planting of a bomb at the Bank of England (*The Suffragette*, vol 1, no 27, 18 April 1913, p 433). When women became militant, they released themselves from the stronghold of polite, dignified, timid – and above all passive – womanhood, and realised their power:

> It is right for (women) to be fierce as well as mild, to be strong as well as gentle. While they are mild and gentle towards their friends, they must be fierce and strong before their enemies and all who despitefully use them. . . It is not right for women, any more than for men, to have characters of tepid milk and water, to be incapable of a divine rage and to be impotent to resist oppression. (Pankhurst, 'Militancy a Virtue', *The Suffragette*, vol 1, no 13, 10 January 1913, p 186)

> A suffragist who becomes militant . . . wins a new freedom and strength of spirit. When the vote comes, it will set a seal upon a liberty already hers. (Pankhurst, 'Shall Women Fight?' *The Suffragette*, vol 1, no 3, 1 November 1912, p 30)

The suffragettes were criticised on all sides for abandoning the male-defined image of patient, self-sacrificing womanhood. Week after week, Christabel devoted a considerable amount of space in *The Suffragette* to confronting the critics of women's militancy – the Liberal Government, the Labour Party, the non-militant suffragists[12] – and she was quick to draw out the double-standard contained in all their arguments. They weren't condemning militancy *per se* – only *women's* militancy. It was appropriate for men to be militant since aggression was in the 'nature' of men – but it was wrong/unnatural for women:

> Men will . . . admit other men's right to rebel. It is only to women that they deny that right. That is to say women may not vote and they may not even fight for the vote. (Pankhurst, 'The Anger of Women', *The Suffragette*, vol 2, no 60, 5 December 1913, p 174)

> . . . anti-militant suffragist women are all in favour of militancy for men. . . It is only in their own sex that they preach a slave morality of submission to injustice. . . What is this but a double standard of morality.' (Pankhurst, 'Militancy Wins', *The Suffragette*, vol 2, no 58, 21 November 1913, p 126)

The critics did not concern themselves with the minor details – like the difference between men's wars and women's militancy – but Christabel was determined to expose the bad faith of those who accepted the 'outrages' of war but condemned the suffragettes' actions:

> Outrages upon women are, as everybody knows, the accompaniment of ordinary warfare. . . Which are the more precious – letters or lives?. . . Whoever has lost a letter in the protest. . . if he is a wise man . . . will insure himself against all such loss in the future by compelling the government to give votes for women. ('Burnt Letters', *The Suffragette*, vol 1, no 8, 6 December 1912, p 114)

> The Government use brute force to keep women in subjection. The anti-militant women bow down before brute force. The women in prison refuse to let brute force rule the world. They defy and by defying they are conquering it. ('The Remedy', *The Suffragette*, vol 3, no 88, 19 June 1914, p 162)

It is quite easy for historians to sensationalise the militant activity of the suffragettes. Without access to the primary sources – for example, papers like *The Suffragette* – readers are not in a position to find out the suffragettes' own rationale for their actions. They rely completely on the interpretative accounts of historians, backed up by a mass media-induced familiarity with guerrilla warfare, political coup d'état, 'terrorist' bombings and hi-jacks. David Mitchell exploits the susceptibility of his readers to the limit. Determined to malign suffragette militancy completely and to use it to reinforce his autocratic image of Christabel Pankhurst, Mitchell presents his audience with a two-sided picture. Readers are led to visualise both: bands of irrational women taking their frustration out on anything and everything without plan or forethought – and a para-military operation, planned with precision and led with total authority by 'Queen' Christabel:

> Here, probably was her [Christabel's] main contribution to the women's movement, then and now: the 'terrorist' touch, the taste of blood. Though free-lance militants – Mary Leigh, Emily Wilding Davison, Sylvia Pankhurst (to whom a contemporary parallel might be Pat Arrowsmith) – pioneered guerrilla gestures, hit-and-run terrorism was put on a para-military footing by Christabel and her squads of very young ultra suggestible bravadoes. (Rose Dugdale or Patty Hearst would be parallels here). (Mitchell 1977, p 321)

Mitchell's portrayal of suffragette militancy is designed to do three things: to divest it of its intended meaning; to replace its meaning with an image of anarchic terrorism; and to demonstrate the full implications of Christabel's tyrannical ruthlessness in her role as military chief-of-staff. The one thing that readers must now know is that the militants were intelligent and brave, fully conscious of the nature of their oppression in a male-dominated society, and *determined* to do something about it.

Conclusion

If we move out of the realm of mystified individual psychology and place Christabel Pankhurst's behaviour and that of the militant suffragettes in general, in the context of a radical feminist critique of male-dominated society, it becomes immediately apparent why both traditional male historians and socialist historians may be motivated to stand in judgement over Christabel and thereby discredit the movement of which she was a part. Christabel's insistence on seeing *men* as the enemy and an autonomous feminist movement as fundamental to the challenge to male power threatens the position, not only of traditional patriarchs, but also of committed socialists.

However, it is not enough for us to 'understand' why historians have been led wilfully to misrepresent the militant suffragette movement and the contributions of individuals within it. Nor is it sufficient for us to be aware of how those with the power to name 'the truth' have been in a position to impose their views. Contemporary feminists must recognise that we have a responsibility to our foremothers, and ultimately to ourselves, to reclaim a feminist tradition of autonomous thought and practice.

Certainly, it is essential that in engaging with the ideas and experiences of earlier feminists, we bear in mind obvious context-determined differences between their analyses and ours and do not simply present them as objects to be admired and copied by feminists today. Obviously, we will feel inclined to argue with them as we argue with one another – but laying down 'judgement' is another matter altogether. Let's leave 'judgement' to men who have the power to insist that they know better and who have a vested interest in denying the validity of feminist challenges to patriarchy – past *and* present. There can be no such thing as feminist judgement of feminism, in a patriarchal society. If we condemn the deeds of our foremothers, we sign our own death-warrant. Alternatively, if we research their work – reassess it, reclaim it, – we reinforce our own efforts as feminists today. Reclaiming Christabel Pankhurst is not about endorsing everything she did and said, it is about claiming her as one of us – a woman who defied the patriarchy – and thereby legitimating the ideas and activities of contemporary feminists. If we judge our foremothers 'wrong' and 'mis-guided', we accept that judgement of ourselves.

Notes

1   Secondary sources on the suffrage movement include works by Fulford (1957); Kamm (1966); Liddington and Norris (1978); David Mitchell (1967, 1977); Morgan (1970); Raeburn (1974); Ramelson (1967); Rosen (1974); Rover (1967); Rowbotham (1974).

2   For an excellent feminist account of 'Black Friday' and male violence against the suffragettes, see Morrell (1981).

3   See the section: 'The enemy is *male* power'.

4   Ray Strachey, a non-militant involved in the National Union of Women's Suffrage Societies (NUWSS), called her account of the Suffrage Movement, *The Cause. A Short History of the Women's Movement in Great Britain* (1979).

5   See especially, *The Woman's Dreadnought*, March 1914–July 1916 and *The Worker's Dreadnought*, July 1916–June 1924, both edited by Sylvia

Pankhurst. For a specific reference, see *The Women's Dreadnought*, vol 2, no 52, 18 March 1916, p 443, and more recently, Dale Spender, 1982(b).

6   For references to *ILP News*, *Clarion* and *Labour Leader* see David Mitchell (1977, pp 232–33).

7   The only man to be closely associated with the work of the WSPU was Emmeline Pethick-Lawrence's husband, Frederick. Although he donated money to 'The Cause' and co-edited *Votes for Women* with Emmeline P-L, Frederick was excluded from membership of the WSPU and did not have a say in its decisions.

8   See especially, editorials and articles in *The Common Cause* (April 1909 to January 1920), official organ of the NUWSS.

9   Like the militants, the non-militants also mobilised large numbers of women. At the outbreak of the First World War, there were 602 societies affilited to the NUWSS in Britain (*The Common Cause*, vol 6, no 279, 14 August 1914, p 385).

10   While the campaign of active militancy was in progress, other militants, notably the women of the Women's Freedom League decided to develop the forms of passive resistance which had been used in the early phase of the militant struggle (1905–1908). See *The Vote* (October 1909 to November 1932), the official organ of the WFL for an on-going account of their campaign.

11   See *The Suffragette*, October 1912 to July 1914, for a weekly bulletin of militant direct action.

12   *Ibid.*, for Christabel's ideas on militancy and her response to the anti-militants.

Alice Paul:
The Quintessential Feminist
(1885–1977)

Jean L. Willis*

Born into a prominent Hicksite Quaker family in Moorestown, Burlington County, New Jersey on 11 January 1885, Alice Paul carried the banner of equal rights for women with an intellectual vigour that contributed to the ratification of the Nineteenth (Woman's Suffrage) Amendment and the serious and controversial consideration, over a period of more than 50 years, of an Equal Rights Amendment to the United States Constitution. Among her other achievements were the passage of an Equal Nationality Act in the United States in 1934 and incorporation of an Equal Rights statement in the United Nations Charter in 1945 and of Title VII in the Civil Rights Act of 1964 in the United States outlawing, among other things, discrimination in employment on the basis of sex. Her death in Moorestown on 9 July 1977, marked the end of a stage in the twentieth-century struggle for women's rights not only in America, but throughout the world.

The oldest of four children of Donald Paul and Tacie (Parry) Paul, Alice had two brothers, William and Parry Haines Paul, and a sister, Helen. Her Quaker ancestors on both her paternal and maternal sides came to America in the seventeenth century. Her maternal grandfather, William Parry, was the Speaker of the New Jersey House of Assembly in 1855, a Judge of the Burlington County Court and a founder of Swarthmore College. Her father was a well-known business man in Burlington County.

A brilliant student, Alice graduated first in her class from Friends' High School and from Swarthmore College in 1905 where she majored in biology, but she became interested in political science in

*Dr Willis wishes to acknowledge the financial support of the Educational Foundation program of the American Association of University Women, through an Individual Member Research Grant for 1981–82.

her senior year. She received a Master of Arts degree from the University of Pennsylvania in 1907 in sociology with a minor in economics and political science. She said that Professor Simon Patten's lectures on economics had great influence on her. In 1912 the University of Pennsylania conferred the PhD upon her for a dissertation on the Legal Position of Women in Pennsylvania. She held three law degrees and in addition, she had studied under famous scholars in the field of sociology and economics, such as St John Heath, Sidney Webb, W. Westermarck, Graham Wallas, G. Lowes Dickinson, and L. T. Hobhouse while a student at the University of Birmingham, England, and the London School of Economics from 1907 to 1909.

Alice's academic achievements were incidental, however, to the driving force of her life, the achievement of equal rights for women. As a Quaker, she was accustomed to the relative freedom women possessed in meetings and to the responsibility given to them as missionaries abroad. The distinguished Quaker feminist, Lucretia Mott, was a frequent visitor in her grandfather Parry's house in Moorestown. Her religious background led her into social work after graduating from college. She was awarded a College Settlement Association Scholarship and became a resident worker in the New York College Settlement and a visitor for the New York Charity Organisation Society. The Women's Trade Union League left part of their work in charge of the Settlement in the summer of 1905, and 'Alice undertook the task of organizing the milliner's union'. The next year she obtained a diploma from the New York School of Social Work and while studying at the University of Pennsylvania became a visitor for the Charity Organisation of Philadelphia. In June 1907, she went to Germany for further study of social conditions and was involved with German social workers who were concerned with the poor. She continued her work among the poor in a Quaker social work school in Birmingham and in the Canningtown Settlement in London in 1907 and 1908. Not content to observe, she became a participant, taking a job in an automobile factory in London and working and living in the same manner as her fellow employees.[1]

As Alice Paul remarked at the end of her life, she soon became disenchanted with work to alleviate conditions among poor women because they did not result in any change. Political action was required so that those who battled with poverty could find the means of controlling their own lives. By 1909 she was ready to join in the political activities of Mrs Emmeline Pankhurst's Women's Social and Political Union which she felt was the most up-to-date in its political propaganda. Under the auspicies of the WSPU, many public demonstrations and processions took place in England and in Scotland in order to obtain the vote for women. Alice Paul participated in a number of them, being arrested seven times and three times imprisoned. She went on a hunger strike each time she was jailed, and once was forcibly fed. Alice Paul made the major decision of her life as a Quaker when she joined the WSPU's suffrage deputation to Prime Minister Asquith in the Spring of 1909. She shed her Quaker pacifism in the cause of equal rights for women. She put her superb intellectual energy into the struggle for equality for women and never deviated from that goal for the rest of her life.

When she returned to the United States in 1910 and began studying for the PhD at the University of Pennsylvania, she became a member of the Philadelphia branch of the National American Woman Suffrage Association, and upon completion of the doctorate in 1912 was taken to the national convention of the NAWSA by Mrs Lawrence Lewis. Alice Paul was prompted to action and formed the Congressional Committee of the NAWSA to work for the passage through Congress of a suffrage amendment. She opposed the slow process of gaining the vote for American women state by state, and the complicated Shafroth-Palmer amendment to the United States Constitution introduced in 1914 to allow referenda in a state, upon petition to a legislature of only 8 percent of the voters who had voted at the last Presidential election. The wording of the suffrage amendment was the same as the original Susan B. Anthony Amendment of 1878. It states: 'The rights of citizens of the United States to vote shall not be denied or abridged by the United States or by any State on account of sex.' By clever direction she spiked the attempt of opponents in the Congress to include a seven-year limit on ratification.

Alice Paul saw the importance of not wasting the lives of generations of women on those state referenda to male voters. When she went to Washington in 1912, she laid her plans skilfully. Carrie Chapman Catt told her in 1912 that it could not be done. The difference led to separation of the efforts of these two remarkable women. An attempt made by Zona Gale in 1917 to bring them together again failed. Mrs Catt headed the NAWSA and Alice Paul the National Woman's Party, formed in 1916 and incorporated in 1918, which had evolved out of the Congressional Committee of NAWSA and the Congressional Union for Woman Suffrage. Mrs Catt had preferred the Shafroth-Palmer to the Anthony Amendment. By late 1917 Mrs Catt's organisation voted at their Louisville Convention to back the Federal Amendment and withdrew the Shafroth-Palmer.

However, she and Alice Paul never met again.

Employing the tactics she had learned in Britain, Alice organised a procession in Washington on 3 March 1913 – the day before President Wilson's inauguration. Other processions had occurred earlier in emulation of the English suffragettes, especially in Boston, but never by approximately 10,000 women, and never as a rival event to the welcoming of a new President. As the British did, she held the party in power responsible for the government's action on woman suffrage. She organised women voters in the suffrage states to defeat Democratic candidates, beginning in the Congressional elections of 1914. She marshalled delegations of women from the non-suffrage states to present their case to President Wilson. She and many of her followers in the National Woman's Party picketed the White House beginning in January 1917, and this became a thorn in the flesh of President Wilson after the United States entered the Great War in April 1917. While in prison for her picketing activities, she went on a hunger strike and was sent to the psychiatric ward of the District of Columbia jail. She succeeded in encouraging her followers to burn President Wilson's war speeches on liberty, freedom, and democracy, and endure a period in jail for their actions.

Each of these policies was protested from both within and without the movement, but each proved in the end excellent political strategy and, at the same time, had a tremendous re-enlivening influence on the suffrage struggle. Those who supported Alice Paul suffered so from the widespread criticism that they gained the power and faith of crusaders (Crystal Eastman in University of California transcript). The more conservative suffragists who opposed these policies, especially the fine organiser and intellect, Mrs Catt, were driven to more and more effective action along their own lines. The movement developed with sudden speed from the differences within its ranks. By 1917, Mrs Catt was converted to working for the Anthony Amendment to the Federal Constitution. Pressure on both the President and Congress resulted in passage of the Federal Amendment by both houses on 4 June 1919. Alice Paul and the National Woman's Party which she headed at the time kept up pressure on the various states for ratification of the Anthony Amendment. She did not use a grass-roots approach; rather, she concentrated on a few key women or men in each state who could exert pressure at the critical moment. Their efforts were crowned with success in August 1920 when Tennessee became the thirty-sixth state to ratify.

The NAWSA disbanded at the time of ratification, most of its members forming a new organisation, the League of Women Voters, to encourage intelligent use of the vote and to engage in what has since been called social feminism; i.e., to improve the conditions of women, children and men in American life. The National Woman's Party whose mother organisation, the Congressional Union, had been eased out of NAWSA, considered suffrage only the first step and, after reorganisation in 1921, set about framing an Equal Rights amendment to push through Congress. What Alice Paul and the NWP sought was not just an end to discrimination in employment, salary and so forth, but the basic freedom for all women to be free to make a choice. To them, the ideal of the free individual implied equality. They sought total legal equality for women.

Alice Paul was stunned when in 1923 she drafted and submitted to Congress the first Equal Rights Amendment, by the fact that not all women wanted equality. Often called the Lucretia Mott Amendment, it reads: 'Men and women shall have equal rights throughout the United States and every place subject to its jurisdiction.' In the early 1920s, the National Woman's Party was the only organisation in the United States supporting equality. The Woman's Trade Union League, the Consumers' League, the Women's Bureau of the Department of Labour, the American Association of University Women, and social workers active in the passage of protective legislation for women, all opposed it. The National Federation of Business and Professional Women's Clubs did not support it until 1928. The opposition of Eleanor and Franklin Delano Roosevelt in New York State and later on in the White House did immeasurable damage to this cause.

The National Woman's Party continued throughout the 1920s and the 1930s to work not only for the Equal Rights Amendment in the United States, but for its international parallel, the Equal Rights Treaty in the League of Nations, and for the more limited Equal Nationality Treaty which dealt only with citizenship. Alice Paul divided her time between the United States and Europe in the years between the World Wars, much of it spent in Geneva, headquarters of the League of Nations. She also guided and consulted with members of her party in activity for equal rights in Latin America. She succeeded in having the Equal Nationality Treaty, which had been adopted at Montevideo in 1933, accepted by the League of Nations and the Equal Nationality Act passed in the United States in 1934. Her final achievement in these years was the founding of the World Woman's Party in Geneva in November 1938, with the National Woman's Party as its American section. The 38 incorporators, who were all NWP members, elected Alice Paul president and chose an international board of 30 directors. The World Woman's Party was to combine the various groups of European and Asian feminists, but the outbreak of the Second World War shattered that possibility.

Returning to the United States in April 1941, Alice devoted the remainder of her life to ratification of an Equal Rights Amendment to the Constitution. Until 1962, she divided her time between Party headquarters in Washington, DC and her home in Vermont. After that she conducted her systematic drive mainly from her cottage in Ridgefield, Connecticut. Her campaign was injured by dissension within the leadership of the National Woman's Party and led to a conflict that reached the courts at the end of the 1940s. Alice Paul's tactics were questioned by women who had been her devoted followers in the early years of the struggle. Nonetheless, she and the Party weathered the storm and saw the passage of an Equal Rights Amendment through Congress by March 1972. The wording differs from that of the 1923 Amendment. It states: 'Equality of rights under the law shall not be denied or abridged by the United States or by any State on account of sex.' Alice had high hopes that ratification by the required number of states (38) would be achieved. She had agreed to the change in 1943 because she had become convinced that the amendment would not pass with her wording. Unfortunately, at the time of her death in 1977, only 35 states had ratified, and several of them had rescinded their ratifiction. The time limit for ratification, 30 June 1982, will pass without the amendment's being added to the Constitution.* It should be noted that she disapproved of the second section of ERA because it did not include enforcement by the several states but only by Congress.

In order to understand Alice Paul's feminist theories, one should accept the fact that her lifelong activity on behalf of equal rights for women constituted a religious movement, not in the sense of founding a formal church, but in seeking personal and worldwide liberation of both women and men so that truly spiritual relationships might develop between human beings (Frances Willis, 1976). She spoke, she wrote, she performed and directed others in public life in the Americas and in Europe for more than 60 years, but no political label can justly be applied to her. She was not a conservative. She was not a radical. She was not a member of the Progressive Party in the United States in the years before the Great War, although her family was

---

*Editor's note: this is in fact the case.

always Republican – with the exception of Uncle Mickle Paul who was President of the Democratic Club of Pennsylvania, and who sent her a telegram in 1914 questioning the wisdom of her decision to attack the party in power. She maintained to the end of her life that the movement for women's rights she led so magnificently was classless, was not (at least as a result of her efforts) a phenomenon of upper and upper middle-class, talented and educated women. She said she merely sought to bring into her National Woman's Party enthusiastic, eager, and devoted women. Frail-looking in her early years and soft-spoken, she appeared shy and retiring and was not in any way charismatic, and yet she compelled attention and devotion as she looked people straight in the eye and asked them to work for women's rights. She was an aristocrat of the spirit.

Alice Paul's earliest experience was in the bosom of a respected Quaker family. Her values were those of the Society of Friends, albeit of the more liberal followers of Elias Hicks who rejected the evangelical elements of American Quakerism. Quakers believed in equality, simplicity, and informality in dress and language, opposed ceremony of any kind, and practised toleration because they believed all human beings are basically good. The Hicksite faction, which separated from the orthodox at the Philadelphia Yearly Meeting in 1827, stressed the inward manifestation of divine light and Christ in human beings as the hope of glory. There was no music, no dancing in her young life. Only the Irish maids of the Paul household danced. Alice substituted an interest in sports to which she applied herself with zeal, having some success with tennis and basketball. A classmate at Swarthmore recalled her persistence in practising until she had mastered the game of basketball. Once she gave herself to the suffrage struggle in Britain, there was no turning back. She possessed the urge toward martyrdom of some seventeenth-century Quakers – including at least one of her ancestors who was imprisoned in England – but she added a political twist. When she went on a hunger strike in 1917 after her arrest for picketing the White House, she said she did so because she wanted to be considered a political prisoner (Newspaper article in Newark Public Library, dated 24 October 1917). She and her followers who were arrested maintained they were not disturbers of the peace and had not violated any law.

When in the 1920s American women failed to respond to her call for an Equal Rights amendment, Alice Paul continued her campaign, working with her lobbying group, the NWP, either as one of its officers or in collaboration with other of its chairpersons and state leaders, the most able of whom were Jane Norman Smith of New

York and Florence Bayard Hilles of Delaware (Becker, 1981, pp 33, 35). At this time, the membership in the Party was approximately 9,000. Its funds averaged about $46,000 a year from 1923 to 1929, but in the early years of the Depression, its average yearly income fell to about $13,500 (Becker, 1981, p 38).

Alice chose to ignore the waning of the progressive spirit which was so widespread in the United States during the first decade or so of the twentieth century. The desire for and a belief in their ability to bring about change had swept both women and men along the path to ratification of the suffrage amendment. The participation of the United States in the Great War 'to make the world safe for democracy' had also helped. President Wilson, who had originally opposed the Federal amendment, could not resist the pressure and by 1919 had asked Congress for its passage. Furthermore, Alice chose to ignore or was oblivious to the threat that suffrage posed to American women's place in the family. She failed to appreciate how radical suffrage really was. It was at the core of feminism in that it asserted that women were individuals with a self-interest independent of their subordinate role in the family (Degler, 1980, pp 343–60).

The 1930s witnessed the submersion of feminist issues in the world-wide economic depression and the rise of fascism. The strategy Alice pursued was always of the most rational and direct nature. It was clear to her that women were individuals and should have the same freedom as men. She did not address the issues of birth control, i.e. abortion, or even women's sexuality, and was concerned that the radical women of the 1960s might alienate support by emphasising these issues (Gallagher, 1974, *American Heritage,* article). She thought, as Westermarck had taught in a course on human marriage, that women, because they are the raisers of children, were peace-loving and constructive (University of California transcript). But at the same time, she said that even if women did want to do many things that she wished they would not do with their freedom, it was not her business to tell them what to do with it, but to see that they had it (University of California transcript). She did not consider the women's liberation movement of the 1960s to have done for equal rights what the NWP group had done for suffrage because the women's liberation groups sought *many* changes and many personal changes, whereas the NWP was concentrated on a single issue, in the public sphere.

Alice Paul succeeded in giving crucial aid to the achievement of woman's suffrage because her goal and tactics were in tune with a progressive America from 1912 to 1920. Although she was *sui generis*

– there was no one remotely like her on the American scene – the time had come to give women the vote in the United States, and her political tactics dovetailed with those of the Republican and Democratic parties in America at that time. It was a time for changes and reforms. By insisting on a federal amendment, she caused discussion that acted as a catalyst to action on everyone's part.

Such was not the case in Alice Paul's campaign for ERA. In the 1920s and the 1930s, Americans – especially American women – had other ideas in mind. She swam against the mainstream and appeared outrageous to most people in public and private life. She supported the opinion of the Supreme Court in *Adkins* v *Children's Hospital* in 1923 when it found a ten-hour law governing women's work in the District of Columbia unconstitutional. No other feminist did so. She judged every political leader on the basis of her or his stand on equal rights. She stood apart from most women in the 1930s. Moreover, the Equal Rights Amendment would take something away from women as the suffrage did not. The vote added to the power of women if they chose to use it. While it did challenge the nineteenth-century doctrine of the two spheres in terms of emphasising the individuality of women as opposed to their subordination to the interests of others in the family, it did not require a major change in their relations with others as ERA does. But by the early 1970s, many women had come to see that the protective legislation of past decades was crippling, demeaning, or actually unnecessary.* The General Federation of Women's Clubs decided to support ERA in 1944. Mrs Roosevelt came over in the late 1940s. In 1970, Esther Petersen said she would not oppose it. The American Association of University Women announced its support in 1971. With the changes in the American economy and in the American family that had seen single and married women enter the workforce in greater numbers than ever before, the attitudes of American women changed. It was the support and effective lobbying of women's organisations that were instrumental in Congress's passage of ERA in 1972 and its ratification by 30 states within a period of a year.

The momentum was soon lost, however. The efforts of women (such as Phyllis Schlafly) have served to divide and weaken women's work for equal rights. And the money available to women such as Phyllis Schlafly (from the new but patriarchially 'old' right) dwarfs the puny sums raised by Alice Paul and the National Woman's Party: the

---

*Editor's note: It was also often an excuse for making women economically subservient.

money permits television and radio broadcasts which reach many more millions than did the processions and other tactics of the older workers for women's rights.

To see Alice Paul, and her life's work, as unsuccessful, is however, to miss the point of much of her philosophy and many of her practices. Her intellectual attainments were outstanding and she gave her mind solely and singly to the struggle for equal rights. She insisted that this was a fundamental and necessary guarantee, for women, who could then in the absence of discrimination be free to choose the ways in which they wanted to live. To her, equal rights were structurally denied and this had to be remedied by structural means.

In her analysis of the problem and her determination to act to bring about change, she made her own *personal* choice which defied convention and announced to women that it was possible to act for change.

Notes

1   Memorandum of biographical detail on Alice Paul, Schlesinger Library, Radcliffe College, mss collection A–116, Jane Norman Smith Papers, box 5, F108.

Select Bibliography of Alice Paul

The transcript of 'Conversations with Alice Paul: Woman Suffrage and the Equal Rights Amendment', on oral interview conducted by Amelia R. Fry in November 1972 and May 1973, under the auspices of the University of California Oral History Project (1976) represents the most comprehensive material now available. A shorter interview conducted by Robert S. Gallagher about the same time for *American Heritage, The Magazine of History* and published in the February 1974 issue of the magazine as 'The Fight for Women's Suffrage: An Interview with Alice Paul' is illuminating.

A fine collection of papers for study of Alice Paul, the NWP and the Woman Suffrage and Equal Rights Amendments is located at the Schlesinger Library, Radcliffe College, Cambridge, Massachusetts. Especially helpful are the Alma Lutz and Jane Norman Smith Papers.

A microfilm edition of the National Woman's Party Papers from 1912–1974, including the World Woman's Party Papers (1938–1958) has been made available by Microfilming Corporation of America (Sandford, North Carolina, 1977). A major new edition to the NWPP, focusing on the 1913–1920 suffrage movement, was presented for sale by Microfilming Corporation of America in 1980.

A collection of newspaper clippings on Alice Paul from the *Newark News* over the period from 1909 to 1972 can be found in the Newark, New Jersey, Public Library. It indicates the public interest she aroused, especially early in her career.

The best books to begin reading about Alice Paul are Doris Stevens's *Jailed for Freedom* (1920) and Inez Haynes Irwin's *The Story of Alice Paul and the National Woman's Party* (1977 reprint), both histories, by participants, of the intensive campaign for the suffrage amendment.

Susan D. Becker's *The Origins of the Equal Rights Amendment* (1981, Greenwood Press, London) is the best study of its subject in print.

Carl Degler's *At Odds* (1980, New York and Oxford) traces the history of women and the family in America from the Revolution to the present and throws light on the problems that Alice Paul's singular devotion to absolute legal equality for women posed to the majority of American women.

Frances Fitzgerald's article on 'The Triumphs of the New Right' in the 19 November 1981 issue of *The New York Review of Books* provides the best interpretation of the failure to ratify ERA.

Frances Willis's unpublished term paper entitled, 'The Categorization and Functions of Women's Liberation as a Religious Movement' contains, without any reference to Alice Paul, the best statement of what the great feminist was seeking all of her life. The paper was written in May 1976 for Dr Ruth Whitney in a course on Religion and Society at Douglass College, Rutgers University, New Brunswick, New Jersey.

Virginia Woolf:
The Life of Natural Happiness
(1882–1941)

Naomi Black

It is now generally accepted that Virginia Woolf was a feminist and, furthermore, that she was a feminist writer. This has not always been the case. Many of those who recognised the strength of her personal beliefs about the situation of women nevertheless denied that those beliefs had any significance for her work. And even those who came to see that her feminism permeates her work have often differed substantially in their interpretations of it. Thus, although friends, relatives, and critics have been prepared to agree that Virginia Woolf wanted equality for women, they have read equality as meaning simply the vote, or women's access to education and to the professions, or an androgyny that would obliterate male–female distinctions, or even a separatist women-only society of amazons or lesbians. By and large, however, commentators have agreed in deriving both the origins and the programmes of Virginia Woolf's feminism from her own personal experience. Finally, with few exceptions, those discussing such topics have agreed that Virginia Woolf was not political, and that she was not significantly involved with the women's movement of her day.[1] In my view, however, almost all of these interpretations are mistaken.

Virginia Woolf *was* a feminist, of course. Her occasional disavowal of the term is both ironic and complex. In *Three Guineas* (1938), in a famous and much misunderstood passage, she attacked the word 'feminist' as 'a vicious and corrupt word that has done much damage in its day and is now obsolete,'[2] and she urged that it be burned and banished. But the passage continued, to explain that women like Josephine Butler should not be labelled feminists because they were 'fighting the tyranny of the patriarchal state' rather than merely seeking women's rights (V. Woolf, 1938, pp 184, 186). Such a statement is not a disavowal of feminism but a distinction among its different varieties. Virginia Woolf's own variety of feminism is my topic here. That system of beliefs constitutes her politics.

In addition, Virginia Woolf did have important connections with the women's movement. She worked for it, more than has previously been realised, she followed its progress with interest and affection, and her feminist writing was much influenced by it. When she criticised individual feminists or groups, she did it as one who sympathised but who saw the human absurdities that are particularly blatant in those serving a Cause.

On the other hand, Virginia Woolf accepted the judgment that she was not political. 'Virginia was the least political animal that has lived since Aristotle invented the definition,' wrote Leonard Woolf, the 'political' member of the family (L. Woolf, 1967, p 27). She agreed. 'I can't believe in wars and politics,' she wrote in a letter in 1900. 'I refuse to go into politics – for one thing I cant [*sic*] grasp them,' she repeated in 1936. And again, towards the end of her life, 'But then of course I'm not a politician' (Nicolson and Trautman, 1975–80, vol I, p 325; vol VI, pp 28, 478). But in this she was wrong. In fact, Virginia Woolf, who accepted current notions of politics, was involved politically in a way very typical of women. She worked at different levels, with different organisations, and for different goals than have been usually accepted as political. Most important, in her feminist writings she expressed the very political feminism of such groups as Britain's non-militant suffragists and their descendants. It is not a coincidence that these 'social' feminist groups are the ones with which she was associated.

Virginia Woolf was a professional writer, a very hard-working one who published 20 books in her lifetime, not to mention hundreds of pamphlets, essays, and book reviews that have since been collected in more than six volumes. It is in her writing that we find her feminism – her politics. And it is on her feminist writing that I shall concentrate here, particularly the polemical *Three Guineas*, first published in 1938. But first it is worth looking briefly at Virginia Woolf's relationship with both the conventional politics and the women's movement of her time. The misunderstanding – and the long undervaluation – of her feminism is connected with the misunderstanding of what today seems clearly political behaviour.

It is not difficult to understand why Virginia Woolf's contemporaries, and even she herself, were ready to dismiss her as apolitical. Her interests and occupations did not fit the classical Aristotelian definitions of politics as activities relating to public governance (Okin, 1979). Unambitious for office, she was like many other women in being willing to remain at the grass-roots level of politics, in her case the Rodmell Labour Party of which she was even secretary for a time (L. Woolf, 1967, p 27; Q. Bell, 1972, vol II, p 186). Even in that context, the issues that attracted her attention and the solutions that she preferred were not the ordinary ones. Nor were her interpretations of what was taking place. Her nephew, Quentin Bell, has recorded that she found baffling and even irrelevant his youthful Marxist explanation of conflict in terms of 'the world economic crisis', and his advocacy of tactics like the United Front. In his biography of his aunt, Bell expresses the exasperated response of 'political' men to Virginia Woolf's insistence on stressing the issue of women's rights and, even worse, on linking that issue to the fascism that was the over-riding problem of the thirties. 'The connection between the two questions seemed tenuous,' he wrote, 'and the positive suggestions wholly inadequate.' He finally, in effect, shrugged his shoulders and concluded that it was all 'her instinctive reaction, the feminine as opposed to the masculine – "the beastly masculine" – reaction' (Q. Bell, 1972, vol II, pp 186, 187, 205). For him, as indeed for Virginia Woolf herself, the only recognisably 'political' issue related to women was the franchise, and by 1928 women in England were able to vote on the same terms as men. Virginia Woolf's continuing insistence upon issues related to women was therefore perceived by him, by her, and by others as non-political. Her association of the situation of women with fascism (as in *Three Guineas*) was worse, evidence of eccentricity and incompetence. Leonard Woolf himself dealt with the paradox of his wife's combination of activism that was almost political, and attitudes that he believed were not, by noting that she was 'intensely interested in things, people, and events, and . . . highly sensitive to the atmosphere which surrounded her' (L. Woolf, 1967, p 27). The diagnosis of Virginia Woolf's feminism as literary and personal is the same as Quentin Bell's. Before him, it was articulated by his father, Clive Bell (C. Bell, 1958, p 101). It was also the view of Nigel Nicolson, son of Virginia Woolf's dear but non-feminist friend, Vita Sackville-West (Nicolson and Trautman, 1975–80, vol V, p xviii).

Ironically enough, contemporary feminists are not without some responsibility for the continuation of explanations that derive Virginia Woolf's feminism, apolitically, from her own life. Her father was certainly a patriarch and even a tyrannical one, but her objections to the patriarchy go well beyond her somewhat mixed feelings about Leslie Stephen, just as her pacifism has other, more significant, and certainly older roots than sharing her sister's grief at the death of

Julian Bell in the Spanish Civil War.

Today it is important to insist that Virginia Woolf's feminism was indeed political. To say that it was personal and idiosyncratic is to minimalise and misrepresent it. Equally, to say that the women's movement was only the battle for the vote, that equality of status was its goal, and that it had achieved these in Britain by 1928, is to marginalise the programmes and beliefs of the historical women's movement along with those of Virginia Woolf. For Virginia Woolf, feminism meant more than the vote, and more also than sisterhood, shared grievances, mutual support, and independent achievement. It meant, specifically, the beliefs that make up social feminism.[3]

Feminist organisations can be historically explained in terms of two different, though closely related sets of beliefs: what has been called 'political' or 'equal rights' feminism as differentiated from 'social' or 'maternal' feminism. Both have repeatedly been important throughout the industrialised world, and they still co-exist today (Black, 1978, 1980). The better known is the equal rights feminism which achieved its greatest visibility in the suffrage campaigns of the early twentieth century; it still animates important segments of the American Women's Movement, such as the campaigns for the Equal Rights Amendment. For this kind of feminism, the basic argument for women's rights is that women are essentially the same as men, or would be if given the chance. It is the position of John Stuart Mill's *The Subjection of Women.** Equal rights feminist organisations seek to abrogate the legislative and other arrangements that prevent women from sharing the opportunities to which human beings are entitled.

By the late nineteenth century the vote had come to be the major symbol of women's disadvantages. In an argument about justice, suffrage stood for equality. The furthest extension of such a position was the belief that any differential treatment of women is a demeaning handicap; equal rights feminists sometimes oppose any form of maternity leave or benefits.

Even in the great suffrage coalitions, however, most activists did not advocate woman suffrage mainly for symbolic reasons, or even as a citizen's tool for self-protection. For the large majority of the women's movement the arguments for improving women's status were based on beliefs about the *differences* between women and men. Among those holding these views there are disagreements about

*Editor's note: It was not the view of his wife, Harriet Taylor, see Alice S. Rossi, 1973.

whether women's distinctive qualities are innate, or whether they are the cumulative product of women's experiences with child-birth, child-care and home-making. In either case, social feminists believe that women have produced a set of values and practical skills that are excluded, along with women, from the larger society that is organised and run by men. The female virtues are nurturant, co-operative, and peaceful. The female skills are productive of orderliness, plenty, and security. An authoritative public role for women is therefore necessary in order to improve the defective social system. The vote was the necessary instrument for women's public service, which would transform the state. In the late nineteenth and early twentieth century, such arguments persuaded extremely conventional women that it was proper to act aggressively to obtain a public role. Today, it persuades many feminists of the necessity for women to play a far larger part in politics than has yet occurred.

An important part of the social feminist rationale has always been the relationship of women to violence and especially to war. Some social feminists were prepared to argue that females or mothers were somehow constitutionally incapable of violence. A more moderate view, widely accepted among suffragists, was that women's socialis-ation would keep a government run by women from being imperial-istic or warlike: women, who give life, are not so careless of it. Among those who accepted this argument, it was one of the most compelling reasons for the participation of women in public life. In 1916 Virginia Woolf expressed the connection in a letter:

> I grow steadily more feminist owing to *The Times*, which I read at breakfast and wonder how this preposterous masculine fiction [the war] keeps going a day longer–without some vigorous young woman pulling us together and marching through it. (Nicolson and Trautman, 1975–80, vol II, p 76).

The majority of the British suffrage movement accepted social feminist arguments, often along with equal rights ones. Even the militant suffragettes, the members of the Pankhursts' Women's Social and Political Union, believed in the distinctiveness and superiority of women's values and capabilities, though they were far from eschewing warlike behaviour. Certainly most of the members of the very large coalition of non-militants, the National Union of Women's Suffrage Societies, based their activism on such arguments.[4] So did the Women's Co-operative Guild which united wives of relatively prosperous working men. In addition, the Women's Co-operative Guild was one of the constituent units of the

People's Suffrage Federation, a coalition mainly of working women's organisations which seems to have been the 'adult suffrage' group with which Virginia Stephen worked in 1910. These were the women's organisations with which Virginia Woolf was associated.

Virginia Woolf's practical connection with the WCG and with the NUWSS seems to have been greater than has been suspected. For instance, she attended the Guild's annual conferences in at least 1916 and 1922, and from 1916 to 1920 she organised and ran meetings of the local Guild in her house in Richmond. Her correspondence and her diaries show her continuing interest in the Guild, of which the most visible evidence is her 'Introductory Letter' to a collection of Guildswomen's memoirs published by Hogarth Press in 1931. This 'Letter' is one of Virginia Woolf's important feminist texts; its preparation involved careful consultation with Guildswomen and with her long-time friend, Margaret Llewelyn Davies, secretary of the group for 24 years. As to the non-militant suffragists of the NUWSS, we can now trace a relationship between Virginia Woolf and its successor, later renamed the Fawcett Society, that lasted until her death. We know that she wrote at least one article for their journal, *The Woman Leader,* and that she at least considered giving them the manuscript of *A Room of One's Own* to sell. In 1930 she gave under their auspices, at a celebration for the feminist composer Ethel Smyth, a speech entitled 'Professions for Women' that was the first version of *Three Guineas.* A series of references in letters, and diaries, testify to Virginia Woolf's fondness for the library at 'Marsham Street'; she solicited funds for it from friends, used it extensively in research for *Three Guineas,* and had from 1938 until her death a standing arrangement by which she purchased books they requested for the library.[5]

All in all, even Virginia Woolf's relatively brief involvement with the suffrage campaign seems more significant than it is usually rated. It seems particularly important that her association, even then, was with and via essentially social feminist women's organisations. For the supposed 'invalid lady of Bloomsbury' she shows a remarkable amount of organisational participation – but with organisations neither she nor her associates thought of as political. Hence, again, the tendency to dismiss her as apolitical. And, even in connection with those groups, she did not show a degree of volunteer commitment comparable to that of some of her other women friends. In the People's Suffrage Federation, in the WCG, in the organisations and successors of the suffrage battle, there were women who contributed their full attention over long periods of years. Virginia Woolf's main concern was always her writing. This, her ill-health, and her husband's concern for her well-being, meant that political activity, however defined, was far from the centre of her life. But in her writing, and especially in her specifically feminist writing, we can see both the influence of the groups she was associated with, and the influence of the social feminism she shared with them.

The simplest versions of social feminism were naively biological in inspiration. Maternity was given credit for creating in women a purer, finer nature than men's. When feminists became aware of how such views had been used to restrict women, they reversed the argument so that innately womanly qualities became the justification for a public role for women. In Virginia Woolf's more subtle discussions it is not simply women's nature that creates their virtues, nor is it simply society that keeps them confined. Certain irreducible female characteristics supply the material with which social structures work. Society has kept women in the home, but women's own reproductive and sexual nature has facilitated the process. In *A Room of One's Own*, Shakespeare's doomed, imaginary sister Judith was initially able to over-ride the social barriers to female achievement. But she paid with psychological distress, pregnancy, and finally death. This is why *Three Guineas* presented mothers' allowances as one of the reforms basic to the transformation of society; this policy represents economic independence and financially expressed reward for the one area of activity that is distinctively and permanently female.

Because for Virginia Woolf the situation of women was not to be attributed exclusively to either their natures or social institutions, her assessment of the domestic, female realm was more complex than the usual social feminist ones. The policy measures she supported were those of the women's movement of her time, but her rationale was slightly different, closer to the arguments of today's feminists. In particular, she was unusual in noting the defects of private as well as public life.

The Victorians and Edwardians tended to idealise the home as the refuge from the brutalities of public life under industrial capitalism. There is a good deal of validity in the ideal of the 'Angel in the House', which still survives in the media myth of the happy family clustered at the table around the bountiful, smiling mother. Virginia Woolf certainly responded to its appeal. In *Monday or Tuesday* she imagined 'A Society' of young women deciding that while men were supposed to make 'good books', women had the superior vocation of making 'good people'. In this story men are compard to the barren cactus of which only the Aloe blooms, and only once in a hundred years; it is the women who are the life-givers and the life-enhancers (V. Woolf, 1921, pp 32, 20). Julia Stephen had been the essential centre of an almost stereotypical patriarchal family which fell apart after her death, as her daughter was well aware. As in the 'Introductory Letter' she had extolled the virtues of working-class wives, in *Three Guineas* she praised upper and middle-class women, translating their affective role into the imagery of stirring pots and rocking cradles. In addition, Virginia Woolf argued that, along with nurturance, women had been able to exercise the virtues that were the result of exclusion from formal education and economic independence. Women's specific virtues were 'poverty, chastity, derision and freedom from unreal loyalties'. This amounts to disinterestedness and integrity – good qualities for running a family, essential conditions for creativity and the avoidance of conflict in both private and public life.

At the same time Virginia Woolf had a good deal to say about the vices produced in the women who were shut up in the private world of the family in a condition of economic, physical, and psychological dependency. The domestic realm was better in many ways, for it had developed, at least in women, certain clearly superior qualities. Women had also escaped the public vices. But they had developed the characteristic defects of slaves: manipulativeness, deceit, pettiness, ignorance, indifference, ineffectiveness. The imagery of master and slave is pervasive in Virginia Woolf's feminism. In a public letter to 'Affable Hawk', Desmond MacCarthy, she described the relationship of men to women as 'half-civilised barbarism [that amounts to] an eternity of dominion on the one hand and of servility on the other' (A. Bell, 1977, vol II, p 342). The slaves even bear some responsibility for the situation. In 'Thoughts on Peace During an Air-Raid' she wrote of red-lipped, red-nailed consumer women as 'slaves who are trying to enslave'. 'Hitlers are bred by slaves', she said, reflecting the role that women play in reinforcing the patriarchy and in raising new generations of patriarchs and of their female dependents (L. Woolf, 1966–67, vol IV, p 174).

Yet if it is degrading to be either slave or master, the masters clearly have the advantages. In the home, they have the first call on all resources and the deciding voice about shares. In the public world, only men are allowed to acquire wealth, power, education, self-confidence, and, above all, the possibility of creativity. They have done a very bad job of using these possibilities; they have not shown much good sense about their own lives and happiness; but they have had chances, simply because of their sex. Their heaviest burden, which they do not recognise, is the values they necessarily acquire from the institutions that are the route to public success. As young men move through education and apprenticeship they become accustomed to competition, hierarchy, and aggressiveness. They become committed to the profit motive, until even the potentially valuable qualities of ambition and patriotism are corrupted. On a national scale, the result is a public life that is heartless, exploitative, and uncreative. Internationally, the result is recurrent wars. And the men bring the attitudes and practices of public life back into the home, domineering over and despising the women who share neither advantages, training, nor values with them.

Or is it the other way around? Virginia Woolf suggested also that the process began in the patriarchal family with its unquestioning acceptance of ascribed characteristics as a basis of status. Today, after the Second World War, it is more acceptable to point to the authoritarian family as important for an authoritarian and warlike society. What Virginia Woolf was saying was more extreme. For her, *every* family is essentially authoritarian because it is patriarchal, and *every* known society is also patriarchal, authoritarian, and ultimately warlike. Instead of the jargon of 'authoritarian', of course, she used the provocation of the polemical references to fascism.

In Virginia Woolf's views, shared by some feminist theorists today, both of the divided realms of human actitivy are pathological. Women have made better use of the separation in that they have developed the attitudes, practices, and values that can possibly redeem public life. But women have not benefitted personally. Men have achieved remarkable efforts of creativity under difficult conditions. But they too have benefitted personally far less than ought to be possible. In neither realm is there an adequate model for the future, although even the defective family is less undesirable than the existing world of politics and economics. And how are the private virtues, produced by exclusion, to be transferred to public life? In particular, how are women to manage to become educated, rich, publicly active, and powerful, without becoming just like the men they are replacing or joining? 'Lopsided education' and 'specialised and arduous careers' are no respecters of sex (Leaska, 1978, p xliv). Virginia Woolf was well aware of the risks and lures of co-option. She loved social life and raged in her Diary over slights such as the absence of an invitation to sit on the Board of the London Library; when she ridiculed and rejected public regalia and the range of rewards for acceptable achievement, she was conscious of how tempting they could be (A. Bell, 1977—, vol IX, pp 297, 8).

But on the whole, like a good social feminist, Virginia Woolf believed that women would be able to make the necessary adjustments. She wrote in 'The Leaning Tower', 'In future we are not going to leave writing to be done for us by a small class of well-to-do young men who have only a pinch, a thimbleful of experience to give us.' The phrasing of the sentence puts emphasis on 'men'. Although she was talking to a group of working-class men, the piece and her comments on it make it clear that among the excluded she placed all women. She was part of the group about which she wrote, 'We are going to add our own experience, to make our own contribution.' (L. Woolf, 1966–67, (a), vol II, p 181; Nicolson and Trautman, 1975–80, vol VI, p 467–468). The relevant female experience was related, not just to 'being despised' but also, more importantly, to women's particular version of reproduction and sexuality. The earliest Diary reference to a 'sequel' for *A Room of One's Own* described it as 'about the sexual life of women: to be called Professions for Women perhaps' (A. Bell, 1977–, vol IV pp 298, 6). On the other hand, the lives of women so carefully documented and analysed in *Three Guineas* and in all of Virginia Woolf's articles and reviews concerning women often seem offered as specific examples of the traps of assimilation and how they might be avoided: 'By considering the experiments that the dead have made with their lives in the past we may find some help . . .' (V. Woolf, 1938, p 113). The examples are most often used to show the risks that correspond to the excesses caricatured in the illustrations to *Three Guineas* and recounted in the failure of 'successful' women like Mrs Humphry Ward and Ella Wheeler Wilcox. The real successes are of less use, for they occurred in the present unsatisfactory world. Yet Virginia Woolf longed for more biography, and urged contemporary feminists to write down their lives. To Ethel Smyth, an intimate friend, she wrote explicitly of how important it was to have candid records of women's sexuality (Nicolson and Trautman, 1975–80, vol VI, p 453).

Women's experiences can thus provide a guide for the content of the desirable egalitarian future. At the same time, it is necessary to destroy the structures within which these experiences were accumulated. *Three Guineas* is full of images of burning and destruction, with the feminists dancing around the flames that consume the patriarchy. The Angel in the House was unselfish, even lovable, but Virginia Woolf spoke of killing her. In the same talk that became *Three Guineas* she warned her audience of young women about the obstacles they would face, the efforts and resources that men would put into maintaining control. Men had, after all, 'a trememdous tradition of mastery' (Leaska, 1978, p xliv). But she assumed that women would win – be easy with those poor men, be amused, not angry: 'If we could free ourselves from slavery we should free men from tyranny' (L. Woolf, 1966–67, vol IV, p 174). To encourage her listeners, she pointed out the potential for men; even now, there are some men 'with whom women can live in perfect freedom, without any fear' (Leaska, 1978, p xliv). She believed that women were in the process of breaking free from their limited and limiting roles, starting to produce a world of people who would be neither patriarchs nor angels. In such a world there would be no distinctions of status on the basis of ascribed characteristics such as gender. There would be no masters and no slaves. As a major consequence there would be no wars.

In a way, the critics of *Three Guineas* were correct in thinking that the book is not really about the prevention of war. The solution to war is easy: pacifism. But according to Virginia Woolf only women are pacifist, and mainly for the wrong reasons and in the wrong ways. What would a truly pacifist *society* be like? In 1938 the vocabulary was lacking for the answer that such a society would have to be non-sexist. The use of the term 'fascist' was misleading. Its opposite was 'democratic' but since the days of Aristotle the notion of democracy had been able to coexist very comfortably with complete subordination of women. However, whatever the terminology used, the existence of violence is not the main reason for wanting to end such a society and to reform the family that is its constituent unit. Instead, it is what a peaceful egalitarian society would be like in positive terms. And for her goal the pacifist, supposedly apolitical Virginia Woolf gave a description very like that of Thomas Hobbes. The purpose of government, wrote the author of *Leviathan* is 'to live delightfully'. Virginia Woolf called it 'the life of natural happiness' (Lamprecht, 1949, p 143; Nicolson and Trautman, 1975–80, vol VI, p 380).

Viscountess Rhondda, who had been a militant suffragette, wrote in response to *Three Guineas* to say that she was sure that women were as capable of violence as men: 'In my heart I find, it seems to me, such echoes of all the pride, vanity and combativeness I ever see in men.'Virginia Woolf wrote back as follows:

[Such feelings] are in us of course; I feel them pricking every moment. But again they have so little encouragement in us; surely, with the great example of what not to be blazing in front of us, we can damp them down before they get a hold. If we emphasise our position as outsiders and come to think it a natural distinction it should be easier for us than for those unfortunate young men . . .

Virginia Woolf compared herself to her 'old half-brother . . . who shot and rode and owned several acres'. Even more to the point, she reminded Lady Rhondda of how even that wealthy peeress had encountered difficulties as a woman trying to break into the world of journalism:

> But isn't that too a proof of what I say–I mean, as a woman shut out from so many of the newspaper sanctuaries you have to fight to enter; and thus don't think, as those within naturally do, how to shut others out. (Nicolson and Trautman, 1975–80, vol VI, pp 236–37).

Virginia Woolf was demonstrating what the real meaning could be for the 'Outsiders' Club' which she suggested as the solution to the problems of co-option. This association without rules and officers, and therefore without hierarchy or status, suggests a fore-runner to the 'structureless' (in hierarchical terms) consciousness–raising groups of the present women's movement. It would operate as a network of support structures within which, like Virginia Woolf and Lady Rhondda, women could remind each other of what their shared history and personal experiences meant. Feminists who read *Three Guineas* wrote and asked if they were 'Outsiders'. Of course, responded Virginia Woolf, who felt herself to be one. She also made it clear that she thought of the women's movement as a first approximation to the Outsiders' Club. Perhaps her experiences with the movement were one of the bases of her confidence that the cause of women would triumph.

In a letter written a year before her death, Virginia Woolf speculated on how the Outsiders could try to bring about the conditions they so much wanted in the post-war world:

> . . . sharing life after the war: pooling men's and women's work: about the possibility, if disarmament comes, of removing men's disabilities. Can one change sex characteristics? How far is the women's movement a remarkable experiment in that tranformation?

Wondering if it would be possible to 'alter the crest and spur of the fighting cock', she found the impact of the war encouraging, for it had removed a great deal of the lure and glamour of militarism. She ended hopefully:

It looks as if the sexes can adapt themselves; and here (that's our work) we can, or the young women can, bring enormous influence to bear. So many of the young men, could they get prestige and admiration, would give up glory and develop whats (*sic*) now so stunted . . . (Nicolson and Trautman, 1975–80, vol VI, p 380).

Virginia Woolf thus pushed the ideas of the social feminists to their natural conclusion, the transformation not just of women's role, but also of society and finally of men. One hostile contemporary response to *Three Guineas* had lamented that it would destroy the existing civilisation (Leavis, 1938, p 212). Virginia Woolf's point was just that: the need to end civilisation as we know it, to the extent that it depends on fascism in the family and in the state, the unpaid devotion of women in the home, the exploitation of women in the workplace, and the implicit structure of values that favours competition, hierarchy, and violence. 'But what about *my* civilisation?' she asked (A. Bell, 1977–, vol IV, p 298).

The social feminist image of the transformed world is a radical one. Virginia Woolf thought that she was incapable of working out the details of how to produce it. Here, once again, she can be seen accepting the image of herself as somehow apolitical. In a letter to Ethel Smyth she wrote typically: 'But then of course I'm not a politician, and so take one leap to the desirable lands' (Nicolson and Trautman, 1975–80, vol VI, p 478). She thought her role was to supply the vision, as indeed she did. Yet in her feminist works she included the specific measures that the women's movement of her day thought were necessary stages along the road to the 'desirable lands'. The list is a long one, and it corresponds point by point with the practical demands made by organised groups of feminists. Much of what it contains is still being asked for today, reappearing in documents like 1975's American National Women's Agenda, and the 1980 programme of the Day of Action of some 60 member groups of the British Women's Movement. It is worth listing them rapidly here, for they represent the specific policies derived by social feminists.

In *A Room of One's Own,* the least concrete of her feminist works, Virginia Woolf asked on behalf of women for economic independence and privacy, as well as for control of marriage and of reproduction (Shakespeare's sister), and the possibility of advanced education. This last includes both access on equal terms and the possibility of such essential related conditions as travel and leisure. The 'Introductory Letter' to *Life as We Have Known It* endorsed working women's demands such as the vote on equal terms with men, reformed divorce laws, minimum wages, and modernisation of household equipment. In *Three Guineas,* she added a woman's party in parliament, a women's newspaper, progressive education (non-hierarchical and including the history of women), pensions for single women, salaries for wives, and childbirth anaesthesia. The last should probably be seen as equivalent to today's demands for more humane childbirth arrangements in which mothers have a larger role; the preceding point looks like wages for housework but is probably Mothers' Allowance. In addition, *Three Guineas* included sustained argument for the full and equal admission of women to the senior, influential, and well-paid professions; she discussed the Church and the Civil Service at length. In the interim, women should be admitted on equal terms to the existing traditional educational institutions. As she measured and counted the precise level of women's share in, for instance, scholarships at Cambridge, the reader may sense an advance warning of affirmative action techniques, although this would be anachronistic for 1938. Virginia Woolf was listing the measures that a rich woman could help bring about, along with the public policies that women's organisations had thought possible and campaigned for. One of her major concerns was to produce some rich (and therefore powerful) women who would see such changes as urgent.

Virginia Woolf thus bridged the older and the newer, present-day women's movements. The new movement is mistakenly likely to think that feminism began in the last few years (see Dale Spender, 1982[b], 1983). But when its members respond to Virginia Woolf's message, they are also implicitly recognising their relationship to the groups who were the context and in part the source of her feminism. The values of social feminism that she accepted still form a major part of the beliefs of feminists today. To begin with, she articulated the older and continuing beliefs: the emphasis on the differences between men and women, the belief that male domination has deformed public life, the hopes for the results of women's impact on public life, the importance of the specific reforms the movement has supported and continues to support, and the notion of women as nurturers and therefore peace-makers. She also added a number of concerns that were not as important for the older movement or were even alien to them, but which are of increasing importance today: hostility to the patriarchal family, fears of co-option and assimilation, sexual issues, and the reliance on the women's movement as a continuing source of support for women even after legal equality has been acquired. The older and the newer movements do not interpret the continuing issues in the same way; necessarily, views have changed about the nature of sexuality and maternity, about education and women's history, and about fascism and war. But there are clear continuities of both ideas and organisations.

Virginia Woolf's associations with the women's movement as well as her explicitly feminist writings make it clear that she was indeed, not just an equal rights feminist, not just one with a political orientation, but a social feminist as well and conscious of how power and institutions explain the disadvantages of women. Why, then, was she so long considered only a feminist in a personal sense, and why was she later believed to be committed only to limited forms of equality, to androgyny, or to female separatism?

The answers, that can only be briefly sketched out here, seem related to how her work was analysed. In the period when she was studied mainly as a novelist, her fiction was appreciated because of its technical innovation. Those novels which were most admired in her period of greatest acclaim were in striking contrast with the 'realistic' novels of social protest or commentary; their message and commitments were not easily recognised, especially by an audience for whom feminism meant suffragism. Virginia Woolf encouraged such naive dismissal of the ideas in fiction by her own insistence that propaganda damaged creative writing. Yet even when attention turned to her non-fiction, the message was often misunderstood. E. M. Forster, in the Rede Lectures, gently chided her for the lack of any 'great cause'. For him feminism had harmed her works, and he thought the 'cantankerous' *Three Guineas* was 'the worst of her books'. He does not seem to have considered her novels feminist at all (Rosenbaum, 1975, pp 207, 215).

Even in *A Room of One's Own,* which just about everyone likes, only part of the argument is usually noticed. Readers agree with the case she puts, that creativity depends on freedom from self-consciousness and on the ability to use all dimensions of the mind and personality. They are still far less responsive to the accompanying insistence that such conditions are, for material and psychological reasons, peculiarly difficult for women to achieve. She would not accept statements that women in general in the twentieth century, or even she in particular, shared the privileges and freedoms of men yet. Her analysis of the persistence of constraints on women did not fit easily into the equal rights feminism so widely accepted. It was easier to read *Room* as showing how the previously excluded women were moving into the mainstream of what would then somehow become an androgynous society. This was the argument made by Winifred

Holtby in a study of Virginia Woolf written before the publication of *Three Guineas*. She admired Virginia Woolf but said that from her viewpoint the author's 'vision of [sex] segregation is excessive'. Virginia Woolf underestimated the extent to which women were becoming integrated into 'the professional world, the political world, the world of business', the extent to which, 'to the mature human being . . . this matter of maleness and femaleness' was already unimportant. Such an interpretation saw the 'Introductory Letter' to *Life as We Have Known It* as Virginia Woolf's 'furthest excursion into political writing . . . recognising the part played, even in the artist's life, by the practical, material conditions of living' (Holtby, 1932, 1978, pp 58, 91, 184, 186). This account, which limited the meaning of *A Room of One's Own,* thus distorted the 'Introductory Letter' quite badly. After the appearance of *Three Guineas* it ceased to make any sense.

Three Guineas, a much less appealing and charming book in any case, was either dismissed or in its turn distorted. Even post-war feminists, who were sympathetic to its viewpoint, found it hard to accept the radical transformative vision of social feminism, and Virginia Woolf's subtle and discouraging account of the dangers and opportunities available for women. It was much easier to read the book as a simple affirmation of the female values; the segregation that had been imposed on women could now be glorified. Men still tend to react with varying degrees of discomfort to what they see as a caricature of 'the evil patriarch as Virginia Woolf saw him . . . a twisted monster'. These are the words of Herbert Marder, who was one of the earliest critics to be aware of the importance of feminism for Virginia Woolf. Even Marder concluded by rejecting *Three Guineas* and its argument as 'morbid'. His final judgment on the feminism of *Three Guineas* was that it was an aberration:

> Virginia Woolf's main emphasis in her feminist writings . . . was on self-reform, and on art as a means to that end. Novels and tracts alike grew out of a preoccupation with her own spiritual dilemma . . . When she deserted art for propaganda, as in *Three Guineas,* her self-absorption got the upper hand . . . Virginia Woolf's direct attack on social evil is too shrill and self-indulgent to succeed, even as propaganda. (Marder, 1968, pp 91, 176, 175)

Oddly enough, it was some of the critics most hostile to *Three Guineas* who best understood its meaning. In a hysterical review that called the piece 'babblings', 'unpleasant self-indulgence' motivated by class bias and 'sex hostility', Q. D. Leavis recognised the implications of Virginia Woolf's social feminism:

> Then there are the unfortunate men . . . They must from the start share the work of tending their offspring. A thorough-going revolution in their wage-earning pursuits, and so a regular social reorganisation must follow. (Leavis, 1938, pp 204, 205, 209, 211)

This was the message of a feminism that has been labelled social but is obviously political, and which has not yet finished having its impact.

Virginia Woolf's feminism was political because it responded to notions about power and social structure, and because it reflected a specific organisational and programmatic history. The vehemence of attempts to represent this sort of feminism as apolitical and marginal shows just how essentially radical it is. War and the patriarchy continue, if perhaps with rather less support than before the days of the women's movement. There is a long way to go yet before women even have their own rooms, which means economic independence and political equality. The equal rights feminists had this as their goal. The social feminists wanted more. Today, they are still looking forward to the time of 'The Knock on the Door', which was one of the early titles for *Three Guineas*. That was the goal of politics for Virginia Woolf: the man's step on the stair as he comes to consult the woman, the door opened by the women, and 'the most interesting, exciting, and important conversation that has ever been heard' (Leaska, 1978, p xliv). The 'life of natural happiness' will be possible in the society where that conversation takes place, for it will be the long-awaited, permanently peaceful community of equals.

Notes

1   Two interesting exceptions are Berenice Carroll, 1978, ' "To Crush Him in Our Own Country": The Political Thought of Virginia Woolf', *Feminist Studies,* 4, no 1, (February), and Jane Marcus, 1977, ' "No More Horses": Virginia Woolf on Art and Propaganda', *Women's Studies,* 4. However, neither Marcus nor Carroll discuss Virginia Woolf's practical political involvements. James Naremore, 1979, in 'Nature and History in *The Years*' in Ralph Freedman, ed., *Virginia Woolf: Re-evaluation and Commentary,* University of California Press, Berkeley, is very perceptive in his analysis of *Three Guineas.*

2   Feminism can be defined in both personal and organisational terms. It includes the desire not to have women judged inferior or lacking by male standards, and the insistence that women not be disadvantaged in

comparison to men. The definition of feminism understood here is close to the one found in Linda Gordon, 1976, *Woman's Body, Woman's Right: Birth Control in America*, Grossman, New York.

3   Social feminism should not be confused with the socialist feminism which sees the end of capitalism as the remedy for the disadvantages of women. Virginia Woolf was a socialist in the sense that she was opposed to capitalism, but her feminism had a separate source, in her analysis of the nature of patriarchy. For social feminism, see J. Stanley Lemons, 1975, *The Woman Citizen: Social Feminism in the 1920s*, University of Illinois Press, Urbana, Ill.

4   The National Union of Women's Suffrage Societies only reluctantly decided to support the First World War, accepting the argument that this war would make it possible to end militarism, at least in Germany. After the war they reverted to pacifism. The Women's Co-operative Guild was always unrelentingly pacifist. See the NUWSS statement cited from the *International Women's Suffrage News* by Arnold Whittick, 1979, *Woman into Citizen*, Atheneum with Frederick Muller, London, p 296, and Ray Strachey, 1931, *Millicent Garrett Fawcett*, John Murray, London.

5   More detail about Virginia Woolf's association with the women's movement may be found in my 'Virginia Woolf and the Women's Movement', in Jane Marcus, ed. 1983, *Virginia Woolf: A Feminist Slant*, University of Chicago Press.

Vera Brittain:
Feminist in a New Age
(1896–1970)

Muriel Mellown

That the final passing of the Equal Franchise Bill in 1928 meant not an end but a fresh beginning to the women's movement was indicated clearly, though unconsciously, by Stanley Baldwin himself as he announced his government's introduction of the bill. 'I would rather', he declared to the mass rally at Queen's Hall, 'trust a woman's instinct than a man's reason.'[1] Among those who felt the tremor pass through the female part of the audience was Vera Brittain, lecturer, journalist, novelist, and a principal voice for feminism in the new age following the attainment of the vote. Born in 1893, ten years before Mrs Pankhurst founded the Women's Social and Political Union, she belonged to the first generation of women to succeed to the rights won by the suffragettes and by that long line of nineteenth-century figures who had worked for the advancement of women. Always at the centre rather than on the fringe of events, and a confirmed internationalist in outlook, Vera Brittain was actively involved in both world wars, in the rise of British socialism, in the peace movement, even in the independence of India and the emergence of the Third World. Amid all these changing events she remained remarkably constant in her philosophies, the centre point of her thinking being from first to last her belief in and work for the women's movement.

Brittain's feminism began with her struggle for a university education. The daughter of a Staffordshire paper manufacturer, she received the education considered appropriate for a young lady – being taught by a governess at home, followed by five years at a boarding school in Surrey. Her parents then automatically assumed that, while her brother went up to Oxford, she would enter their social circle in Buxton and eventually make a suitable marriage. But Vera Brittain was not of the stuff to accept such a scheme. Encouraged by her reading of Olive Schreiner's *Woman and Labour*

(1911), which first made a feminist of her, she determined to escape the intellectual stagnation of provincial life and persuaded her reluctant father to send her to Oxford. She went up to Somerville in the inauspicious month of September 1914, intending to ignore events in Europe. But her plans, like those of an entire generation, were shattered by the realities of the war she had tried to forget. With her fiancé, Roland Leighton, and her brother both in the army, she could not remain in the Oxford backwater, and at the end of her first year she left for three years of nursing as a VAD in England, Malta, and France. By the end of the war she had lost her brother, her fiancé, and her two closest friends, and she had seen at first hand the horror of a civilisation crashing into chaos. In numb despair she viewed college as 'the one thing left out of the utter wreckage of the past' (*Testament of Youth*, 1933, p 468) and decided to return to Oxford.

It was not at first easy. Brittain experienced the problems of readjustment now fully recognised but in those days practically ignored. She suffered depression, tension, and a nightmare sense of hostilities around her. But from her two remaining years at Oxford she made certain gains which determined the course of her life. First was her friendship with Winifred Holtby, which continued until Holtby's premature death in 1935. Next, for the first time she was able to become an active participant in a women's cause. During those post-war years Oxford was shaken by the last stages of the campaign for degrees for women, a campaign which ended in October 1920, as the first women received their degrees in the Sheldonian Theatre side by side with men. Brittain threw herself wholeheartedly into this cause, supporting it, as she said nine years later, 'by the ardent outpourings of my propagandist pen in any column then open to women students' (*The Nation*, 14 February 1931, p 631). At Oxford, too, Brittain first knew the stimulating companionship of other writers. In 1920 she was co-editor, with C. H. B. Kitchin and Alan Porter, of *Oxford Poetry*, where her work appeared beside that of Robert Graves, Edmund Blunden, L. A. G. Strong, L. P. Hartley, Roy Campbell, Richard Hughes, and Winifred Holtby. When she left Oxford in 1921 she had decided on a life-time career as a writer.

Early in 1922 she and Winifred Holtby settled in London, and she began to gain the first footholds in that career. Her initial successes were in lecturing rather than in journalism. As a speaker for the League of Nations Union she found herself much in demand and was soon giving as many as four speeches a week. But her real goal was writing, and within two years she had published a number of journal articles and two novels, *The Dark Tide* (1923) and *Not Without*

Honour (1924). Neither her marriage in 1925 to the political philosopher George Catlin nor the birth of her children in 1927 and 1930 deflected her from her career. In the following years she became a highly successful free-lance journalist, contributing frequently to such publications as the *Manchester Guardian*, the *Yorkshire Post, Time and Tide*, and the *Nation*. Full-length feminist studies at this time were *Women's Work in Modern England* (1928), a review of the fields of employment open to women, and *Halcyon, or The Future of Monogamy* (1929), a tongue-in-cheek 'history' of marriage in the nineteenth, twentieth, and twenty-first centuries. To these years too belonged Brittain's first major literary successes, her autobiography *Testament of Youth* (1933) and the novel *Honourable Estate* (1936).

During this period Vera Brittain became associated with the considerable number of active feminists then working in London. In 1920 Lady Margaret Rhondda, assisted by a group of women, including the writers Rebecca West, E. M. Delafield, and Cicely Hamilton, had founded the feminist journal *Time and Tide*. Lady Rhondda had already gained success in the male-dominated business world as assistant to her father, the Viscount Rhondda, coal merchant and politician. As she explained in her autobiography (Rhondda, 1933), she designed the review in order to propagate the new ideas which she saw as the only salvation for society in the future. The next year she also inaugurated the feminist organisation known as the Six Point Group, which took its name from its six goals: pensions for widows, equal rights of guardianship for parents, improvement of the laws dealing with child assault and with unmarried mothers, equal pay for teachers, and equal opportunities in the Civil Service. Vera Brittain and Winifred Holtby began to work for the Six Point Group shortly after their arrival in London, and the connection brought them into the mainstream of post-war feminism. Winifred Holtby became a director of *Time and Tide* in 1926, and Vera Brittain was a regular contributor. By the 1930s they were established as prominent members and feminist leaders in a circle of well known writers and journalists.

The years between the wars saw Brittain's most active involvement in the women's movement. Her life took a different turn as the threat of a second world war came closer. Early in 1937 she became a sponsor for Canon Dick Sheppard's Peace Pledge Union and committed herself to the cause of pacifism. She tells the full story of that commitment in her second autobiography *Testament of Experience* (1957). Throughout the war 'men's politics' determined her course and pacifism claimed her exclusive attention, and only after 1945 was she free to resume her work for the advancement of women. In the last stage of her intellectual development she combined the ideals of feminism and pacifism, bringing to both an ever-deepening sense of internationalism. She had always transcended the narrow confines of mere nationalism and embraced the European and American perspective; now her vision was further enlarged by travel and lecture tours not only in Europe and America but also in India and South Africa. Such works as *Lady Into Woman* (1953), *The Women At Oxford* (1960), *Pethick-Lawrence* (1963), *Envoy Extraordinary: A Study of Vijaya Lakshmi Pandit and her Contribution to Modern India* (1965), and *Radclyffe Hall, A Case of Obscenity?* (1968) betoken the range of her interests and her abiding loyalty to the women's movement.

On her death in 1970 Vera Brittain left behind, in addition to innumerable newspaper and journal articles, 29 books, including five novels, two volumes of poetry, two autobiographies, biographies, travel books, and a variety of social studies. This diverse material is marked by a remarkable intellectual consistency. Whatever the form of her work, Brittain wrote – even in her fiction – to express her views on life and in particular her views on women. During the early years in Oxford and London she formulated distinct theories about woman's position and autonomy and the rights of woman to think, to act, and to be heard. At Oxford she had received an historian's training, and her historical sense allowed her to see the long tradition of female oppression which she was combating. As she espoused the feminist cause, she brought to bear the keen intelligence which had enabled her – without tutoring, guidance or instruction – to win a Somerville Exhibition. Her theories are consistent, precisely thought out, and clearly articulated into a coherent system.

Vera Brittain's ideas reflect the new direction of the feminist movement in the 1920s. Women now had won the right to an education and the power of the vote. In the second stage of the women's movement the need was to utilise these gains in order to effect extensive legal and social reforms and Vera Brittain devoted much of her life to this end. The basis of her efforts was a set of six distinct, specific goals: sweeping changes in human attitudes, a new concept of marriage, the advancement of women to professional and economic equality, the improvement of social services for women, radical developments in sexual morality, and a new understanding of women's psychology and capacities. These six goals constitute the main planks of her feminist theory, which was aimed at ending sexual inequality.

The first goal, a change in human attitudes, was the necessary foundation for all other reforms since old traditions and patterns of thought formed the primary obstacle to progress. Brittain was well aware that such changes were harder to bring about than changes in the law because the effect of centuries of conditioning had to be dispelled. The corner-stone of her feminism, then, was her attack upon 'the ancient conventions and prejudices which keep women in inferior positions' (*Women's Work*, p 37). The barriers she sought to overcome were twofold, involving both men and women. Granted, by the 1920s male attitudes to women had undergone considerable change, yet old attitudes die hard. Vera Brittain had grown up in a world where to the average man only three attitudes to women were possible. The first – and the most common – was that of contemptuous amusement, signified by the smirk, the furtive snigger, the sly nudge, which accompanied any reference to women, sex, marriage, or childbirth. Still not unknown in the 1920s, it stood in the way of any serious attempt to reform social services or move towards equality for women. The second approach took the position that women were delicate, decorative creatures, to be treated with gallantry but strictly excluded from any serious business in life. According to this view, no real education was necessary for women since their province was the drawing-room and superficial cultural accomplishments. The third attitude was one of indifference, a simple refusal to recognise the rights of women in matters of legislation and reform. Such attitudes were not just the legacy of the Victorian era; their roots went back to the Middle Ages when women were regarded with strange ambivalence – simultaneously hated and venerated as representative of both Eve and Mary.

In all their manifestations these views stemmed from the long tradition which saw women as lacking the ability to reason. Such a lack – the argument went – precluded any kind of political, economic or social equality for women and required their exclusion from all major decision-making in either family or national life. Vera Brittain first became conscious of these views when as a girl she fought to free herself from the provincial life of Buxton and gain admission to Oxford. The following years confirmed her recognition of the customary denigration of women. In opposition to the common estimates, she based her entire feminist theory upon the principle that woman is a thinking, reasoning being, endowed with the same intelligence and intellectual power as man. Throughout her life, then, she attacked the lingering prejudices which hindered the advancement of women and prevented an acknowledgement of their real abilities.

No less significant than male prejudice was the female sense of inferiority which it had bred. A major part of Vera Brittain's life work was to change this attitude, still prevalent in 1953 when she was writing her study of the women's movement *Lady Into Woman*. Since women in large numbers had even then not risen to the challenges of responsibility, they remained under-represented in parliament and local government and consequently deprived of full and equal status. Recognising the necessity of economic independence, what was needed, she declared, was that women should shed their traditional acceptance of a secondary role and avail themselves of the opportunities and powers they now possessed. Writing of an article in the *Manchester Guardian* entitled 'Abolishing that Five-pound Look', she commented: 'Today that five-pound look has become a ten-pound look, but it is not yet a hundred-pound look, still less a thousand. Only when women in sufficient numbers acquire a thousand-pound look will they endow their institutions and produce their Shakespeares' (p 126). In other words, she exhorted women to develop the self-confidence and assertiveness necessary for equality and for self-realisation.

In working towards her second goal, a new concept of marriage, Vera Brittain made possibly her most significant and original contribution to feminism. She maintained that a complete revision of traditional attitudes was essential if women were to achieve equality, and therefore happiness, in marriage. In the old-style marriage women were the victims in a relationship in which 'the Jehovah-like spouse . . . eclipsed and absorbed his young wife's personality, himself dictating her tastes, her occupations and even the number of her children' (*Halcyon*, 1929, p 84). In contrast to this Brittain put forward the idea of marriage as an equal partnership, in which the wife was accepted as 'an intelligent, independent companion' (*Lady Into Woman*, 1953, p 10) and women were no longer forced into the roles of 'either slaves, toys, exotic greenhouse plants, or carefully-reared animals' (*Halcyon*, 1929, p 86). In her novel *Honourable Estate* she illustrated both types of marriage. The old-style marriage is represented by Janet and Thomas Rutherston, characters based in part upon Brittain's parents-in-law. The marriage, depicted in painful detail, reveals the failure in personal relationships which inevitably accompanies male domination. Thomas, a domineering, selfish clergyman, believes that his wife's duty is to attend to his happiness. He denies Janet any rights of privacy or possession: he reads her diaries, he manages her small private income, and he selects her doctor. Identifying his sexual desires with traditional morality, he maintains that her function, sanctified by God, is to bear a large number of children. Any rejection of these wifely duties he interprets as rebellion not just against society but against the divine will. By contrast Denis Rutherston and Ruth Alleyndene, of the younger generation, consciously work to build an equal marriage in which Ruth retains her independence and pursues her own career as a politician.

The emphasis on Ruth's career indicates Brittain's deep conviction that under no circumstances should marriage deprive a woman of the right to work. Brittain rejected vehemently the convention that married women should abandon independent work and dedicate their talents to the careers of their husbands. Following Olive Schreiner's sentiments in *Woman and Labour*, she regarded meaningful work as the only sure way of giving significance to one's life and the only unfailing source of happiness.[2] In her view, if a woman lacks the opportunity to work, she is robbed of both economic independence and emotional satisfaction. One of the chief purposes of *Women's Work in Modern England* was to counter the tendency – widespread until the Second World War – to discourage women from continuous work after marriage. In *Lady Into Woman* Brittain described one of the greatest achievements of the woman's movement to be the ending of prejudice against working wives and the disappearance of the lady of leisure who knew only the empty satisfaction of futile drawing-room accomplishments.[3]

With all this insistence on the married woman's right to a career outside the home, Vera Brittain also recognised that homemaking and motherhood are legitimate, valuable forms of work. Before the war she directed her efforts mainly at repudiating the convention which tied married women to domesticity. Her priority stemmed from the marriage-bar which forced women to give up their jobs on marriage. After the war, when the marriage-bar was less common, she turned her attention to the rights of women who deliberately chose to work within the home. She maintained that their services should give them a legal right to a proportion of their husbands' incomes, and she pointed to the example of the Scandinavian Code, which ensured for homemakers the economic advantages and protection enjoyed by other members of the work force (*Lady Into Woman*, pp 164, 170, 180).

Brittain's theorising on marriage extended to a practical concern with day-to-day living, and she defended any innovation which might improve the state of marriage. In particular, she noted the need for more flexibility in domestic life. She favoured labour-saving devices which would reduce domestic toil, stressed the need for husbands to participate in housekeeping, welcomed the advent of radio and television as an enhancement of home life, and advocated privacy, temporary separation, and holidays apart for husbands and wives.[4] Along with these new ideas, she rejected the convention which identified motherhood 'with the four S's – sentiment, suffering, sacrifice, and stupidity . . . so long . . . considered the appropriate adjuncts of maternity' (*Halcyon*, 1929, p 67).

When she wrote *Lady Into Woman*, Brittain believed that her ideal of marriage was fast becoming a reality. Indeed, as she looked at modern marriages and contrasted them with those she had seen in her girlhood she could not but emphasise the progress that had taken place. However, her awareness of the gulf between past and present led her to overestimate the extent of the gains. True, the worst extremes of husbands such as Thomas Rutherston belonged to the past. Yet the equal partnership she envisioned, if it existed at all in the 1950s, was to be found only in isolated cases. In the great majority of marriages the old prejudices and customs and inequalities survived. A long road lay ahead before equal marriages would be accepted throughout the entire social structure. Although women have proceeded further down that road in the past 30 years, the goal still belongs to the future.

Feminist precept and practice have seldom been more completely linked than in Vera Brittain's own marriage to George Catlin. Brittain believed that her marriage might set an example and pave the way for other women. In the last chapter of *Testament of Youth*, which deals extensively with her approach to marriage, she expresses her hope that 'the future of women, like the future of peace, could be influenced by individual decisions in a way that had never seemed possible when all individuality was quenched and drowned in the dark tide of the War' (p 654). Similarly when she referred in *Halcyon* to the value of the experiments in marriage made by a few enlightened couples she must have been thinking of herself and her husband (p 47). Motherhood too she considered a vital challenge which she accepted as a pioneer who might suggest to future generations a way of reconciling the claims of marriage and a career (*Testament of Youth*, 1933, p 653).

Throughout her married life Brittain lived up to this determination to establish a precedent in her personal life. She spent her first year of marriage in Ithaca, New York, where her husband held a professorship at Cornell University. However, she decided that residence in London was essential to success in her career, and as a result they agreed to try what she called 'semi-detached marriage',[5] an arrangement by which they would live apart for several months each year. It was a commuter marriage between two continents which would be impressive even by today's standards. The arrangement continued even after her children were born, and despite interruptions and discouragements, Brittain produced her two greatest successes, *Testament of Youth* and *Honourable Estate*, while both her children were under ten years old. Catlin's resignation from his professorship at Cornell in 1935 did not bring an end to the semi-detached style of living. As the years passed, each partner combined personal independence and careers involving world travel with commitment to one another. In the matter of marriage and motherhood, Brittain's life speaks as much to us today as does her writing. Fifty years ago she faced and overcame problems still considered exclusively modern. In that fact by itself she deserves our respect.

Vera Brittain's third goal was equality for women in education and employment. She saw that the struggle at Oxford extended beyond the limits of a single university, since 'it represented the quintessence of the whole movement for women's emancipation, the contest for the equal citizenship of the mind' (*Women At Oxford*, 1960, p 16). As with other issues, Brittain did not cease her efforts once the goal of degrees was reached; she continued to stress the poverty of women's colleges and the need for endowments and gifts.[6]

One of Brittain's chief objectives was to encourage women to make direct use of any professional training they had acquired, and her main efforts were aimed at equality in employment. Her book *Women's Work in Modern England*, developed from a series of articles which first appeared in the *Outlook*, was conceived as a deliberate weapon in the struggle for equality. In the 1920s the doors which had begun to open for women during the war were closing again. Their services no longer needed, women were being pushed back once more to drawing-room or kitchen. The chief efforts, therefore, had to be in the area of employment. In an article for the *Nation* Brittain remarked that women's interest in articles giving career information 'indicates clearly the logical development of feminism in the new decade. Political equality is Dead Sea fruit unless it leads to economic equality' (The *Nation*, 3 January 1931).

Brittain's aims in *Women's Work* were first to encourage women to pursue careers and second to expose sex discrimination. The book is a survey of the employment then open to women, giving details about the necessary training, the prospects, and remuneration. While Brittain pointed out that in every field women occupied the lower echelons and were paid at lower rates than their male counterparts, she attacked most forcefully the professions of teaching and the Civil Service, both earlier singled out as targets by the Six Point Group. She contended that the flagrant disregard for women's rights in teaching produced especially far-reaching effects since this was traditionally the chief female profession. At that time most education authorities required women to resign from their posts on marriage, a practice which continued up to the Second World War. Moreover, it was impossible even for unmarried women to advance as far or as fast as men – largely because of men teachers' refusal to serve under a woman head. Generally the most a woman could hope for in a mixed school was the headship of an infant school or – under extraordinary circumstances – the deputy headship of a secondary school, serving under a headmaster. The early feminist efforts in these areas did eventually produce results, though only after heavy opposition. In the 1960s the Civil Service and teaching granted equal pay to women, ahead of business and industry and in advance of the Equal Pay Act of 1970.

The major goals of working women have always been equal hiring practices, equal pay, equal rights for promotion, and equal rights to work after marriage. Brittain worked consistently for all these. As in her views on marriage, so in her theories about women in the labour market, she was far in advance of her time and in some respects of ours too. She argued that women with children 'have the right to demand that conventional employment regulations should be modified for their sake' (*Lady Into Woman*, 1953, p 180), and she supported a wide range of innovations which would make permanent and equal work possible for women. Her suggestions included maternity leave, state nursery schools and baby-sitting services, part-time work for women with young children, refresher courses for women who wished to rejoin the work force, and even sabbaticals for wives.[7] Repeatedly, too, she proclaimed the need for women to organise in order to attain their objectives. Organisation had been the method by which men had endeavoured to keep women in a depressed condition. It was up to women, then, to adopt the same tactics to increase their bargaining power.[8]

Brittain's next goal, social reform achieved through political action, was based upon a somewhat different approach to women's problems. In giving first priority to equality Brittain was in accordance with the Six Point Group and its motto 'Equality First', as well as with the tradition of the nineteenth-century feminists. But a new type of feminism was also developing which concentrated on social reforms designed to recognise the needs peculiar to women. This type of feminism was most fully represented by Eleanor Rathbone, who led the fight for family allowances in Parliament. While Brittain gave her chief allegiance to the traditional feminism, she also saw the value of the new approach. Indeed, looking back in 1953, she conceded that perhaps traditional feminists had erred in stressing equality and sometimes ignoring the fact that as mothers, not as workers, women performed 'an important national service, comparable from the State's point of view with conscription, which deserved special privileges' (*Lady Into Woman*, 1953, p 168).

As a socialist Vera Brittain had always supported social reform, particularly in matters which affected women. She joined the Labour Party in 1924 and politically she stood to the left of the party. As a feminist she considered the welfare state itself a development of the women's movement, since it indicates a shift from the power politics of a male-dominated world to the welfare politics of a world in which women are able to exercise direct influence. The social services provided by the welfare state benefit both sexes, but in many instances their most immediate impact is on the lives of women. One of the reasons for Brittain's championship of the welfare state was her sense that in it women have become ends in themselves and not means to the ends of men (*Lady Into Woman*, 1953, pp 8, 29, 224).

In the field of social reform Vera Brittain was primarily concerned with family planning clinics, a national maternity service, and state nurseries and nursery schools. From the start she had stressed the liberating power of birth control, and she had attended in 1922 the earliest meetings of Marie Stopes's Society for Constructive Birth Control. Birth control more than any other single factor has freed women from traditional limitations, enabled them to reject traditional roles, and given them control over their own lives. Yet in the 1920s and 1930s officials of church and government alike still opposed it, and many medical officers refused to permit birth control information at public clinics. Brittain fought this in *Halcyon* and in such articles as that for the *Nation* where she cited the case of a Mrs Wise, on trial for the murder of her fifth child, an infant of nine months, and already again pregnant. As Brittain pointed out, Mrs Wise was herself a victim, the real criminal being 'cruel, obstructive prejudice' against provision for adequate family planning among all classes of society (*The Nation*, 24 January, 1931).

Personal experience as well as socialist and feminist conviction underlay Brittain's support of a national maternity service and state nursery schools. A powerful element in her feminism was that gift of sympathetic imagination which enabled her to identify with the mass of women throughout the nation. For example, the difficult birth of her first child and her problems in raising the frail, delicate infant led her to campaign for better health and maternity services for all. Her recognition of the need for a national maternity service is expressed in *Testament of Experience* with a fury possibly unique in her writings: 'At such times I was filled with a vehement anger. I wanted to batter down the walls of the Ministry of Health; to take the Minister himself and give him a woman's inside, and compel him to have six babies, all without anaesthetics. . . Sometimes I gripped the chair in impotent rage because one woman could do so little' (p 52). Similarly her own experiences as a working mother, forced to combine professional responsibilities with all the interruptions and upheavals of domestic life, led her to advocate the establishment of state nursery schools for all classes of women.

In her resistance to prejudice and her stand on marriage, equality, and social reform Vera Brittain sought practical, clearly defined goals. Her fifth goal, a radical shift in sexual morality, was more subtle, but just as important and perhaps even more revolutionary. On the most pressing moral issue of the 1980s, that of abortion, she has little to say, though her views may be partly inferred from her sympathetic depiction in *Honourable Estate* of Janet Rutherston's attempts to bring about an abortion. Her main concern, however, was the removal of double standards of sexual morality. She first recognised those standards when as a girl she heard her father amuse a guest with an account of how his mother had found her unmarried cook in labour and had turned her out of the house at midnight, with the result that her child was born in a cab as she was on her way to the workhouse. The episode provided a revelation that Brittain never forgot. The chapter on 'Women and Sex Morals' in *Lady Into Woman* traces the gradual disappearance of the old standards which had equated all morality with sexual morality (and a double standard of sexual morality at that) and which had blandly countenanced outrageous social and legislative injustice in the area of sexual offences against women.

Brittain's theorising on morality is most noteworthy in her approach to homosexuality which while dated today in terms of its origins in a biological frame of reference, was very much in advance of its time and was a courageous public stance to take. Her first defence of homosexuality developed in connection with Radclyffe Hall's *The Well of Loneliness*. On 10 August 1928 she reviewed the novel in *Time and Tide*, describing it as 'a plea, passionate, yet admirably restrained and never offensive, for the extension of social tolerance, compassion and recognition to the biologically abnormal woman' ('Radclyffe Hall', 1968, p 48). As a result, she was one of the 39 witnesses assembled to defend the work in the obscenity trial brought against it. Forty years later, in the last book she published, she did not substantially revise her opinion and reiterated her admiration of the book's honesty and the author's courage in presenting her case to an intolerant public. Looking back across the years, she saw modern society as indebted to Radclyffe Hall for initiating free, open discussion and for bringing 'the individual practices falsely and cruelly labelled "vice" out of the region of the furtive snigger, and the darkness of the hidden places where the real obscenities of human life crawl under stones, into the light of day' *Radclyffe Hall*, 1968, p 157–58).

In *Honourable Estate* Brittain made her own plea for a new attitude towards homosexuality. In the novel she traces the history of Gertrude Campbell, a brilliant dramatist who despite her powerful intellect is still tied down by the restrictions of a male-oriented society. The one real joy in Gertrude's life comes from her passionate love for Janet Rutherston. Yet the two women, hampered by the conventions and ignorance of their time, fail to come to terms with the nature of their attachment. As a result, Gertrude breaks off the friendship and ends her life as a deeply unhappy woman. No less striking is the description of the homosexual relationship of Richard Alleyndene and Valentine Jessel with its disastrous ending. Homosexuality is only a secondary theme in the novel; nevertheless, Vera Brittain's treatment of the subject is as revolutionary as Radclyffe Hall's and makes a bold attack on conventional subterfuge, prejudice, and intolerance.

Vera Brittain's final goal was to bring about through her writings a fresh understanding of women's psychology and abilities. In her view female psychology is distinguished from male by a capacity for friendship and loyalty and by a deep-seated instinct for peace. Her understanding of the importance of friendship among women is most completely revealed in *Testament of Friendship* (1940). Though primarily a biography of Winifred Holtby, this work was also designed to explore the subject of women's friendship, just as *Testament of Youth* was written to attest to the role of women in war. In the prologue Brittain explains: 'From the days of Homer the friendships of men have enjoyed glory and acclamation, but the friendships of women, in spite of Ruth and Naomi, have usually been not merely unsung, but mocked, belittled and falsely interpreted' (p 2). Thus the work is not only a glowing tribute to Holtby but also a powerful and detailed analysis of their friendship and the gamut of emotions it involved. Its main theme is that 'loyalty and affection between women is a noble relationship' (p 2). Years later Brittain must have had herself and Winifred Holtby in mind when she wrote in *Radclyffe Hall* of the 'intensity of love which can exist between woman and woman'. That she was not speaking only of an erotic relationship is made clear by her comment: 'Such love can exist between mother and daughter, sister and sister, or friend and friend; its distinction lies in its intensity, and its freedom from selfishness or the desire to possess' (p 45).

Yet the biography is more than an account of the relationship of Vera Brittain and Winifred Holtby. Holtby's warm, sympathetic, outgoing nature brought her many friends, and the book describes the full range of her connections – with Stella Benson, Dot McCalman, Jean McWilliam, Phyllis Bentley, Storm Jameson, and many others. In fact, the work becomes a celebration not merely of individual relationships but also of women's friendships in general. In short, it records the commitment to women which has always been a part of the women's movement. That commitment reached a peak with the suffragettes. In her biography of Pethick-Lawrence, Brittain quotes Christabel Pankhurst's obituary of Emmeline Pethick-Lawrence, where she recalled Emmeline's favourite saying, 'It's women for women now' and her belief that only 'this loyalty of women to women' finally won the vote (1963, p 200). In *Testament of Friendship* Brittain was testifying to her own sense of and faith in that loyalty.

The final element in Brittain's theory establishes the link between her feminism and her pacifism. Pointing to a sharp distinction between male and female characteristics, Brittain associated the male principle with power, tyranny, and aggression, the female with love, compassion, forbearance, and tolerance, in short, with the instinct for peace. Two factors, according to Brittain, underlay this development in women, one fixed, the other susceptible to gradual change. Women's reproductive function predisposes them to create and preserve life, and so the wanton destruction of human life is contrary to their biological urge. In addition, through the centuries women have been preoccupied with individual relationships and family life, learning the value of co-operation rather than competition. She contended that as a result women can make their most notable contributions to public life through their inclination to peace and their 'sensitive comprehension of human problems' (*Envoy Extraordinary*, 1965, p 14). Her chief exemplar of this special contribution was Mrs Pandit, Indian stateswoman and sister of Prime Minister Nehru. In her Brittain saw 'the symbol of a future society which would recognise that woman's contribution, modifying the aggressive patterns laid down by man, was essential to human survival' (1965, p 116). But even as she identified characteristics exclusive to women Brittain also looked to a future which would see a synthesis of the separate qualities and the emergence of an 'organic type of human being' (*Lady Into Woman*, 1953, p 11). Emancipation of woman would, she realised, mean also emancipation of man. His 'willing and intelligent' entry into spheres previously regarded as strictly female would become accepted, and he would at last be able to shed the stereotyped role forced upon him by society and live according to his individual nature (1953, p 9). Such a development could only add to the sum of human happiness.

In connecting women with work for peace Brittain was again allying herself with a long tradition. She became aware of this tradition as she read *Woman and Labour*, in which Schreiner identified women's struggle with the crusade for peace. Among the suffragettes Mrs Pankhurst, although an enthusiastic supporter of the war effort, knew that violence is contrary to women's basic instincts.[9] Sylvia Pankhurst remained a pacifist throughout the First World War, on one occasion suffering arrest for addressing an anti-war meeting. Emmeline Pethick-Lawrence was also a concerned pacifist. One of the founders of the Women's International League for Peace and Freedom (of which Vera Brittain was a lifetime member), she believed that it was up to women to 'rise up and deliver their children from the terrible convention of war, divorced as it is in this scientific age from reason and common sense' (*Pethick-Lawrence*, 1963, p 77). Her husband, Frederick Pethick-Lawrence, served as a conscientious objector in the war. Throughout her life Brittain remained committed to work for peace. Even during the dark days of the Second World War, when she suffered humiliation and social ostracism for her beliefs, she did not waver in her conviction that war is never truly justified. One of her supports at that time must have been the consciousness that her attitudes and experiences had been shared through the years by a number of like-minded feminists.

Vera Brittain's six specific goals formed a firmly conceived theory which was in fact almost the classic feminist theory. It rested primarily on a recognition of women's capacities and an understanding that the conventional role forced on women deprived them of the means of living up to these capacities and achieving full self-realisation. Brittain saw that women are equal to men in intellect, reason, and imagination, but have been consistently denied equal opportunities to exercise and extend their mental faculties. As a result, for many women the faculties had atrophied, and only a few outstanding figures – the George Eliots and Florence Nightingales – had even begun to live up to their potential. After centuries of conditioning the majority of women had come to accept the male estimate of their inferiority and to acquiesce in their position as second-class citizens.

A second element in Brittain's theory was her critical awareness of the inaccuracy of the traditional views of women. One of her most important contributions to the women's movement was her endeavour to dispel the old convenient myths about women that had prevailed through so many generations. The first of these stemmed from the Middle Ages. In that devout, confused, and violent age arose the chivalric concept of women as too good and too noble to participate in the rough, hurly-burly world of business and politics – that is, in the real world of action and decision. The legacy of the Middle Ages continued to the nineteenth and twentieth centuries: it was reflected in Gladstone's notion that women were too pure and elevated to vote and in the reactionary stance of Mrs Humphry Ward and her followers in the Anti-Suffrage League; it even underlies some of the contemporary opposition to women's rights. It was an attitude that Brittain's clear-sighted realism utterly repudiated. Yet another myth which Brittain attacked was that in the home woman will find true happiness and satisfaction. This myth gained its widest currency in the nineteenth century with the stress on domestic virtue inculcated by that seemingly most devoted of wives and mothers, Queen Victoria herself. Brittain saw that the image of woman as contented to care for husband and children and to live her life through them simply did not meet the facts of female experience. For herself, she knew that she had to work and gain personal fulfilment if she were to remain true to herself and capable of love for others. And she had only to look at the unhappy marriages in her immediate family – at her mother-in-law and the aunt who after years of marital misery committed suicide – to see the rejection of the myth as a prime necessity in women's liberation.

Finally, Brittain's theory involved the fundamental recognition of female oppression and a determination to end that oppression. The contributions of women in the First World War and the attainment of the vote had raised hopes that real progress might now come, but these hopes were soon dashed when women, bound by centuries of conditioning, were coerced back into the domestic life. Vera Brittain recognised the oppression of women in all spheres. At work they occupied lower positions than men, received lower wages, and were denied opportunities of advancement. At home they deferred to husbands and sons, cooked, cleaned, and laundered (or supervised female servants in these activities), but had no part in major decisions or in financial management. Brittain devoted much of her life to exposure of this subjugation and to an insistence that society must change to accommodate women's rights.

This feminist theory arose mainly from Brittain's personality and education. By temperament and inclination she was from the start a feminist. The young girl who, as she recounts in the first chapter of *Testament of Youth*, found herself ill-at-ease and dissatisfied with the supposedly typical feminine interests of her companions at school was already consciously moving in the direction which she would follow throughout her life. The same impulse underlay her insistence on a university education. Disregarding convention and defying her parents' wishes, she sought a life-style which would provide intellectual satisfaction rather than the empty diversions of drawing-room society. This natural bent to feminism was reinforced by the years at Oxford. There Brittain's keen intellect was further sharpened by contact with others of similar capacities and attitudes. The resulting mental enrichment confirmed her determination to think independently, judge independently, and accept nothing without question.

The ideas suggested by personality and education were strengthened by Vera Brittain's experience as a wife and mother. Even in her own genuinely liberated marriage she felt the constraints of domesticity. From her own life she knew that wifehood and motherhood alone cannot give happiness, that the thinking woman, like the thinking man, needs outlets for her energies, talents, and intellect. Yet Brittain was always able to move beyond the personal to the general. She was able, moreover, to identify not only with the educated middle-class woman but also with the poor, with those who were twice victims – by reason of their sex and their social class. In this way she assumed the position of the political activist whose theories are combined with positive work for social change. Brittain's ideas also owe something to the work of other feminists. Her reading of Olive Schreiner first gave her a reasoned statement about the needs and rights of women. Her friendship with Winifred Holtby, her work for Lady Rhondda, and her association with the feminists of her day, all strengthened her determination to press forward in the task which she had set herself. But their influence mainly corroborated ideas already formed. In fact, except in *Lady Into Woman* and *The Women at Oxford*, Brittain has surprisingly little to say of the great feminists of the past. Yet it is perhaps indicative of her highly individual approach to human problems that her theory should rest on independent thinking rather than on the systems of others. She remained always a creative and original thinker.

Vera Brittain was most active as a feminist in the 1920s and 1930s. During the war she directed her efforts to the service of pacifism, and thereafter, though she continued to work for women, she began that long slide into obscurity which lasted until recent years. There were several reasons for her disappearance from view. Possibly the first was her pacifism. Never a popular philosophy, pacifism cost her both friendships during the war and reputation after it. A contributing factor was the social climate in England after 1945. As after the First World War, women returned from the schools, the factories, the farms, the battle-lines where they had served – back to the home. A weary nation sought only to rest. And it still had to pay the cost of the war – no longer in human lives but in the economy. The shift to the welfare state under the Attlee government was a social imperative, but few in those hard and bitter years were ready to confront the social upheaval which would come with a true apprehension of feminism. It was simply easier to shelve the issue. Thus Brittain fell victim to that conspiracy of silence which, rather than suppressing, ignores the works of feminists. It is worth noting that her present rediscovery owes more to her experience as a VAD nurse than to her feminist theory, and even today many readers know more of the young girl who went to war in France than of the mature woman who fought for women.

For Vera Brittain the goal of the women's movement was at its deepest level the 'recognition of woman's full share in a common humanity' (*Lady Into Woman*, 1953, p 8), a goal which she equated with four basic freedoms of woman: to be educated, to be a full citizen, to work, to regulate the size of her family (*Lady Into Woman*, p 163). Some – though by no means all – of her specific objectives have now been attained. She herself in 1953, looking down the long road which women had travelled in 50 years, could mark with satisfaction the vast difference between the woman of the 1950s and the lady of half a century earlier. Yet because of her astonishing modernity her personal and public life continue to exercise a fascination for the present day feminist. In her feminism, both practical and theoretical, she seems more like one of us than a member of an older generation, and her ideas, her ideals, and even – or especially – the details of her life anticipate our own. But Vera Brittain's significance for us today goes deeper than this. Her real legacy to the modern thinker lies in her state of mind, her philosophy of life, and her method of approaching human problems.

The centre point of Brittain's approach to life was her unyielding faith that human nature can change, and can change for the better. In her view human beings are not fallous irretrievably enmired in guilt and corruption, nor are they passive creatures swayed by forces beyond their control. Rather, they are capable of growth and improvement. And as they grow and improve, so civilisation advances. It was a view that she first formulated at Somerville and the thesis that underlies the final meditation of Ruth Alleyndene at the end of *Honourable Estate*. Reflecting on the sorrows of the past and the dangers of the future, Ruth is obviously the speaker for Brittain herself: 'Hatred and cruelty and perhaps even war will come again, in my children's time and the time of their children; they're the dark forces from our barbaric beginnings which are always being conquered and always rising again. But with every generation we know them better for what they are. We know more clearly what we should withstand and how we should build' (p 599). By 1953 Brittain's conviction had lost none of its firmness: 'The history of the past fifty years has shown that human nature does change in its attitude towards cruelty and injustice' (*Lady Into Woman*, 1953, p 160).

Let it not be thought this was a facile optimism. Vera Brittain had witnessed more evil, experienced more suffering, and known more personal tragedies than most of us have. She had nursed in France in the First World War, been present throughout the bombing of London in the second, and lost through death all her closest friends. Despite these disasters her faith in the ultimate progress of civilisation was rooted in her positive belief in the power of human reason and the strength of personal commitment. Beneath the feminist and pacifist ideals lay the great tradition of western humanism, which increased her confidence and supported her philosophy. Her belief that human beings must control their lives through the exercise of reason first led her to switch from English to history at Oxford. Her decision was based upon her wish to 'understand where humanity failed and where civilisation went wrong' (*Testament of Youth*, 1933, p 472). The end she proposed, though not the means, was essentially the same as that of George Catlin, who in the same years determined to ascertain the causes of war through a study of the psychology of power politics. As time passed, Brittain's conviction grew that positive good may be won from suffering and evil only by the deliberate application of reason and by an intellectual attempt to understand the causes of human disasters and disorders. Hers was a peculiarly modern adaptation of the old adage that suffering brings wisdom. For her wisdom was not passive endurance, blind acceptance of fate or providence; instead it was the conscious use of intellect to learn from defeat and to assist the ongoing march of civilisation.

Yet intellect and intelligence alone are not enough. Courage, faith, loyalty to a cause are also needed. These were the qualities Vera Brittain demonstrated in her own life. Pervading the entire body of her work is her sense of dedication. In the final reckoning it is her absolute integrity – both intellectual and emotional – that counts the most. Never faltering in her attempt to make justice prevail, in her championship of the oppressed, her devotion to peace, and her commitment to women, she played her part in that advance of civilisation in which she believed so firmly.

Notes

1   Vera Brittain refers to this episode on at least three occasions: *Honourable Estate* (1936), p 527; *Lady Into Woman* (1953), p 13; *Pethick-Lawrence* (1963), p 93.

2   Typical comments on the significance of work are found in *On Being An Author* (1948), p 146, and *Lady Into Woman*, pp 8, 231, 234.

3   Similar views on the leisured woman are stated by Lady Rhondda in *This Was My World* (1933), and *Leisured Women* (1928).

4   See *Women's Work in Modern England* (1928), pp 44–45, 112; *Halcyon* (1929), pp 53–59; *Lady Into Woman*, pp 170–173, 181.

5   *Halcyon*, p 46; *Testament of Youth*, (1933), p 658; *Testament of Experience* (1957), p 39.

6   See, for example, 'A Woman's Notebook', *The Nation*, 17 January 1931, pp 508–09.

7   See *Women at Oxford*, (1960), p 233; *Lady Into Woman*, pp 168–169, 180–181.

8   See *Women's Work in Modern England*, p 17; *Lady Into Woman*, p 146.

9   Vera Brittain quotes her statement at the Old Bailey Conspiracy Trial: ' "We cast about", she said, "to find a way, as women will, that would not involve loss of human life and the maiming of human beings, because women care more about human life than men, and I think it is quite natural that we should, for we know what it costs." ' *Lady Into Woman*, p 199.

Select Bibliography of Vera Brittain

Women's Work in Modern England, Noel Douglas, London, 1928.
Halcyon, or The Future of Monogamy, Kegan Paul, London, 1929.
Testament of Youth, Victor Gollancz, London, 1933; Virago, London, 1978.
Honourable Estate, Macmillan, New York, 1936.
Testament of Friendship, Macmillan, London, 1940; Virago, London, 1980.
On Being An Author, Macmillan, New York, 1948.
Lady Into Woman, Macmillan, New York, 1953.
Testament of Experience, Victor Gollancz, London, 1957; Fontana Paperbacks, London, 1980.
The Women at Oxford: A Fragment of History, Macmillan, New York, 1960.
Pethick-Lawrence: A Portrait, Allen and Unwin, London, 1963.
Envoy Extraordinary: A Study of Vijaya Lakshmi Pandit and her Contribution to Modern India, Allen and Unwin, London, 1965.
Radclyffe Hall; A Case of Obscenity? Femina Books, London, 1968.

Other Sources

Brittain, Vera and Geoffrey Handley-Taylor, eds, *Selected Letters of Winifred Holtby and Vera Brittain (1920–1935)*, A. Brown and Sons, London and Hull, 1960.
Catlin, Sir George, *For God's Sake, Go!*, Colin Smythe, Gerrards Cross, 1972.
Rhondda, Margaret Haig, Viscountess, *Leisured Women*, Hogarth Press, London, 1928.
This Was My World, Macmillan, London, 1933.

Mary Ritter Beard:
Woman as Force
(1876–1958)

Ann J. Lane

When I was a graduate student of United States history, studying and living in New York City in the late 1950s, I did not know that Mary Ritter Beard had ever written any books on the history of women. I learned about the craft of history from eminent historian and teachers at Columbia University, and they had, naturally, introduced me to Charles A. Beard's classic study, published in 1913, *An Economic Interpretation of the Constitution,* as they should have, but they did not introduce me, perhaps because they themselves were unaware, to Mary Beard's *Woman as Force in History,* published in 1946. It was not until this current phase of the woman's movement, within the last 15 years, that Mary Beard's work and life have become enormously meaningful to me. Still, she has yet to receive the recognition that she has long deserved or acceptance by contemporary feminists, although her central ideas have profoundly shaped the way we today think and write about women and men in society.

The thesis that became Mary Beard's song through her life asserted that women have always been a very real, although neglected, force in society. The myth that women were or are only a subject and oppressed sex is not only wrong, she argued, but it is counterproductive, because as women accept that designation of themselves and their pasts, their collective strength is undermined. The very notion of oppression imprisons women's minds and oppresses them. But women can be freed from that ideological bondage by discovering their own powerful, creative history and using that knowledge to create new social relations. She saw her job, her intellectual work, as political, designed to reach all women and persuade them of the power of their pasts and therefore their futures.

Women are made to seem invisible, she said, not simply because history has been written by bad men or because women have been invisible, but because these men, as well as most of the professional women and radical feminists of her day, focus their concern on those areas of the community in which men predominate. Beard placed herself in opposition to the militant feminists of her time who called for absolute equality; such simple-minded slogans, she insisted, deny the power and force of the total community of women, deny the existence and value of a distinct female culture.

Mary Beard devoted her energies to reconstructing women's pasts in an effort to end that invisibility; yet she is herself a demonstration of it. She still remains largely neglected or relegated to the status of Charles Beard's wife and collaborator – a true but hardly adequate description. She was a political activist identified with the most radical wing of the American suffrage movement; she was a committed feminist, despite her criticism of the militants; and she was a highly productive scholar. Her intellectual work – she wrote six books alone and collaborated with her husband on seven others – is sufficiently important to provide a respected place for her among feminists.

She was of the generation that came of age at the turn of the century, when American reform movements were undergoing change, when, as one historian wrote, 'the critical intelligentsia in the United States' was formed (Hofstadter, 1970, p 184). The Progressive Era, as it came to be known, stimulated outcries against abuses by big monopolies, concern for the survival of democratic government, and efforts to institute municipal reform. From that period came the literature of exposure by such writers as Upton Sinclair and Theodore Dreiser; during the same period the settlement house movement was established by reformers like Jane Addams. In the universities, formalist approaches were shattered: by Thorstein Veblen in economics, by John Dewey in philosophy, and in history by James Harvey Robinson, Arthur M. Schlesinger, and Charles and Mary Beard. The writers of this New History stressed the needs of the contemporary world; they challenged the primacy of military and political explanations by examining economic and social factors; and they showed new respect for the history of ideas. Mary Beard belongs with this new breed of critics and writers. Her work deals with the fundamental matter of history-writing. She used her energies to assert and demonstrate the centrality of women in history and the need to incorporate that conception of women in history, into the mainstream of historical writing.

Mary Ritter was born into a conservative, Republican, middle-class world in Indianapolis, Indiana, in 1876. Her father, Eli Foster

Ritter, was an attorney by occupation and a zealous Temperance advocate and stalwart of the Methodist Church by commitment. About her mother, Narcissa Lockwood Ritter, little, predictably is known, but enough to suggest that she might have been the model years later for Mary Beard's formidable but invisible female life-force.

Mary, along with her three brothers and a sister, attended DePauw University, not far from her home, where she met and in 1900 married her college-mate, Charles Austin Beard. The young couple settled in Manchester, England, a centre of labour and feminist ferment, and both movements absorbed their energies. Charles Beard helped found Ruskin Hall in Oxford, a college designed for working-class men. Mary Beard discovered the militant woman's movement, and through her active participation she met and worked with leading English radical suffragists, including Emmeline Pankhurst, who later visited the United States on a trip sponsored in part by Beard.

The Beards returned to the US in 1902, and both entered Columbia University as graduate students, but Mary Beard soon left her studies in Sociology. By then the mother of two children, she chose to work actively in the struggles for woman suffrage and trade union reform. She was a close friend of Alice Paul, and when Paul left the National American Woman Suffrage Association (NAWSA) to form the militant Congressional Union (the name was later to change to the National Woman's Party), Mary Beard moved with her. As she had in England, she allied herself with the most militant wing of the suffrage movement. Mary Beard's seemingly staid later career as a writer and historian and her outspoken criticism of what she called the 'intransigent feminists' obscure her radical political commitment in this period.

Although Beard stayed with the woman suffrage movement for years, writing, speaking, propagandising, she was slowly detaching herself from the role of activist and moving toward the role of analyst and critic. There was no sudden break, merely a drifting away from conventional political action.

The break finally did come with the battle for the Equal Rights Amendment, undertaken by the National Woman's Party after the suffrage amendment was won in 1920. Although perhaps difficult to understand today, Mary Beard was only one of many feminists to oppose strenuously the ERA. Her opposition was shared by many distinguished and committed feminists, particularly those in the labour sector. They argued that while all workers were exploited, women were particularly victimised, and that protection of children and then women was the first step towards a more humane reformation of the total society. They also believed that women, most of whom were mothers or would be mothers, required different treatment, that a special set of conditions had to be granted to women for their protection. Many of these anti-ERA feminists had struggled for years to bring about protective labour legislation and, if they were not entirely satisfied, they were convinced that the gains they had achieved were better than none.

To Alice Paul the principle of equality and absolute justice was a necessary ideal around which to organise and struggle; concessions along the way would only hinder ultimate success. To Mary Beard, the world was imperfect, and survival for the moment required the recognition that men and women had different social roles and therefore different needs. Whatever the ultimate goal, people live one day at a time. To Alice Paul, keeping an eye on day-to-day needs crippled one's long-range goals.

Charles and Mary Beard were partners for almost 50 years, raised two children, established a warm, loving and exciting home and shared a political commitment that carried them often into the public arena. And they collaborated on major works. The Beards' first joint venture, *American Citizenship*, appeared in 1914. In 1920 they issued *The History of the United States*. The first two volumes of their monumental history of the nation appeared in 1927. The total work is titled *The Rise of American Civilization*. In 1939 appeared another two volumes of *The Rise*, and in 1942 came the concluding volume. As much as any book can change people, *The Rise of American Civilization* shaped the thinking of generations of Americans. It is probably still the most popular work in American history written in the twentieth century. While it is not possible to determine who wrote which lines, it is also not necessary. Their books were genuinely collaborative efforts that reflected the thinking of both, although the inclusion of material on the significant role of women in American life and the sizeable slice of cultural and literary history were Mary Beard's contributions. *A Basic History of the United States,* their 'last will and testament to the American people,' said Charles Beard, was published in 1944.

With considerable experience in the realities of reform and radical politics, they were determined to make history accessible to the ordinary reader without demeaning the demands of critical scholarship. As a result, their books have a scope and a vision that transcends the academic's usual concern for specialisation. Most important, they sought to use their intellectual gifts in the service of humanity.

Mary Beard published two books alone while she was still deeply involved in activist politics. The first, *Woman's Work in Municipalities,* published in 1915, was a lengthy essay in the tradition of good muckraking literature, demonstrating, as the title idicates, the varied and essential work of women in cities. In 1920 she produced *A Short History of the American Labor Movement.* Her only other book that did not deal with women was a long essay, *The Making of Charles A. Beard,* which was published in 1955, seven years after her husband's death.

In 1931 Beard's *On Understanding Women* appeared. She was 55 when this book was published, and was entering, as is characteristic of many women, her most creative period. In 1934 she wrote an extraordinary 50-page pamphlet entitled 'A Changing Political Economy As It Affects Women', which was a detailed syllabus for a Women's Studies course, the first of its kind that I know of. The same year she edited a reader, *America Through Woman's Eyes,* which illustrated how American women were an integral part of the development of the nation from its inception. The same year, 1934, she co-authored with Martha Bruère, *Laughing Their Way: Women's Humor in America* – a book that has not lost its revelance today when women are – still – charged with a lack of humour!

The collaborative work with Charles Beard may have been influential in many ways, but what Mary Beard was trying to accomplish on the subject of women seemed not to be well understood. By now women had had the vote for years and yet their recognition of their own vital history and active past was as distant as ever. Characteristically, Mary Beard lamented a little, deplored the meagre impact her work had made, and then began a project aimed at confronting the abysmal ignorance that still overwhelmed women.

In an effort to create some active, real demonstration, Beard moved to the idea of establishing a women's archive, an idea influenced by the Hungarian pacifist-feminist Rosika Schwimmer. For the next five years Mary Beard tried to establish, finance, organise, structure, house and publicise what became known as the World Center for Women's Archives.

How could truth be established, she wrote, if women's lives in the past were not known? How could links between the past and present, the present and future, be joined and understood if women were omitted from the record? It was time for women to think about their culture and their relationship to it, but the materials upon which to do that type of thinking were not available. The circular for the WCWA read in part:

> In the furnace room, attics and cellars, in fading heaps crumbling
> with age, source material pertaining to women's aspirations,
> struggles, achievements, contributions and failures, remains
> hidden in large part.

The object of the World Center was to assemble and preserve such
source material, the guiding principle being 'the projection of
woman's personality out of the shadows of time into the living force
which is woman in fact, into written history.' All the material was to
be housed in one centre, which was envisioned as a clearing house of
information on the history of women. The then prevalent idea that
women's history began with the vote was persistently seen by Mary
Beard as 'injurious . . . for men and women'. It continued because
documentation of humanity's total view was not accessible.
Unhappily, the World Center dissolved in 1940, for a variety of
financial, institutional and political reasons, its holdings being
distributed to various libraries.

In the spring of 1941 Mary Beard was intrigued by a new project, a
feminist critique of the *Encylopaedia Britannica,* financed by the
Encyclopaedia itself, and carried out by a staff of three women Beard
selected. A final report, submitted after 18 months, a fascinating
40-page document, is filled with provocative and exciting ideas for
further research. Many of the notions that appeared earlier in *On
Understanding Women* and later in *Woman as Force in History* are
evident in the way she approached the suggested revisions of the
Britannica. In addition to pointing to significant women who were not
included, the report reflects a recognition of the historical significance of sexual differentiation over time, in, for example, the
evolution of certain industries such as spinning and weaving, and in
distinct male and female language patterns. It highlights new ways of
looking at old material, stressing, for instance, the powerful role of
women in medieval convents and the creation, by those nuns, of the
first hospitals. Among the most fruitful insights, the report suggests
that earlier, traditional powers of women were reduced in modern
times, partly as a result of the development of institutions, such as
congresses, universities and medical schools, that could, for the first
time, exclude women.

The report also pointed to the Protestant as well as male bias of the
Britannmica. The document was submitted on 15 December 1942,
and received by the editor-in-chief with appreciation. Despite his
assurance that the 'long neglect of women in the compendium' would
be rectified, the criticisms raised in the report are as pertinent today

as they were 40 years ago.

At the age of 70, Mary Beard said in a public address: 'I'm not a "woman of achievement" or a "career woman" or a PhD . . . I'm a woman who works. Works at what? Works at self-education, and I've been brash enough to write my feelings.' Careers meant to her legitimation by the established experts, whoever they were at the time, but since she denied their legitimacy, at least as far as women were concerned, she repudiated their system of credentials. It was not merely that she believed it possible for a woman to get educated outside the university, she thought it likely that only outside the university could a woman be truly educated! College stifled the imagination of all its inhabitants, but of women even more so. More than the neglect that women suffered in the college community, Beard detested and feared the trap of imitation. In terms that would be understood today by those who have established women's studies courses, Beard claimed that whatever men had – the position, appointments, the courses, the status, the careers – women came to demand for themselves, and were caught in the trap of a structure they were trying to transform.

Yet she knew that there were many sympathetic young women in colleges; there were skilled and concerned librarians and archivists. There were knowledgeable and influential women faculty. There were even some approachable college presidents. So in her later years she turned her attention to the college community in an effort to persuade those within it of the value of her historical analysis.

Most of all she tried to reach students, to inspire them with her ideas of what constituted an equal education. It was not a separate education for women that she wanted but a new approach to learning about women; that new approach would be as valuable to men as to women. The gender of the student body made little difference. Women needed to locate themselves in their historic past and to learn to think about their meaning in history, just as they are taught to learn about the meaning of men in history. The 'suffragists at the wailing wall' helped to make women feel powerless by focusing entirely on subjugation and oppression.

Beard knew that the re-education of women would be a long, slow, often futile task, but it never seemed to have occurred to her to stop. On one occasion she referred to her 'obsession', and nothing less than that could have so long sustained her. She was essentially alone in her efforts to project a new, different image of women, and she battled the anti-woman forces, as well as most of the militant feminists.

Her life was a crusade for women's minds. In 1949, still poking around with new ideas, she played with the notion of an 'academy of women'. She spoke to anyone who would listen. She never wavered in her belief in the important historical role of women at the very moment when the feminists around her continued to reiterate the view of women, past and present, as powerless.

Mary Ritter Beard had a mission. She called it Women in Long History, and she was determined to be heard. She had a tenacious, persistent, dogged, unyielding evangelical passion that would not be silenced. She spent 40 years of her life looking at history differently, putting women in the centre of it and seeing how the contours of the world's story altered. Many of her ideas have appeared in the last few years in contemporary feminist scholarship, though her life and her work are not yet an acknowledged part of our legacy.

In *Woman's Work in Municipalities* she tells a 'story of women's achievement and visions' in the establishment in the United States of the first kindergartens, public libraries, adult education programmes for immigrants, industrial training schools, the first programmes for public health, municipal recreation, housing reform and the new field of social work. What emerges from this book is a very different picture of the early years of the twentieth century from the traditional one that stresses national politics, diplomacy, two-party politics and the growth of major corporations.

The first book-length statement of Beard's theoretical proposition that woman is 'the elemental force in the rise and development of civilisation' appeared in *On Understanding Woman* in 1931. As an extension of her 'responsibility for the continuance and care of life,' Beard asserted in this book, woman invented the domestic arts, and in this way is responsible for 'launching civilisation'. Woman's crucial role in the maintenance of life and the creation of culture is not understood, she said, because historians focus their attention on the emergence of class divisions, ignoring gender as an analytic or historic category. But however much women as a group are dropped out of history-writing, they 'remained in the actuality'. And whatever legitimacy there is to the criticisms voiced by the feminists, said Beard, those grievances are not rooted in the inherent relationship of men and women but rather reflect given conditions at a particular time. At some point the 'sex antagonism' of the militant feminists, bearing the 'wound of honourable battle', will achieve its goal and cease to exist. Then, Beard concluded, 'the eternal feminism . . . at the centre of all things – that is, the care of life' will remain.

Woman as Force in History: A Study in Traditions and Realities, published first in 1946 and then again in 1962, 1971 and 1973, is Mary

Beard's most famous book. It represents the culmination of her years of study and stands as the mature statement of her thesis. Many of the ideas and themes developed earlier are pulled together and deepened in this major work. Her analysis of the ideas of William Blackstone and their impact on American feminism occupies a significant portion of what is new and of immense value.

The false and tyrannical idea that women have always been a subject sex was aided in part by the interpretations of the American feminist movement in the middle of the nineteenth century, said Beard. The authority cited to support this proposition was Blackstone, author of *Commentaries on the Laws of England,* published in 1765. In his chapter entitled 'Of Husband and Wife,' which is frequently referred to by feminists, Blackstone asserts that woman was civilly dead at marriage and that her 'very being or legal existence' is consolidated into that of the husband.'

Mary Beard then challenged the interpretation of that phrase used by feminists 100 years later. She argued that Blackstone's language was meant to be taken metaphorically, not literally, that he was attempting to introduce some literary flavour into a dry subject; that he was, in any case, referring only to married women; and, most importantly, that when he used the phrase 'in law', he meant precisely and only 'in Common Law'. According to Beard, those readers trained in law, for whom he was writing, understood all of these qualifications. The Common Law was, Beard said, 'only one branch of English law'. Other laws of England which could and did modify the Common Law included Acts of Parliament and old customs, which were often left undisturbed. Most important, there was Equity, which was administered by a special court and which provided, 'in the name of justice, remedies for wrongs for which the Common Law afforded no remedies'. Many powers denied to women under the Common Law were, said Beard, granted women under Equity. In addition, there were many private agreements of men and women which rarely even were brought to court, but which regulated much of ordinary daily affairs.

American feminists, misunderstanding the technical aspects of Blackstone's legal writings, adopted the theory of total legal subjugation as the foundation for the Seneca Falls Declaration of Sentiments and Resolution in 1848, and in so doing 'they adopted a fiction about human behaviour'. In times past, Beard went on, theologians and moralists insisted that woman was evil and ought to be subjugated to man, but it was the feminist manifesto, using Blackstone's dictum as evidence, that argued that woman had, in fact, been subject to man.*

Much of the rich detail of *Woman as Force* is evidence Beard offered to demonstrate the validity of her thesis. In the Middle Ages, for example, she said, sharp class lines determined how one behaved and what rights one had, but sex distinctions, even when they were encoded in law, were so often defied in practice that it is not possible to use any single formula to describe woman's role. Women in the ruling class, she said, exercised enormous power. It was not until power passed to parliaments, which were elected by men and composed of men, that women were excluded from the exercise of power.

Beard claims that in pre-capitalist societies women had most of the privileges and burdens assigned them by their class, and that when women suffered it was largely because of their class position, not their sex. It was with the development of capitalism, she insisted, that discrimination on account of sex, regardless of class, became pervasive. It was in this time that women were driven out of the professions, out of politics, out of power. The feminist movement, which was born during this period of diminished rights, assumed that such restrictions had always existed. Then they concocted a description of the past that was profoundly untrue.

Mary Beard's repudiation of the traditional feminist view of history is important; it has also been largely ignored. To test the validity of her interpretation requires the kind of empirical work that is only now being undertaken, and much of which seems to substantiate her ideas.

Another theme that reappeared throughout her work is the acknowledgement of the power of collective action and community cohesiveness as a means to offset formal powerlessness. For instance, in a 1914 article entitled 'Legislative Influence of Unenfranchised Women', she examined how women without the vote still wielded influence and expressed their collective will. From her own early experience in the suffrage and trade union movements she knew that people without ready access to sources of power still have avenues of strength that have little to do with that conferred by established authority. In the same way women, denied formal learning, never-

*Editor's Note: In some respects Mary Beard has been misled as were her foremothers who were also dependent on male-controlled sources. Beard does not refer to Matilda Joslyn Gage; who was very much one of those nineteenth-century feminists, and whose thesis so closely resembled Beard's that it is astonishing. Gage was certainly not of the 'mould' that Beard describes – yet the theses of both are substantiated by their own – tragic – disappearances.

theless were able, depending on their class position, to achieve a substantial education, through any number of informal means.

She addressed herself to the everlasting question, which has taken many forms: why, with all the leisure they have are American women not in the front ranks of intellectual excellence? In an article that appeared in 1929 she suggested that perhaps it is *because* of all the leisure, perhaps it is 'work and responsibility' that are the underlying impulses to serious intellectual work. When women are caught up in the major social and intellectual struggles of their time, they do indeed write seriously about them. 'Great thinkers and writers have never been spectators,' she said, and thus, if the greatest heights of intellectual endeavour are to be achieved by women, 'they will be reached only through the avenue of experience, thus far denied them.'

Beard's askew angle of vision enabled her to see fresh that which historians and social critics have long looked at but not noticed. For instance, 50 years ago she commented upon the convents in the Middle Ages as refuges of female autonomy, a notion only recently making its way into feminist scholarship.* In the same way she advised that we study the subject of gossip, not as a trivial matter, but as a way of understanding how women bind together; she also urged that others examine the history of bathing, cooking and laundering as distinctly female enterprises and legitimate ones for careful study.

She also looked at men differently. In an article that called attention to the importance of the single person in society – the divorced, widowed and unmarried – she examined the role of men in the context of family life, although it is women who are commonly placed in a family setting. In this striking article, written in 1934, she focused on SS troops, as a category of single men, describing their movements as 'essentially a dynamic of unmarried males'. After the First World War, she said, power went begging in the streets, where it was picked up by soldiers. Hitler surrounded himself with men 'of sadistic temper, unaffected by the restraining influences which education, jobs, families and public obligations exert'. This handful of 'undomesticated men' is supported by a 'romantic youth movement, naturally violent and composed of men just reaching manhood, all poor, all jobless . . . all resentful'. With 'the rage of tigers, they leaped over the barriers which civilised nations had erected for human behaviour'.

*Editor's Note: Again, Gage had done all this in 1893 but Beard did not know of the existence of such work.

In the United States too, she pointed out, in the midst of economic crisis, there are 'hordes of young men and women wandering about . . . like nomads, in search of sustenance and comfort', and we should never forget 'how thin is the veneer which civilisation spreads over mankind's natural urges'. What is particularly engaging about this article is the overriding insistence that men as well as women need roots and domesticity if domestic tranquility and social stability are to be maintained.

Beard's belief that the struggle to eradicate oppression is, ulti-mately, a struggle for women's *minds,* places her today in the front lines of feminist belief. She recognised that the success of revolution, any revolution, depends on changed consciousness, on the ability to shatter what Emma Goldman called the inner tyrants, the ones we internalise.

What then, finally, is the significance of Mary Ritter Beard's body of work? Much feminist writing in the last years echoes her legacy if not her name: the central place of changed consciousness; the power of informal collective action and the great strength of female com-munity; the recognition that certain historical changes that are good for many men, such as expansion of political and educational oppor-tunities, may for the moment make it even worse for those who are denied those new opportunities; the faculty to look at men, as well as women, with different eyes, sometimes to see men as the 'other'; the woman-centredness of her vision. Why then have so many feminists not acknowledged her contribution?

Her work is not so easy for feminists to use in ideological struggle. If women have been as powerful as she says, then why the complaints, the grievances? Beard's position may seem to have an anti-feminist tone, although such an inference is not what she intended or what is truly in her work.

Still, in her overstatement she does minimise the reality of sub-jugation, although she knew well the circumstances under which women have lived. She did not believe the world was ever a just place for women. Her overstatement comes inevitably with long-overdue compensation. More important, her overstatement is part of her ideological effort. Women through time, as a mass, constitute a force that is limited only by the ignorance of those who do not recognise its power, she believed. If women only knew how much they had con-tributed to the world's wealth, arts, beauty, science and technology, Beard felt, that knowledge would provide them with a tool of much greater value than the simple cry for equality. Whatever retards that growth of self-consciousness, self-confidence and self-knowledge she rejected categorically. So she minimised the negative.

There remain many serious theoretical flaws in her construct. She was not entirely successful in creating a theoretical model to explain what she was able to describe with such rich texture and detail. Still, it is only very recently, and with not much more success, that these questions have been addressed by feminists.

Mary Beard's language is difficult to read. Her style is heavy and often pedantic. More seriously, her work suffered from intellectual isolation. The criticisms upon which one sharpens one's work were missing. Her books were greeted with flattering platitudes, hostile assaults, or they were ignored. Perhaps if she had been caught up in the dialogue of a university seminar, if her work had been subjected to criticism from colleagues, she might have examined and resolved some of the stylistic and substantive shortcomings. She knew better, she was better, but nobody engaged her in serious debate. High up on the list of grievances women have suffered is the deadly effect of not being taken seriously.

In her early activist years Mary Ritter Beard associated with the radical wing of the woman's movement in England and in America. When she left the political arena to devote herself to intellectual tasks, her work became even more radical. She sought her goals differently; she tried to reach the larger community of women in a variety of ways: speeches, radio addresses, articles in popular journals, women's courses in college, an international women's archive, a critique of the *Encyclopaedia Britannica,* as well as the many long and serious books.

Without much support from the woman's movement, without a large body of ideas upon which to build, without models of any kind to follow, virtually alone, she audaciously placed women at the centre of history and society, and then she insisted that the world look again from her perspective. I believe her force was substantial and far-reaching, although not immediate and often not tangible. Intellectuals and academics may deny the impact of women in general and Mary Beard in particular, but the world altered nevertheless. In this sense, Beard's life and work embody her thesis: women are neglected in the writing of history, but the effect of their existence is a reality of history. The echo of her voice has never been lost.

Simone de Beauvoir:
Dilemmas of a Feminist Radical
(1908–   )

Mary Evans

Any collection of essays on feminist writers inevitably includes Simone de Beauvoir, since until the resurgence of feminist writing in the late 1960s and 1970s de Beauvoir's *The Second Sex* stood almost alone in the post-war world as an assertive feminist challenge to the prevailing ideology of 'Kinde, Küche und Kirche' which defined the place of women as the home and their natural role as that of the care of men. Although it would be wrong to suppose that all women subscribed to this ideology, or that feminist institutions and activities did not exist in the 1950s and early 1960s, de Beauvoir's work did stand out at the time for its fierce rejection of the belief that women's subordination is a natural, given, state.[1] *The Second Sex* roundly and utterly condemned this view; 'women are made, not born', thundered the author, marshalling an enormous amount of evidence to demonstrate the social processes through which women acquire those characteristics of orthodox femininity which carry with them an automatic submission to male interests and definitions of normality. From the date of its first publication in 1949, *The Second Sex* became an immediate best-seller, a widely read and influential book, fiercely attacked in some quarters in a way which only served to suggest its opponents' fears of it's likely effect.

Yet for all its considerable importance, and precisely because of its influence, it is important that contemporary feminists should examine some of the views propounded by de Beauvoir, both in *The Second Sex* and her other work. Anti-feminist, and right-wing, criticism of de Beauvoir exists in considerable quantities; rather less available – indeed, almost absent – is any feminist discussion of de Beauvoir's work. This is particularly unfortunate since in her writing de Beauvoir does put forward views which might well lead feminism into some unfortunate dead ends. If every generation of feminists is not to have to 're-invent the wheel' (in Catherine Stimpson's particularly vivid phrase) it is surely essential that the great works of the feminist tradition are examined critically in order to establish how feminism might both develop and overcome some of its inevitable contradictions. I shall examine three aspects of de Beauvoir's work which I would argue are as crucial for contemporary feminism as they were when *The Second Sex* was first published, namely: de Beauvoir's analysis of the causes of women's subordination, her discussion of female sexuality and of women's capacity for reproduction and motherhood, and her understanding of the nature of feminist politics.

One of the essential elements of all de Beauvoir's work is the training which she acquired in academic philosophy, and the essentially bourgeois and competitive education which she received. An extraordinarily gifted student, de Beauvoir studied philosophy at the Sorbonne, receiving first a degree in the subject and then the coveted *aggrégation* – the French qualification which allows its holder to teach a particular subject in either a *lycée* or a university. Infinitely more difficult, and of a far higher status than the Anglo-Saxon equivalent of a post-graduate certificate or diploma in education, the *aggrégation* assures – and assured – its holder a firm place in French society. Thus from the age of 22 she was guaranteed an entry into the academy. Whilst Anglo-Saxon audiences often over-estimate the importance which the French assign to intellectual life, assuming that every peasant and factory worker is a vigorous and well informed participant in academic debate, it is nevertheless the case that the centralised organisation of the French educational system assures those individuals whom it admits to the teaching profession a secure place in bourgeois society.[2]

Hence de Beauvoir, from a relatively early age, gained for herself a social role and position of some considerable prestige and reward. The agony of passing the necessary examinations is well documented in *Memoirs of a Dutiful Daughter,* but the book ends on a note of triumphant emancipation: de Beauvoir passes all tests with flying colours and is able to embark on a life in which she will *épater le bourgeois* from a secure place within bourgeois society. But the break between *Memoirs of a Dutiful Daughter* and *The Prime of Life* (the second volume of her autobiography) is as much sexual as professional: now a fully qualified teacher with an independent income de Beauvoir could embark on a fully consummated love affair with Jean-Paul Sartre, the first stage of a partnership which was eventually to transcend existing definitions of a relationship between a man and a woman. When in *The Times*'s obituary on Sartre, de Beauvoir was described as his 'mistress', the mis-naming of the relationship (and the assumption of female economic dependence which the word often implies) was a remarkable reflection of the narrowness of orthodox definitions of heterosexual relationships.

Their relationship has been fully documented by de Beauvoir, both in her autobiography (*Memoirs of a Dutiful Daughter*, *The Prime of Life*, *Force of Circumstance* and *All Said and Done*) and, in a fictional form, in her novels. The development of the relationship, its trials and problems, not the least of which was the *vie à trois* between de Beauvoir, Sartre and Olga Kosakievicz, are all outlined. If the omissions are sometimes glaring, then they are no less significant in indicating de Beauvoir's view of what is private about a very public life. On one subject however, she is far from reticent. It is that of the philosophical system which she and Sartre embraced, and to which he devoted the greater part of his life. The particular philosophical system in question is that of existentialism, and yet whilst it is undeniably true that Sartre did develop certain ideas within philosophy into a coherent conceptual system described as existentialism, it is also the case that Sartre, particularly in his later life, came to abandon some of the individualistic elements of existentialism and attempted the construction of a system of thought in which personal freedom could be reconciled with more utilitarian, and socialist, aims of achieving a just, and non-exploitative, system. For both Sartre and de Beauvoir the Second World War was crucial in demonstrating that individuals cannot always define their own fate, and that the search for personal autonomy has to be accompanied by a battle for a form of society in which individual liberties are safe-guarded. In a revealing passage in *The Prime of Life* de Beauvoir writes that at the outbreak of the war she was much impressed by an acquaintance who remarked that the war 'does not change my attitude to a blade of gress' (1965, (a), p 599). Yet she also acknowledges that for her the war changed everything:

> After June 1940, I no longer recognised anything – objects, people, seasons, places, even myself . . . The earth turned, and revealed another of its faces to me. Violence and injustice were let loose, with every kind of folly, scandal and horror. Not even victory would turn back the clock and revive the old order that had been temporarily disrupted: it ushered in a new era, the post-war period. (de Beauvoir, 1965, (a), p 599)

Clearly, what the war demonstrated to both de Beauvoir and Sartre was that personal freedom and liberty cannot exist within an un-free society, and that those individual choices and modes of self expression which they so valued had to exist within a general context of respect for individual freedoms if they were to be anything except meaningless. The right to express oneself freely, to publish dissenting works, to be critical of the *status quo* or to live in an unorthodox or deviant manner, were all threatened, and curtailed, by the German occupation. It did become impossible for radical and critical intellectuals to write and publish and a variety of measures severely limited intellectual freedom for the duration of the Occupation. De Beauvoir herself was sacked from her teaching post for refusing to persuade one of her pupils to follow a course of action which she found morally repugnant.

The general limits imposed on intellectuals by the Occupation were clearly neither as harsh or punitive as those invoked against other sections of French society – in particular, the Trade Unions and the Communist Party. From the evidence provided in *The Prime of Life* it is obvious that a kind of clandestine intellectual activity was maintained in Paris. But what was demonstrated by the war was that people are not always free to make their own choices, that constraint is a very important part of human existence and that freedom, and personal self-definition, is for the majority of humankind, not a matter of rational choice. For de Beauvoir and Sartre, pre-war life had allowed enormous freedom. Even given their need to maintain themselves, they had both largely defined the pattern, organisation and nature of their own lives, and associated freedom largely with the freedom to make decisions of a personal and abstract kind.

It is therefore hardly surprising, given the traumatic impact that the war had on de Beauvoir, that in her first major post-war work, *The Second Sex*, she should turn to an examination of constraint, and in particular the constraints on women. Yet the work is a curious amalgam of existentialism and materialism, as if de Beauvoir's residual, pre-war beliefs in limitless personal freedom had not quite come to terms with the experiences of the war and the German occupation. The book provides a very full account of de Beauvoir's analysis of the nature and causes of women's subordination and marks an important transition for its author – that for the first time in her life she admitted she was not just an isolated individual but a member of a general category, and hence defined in certain ways. She writes of her views of being a woman before writing *The Second Sex*:

   . . . far from suffering from my femininity, I have, on the contrary, from the age of twenty on, accumulated the advantages of both sexes; after *She Came to Stay*, those around me treated me both as a writer, their peer in the masculine world, and as a woman; this was particularly noticeable in America: at the parties I went to, the wives all got together and talked to each other while I talked to the men, who nevertheless behaved toward me with greater courtesy than they did toward the members of their own sex. (de Beauvoir, 1965, (b), p 189)

Many contemporary feminists might well baulk at some of the underlying assumptions of this passage and suggest that what de Beauvoir is actually saying is that since the age of twenty she has been able, because of her exceptional achievements in a male world, to give up talking to boring wives and talk instead to their fascinating husbands, who are pre-occupied with the major issues of the day. Even more severe critics might suggest that the passage has something of an air of Aunt Tom about it.

However, the essential issue about *The Second Sex* that concerns us here is de Beauvoir's account in the book of the cause of women's oppression. The book opens with a long account of female biology, in which the sperm and the ova compete for attention with Heidegger and Hegel's musings on the nature of male and female subjectivity. De Beauvoir's distinction between male and female mammals is essentially that 'the female is the victim of the species' (de Beauvoir, 1964, p 18), and she goes on to explain exactly why she thinks this is the case:

> . . . the fundamental difference between male and female mammals lies in this: the sperm, through which the life of the male is transcended in another, at the same instant becomes a stranger to him and separates from his body; so that the male recovers his individuality intact at the moment when he transcends it. The egg, on the contrary, begins to separate from the female body when fully matured, it emerges from the follicle and falls into the oviduct; but if fertilised . . . it becomes attached again through implementation in the interns. First violated, the female is then alienated – she becomes, in part, another than herself. (de Beauvoir, 1964, p 19)*

It must be allowed that in this passage de Beauvoir is describing mammals in general rather than human beings in particular and thus we should not assume that her interpretation of the consequences of the savage battle between the ovum and the sperm in all mammals is necessarily the same for all human beings. Nevertheless, it is very

---

*Ruth Herschberger, 1946, p 19 provides an alternative and dramatically different version in 'Matriarchal Society writes Biology'.

difficult to see how we can avoid the conclusion that de Beauvoir is asking us to assume that what occurs between every male and female rabbit (or rather, between their biology as distinct from their existentially constructed selves) also occurs between human beings: that female human biology is naturally of a kind which entails surrender to the male, self-alienation and loss of autonomy. Indeed, in a chilling sentence only a few pages after the discussion of the metaphysical *angst* of the female rabbit de Beauvoir announces that, 'Woman, like man, is her body; *but her body is something other than herself*' (1964, p 26, my emphasis).

The emphasis is an indication of the surprise that confronted me when re-reading the passage. Perhaps many contemporary feminists will share the same sense of astonishment: that one of the founding mothers of modern feminism could make such a suggestion, redolent as it is of male-defined assumptions about the 'normal' male and 'abnormal' female. To a generation (or at least part of a generation) well read in works such as *Our Bodies Ourselves* (1971), *Sexual Politics* (1970) or any feminist book on the medicalisation (and masculinisation) of female sexuality and reproductive capacity, it is astounding to find within the feminist tradition such an uncritical acceptance of male definitions of female sexuality.

But throughout de Beauvoir's discussion of female biology we are faced repeatedly with essentialist arguments about the nature of female biology. We are told, for example, that 'it has been said that women have infirmity in the abdomen' (1964, p 27) but we are never allowed to speculate on who said it, or for what reasons. The account de Beauvoir provides of menstruation surpasses many histories of the Inquisition in its catalogue of horrors; again, no questions are asked about the conditions in which women's biology becomes problematic or troublesome. It is true that at the conclusion of the section on biology de Beauvoir allows that 'the facts of biology take on the values that the existent bestows upon them' (1964, p 33), but she has already stated what for her are the 'facts' of biology. They are that:

> Woman is weaker than man; she has less muscular strength, fewer red blood corpuscles, less lung capacity; she runs more slowly, can lift less heavy weights, can compete with man in hardly any sport; she cannot stand up to him in a fight. To all this weakness must be added the instability, the lack of control, and the fragility already discussed: these are facts. (de Beauvoir, 1964, p 31)

We are confronted therefore, in de Beauvoir's analysis of the implications of female biology with two somewhat disturbing themes:

that there is an absolute polarity between women and men and that women's biology implicitly carries with it the taken-for-granted assumption of women's physical weakness, the most important element of which is, for de Beauvoir, woman's inability to transcend her biology. Women, it would appear, are trapped within their bodies in a way which men are not. Moreover, this condition apparently applies to all women, and they all suffer their physical weakness relative to that of men. Hence de Beauvoir does not question why the physical strength of men and women should be an issue and places the debate about male and female biology very much in competitive terms: women run more slowly, lift less heavy weights and so on. What is suggested is a kind of perpetual Olympics in which the ability to run more or less fast for the bus whilst carrying heavy packages carries with it crucial results for the determination of an individual's life chances.

But de Beauvoir's account of the physical differences between the sexes is only part of her attempt to locate the causes of the subordination of women. She turns next to what she describes as the 'psycho-analytic point of view', and having, in the previous chapter, given us a particular reading of the implications of female biology now criticises another interpretation of biological data. She rejects flatly Freud's theory of sexual development in explicitly existential terms:

> Whan a child takes the road indicated by the one or the other of its parents, it may be because the child freely takes up their projects; its behaviour may be the result of a choice motivated by ends and aims. (de Beauvoir, 1964, p 46)

In defiance of the arguments of the previous chapter – in which we are told that women have very little choice about their self-determination because they are trapped in feeble, badly functioning bodies – it is now suggested that women, and men, can choose their destiny in life, and choose it at a relatively early age.

But when de Beauvoir turns to examine Engels, and historical materialism, we discover that not only do human beings have certain innate physical differences, they also have certain innate psychological characteristics. They do not have the characteristics imputed to them by Freud, but

> . . . (female enslavement) is a result of the imperialism of the human consciousness, seeking always to exercise its sovereignty in objective fashion. If the human consciousness had not included

the original category of the Other and an original aspiration to dominate the Other, the invention of the bronze tool could not have caused the oppression of women (de Beauvoir, 1964, p 52)

However, as perhaps comes clear from reading the above passage, it now becomes essential that we stop and ask exactly who human beings, and the Other, are. In the extract quoted above, de Beauvoir asks us to agree that the 'human consciousness' has a natural tendency to attempt to dominate others. But implicit in the term human being as it is employed here by de Beauvoir is the assumption that all human beings are male, who dominate (because of 'natural' characteristics) women. We are asked to accept that back in the primeval childhood of human history, a major motivating force for human (ie male) action was the desire to institutionalise the Other as the female. What de Beauvoir reads into Engels – and inevitably Marx and historical materialism – is a theory of the human, male, personality possessing certain given psychological characteristics. Whilst both Marx and Engels assumed that all human beings have a capacity to create and impose order on the world, this does not mean that they also assume an innate tendency towards domination. Indeed, probably the most important element of Engels' argument in *The Origin of the Family, Private Property and the State* is his attempt to show how entirely non-natural forces – that is, the development of primitive technology and the means of controlling and organising subsistence agriculture – led to the situation in which social relations between the sexes took on a form of subordination and domination. In eliminating a crucial stage of Engel's discussion – that of the development of class society – de Beauvoir must be accused of a serious misunderstanding of Marxism.

One inevitable result of de Beauvoir's account of pre-history is that her analysis of relations between the sexes tends throughout *The Second Sex* towards a form of existential radical feminism. As suggested earlier, the book does assume a very rigid dichotomy between the interests and behaviour of men and women, and the explanation given for this is the 'natural' desire of men to dominate women. This account of sexual relations is very close to certain forms of what some term radical feminism, the only significant differences being the terms in which the argument is couched and the solution which de Beauvoir offers to breaking a pattern of female submission and domination. Almost perversely, she does not argue for female separation; on the contrary, she argues for women to become rather more like men: to assume those characteristics – of rationality and personal autonomy and independence – which she assumes to be typical of men. Her account of what men and women are like, and what masculinity and femininity represent, is not therefore one which many contemporary feminists (radical or otherwise) would necessarily accept, but it is a most important illustration of the problematic search which feminists have always faced for the 'true' female nature.

An essential element of the search for the 'true' female nature which contemporary feminism emphasises is that women possess certain characteristics – a capacity to nurture and care for others – which have been consistently devalued by male cultures and ideologies. Moreover, contemporary feminism stresses as a positive attribute women's ability to bear children, and argues that women's reproductive capacities have been, and are, misunderstood, mistreated and often feared by men. It is thus an important assertion by feminists that women should be able to regain control of their bodies, and reproduction, and define sexuality and reproduction in ways which are not determined or manipulated by men. Many discussions of women's biology, for obvious political reasons, thus tend towards the placing of very positive values on female biology: it is celebrated precisely because it is felt that it has too often been abused.

But this development is relatively recent: previous generations of feminists often sought to do exactly the reverse to their contemporary sisters and, instead of celebrating female sexuality, would attempt to 'normalise' it by invoking a model of what was assumed to be normal, straightforward, sexuality – that is, that of men. This kind of model, of aberrant female and normal male sexuality, is an important part of the discussion of *The Second Sex*, since throughout the book numerous passages suggest that the author sees female biology and sexuality as inherently problematic.

There are two instances in *The Second Sex* where it becomes arguably apparent that de Beauvoir sees female sexuality as problematic and contradictory. The first is her discussion of heterosexuality in the chapter entitled 'Sexual Initiation' and the second the account of maternity in the section on 'The Mother'. In the section on 'Sexual Initiation' de Beauvoir suggests quite unequivocally that female sexual initiation is inevitably 'a violation' (de Beauvoir, 1964, p 359). Moreover, it would appear that any act of heterosexual coition is unwelcome to women: 'To the taboos and inhibitions contributed by her education and by society are added feelings of disgust and denial coming from the erotic experience itself . . .' (de Beauvoir, 1964, p 362). So de Beauvoir is suggesting, quite rightly and more or less uncontroversially that society can shape (or mis-shape) sexuality, but she is also implying that 'feelings of disgust and denial' are an inevitable part, for women, of the physical expression of heterosexuality. What is not openly acknowledged is the issue of deciding the extent to which human sexuality, and its expression, is naturally given or socially constructed. De Beauvoir bravely and admirably describes the appalling consequences for women's sexual enjoyment of the lack of contraception, poor medical care and sexual abuse by men and yet at the same time implies that even with changes and improvements in these areas, heterosexuality would always involve women in submission and subordination.

It is at this point that it is perhaps possible to argue that in *The Second Sex* de Beauvoir came very close to suggesting, implicitly, what later feminists, and most significantly radical feminists, have explicitly stated: namely, that in fact heterosexuality does inevitably oppress women. However favourable a woman's material situation, however pro-feminist the man, the very nature of heterosexuality carries with it inescapable consequences of male domination and female submission (see for example, Adrienne Rich, 1981). This position is not stated explicitly in *The Second Sex*, indeed the conclusion of the book suggests that a kind of friendly heterosexuality is, under certain conditions, possible. But in her fiction de Beauvoir never allows, or portrays, successful relationships between men and women that are still sexually active. There are happy relationships between men and women in which sex no longer plays a part (of which the best example is the relationship between Anne and Robert Dubreuilh in *The Mandarins*) but the relationships in which sexuality is still expressed are uniformly beset with problems and difficulties.

The nature of these problems and difficulties is not, interestingly, the same as is suggested about heterosexuality in *The Second Sex*. De Beauvoir's fiction is more or less entirely about the educated French petit-bourgeoisie, and thus material issues rarely figure as important. All those cares which are described as the lot of women in *The Second Sex* do not, therefore, appear in de Beauvoir's fiction. Since she did not choose to write about poor, frigid, badly educated women with large families, the problems with which the novels deal are more or less exclusively of a metaphysical or abstract kind. And the issue that arises most frequently in de Beauvoir's fiction between men and women engaged in sexual relationships is that of jealousy – an ancient, frequently irrational force of immense power and consuming energy.

So between de Beauvoir's fictional and non-fictional accounts of relations between men and women is an enormous dissimilarity in the identification and discussion of essential problems. In the non-fiction we are given an account of men and women which sets out very clearly women's real disadvantages relative to men, and which, essentially, suggests almost insuperable differences between the sexes. In the fiction, on the other hand, we find both men and women beset by very similar, if not identical, problems: problems about the end of love affairs, sexual jealousy and the need of both men and women to be able to establish in their lives hierarchies of emotional significance and importance. In all, throughout de Beauvoir's fiction, the sexes appear as far from distinct: both men and women suffer from the same kinds of emotional problems and difficulties, and although we can identify in the novels unhappy women, no consistent pattern emerges which suggests that the author always sees women as the victims of men. Often, in fact, the women who are unhappy are portrayed as being victims of their own choices. The over-dependent Paula in *The Mandarins*, and the central character of *The Woman Destroyed* are both desperately unhappy women – but the responsibility for their unhappiness does not lie, the author suggests, simply at the feet of their male companions. In both cases (and particularly so in the case of Paula), the men involved encourage the women to develop more independent and less emotionally dependent lives.

Between de Beauvoir's fiction and non-fiction there is, then, a very real difference in analysis. In the non-fiction, women are, for biological reasons, inevitably weaker than men and imprisoned in a physical body which is constraining and problematic. In her fiction, on the other hand, de Beauvoir almost ignores biology, and material factors, and suggests that the real problem about sexuality is that it carries with it potentially, and often actually, explosive dangers of jealousy and exclusivity. Indeed, a theme that occurs frequently in de Beauvoir's novels is that of the problem of sexual jealousy: the age old triangle provides a theme for *The Woman Destroyed*, *The Mandarins* and *She Came to Stay*. Nor, it must be noted, is the triangle necessarily one of two women competing for one man. In *The Mandarins* the crucial triangle in the novel is between Anne and Robert Dubreuilh and Anne's lover, Lewis Brogan, and it is Lewis who eventually has to reconcile himself to the fact that his love for Anne cannot become a permanent relationship. Despite the affection between them – and the very explicitly stated and celebrated sexual passion – Anne and Lewis part, more or less entirely because of Anne's previous, and in the event, more significant, commitment to Robert.

Anne's choice of Robert, rather than Lewis, is an example of that feature of de Beauvoir's fiction that was stated earlier: the truly successful relationships between men and women are those which are non-sexual, and it is these relationships which should be chosen and maintained rather than passing affairs. But this position raises a number of important issues for feminists, and indeed for anyone interested in the question of how men and women should relate to each other. Most crucially, in *The Second Sex* de Beauvoir gives an account of relations between the sexes which is, for biological and psychological reasons, inevitably a battleground: an analysis which many feminists would accept. In her novels she suggests that sexually active heterosexual relationships are fraught with problems about jealousy, possessiveness and dependence – again, an analysis which many feminists would endorse. Yet once expressed sexuality between men and women disappears, or is not present, the sexes can act together in perfectly harmonious unions – unions which are non-sexual but nevertheless sustaining and happy.

What is not clear in this account of how men and women act, and should act, towards each other, is the extent to which de Beauvoir is arguing that all sexuality is problematic, or if it is only female sexuality, and most particularly female sexuality that is expressed heterosexually, that creates difficulties and tensions between men and women. In *The Second Sex* de Beauvoir states quite explicitly that:

> Feminine sexual excitement can reach an intensity unknown to man. Male sex excitement is keen but localised and it leaves the man quite in possession of himself; woman, on the other contrary, really loses her mind. (de Beauvoir, 1964, p 367)

And the pages of de Beauvoir's novels are scattered with instances of women who, quite literally in some cases, do lose, if not their minds, then at least a measure of their sanity because of their sexual involvements with men. From both *The Second Sex* and her fiction it is, therefore, possible to deduce that de Beauvoir's model of sexuality is one which must be unacceptable to many contemporary feminists: female sexuality is so volatile, and so likely to lead to over-dependence on men and the loss of female autonomy, that it is better if it is not expressed. The great gain of this position – at least as far as de Beauvoir is concerned – is that once expressed female hetero-sexuality is dispensed with, then men and women can begin to be comrades, friends and genuinely co-operative.

There is perhaps, much to be said for such a vision of relations between men and women. Yet what makes this vision one which it is difficult to accept entirely are two features: de Beauvoir's taken-for-granted assumption that male sexuality is normal and unproblematic – and must always be expressed in a desire for sexual relations with women – and the more or less complete absence in either *The Second Sex* or her fiction of any sympathetic treatment by de Beauvoir of maternity and the bearing of children. In the fiction, children are notably absent: Anne Dubreuilh has a daughter and the central character of *The Woman Destroyed* two daughters, but the social relations of parenthood are only minimally explored. Nor is motherhood presented as anything except a chore: again, it is justifiable, and important, for feminists to point out the ambiguities which many women feel about motherhood, but not, perhaps, entirely satisfactory – or helpful as far as women are concerned – for the feminist author to refuse to countenance that the well known responsibilities of motherhood can also provide satisfaction and reward.

The section on motherhood in *The Second Sex* inevitably includes, since it was written in France in the late 1940s, a long discussion about the evils of the lack of proper contraceptive advice and technology for women, and the awful dangers which are presented by illegal abortion. It is one of de Beauvoir's finest achievements that she challenged the traditional chauvinistic pro-natalism of French ortho-doxy, and argued for a liberalisation of the French penal code on contraception and abortion. For this stand, she was subjected to some considerable abuse and hostility – never as great or as dangerous as she faced when she and Sartre opposed French foreign policy in Algeria – but nevertheless public vilification of a real and significant kind. Yet against this brave achievement, of arguing for voluntary, freely chosen motherhood, we must also set de Beauvoir's view of what maternity entails. For example, in one of the more florid passages of *The Second Sex*, de Beauvoir discusses the positive feel-ings of a pregnant woman:

> Her body is at last her own, since it exists for the child who belongs to her . . . (but) this is only an illusion. for she does not really make the baby, it makes itself within her; her flesh engenders flesh only, and she is quite incapable of establishing an existence that will have to establish itself. Creative acts originating in liberty establish the object as value and give it the quality of the essential; whereas the child in the maternal body is not thus justified; it is still only a gratuitous cellular growth, a brute fact of nature as contin-gent on circumstance as death and corresponding philosophically with it. A mother can have *her* reason for wanting *a* child, but she

cannot give to *this* independent person, who is to exist tomorrow, his own reasons, his justification, for existence; she engenders him as a product of her generalised body, not of her individualised existence.(de Beauvoir, 1964, p 468)

She goes on to quote Hegel on the subject of parenthood – 'the birth of children is the death of parents'.

Contained within the passage quoted above, and indeed throughout the section on 'The Mother' we are faced with a view of maternity which is premised, as is *The Second Sex* in general, on a set of assumptions about the Other, and the constant competition between human beings (all of whom are, after all, others to each other) for the power to define the nature of the Other. In her discussion of Engels, we have seen that de Beauvoir suggests that a given feature of human psychology is the desire to dominate others ('the imperialism of the human consciousness') and in the section on maternity we find this assumption appearing again: but now not in what de Beauvoir is saying about men's motivation for attempting to dominate women, but in her analysis of women's motivation for motherhood. Hence her view of motherhood emerges as an instance of the imperialism of the female – a mistaken desire to impose an identity on the world through another. 'Maternity', de Beauvoir writes, 'is usually a strange mixture of narcissism, altruism, idle daydreaming, sincerity, bad faith, devotion and cynicism' (1964, p 485).

Exactly what women have felt about motherhood in the past – and to a large extent the present – is only partially recorded. De Beauvoir's account suggests a widespread dissatisfaction that no doubt contains a great deal of truth – but at the same time she might well be accused of presenting a particularly limited or one-dimensional view of what is arguably a complex experience. Female autobiographies speak, as de Beauvoir rightly points out, of some of the trials of maternity, but female autobiographies, diaries and letters also speak of the positive aspects of motherhood. The written culture of the West is indeed not very well endowed with accounts of women's reactions to motherhood, but it is surely wrong to conclude, as de Beauvoir does, that women are, or have been, silent on the subject. Almost any study of any community will show that amongst women, women speak openly and often critically of their social position as mothers and wives.

A further missing ingredient of de Beauvoir's account of motherhood is any mention of the role that men play in parenthood and she fails to discuss the social and personal aspects of paternity. If motherhood is a mystery to some women, given the arrival of a child who is the archetypal 'other', how much more might that child be an 'other' to a father.

For many contemporary feminists, of whom Adrienne Rich is the best example, the bearing of children is not a demonstration of weakness ar.d vulnerability and negative female sexuality – as it is to de Beauvoir – but of female strength and power. If we compare de Beauvoir and Rich on the meaning of motherhood an enormous shift in feminist values is apparent. De Beauvoir writes:

> It is significant that woman . . . requires help in performing the function assigned to her by nature . . . At just the time when women attains the realisation of her feminine destiny, she is still dependent . . . (de Beauvoir, 1964, p 476)

Rich, on the other hand, positively celebrates female biology, and includes some comments on the attitudes of previous generations of feminists to the body which are particularly pertinent in the case of de Beauvoir:

> Patriarchal thought has limited female biology to its own narrow specifications. The feminist vision has recoiled from female biology for these reasons; it will, I believe, come to view our physicality as a resource, rather than a destiny . . . The ancient, continuing envy, awe, and dread of the male for the female capacity to create life has repeatedly taken the form of hatred for every other female aspect of creativity . . . No wonder that many intellectual and creative women have insisted that they were 'human beings' first and women only incidentally, have minimised their physicality and their bonds with other women. The body has been made so problematic for women that it has often seemed easier to shrug it off and travel as a disembodied spirit. (Rich, 1979, p 40)

Between 1949 when *The Second Sex* was published, and 1976 when *Of Woman Born* appeared, feminism travelled through the revolutions of the coming of affluence to Western Europe, the availability of effective contraception, the so-called sexual revolution and the liberalisation of many public, and institutional, attitudes to sexuality and personal politics. The world in which de Beauvoir grew up disappeared and women faced no fewer, but different problems, from those outlined in *The Second Sex*. Control of reproductive capacity did become possible for many, although by no means all women, and the expanding European economy offered to women the chance of at least a minimal financial independence. At least some of the conditions were created for the existence of that economically independent woman, able to control her own fertility, who is the ideal of *The Second Sex*. Yet given that these conditions now exist, we must ask if the analysis of the position of women given in *The Second Sex* has any longer any relevance for contemporary women.

Since *The Second Sex* is an enormously rich, and wide ranging book, it is inevitable that no single answer exists to questions about its continued usefulness. The analysis of women as 'the Other' in European culture is still as powerful as it ever was – and contemporary feminism is still much concerned to demonstrate that all social institutions and ideological systems are riddled with assumptions about the male being the definitive human being, with woman as the aberrant exception. But the dangers of analyses which make rigid distinctions between men and women – as de Beauvoir's does – are as much a problem for contemporary feminists as they were in the past. A reading, for example, of European literature can demonstrate – as is the case in *The Second Sex* – that male authors have a single view of women. Just as Kate Millett in *Sexual Politics* bases a general case about patriarchal ideology on a discussion of three authors (Mailer, Miller and Lawrence) so de Beauvoir argues (from an examination of Montherlant, Lawrence, Stendhal, Claudel and Breton) that a single myth of the eternal feminine exists in European culture. Cora Kaplan has demonstrated that the case put forward by Kate Millett is far from proven (Kaplan, 1979); similarly it can be said of de Beauvoir that she chooses her authors to fit her case, and that other French writers – for example Flaubert and Balzac – suggest a much more complex picture of male and female behaviour, in which neither sex can be said to have particular, essential, qualities.

But the force of any feminist analysis which sees men and women as distinct, and insuperably separated by biology, must be acknowledged. Yet it is an analysis which as every contemporary feminist knows, is of a highly problematic nature. Feminism is premised on the assumption that there are some concerns – particularly to do with the control of reproduction and the definition of female sexuality – which unite all women. But – and it is a but of crucial, and often diverse, significance – once other areas of human behaviour are examined, it becomes apparent, at least to some feminists, that women are divided in certain ways – not the least of which is in terms of their race or class interests and identification. From the different importance and emphases that diverse groups of feminists attach to the material divisions between women (and of course many feminists deny that any material interests divide women) develop the different political groupings within feminism.

De Beauvoir's work does not fit easily into any one of these groupings. Her political views, at least after the end of the Second World War, have always been avowedly left-wing, and both she and Sartre played a very active part in left-wing, radical organisations and causes. Of the many causes in which she took part, the two most prominent were her opposition to French colonialism in Algeria and her participation in the Russell War Crimes Tribunal, which publicised and condemned the intervention of the United States in Vietnam. More recently, de Beauvoir has taken a leading part in the campaign to legalise abortion in France. No one could question the energy, and the extent, of her political activities: some on behalf of women, and some directed towards the interests of both men and women. On the level of political engagement, therefore, she has led a life of almost unparallelled activity.

Yet *The Second Sex* does not suggest that its author is necessarily a socialist, so much as a radical liberal. Passionately concerned with questions of social justice, especially in so far as they affect women, de Beauvoir nevertheless ignores many of the questions about the social world which materialists, and Marxists, would ask. She demands that women be 'freed', but provides no indication of the kind of conditions which might guarantee that freedom. She clearly sees co-operation and consensus between the sexes as possible, and yet can only envisage this if explicitly sexual relationships between the sexes are minimised or abandoned. Equally, she does not celebrate female sexuality, but asks for the conditions to be created in which women can transcend their physical beings, which as we have seen, in de Beauvoir's view is an unenviable state. Finally, and perhaps most critically, we must ask if de Beauvoir's view of history and culture as it is outlined in *The Second Sex* is not merely an uncritical acceptance of all that men have written about the past. To take, as she does, a male view of the past and re-iterate it as the true version of the emergence of contemporary society is perhaps the most serious disservice to feminism – that far from attempting to re-write history, and rescue the past, and the present, from manifestly patriarchal concerns and interests, she suggests to yet another generation of women that only men formed, and shaped, the world in which we live. The magnificence of the achievement of *The Second Sex* should not detract feminists from examining critically de Beauvoir's model of sexual and psychological normality, or from encouraging women to learn to reject male expectations of normal human behaviour.

Notes

1   In *Only Halfway to Paradise*, 1980, Elizabeth Wilson argues that feminism never entirely disappeared during the 1940s and 1950s. Dale Spender, 1982 (b), documents the number of feminist publications of this period, and in *There's Always Been a Women's Movement This Century* interviews some of the women who were active feminists in the 1940s and 1950s.

2   The domination of the French elite by those from petit-bourgeois and bourgeois origins such as those of de Beauvoir, are summarised by Johnson, 1981, pp 116–135.

Modern Feminist Theorists: Reinventing Rebellion

Dale Spender

This is not a comprehensive analysis of contemporary feminist theory – for such a task would require at least one volume of its own. But the ideas of many feminists of the past have preceded these pages and it is my intention here to provide an overview and to give some indication of if and where modern feminist theorists have links with their foremothers.

Brevity enforces restrictions on my descriptions and explanations for I cannot deal with all the many contemporary feminists who have made their contribution to our current insights. I have referred to women whom I think represent a particular position, but in so doing I have rendered many other women invisible, and have not overtly challenged the 'prominent individual' syndrome. I am not at ease with this situation because it is fundamental to my own beliefs that the development of feminist ideas is a collective process; certainly this has always been my own experience with ideas emerging from discussion and exchange. So it is with some reluctance that I present a partial view of the process, which implies that there have only been a few and not the many who have helped to produce feminist theories.

In such a short space it is not possible to do more than summarise a few of the origins, developments and connections of some of the strands of feminist theory and to show that while feminist forms of analysis are not all the same in emphasis, they nonetheless share a commitment to the politics of exploring, explaining and validating women's experience and to ending women's oppression.

The territory of women's discontent in contemporary times was mapped by Betty Friedan in the early 1960s. That Friedan sought, and treated as real, the experience and explanations of women was in itself a radical departure from the conventional practices of the time and while *The Feminine Mystique* was followed by other publications which adopted a similar frame of reference (eg Mary Ellmann, 1968, Hazel Hunkins-Hallinan, 1968), the consensus seems to be that the scene remained relatively quiet until Germaine Greer and Kate Millett burst upon it in 1970 and ushered in the modern women's movement.[1]

Friedan had started to open the door when she began to question women's role: she argued that all was not well with women and in doing so she helped to establish the basis and the parameters of the modern version of 'the woman question'. She identified one of the fundamental issues which has since become a hallmark of contemporary feminist theory when she stated that while for women a genuine problem existed, it was 'a problem without a name'. Women, insisted Friedan, were informed from the cradle by a multiplicity of sources that happiness lay in homemaking, in love, marriage, children and self-denial. Yet as she observed and as numerous women stated, even though these prescriptions may have been diligently adhered to by a majority of women, many of them did not *feel* happy with their way of life. And in the absence of any public and legitimated knowledge about the widespread phenomenon of female disillusionment, even despair, women in their isolation resorted to blaming themselves for their own inadequacies. If they possessed everything society decreed necessary for their happiness and did not feel happy, then there must be something wrong them them – or so went the rationale in many a suburban home, and it was a rationale that was bolstered by many a male-defined theory of female fulfilment and necessity for feminine adjustment.

Encountering every day of their lives the public and unquestioned knowledge that women in their situation were supposed to be content and fulfilled (and were 'sick' if they were not), these women – and Betty Friedan is among them – were deprived of the knowledge that the problem was not a new one; Charlotte Perkins Gilman for example, had described and explained it all 50 years before. But women had been denied the past and present knowledge which Friedan was painstakingly re-constructing, the knowledge that women's disenchantment, sense of emptiness, was a realistic and rational response to the circumstances in which they found themselves, and far from finding deficiencies in themselves they would be well advised to take a closer look at the circumstances.

While Betty Friedan did not explicitly state that the problem had no name precisely because it was not a problem for men, who as the powerful group are the ones who provide the names, (see Mary Daly, 1973, and Dale Spender, 1980), she did help to set the parameters for the development of the thesis that the knowledge which becomes public and is legitimated in a male dominated society, is the knowledge of men: it is based on their own experience and reflects their own perspective and priorities. Hence the absence of a name and the absence of a body of accepted knowledge in relation to a problem experienced by women.

'The problem without a name', and the 'invisibility' of women's lives and experience, has since become a foundation stone of contemporary feminist thought. It was a major force in the emergence of consciousness-raising groups (see Cassell, 1977) and has become a primary rationale for women's studies courses (see, for example, Joan Roberts, 1976 and Renate Duelli-Klein, 1981). In 1973, Mary Daly was arguing that so extensively was the world defined by men that women had in effect had the power of naming stolen from them; Sheila Rowbotham in the first chapter of *Women's Consciousness, Man's World* (entitled 'The problem without a name'), was assessing the difficulty and even the futility of trying to organise politically around a sense of emptiness, or an absence. While women such as Jean Baker Miller (1974), Ann Oakley (1974, 1980), Dorothy Smith (1978) and Adrienne Rich (1980, 1981) built upon the premise and the implications of women's invisibility, practical examples of how the world was described and explained differently through the eyes – and the position – of women, were provided by Elaine Morgan (*The Descent of Woman*, 1972); Jessie Bernard (*The Future of Marriage*, 1972) and Elizabeth Janeway (*Powers of the Weak*, 1980) among many more.

Implicit in this school of feminist philosophy[2] is the understanding that human beings make sense of the world and act upon that reality, according to the information which is available to them, and even a cursory examination of history reveals (from our present perspective of being in possession of different information and therefore able to construct a different form of 'sense' from our predecessors), that human beings have been capable of believing and acting upon the most extraordinary 'myths'. Nothing, it seems is too fantastic.

When information was filtered through the church, whole communities of average human beings were persuaded to believe in and act upon the premise that vast numbers of women were witches; when filtered through racist regimes, whole societies of ordinary human beings have been persuaded that pigmentation possesses astonishing properties. What many feminists have come to recognise is that in male-dominated societies information is filtered through male-controlled agencies and that community after community has been persuaded to believe and act upon no less extraordinary myths in relation to women. A re-examination of the information made available to women first to get them into the workforce during the Second World War in English-speaking societies – and then to get them out afterwards – makes this abundantly clear.[3]

Being able to generate, validate and control our own knowledge about ourselves and society is then of critical importance to women, for we have been 'victims' insofar as we have been dependent on males for the public knowledge of ourselves. In a male-dominated society the interests of men are not always and perhaps not often compatible with those of women, but while men control information with an eye to their own interest, the knowledge that they produce about women is all that is publicly available, and we are forced to draw upon it to make sense of the world, even though it may do little or nothing to reflect or enhance our lives.

A number of women have focused particularly on the consequences of men defining themselves as the norm, which means that the behaviour of women, where it is different, can be readily classified as 'deviant'. Simone de Beauvoir elaborated the idea of woman as 'Other', even as feared and despised 'Other', and feminists such as Naomi Weisstein (1970) and Phyllis Chesler (1972) – all building on some of the insights used by Friedan – have explored the implications of this practice in relation to women's mental health. When one group in society possesses the power to decree its own experience as the only meaningful, ordered and normal experience, it also has the power to define that which is *outside* its experience as meaningless, chaotic – and abnormal; in other words, says Phyllis Chesler, men have the power to assert and to act upon the belief that women are mad insofar as they do not manifest the characteristics that men have deemed appropriate for them.

Given these understandings, it is not surprising that the modern women's movement should conclude that patriarchy – like many another dictatorship – controls the information available in order to ensure the perpetuation of its own power, that it practises censorship and engages in propaganda on a massive scale, so that its version of sense, and reality, can be unquestioningly accepted.

Contemporary feminists are not the first, of course, to have recognised this aspect of women's oppression and many are the women who have talked of the colonisation of women's minds, and who have expended enormous energy in trying to raise the consciousness of women by presenting them with different information from that provided by patriarchy. Both Matilda Joslyn Gage and Mary Ritter

Beard were passionate in their claims for women to break the mind-set facilitated by patriarchy, to discover and express their own strength which patriarchy (understandably) denied, and to take over and control agencies of information which could reflect women's experience. Before them there was Frances Wright (1795–1852) who insisted on the necessity of 'free enquiry' and who urged women to break their mental chains (see Alice Rossi, 1974, p 115). And before her was 'Sophia, a person of quality' who in 1739 declared unequivocally that it must be observed that so bold a tenet as that of male superiority ought to have better proofs to support it than the bare word of the males who advance it, for as they are parties with so much to gain if their word is believed, this must render their case highly suspect (p 20). She too urged women to cast aside their mental bondage and to generate and establish their own 'truths' of their own existence, which would stand them in good stead.

Always, it seems, while some women have resisted male versions of reality and been 'non-believers' ('heretics' in Cicely Hamilton's terms, 'outsiders' in Virginia Woolf's, and women who are 'disloyal to civilisation' in the words of Adrienne Rich, 1980), others have accepted male definitions and have defended their identity in women's proper place. This is still the case today, and the fact that some women do, and some women don't seek liberation is an area which requires further examination and explanation. What is known, however, is that women have a long tradition of describing male control of information and the way this is used to control women's minds (see Robyn Rowland, 1983, *Women Who Do and Women Who Don't Join the Women's Movement*, for some startling insights). Women who do not acknowledge this tradition and locate themselves within it, are working with considerable handicaps. Women need to know that our ideas are produced – and received – in a male-dominated society and that this influences not just *how* we can explain the world, but what happens to our explanations.

I suspect that knowledge of the existence of Charlotte Perkins Gilman, and her ideas, would have made a significant difference to Betty Friedan in the late 1950s when she was formulating her explanations of women's oppression – for after all, she would have recognised that it had all happened before. Likewise, when arguments are put forward today that women should return to hearth, home and happiness, that they should put more faith in men and look towards a second stage of feminism, we are less likely to be convinced when we can see that this too has all happened before . . . repeatedly. It was a prospect held out to Rebecca West at the beginning of this century, and one which she rejected then (a position which I would wholeheartedly endorse today) when she retorted that 'I am an old fashioned feminist. I believe in the sex war. When those of our army whose voices are inclined to coo tell us that the day of sex antagonism is over and that henceforth we have only to advance hand in hand with the male, I do not believe it' (quoted in Jane Marcus, 1982, p 11).

This cyclical repetition of women's experience helps to substantiate the thesis that men censor women's ideas and explanations, while men are dominant. It is one of the reasons that whenever women have questioned male power (and they have been doing so for centuries) they have attached great significance to consciousness, to the 'personal' as experienced by women in contrast to the 'public' as proclaimed by men, and the modern women's movement reveals its links with past women's movements when it continues within this tradition (see for example Ehrenreich and English, 1978).

This was what Betty Friedan was doing when she began to make clear that so many discontented women in their isolation did *not* know that other women shared similar personal and privatised experience; they did not know this because few, if any, of the information agencies made available knowledge about women's lives from the perspective of those who lived them. Instead, what was known was a version of women's lives which men found acceptable – and convenient!

Within the framework in which great significance has been attached to consciousness however, historically and currently, different responses have developed. Whereas Friedan concentrated on what was left *out* of public knowledge when it was produced by men, Germaine Greer and Kate Millett focused on what was put *in*, for the other side of the invisibility of women is the peculiar and particular way women are made visible under patriarchy. To Millett and Greer, the problem did have a name and the name was male power.

Millett and Greer were enraged by the distorted representation of women. If there was a relatively recent precedent for their stance it was not Mary Ellmann (1968) whose background, like their own was the study of literature, and who coined the term 'phallic criticism' to denote the response women received in a male-dominated society, for Ellmann does not appear to have been particularly influential on either of these writers;[4] Viola Klein seems to be the closest parallel, for it was she who in 1946 examined what men's theories were about women, and what their authority was for formulating them. Needless to say, in the case of Freud, for example, she found that there was little other than personal prejudice sanctified as science and in the main, yet another example of the theory that human beings can convince themselves of the validity of just about anything. But there is still a significant difference between Klein's stand and that adopted by Millett and Greer, for despite the radical and subversive nature of her challenge she still remains largely within the confines of academically respectable discourse. Millett and Greer did not.

They both enter the debate with the determination to demonstrate that men have harboured much malice towards women and they quote male after male from past to present times as documentation. But it is as much the *style* as the content of their protest which is responsible for its force, and this too casts considerable light on contemporary feminist theory.

Going back to the ideas on women's oppression and the part played by consciousness, we find again and again that there has been the claim that women have been required to make men feel good. John Stuart Mill said (and on his own acknowledgement he was informed by the best authority – namely Harriet Taylor, see Rossi, 1970) that it was not sufficient for women to be slaves but that they must be *willing* slaves, the implication being that men do not feel good when obliged to be seen to use force to make women serve them; better by far to have it believed that women *choose* to cater to men's needs and that men themselves are not responsible for the resultant gross inequalities. Under the circumstances the argument that women have only themselves – or their nature – to blame, becomes almost credible.

It was Florence Nightingale who wrote that men took it as a personal affront if the women on whom they bestowed their favours and to whom they ostensibly extended their protection, were not positively cheerful about their self denial and effusive in their delight at making their masters the centre of the universe. By such means, argued Nightingale, men hold women personally responsible for their sense of well being and it is a measure of women's subordination that they accept the responsibility and even feel guilty when their men are not maintained in the good mood which they consider their due (see Strachey, 1978).

And it was Virginia Woolf who in 1928 put the case so eloquently when she said that for centuries, women have been serving as looking glasses for men, reflecting them at twice their natural size. If and when women reflect men at their natural size, in the form in which women see them, argued Woolf, then the male capacity for living diminishes. When women do not enhance the image of men, men may feel cheated, deprived of something they see as their right.

Making men feel good is *work* which women are required to

undertake in a patriarchal society; refusing to engage in such work is a form of resistance. It is not pettiness, petulance or pique, but *politics* which is the basis of women's protest and assertion of anger; rather than finding themselves feeling good, men may be severely discomfited by such rage and can attempt to penalise such rebellious women with counter-charges of 'unfeminine', 'embittered' or 'neurotic'. Women who will not massage male egos are withdrawing their labour – as did the receptionists in New York who refused to smile for a week – and are making a defiant political stand which has a sound theoretical and practical base. This is what Greer and Millett did in 1970.

That this aspect of women's oppression and resistance to it is not fully and freely addressed in our society is nor surprising, given the way information is monitored, but it is an insight nonetheless which has been forged by women for centuries. Elizabeth Cady Stanton and Matilda Joslyn Gage referred to it when they urged women to cease making their emotional and intellectual resources available to men and to get angry at the theft of their resources; the writing of Stanton and Gage reveals that they practised what they preached.

That the stand which Millett and Greer took has not been perhaps the predominant one within feminist theory (with many women being exceptions, Ti-Grace Atkinson, Susan Brownmiller, Michelle Cliff, Mary Daly, Andrea Dworkin, Robin Morgan, Adrienne Rich and Barbara Smith for example) could well be a matter for some regret.

In 1970 Greer and Millett were both aware of the part played by women in propping up patriarchy, and both were intent on removing the veneer of acceptable rationalisations and revealing the nature and extent of woman hatred that is passed off as unproblematic. There is no sugar coating on the pill to make it easier for men to swallow, no glossing over the harsh realities of women's oppression to make it palatable, to preserve male comfort, to gain male approval. The facts as they impinge upon women are laid bare.

'Women have very little idea how much men hate them,' Greer states simply in the opening sentence of her section entitled 'Loathing and Disgust' (p 249). But she makes her statement in the certainty that if women *do* possess the information on how much men hate them they will not be so ready to enhance the male image. In the interest of providing fuller information Greer supplies some of the data missing from the male record and presents a chilling account of male hatred of women in which her analysis of sexual harassment and rape (an 'act of murderous aggression' which is 'enacted upon the hated other' with the intention of humiliating and degrading women, p 251) assumes central significance.

In their analysis of male violence against women Millett and Greer – and the many who have followed them since 1970 – focus on a critical area, where consciousness and physical reality meet. A long formulated feminist principle has been that women's minds, *and women's bodies*, have been colonised under patriarchy, that women's oppression has taken both emotional and physical forms, and as both are inextricably linked, it is no solution to try and attain one form of liberation without the other. Susan Brownmiller, Andrea Dworkin, Catherine MacKinnon and Adrienne Rich have all helped to describe and explain the way male power can be used as a threat to intimidate women but all have emphasised that it is *no idle threat*! In a comparable way in which the white community in America lynched blacks as a means of intimidating, subordinating and controlling the black community (see Ida B. Wells, in Dorothy Sterling, 1979), so has rape, wife battering and sexual harassment been used as a means of controlling women.

The nexus of mind and matter is a complex one; consciousness plays a highly influential role in determining one's view of the world, but at the same time, one's physical circumstances make a significant contribution to the formation of one's consciousness. Even if it were desirable it is not as yet possible to separate satisfactorily the psychological from the material world and to construct two discrete, theoretical entities. Modern feminism reflects the composite nature of women's oppression with some theorists taking consciousness as their starting point and moving towards a consideration of material reality, while others begin with the material reality and move towards an understanding of consciousness.

At the base line of material circumstances women are poorer than men; poverty, says Hilda Scott (forthcoming) is a woman's problem, the world over, and the UN statistics of 1980 substantiate this claim. Women, according to the UN statisticians (who were unlikely to have taken into account the work of emotional management of men) perform two thirds of the world's work, for less than 10 percent of the world's pay, and own less than 1 percent of the world's wealth. And says Scott, if you think women cannot get poorer than that, just remember that the gap between women and men is growing greater every year!

It is indisputable that less than 10 percent of the world's pay and less than 1 percent of the world's wealth is simply not enough to go around for over half the world's population, and the absence of financial autonomy has many ramifications for women who, if they and their children are to survive, must gain access to some of the resources controlled by men. This leads straight into the strategy of women's emotional management of men as women make men feel good, and provide female services in return for support. It is the means by which women are coerced into marriage (or its equivalent) as men ensure that women have little luck at the Labour Exchange, stated Rebecca West in 1912, adding her protest to that of Cicely Hamilton (1909). It is the means by which women work for their survival (see Lynne Spender, forthcoming, and Judith Walkowitz 1980). This structured dependency of women on male approval, in the attempt to earn a living, may be at the work place or in the home, in the public or private sphere and the result is what Adrienne Rich has called 'compulsory heterosexuality', for women are forced into unequal relationships with men as their livelihood.

Perceived in this way it is clear that women are dependent on the good will of men and as the male record of good will to women has been so spectacularly poor, it is feasible to assume that women are obliged to work extremely hard to cultivate it . . . and that they haven't had much success. There seems to be a vicious circle, no closer to being broken now than it was when described by Matilda Joslyn Gage almost a century ago, when she implored women to stop making their emotional, creative and physical resources available to men. However, not many women are in the position of being able to make such a choice. They might possess the knowledge that such a strategy would be desirable but necessity dictates that they 'earn' their way, that they trade their minds and their bodies (in the absence of male-defined material resources) in return for board and lodging – as Cicely Hamilton stated in 1909, and was neither the first nor the last to do so.

To some it seems that the lynch-pin in this system is women's reproductive capacity and that it is because women produce children and are vulnerable during pregnancy and child-rearing that men have been able to take the upper hand and progressively amass their resources which now constitute their power base. Shulamith Firestone (1971), who is frequently misrepresented, has argued that only when women are not engaged in reproduction will the two sexes be the *same* and presumably able to be equal.

There are difficulties in sustaining this line of argument; for me one of the major ones being the recognition that men's record of be-haviour towards women has been so appalling that when women are no longer necessary for reproduction, men may decide that women are no longer necesssary! There is also the consideration that with the possession of different information, reproduction may not be seen to be negative and to constitute a liability – for it is men who have defined resources in material terms and it reflects their own perspective. Reproduction can be defined as positive, as a resource; in the words of Dora Russell (1982), we cannot repudiate some of our most positive and valuable resources, simply because men have been able to use them against us. And in the words of Pauline Bart (1981) who has argued that men have appropriated women's reproductive powers, it is time for women to seize the means of reproduction.

Within most of the economic frameworks men have designed, women's reproductive capacity has been controlled by men and used against them, for at best, most economic theories and forms of analyses have concentrated on production while reproduction has been made invisible and has been almost completely ignored. Trying to insert the value of reproduction into economic descriptions of wealth and its distribution, so that they reflect the realities of human beings and not just of males, has been another feminist goal which has taken a variety of forms. At the risk of leaving intact the existing inequalities among men (for it is patently obvious that men have not distributed equitably among themselves the 99 percent of resources they own), and at the risk of institutionalising women's domestic work, child-rearing responsibilities, and isolation, some have urged that women's work in the home which has for so long been invisible and *unpaid* be given the same status as work performed by men and that wages be paid for housework. There are some advantages in such a scheme, which ideally, would redistribute wealth and provide women with more material resources. But it is doubtful whether the long term gains would be great – or even that men would consent to such an arrangement.

Other feminists, such as Juliet Mitchell (1971) and Sheila Rowbotham (1973, 1974), have been more concerned with tackling the cause at its roots and in overthrowing capitalism which is a fundamental basis of inequality. Capitalism structures inequality for women as well as men, for while men may control the purse strings and no woman may be guaranteed of continued support in return for mind and body, it is clear that women can enjoy access to different sized purses and to different levels of privilege. It is also the case that women are not just unpaid domestic workers but working-class women in the past, and today ever increasing numbers of women, along with the majority of men, are in the paid and exploited work force. For theorists such as Mitchell and Rowbotham there has been the daunting task of articulating the resistance to capitalism while at the same time trying to extend the analysis to encompass women's existence – and specific oppression – for it cannot be accepted that socialism *per se*, or as it is presently practised, is a woman's paradise (see Hilda Scott, 1974).

That women should have economic independence, that they should cease to be economically exploited, is not a controversial issue in feminism, although there are some differences when it comes to formulating the means for achieving this end. Personally, I feel that equality is equality and that feminist goals will not have been realised until all human beings are equal, and this means an end to existing social arrangements which structure inequality – be they based on nationality, ethnicity, class, political position, education, sexual preference, disability or age.

While it may appear to some that there is a gulf between those theories that originate in the context of the psychological realm, and those which originate within the physical world, I suspect that the differences between the two are not so great as some would have us believe, for both theoretical positions recognise that there will be no emotional independence without economic independence and that economic independence of its own – and within the present male-defined value system – will not ensure women's liberation. These theories may begin at different points but because they converge to some extent, because they share a set of assumptions about women's oppression, they reflect diversity, rather than division – another aspect of contemporary feminist theory which helps feminism to take account of its own formation.

Cutting across the apparent differences between the theoretical positions have been a number of debates over the last decade; one example has concerned violence against women, another has involved the significance which should be attached to men. Clearly it is unwise to disregard the oppressors, but equally clearly it is a sound political move to treat them – where possible – with indifference. During the mid-seventies it seems as if the balance were on the side of ignoring the presence of men and there is even a suggestion that feminist research related exclusively to women. Women's experience, however, contains the element of dealing with men, and as Liz Stanley and Sue Wise have said and as Gloria Steinem, Andrea Dworkin and Susan Brownmiller have repeatedly demonstrated, women may know and see much about men which men do not know and see of themselves, and this is information which can be codified and used.

Recently there seems to have been a move towards examining in more detail the problem of men, of male power and male consciousness (see for example, Elizabeth Sarah, 1982) and while keeping in mind the possible pitfall of diverting women's energy into (once more) understanding men, of making the oppressor the focus, increased attention is being given to the morality of mastery and to the threat which male power poses in the world.

Mary O'Brien (1981) has put forward the case that the material reality of reproduction is different for the two sexes and that this gives rise to different forms of consciousness. Dora Russell (forthcoming) is gaining an audience for her ideas on male consciousness (ideas which she has been positing for 60 years), and she refers to men as experiencing a 'flight from the body' in relation to reproduction. This is translated into male attempts to remove from their thought processes all forms of human consideration (that is, to strive for 'objectivity') and to subdue and control the universe through science and technology. Russell traces man's relationships with machines and sheds a different light on women's reluctance to enter technological fields. Man, says Russell, in both capitalist and socialist societies has accepted industrialisation as the new god, and has placed unquestioned faith in the power of machines; man has engaged in humanly and planetary destructive measures in his 'objective' and ahuman attempts to find technological solutions to the problems of human existence.

Refusing to submit to the derogatory meanings which are often applied to women's identification with 'nature', Russell defiantly asserts that women have *not* tried rigorously to rid themselves of the contamination of human consideration from their thought processes, that they *do* see the universe as an organic and interdependent whole, that rather than control and subdue the natural world they want to assert that they are an integral part of it and that there must be harmony among living things; for this reason ecological understandings and pacifist principles are firmly planted in women's consciousness argues Russell, even if they have been eliminated from men's. For Russell, the only possible hope for human and planetary survival lies in the adoption of women's values throughout society (this same stand has been taken by many other women, Vera Brittain, for example, after the First World War).

While many feminist theorists have concerned themselves with the problem of *why* women are oppressed – and possible and plausible explanations range from male fear of irrelevancy to male needs to compensate for lack of reproductive capacity comparable to women's – there are others who are looking at men in the attempt to discover *how* they do it; for Liz Stanley (1982) a central question has been how do men enact oppression on a daily basis, from street harassment to obscene 'phone calls, from sexual violence to emotional abuse; again, it is impossible to divide the phenomenon into psychological and concrete forms.

Likewise many women have looked at power and have tried to disentangle what seem to be contradictory threads. Recognising that what we know has come primarily from those in power, and whose version is therefore very suspect, Elizabeth Janeway (1980) and Robyn Rowland (forthcoming) have alerted us to the perils of believing men's own good opinion of themselves and the power they wield in the institutions of their own making. Power is still a concept about which women have codified very little and it may be that there are some grounds for suggesting that it is a concept which women have avoided analysing; it has been seen as the prerogative of men and it has numerous negative connotations for women, but it could be that patriarchy finds it convenient that we accept men's word on the subject, rather than formulate our own, and make them, their motives and their mechanisms an object of scrutiny.

This is where all feminist theories encounter a problem of major proportions, for all feminists develop theories and attempt to make them available in a male-dominated world. This means acknowledging that we can only make sense with what we know and yet so much that we know is suspect because it has been encoded by men and may work against our own interests. It means that our ideas in the main are still monitored through male agencies (see Lynne Spender, 1983) and we run the risk of having our representations distorted, of our words being used to divide us, or of disappearing. This is particularly the case when we provide information on our own processes, on the controversial issues among us; because of the way society is structured, rather than being perceived as diversity our points of debate over class, ethnicity and sexual preference for example, can be used to discredit us and devalue our movement. But this is part of the pattern of our oppression.

When women's perceptions and insights – in all their diversity – are accorded the same space and legitimacy as men's, oppression as we know it will no longer exist. To the extent that modern feminist theorists have escaped the patriarchal mind-set as outlined by Mary Daly (1978), to the extent that we produce and control our own ideas about our own existence, our minds as well as our bodies, we have broken some of the chains that bind us. To the extent that there are feminist theorists reaching a feminist audience we have moved outside the boundaries of patriarchy. But oppression, as feminist theorists consistently acknowledge, is neither monolithic nor static; it takes many forms and can shift and change. Even while more feminists join the fray, while more information is published on women's lives, while more bridges are built between women who have been divided by racism, classism and heterosexism, the gap between women's resources and those of men, steadily expands. Part of the tradition of feminism, it is worth noting, is to have faith in the belief that *this time* the problem has been exposed, named, and *will be* eradicated.

Notes

1   The National Women's Studies Association Conference in 1980 addressed the issue 'Sexual Politics, Ten Years On'.

2   It should not have escaped attention that all these many books of feminist theory which have existed through the ages, themselves have no name, no category as a genre – another way in which their disappearance is facilitated.

3   The film *Rosie the Riveter* for example, which actually makes use of the propaganda films directed at women during this time, demonstrates that human beings are capable of believing virtually anything and even of having their beliefs dramatically transformed in a short space of time when those who control information find it convenient in the interests of social management and control.

4   Ellmann is mentioned only once by Millett and only once in a footnote by Greer; Viola Klein is referred to by Millett, but not by Greer.

Bibliography

ADLER, Laure, *A L'Aube du Feminisme: Les Premières Journalistes*, Payot, Paris, 1979.

ALBERT, Judith Strong, 'Margaret Fuller and Mary Ware Allen: "In Youth an Insatiate Student" – A Certain Kind of Friendship', *Thoreau Journal Quarterly* 12, July 1980, pp 11–12.

ALLEN, Margaret Venderhaar, *The Achievement of Margaret Fuller*, Pennsylvania State University Press, University Park and London, 1979.

ALLINGHAM, H., and E.B. Williams (eds), *Letters to William Allingham*, Longmans Green, London, 1911; reprinted AMS Press, New York, date n.a.

ANONYMOUS, *An Essay in Defence of the Female Sex*, London, 1696; reprinted 1721.

ANTHONY, Katherine, *Margaret Fuller: A Psychological Biography*, Harcourt, Brace & Howe, New York, 1920; reprinted Arden Library, Darby Pennsylvania, 1978.

ASCOLI, George, 'Essai sur l'histoire des idées feministes en France du XVI siècle à la Revolution', *Revue de Synthèse Historique XIII*, 1906. Cited in Carolyn C. Lougee, *Le Paradis des Femmes: Women, Salons and Social Stratification in Seventeenth-Century France*, Princeton University Press, Princeton, 1976.

ASTELL, Mary. See Select Bibliography, page 38.

BALLARD, George, *Memoirs of British Ladies*, London, 1775.

BANKS, Olive, *Faces of Feminism*, Martin Robertson, Oxford, 1981; St. Martin's Press, New York, 1981.

BART, Pauline, 'Seizing the Means of Reproduction: An Illegal Feminist Abortion Collective – How and Why It Worked', in Helen Roberts (ed), *Women, Health and Reproduction*, Routledge & Kegan Paul, London and Boston, 1981, pp 109–128.

BEARD, Mary Ritter, *Women's Work in Municipalities*, Appleton, New York and London, 1915; reprinted Arno Press, New York, date n.a.

BEARD, Mary Ritter, *On Understanding Women*, Grosset & Dunlap,

New York, 1931; reprinted Greenwood Press, Westport, Connecticut, 1968.

BEARD, Mary Ritter (ed), *America Through Women's Eyes*, Macmillan, New York, 1933.

BEARD, Mary Ritter, 'A Changing Political Economy as It Affects Women', syllabus for a women's studies course, American Association of University Women, Washington, D.C. (mimeographed), 1934.

BEARD, Mary Ritter, *Women as Force in History: A Study in Traditions and Realities*, Macmillan, New York, 1946; reprinted Collier Books, New York, 1962, 1971, 1973; Octagon Books, New York, 1976.

de BEAUVOIR, Simone, *The Second Sex*, 1949; Alfred A. Knopf, New York, 1953; reprinted Bantam Books, New York, 1964; Penguin, Harmondsworth, Middlesex, 1972.

de BEAUVOIR, Simone, *The Prime of Life*, Penguin, Harmondsworth, Middlesex, 1965a; World Publishing, Cleveland, 1962.

de BEAUVOIR, Simone, *Force of Circumstance*, Penguin, Harmondsworth, Middlesex, 1965b; G.P. Putnam's Sons, New York, 1965.

BECKER, Susan D., *The Origins of the Equal Rights Amendment: American Feminism Between the Wars*, Greenwood Press, Westport, Connecticut, and London, 1981.

BEHN, Aphra, *Works*, Montague Summers (ed), London, 1913; reprinted Phaeton Press, Staten Island, New York, 1967.

BELL, Anne Oliver (ed), *The Diary of Virginia Woolf* (4 vols), Hogarth Press, London, 1977–1982; Harcourt Brace Jovanovich, New York, 1978–1982.

BELL, Clive, *Old Friends*, Chatto & Windus, London, 1956.

BELL, Quentin, *Virginia Woolf: A Biography*, Hogarth Press, London, 1972; Harcourt Brace Jovanovich, New York, 1974.

BERNARD, Jessie, *The Future of Marriage*, World Publishing, New York, 1972; reprinted Yale University Press, New Haven, 1982.

BIRCH, Una, *Three Englishwomen in America*, Ernest Benn, London, 1929.

BLACK, Naomi, 'Changing European and North American Attitudes towards Women in Public Life', *Journal of European Integration* 1:2, January 1978, pp 221–240.

BLACK, Naomi, 'The European Communities' Surveys: "European Men and Women"', *Journal of European Integration* 4:1, 1980, pp 83–103.

BLACK, Naomi, 'Virginia Woolf and the Women's Movement', in

Jane Marcus (ed), *New Feminist Essays on Virginia Woolf II*, University of Nebraska Press, Lincoln, 1982.

BLACKWELL, Alice Stone, *Lucy Stone: Pioneer of Women's Rights*, Little, Brown, Boston, 1930; reprinted Kraus Reprint, New York, 1971.

BLANCHARD, Paula, *Margaret Fuller: From Transcendentalism to Revolution*, Delacorte Press, New York, 1978.

BODICHON, Barbara. See Select Bibliography, page 122.

BOETCHER-JOERES, Ruth-Ellen, 'The Ambiguous World of Hedwig Dohm', *Amsterdamer Beiträge zur neueren Germanistik* 10, 1980, pp 255–275.

BOSANQUET, Theodora, *Harriet Martineau: An Essay in Comprehension*, Etchelles & McDonald, London, 1928; reprinted Richard West, Philadelphia, date n.a.

BOYD, Nancy, *Three Victorian Women Who Changed Their World: Josephine Butler, Octavia Hill, Florence Nightingale*, Macmillan, London, 1982; Oxford University Press, New York, 1982.

BOYLE, J., *A Review of Miss Martineau's Work in 'Society in America'*, Marsh Cape & Lyon, London, 1837.

BRAUN, Frederick Augustus, *Margaret Fuller and Goethe*, Henry Holt, New York, 1910; reprinted Folcroft Library Editions, Folcroft, Pennsylvania, date n.a.

BRINK, J.R. (ed), *Female Scholars: A Tradition of Learned Women Before 1800*, Eden Press, Montreal, 1980.

BRINKER-GABLER, Gisela (ed), *Frauen gegen den Krieg*, Fischer Taschenbuchverlag, Frankfurt a/Main, 1980.

BRISTOW, Edward J., *Vice and Vigilance*, Gill & Macmillan, Dublin, 1977.

BRITTAIN, Vera. See Select Bibliography, page 334.

BROWNFOOT, Janice, and Dianne SCOTT, *The Unequal Half: Women in Australia Since 1788*, Reed International, Sydney, 1977.

BROWNMILLER, Susan, 'Speaking Out on Prostitution', in A. Koedt *et al.* (eds), *Radical Feminism*, Quadrangle, New York, 1973, p 72.

BROWNMILLER, Susan, *Against Our Will: Men, Women and Rape*, Penguin, Harmondsworth, Middlesex, 1977; Simon & Schuster, New York, 1975.

BRUÈRE, Martha Bensley, and Mary Ritter BEARD (eds), *Laughing Their Way: Women's Humor in America*, Macmillan, New York, 1934; reprinted Arden Library, Darby, Pennsylvania, date n.a.

BURTON, Hester, *Barbara Bodichon*, John Murray, London, 1949.

BUTLER, A.S.G., *Portrait of Josephine Butler*, Faber, London, 1954.

BUTLER, Josephine E. See Select Bibliography, page 163.

CARROLL, Bernice, '"To Crush Him in Our Own Country": The Political Thought of Virginia Woolf', *Feminist Studies* 4:1, February 1978, pp 99–129.

CASSELL, Joan, *A Group Called Woman: Sisterhood and Symbolism in the Feminist Movement*, David McKay, New York, 1977.

CAVENDISH, Margaret, Duchess of Newcastle, 'Epistle', in *The World's Olio*, London (unpaginated), 1655.

CAVENDISH, Margaret, Duchess of Newcastle, *Sociable Letters*, London, 1664a.

CAVENDISH, Margaret, Duchess of Newcastle, *Philosophical Letters*, London, 1664b.

CAVENDISH, Margaret, Duchess of Newcastle, 'A True Relation of My Birth, Breeding and Life', appended to *Memoirs of the Duke of Newcastle*, London, 1667; reprinted 1907.

CHAPMAN, Maria Weston, 'Memorials', in *Harriet Martineau's Autobiography*, Smith Elder, London, 1877; James R. Osgood, Boston, 1877.

CHAPPLE, J.A.V., and A. POLLARD (eds), *The Letters of Mrs Gaskell*, University Press, Manchester, 1966; Harvard University Press, Cambridge, Massachusetts, 1966.

CHESLER, Phyllis, *Women and Madness*, Allen Lane, London, 1972; Avon Books, New York, 1972.

CHEVIGNY, Bell Gale, *The Woman and the Myth: Margaret Fuller's Life and Writings*, Feminist Press, Old Westbury, New York, 1976.

de CLEYRE, Voltairine, *Selected Works*, Mother Earth, New York, 1914; reprinted Revisionist Press, Brooklyn, date n.a.

CLIFF, Michelle, 'The Resonance of Interruption', *Chrysalis*, No 8, 1979, pp 29–37.

THE COMMON CAUSE, April 1919–January 1920, Official Organ of the National Union of Women's Suffrage Societies. Available for reference, Fawcett Library, City of London Polytechnic, London.

COOTE, Anna, and Beatrix CAMPBELL, *Sweet Freedom: The Struggle for Women's Liberation*, Picador, London, 1982.

COTT, Nancy F., 'Passionless: An Interpretation of Victorian Sexual Ideology, 1790–1850', *Signs* 1:2, 1978, pp 219–236.

COURTNEY, J.E., *Freethinkers of the Nineteenth Century*, Chapman & Hall, London, 1929; reprinted Arno Press, New York, date n.a.

CRABBE, John, 'An Artist Divided', *Apollo*, May 1981, pp 311–313.

DALL, Caroline W. Healey, *Margaret and Her Friends*, Roberts, Boston, 1895; reprinted Arno Press, New York, date n.a.

DALY, Mary, *Beyond God the Father: Toward a Philosophy of Women's Liberation*, Beacon Press, Boston, 1973.

DALY, Mary, *Gyn/Ecology: The Metaethics of Radical Feminism*, Women's Press, London, 1979; Beacon Press, Boston, 1979.

DALY, Mary, 'Foreword', in Matilda Joslyn Gage (1893), *Women, Church and State: The Original Exposé of Male Collaboration Against the Female Sex*, Persephone Press, Watertown, Massachusetts, 1980, pp vii–x.

DEGLER, Carl N., *Is There a History of Women?* Oxford University Press, Oxford, 1974.

DEISS, Joseph Jay, *The Roman Years of Margaret Fuller*, Crowell, New York, 1969.

DELAMONT, Sara, and Lorna DUFFIN (eds), *The Nineteenth-Century Woman: Her Cultural and Physical World*, Croom Helm, London; Barnes & Noble, New York, 1978.

DEROIN, Jeanne, *Cours de Droit Social pour les Femmes*, Plon, Paris, 1848.

DETTI, Emma, *Margaret Fuller Ossoli e i suoi corrispondenti*, Le Monnier, Florence, 1942.

DOHM, Hedwig. See Select Bibliography, page 182.

DOUGHTY, O., and J.R. Wahl (eds), *Letters of Dante Gabriel Rossetti*, Clarendon Press, Oxford, 1965–67; Oxford University Press, New York, 1965–67.

DUELLI-KLEIN, Renate, 'Women's Studies', paper presented to Society for Research into Higher Education Conference, Manchester, December 1981 (forthcoming publication).

DWORKIN, Andrea, *Woman Hating*, E.P. Dutton, New York, 1974.

DWORKIN, Andrea, *Pornography: Men Possessing Women*, Women's Press, London, 1981.

EHRENREICH, Barbara, and Deirdre ENGLISH, *For Her Own Good: 150 Years of the Experts' Advice to Women*, Anchor Press, Doubleday, New York, 1978; Pluto Press, London, 1979.

ELIOT, George, *Letters*, Gordon S. Haight (ed), Oxford University Press, Oxford, 1955–66.

ELLMANN, Mary, *Thinking about Women*, Harcourt Brace Jovanovich, New York, 1968; reprinted Virago, London, 1979.

ENGELS, Frederick, *The Condition of the Working Classes in England*, 1845; reprinted in K. Marx and F. Engels, *Collected Works*, Vol IV, Lawrence & Wishart, London, 1975.

ENGELS, Frederick, *The Origins of the Family*, 1884; reprinted International Publishers, New York, 1942; Pathfinder Press, New York, 1972.

ETHEREGE, George, *Poems*, J. Thorpe (ed), Princeton University Press, Princeton, 1963.

EVANS, Richard, *The Feminists: Women's Emancipation Movements in Europe, America and Australasia, 1840–1920*, Croom Helm, London, 1979; Barnes & Noble, New York, 1977.

FAWCETT, Henry, and Millicent Garrett FAWCETT, *Essays and Lectures on Social and Political Subjects*, Macmillan, London, 1872.

FAWCETT, Millicent Garrett, *Women's Suffrage*, T.C. & E.C. Jack, London, no date.

FAWCETT, Millicent Garrett, 'Introduction' to Mary Wollstonecraft, *A Vindication of the Rights of Woman*, T. Fisher Unwin, London, 1891.

FAWCETT, Millicent Garrett, *Five Famous French Women*, Cassell, London, 1905.

FAWCETT, Millicent Garrett, *The Women's Victory – And After: Personal Reminiscences*, Sidgwick & Jackson, London, 1920.

FAWCETT, Millicent Garrett, *What I Remember*, T. Fisher Unwin, London, 1924; reprinted Hyperion Press, Westport, Connecticut, 1975.

FAWCETT, Millicent Garrett, *Easter in Palestine*, T. Fisher Unwin, London, 1926.

FAWCETT, Millicent Garrett, and E.M. TURNER, *Josephine Butler*, Association for Moral & Social Hygiene, London, 1927.

FENWICK MILLER, Mrs F., *Harriet Martineau*, Eminent Women Series, W.H. Allen, London, 1884.

FIRESTONE, Shulamith, *The Dialectic of Sex: The Case for Feminist Revolution*, Jonathan Cape, London, 1971; Bantam Books, New York, 1971; reprinted Women's Press, London, 1979.

FLEXNER, Eleanor, *Century of Struggle: The Woman's Rights Movement in the United States*, Harvard University Press, Cambridge, Massachusetts, 1959; revised 1979.

FRIEDAN, Betty, *The Feminine Mystique*, W.W. Norton, New York, 1963.

FULFORD, Roger, *Votes for Women*, Faber & Faber, London, 1957.

FULLER, Margaret. See Select Bibliography, page 89.

GAGE, Matilda Joslyn, 'Women as Inventor', *Woman Suffrage Tracts*, No 1, Fayetteville, New York, 1870.

GAGE, Matilda Joslyn, 'Who Planned the Tennessee Campaign of 1862?' *National Citizen Tract*, No 1, 1880.

GAGE, Matilda Joslyn, *Woman, Church and State: The Original Exposé of Male Collaboration Against the Female Sex*, Charles Kerr, Chicago, 1893; reprinted Persephone Press, Watertown, Massachusetts, 1980.

GAGEN, Jean E., *The New Woman: Her Emergence in English Drama 1600–1730*, Twayne, New York, 1954.

GALLAGHER, Robert S., 'The Fight for Women's Suffrage: An Interview with Alice Paul', *American Heritage: The Magazine of History*, February 1974.

GARTH, Wilkinson J.J., *The Forcible Introspection of Women for the Army and Navy by the Oligarchy considered Physically*, London, 1870.

GASKELL, Elizabeth, *Letters*, J.A.V. Chapple & A. Pollard (eds), University Press, Manchester, 1966; Harvard University Press, Cambridge, Massachusetts, 1966.

GEIGER, Ruth-Esthe, and Sigrid WEIGEL, *Sind das noch Damen? Vom gelehrten Frauenzimmer – Journal zum feministischen Journalismus*, Frauenbuchverlag, München, 1981.

GÉRIN, Winifred, *Elizabeth Gaskell: A Biography*, Oxford University Press, New York, 1976.

GILLMAN, Charlotte Perkins, *The Living of Charlotte Perkins Gillman*, Appleton-Century, New York, 1935.

GODWIN, William, *Memoirs of Mary Wollstonecraft*, W. Clark Durant (ed), Constable, London, 1927; reprinted Haskell, Brooklyn, 1969.

GOLDMAN, Emma, *Anarchism and Other Essays*, Dover, New York, 1919; reprinted 1969.

GOLDMAN, Emma, *Living My Life* (2 vols), Dover, New York, 1931; reprinted 1970.

GOLDMAN, Emma, *Red Emma Speaks: The Selected Speeches and Writings of the Anarchist and Feminist*, Alix Kates Shulman (ed), Vintage Books, New York, 1972; Wildwood House, 1979.

GOLDMAN, Emma, *Dancing in the Revolution: Selected Writings and Speeches*, Alix Kates Shulman (ed), Virago, London, 1983.

GOLDSTEIN, Vida. See Select Bibliography, page 255.

GORDON, Linda, *Woman's Body, Woman's Right: Birth Control in America*, Grossman, New York; Penguin, Harmondsworth, Middlesex, 1974; reprinted Viking Press, New York, 1976.

GOREAU, Angeline, *Reconstructing Aphra: A Social Biography of Aphra Behn*, Oxford University Press, Oxford, 1980; Dial Press, New York, 1980.

GREER, Germaine, *The Female Eunuch*, McGibbon & Kee, London, 1970; McGraw-Hill, New York, 1971.

HAIGHT, Gordon S. (ed), *Letters of George Eliot*, Oxford University Press, Oxford, 1955–66.

HAIGHT, Gordon S. (ed), *George Eliot and John Chapman*, Archon Books, Hamden, Connecticut, 1969.

HALSBAND, Robert, *The Life of Lady Mary Wortley Montagu*, Oxford University Press, Oxford and New York, 1956.

HAMILTON, Cicely, *Marriage as a Trade*, 1909; reprinted Women's Press, London, 1981.

HARRISON, Brian, 'Josephine Butler', in *Eminently Victorian*, J.F.G. Harrison *et al.* (eds), Routledge & Kegan Paul, London, 1974.

HAYS, Elinor Rice, *Morning Star: A Biography of Lucy Stone*, Harcourt, Brace & World, New York, 1961; reprinted Octagon Books, New York, 1978.

HELLERSTEIN, Erna Olafson, Leslie Parker HUME, and Karen M. OFFEN (eds), *Victorian Women: A Documentary Account of Women's Lives in Nineteenth-Century England, France and the United States*, Harvester Press, Brighton, 1981; Stanford University Press, Stanford, 1981.

HENDERSON, Leslie M., *The Goldstein Story*, Stockland Press, Melbourne, 1973.

HERSCHBERGER, Ruth, *Adam's Rib*, 1946; Harper & Row, New York, 1970.

HIGGINSON, Thomas Wentworth, *Margaret Fuller Ossoli*, Houghton Mifflin, Boston, 1884; reprinted Haskell, Brooklyn, 1968.

HOFSTADTER, Richard, *The Progressive Historians: Turner, Beard, Parrington*, Vintage Books, New York, 1970.

HOLCOMBE, Lee, 'Victorian Wives and Property', in Martha Vicinus (ed), *A Widening Sphere*, 1932; reprinted Indiana University Press, Bloomington, 1977.

HOLTBY, Winifred, *Virginia Woolf: A Critical Memoir*, Cassandra, Chicago, 1978.

HOUGHTON, Walter E., *A Victorian Frame of Mind*, Yale University Press, New Haven, 1957.

HOWE, Julia Ward, *Margaret Fuller (Marchesa Ossoli)*, Little, Brown, Boston, 1883; reprinted Richard West, Philadelphia, 1973.

HOWE, M.D. (ed), *The Holmes–Laski Letters 1916–1935*, Oxford University Press, Oxford, 1953; Atheneum, New York, 1963.

HUBBARD, Ruth, 'Reflections on the Story of the Double Helix', *Women's Studies International Quarterly* 2:3, 1979, pp 261–274.

HUME-ROTHERBY, Mary, *Women and Doctors: Or Medical Despotism in England*, London, 1871.

HUNKINS HALLINAN, Hazel (ed), *In Her Own Right: A Discussion Conducted by the Six Point Group*, George G. Harrap, London, 1968.

HUNTER, Joseph (ed), *Ralph Thoresby: Diary*, London, 1830.

JANEWAY, Elizabeth, *Powers of the Weak*, Alfred A. Knopf, New York, 1980.

JOHNSON, R.W., *The Long March of the French Left*, Macmillan, London, 1981; St. Martin's Press, New York, 1981.

KAMM, Josephine, *Rapiers and Battleaxes: The Women's Movement and Its Aftermath*, Allen & Unwin, London, 1966.

KAMM, Josephine, *John Stuart Mill in Love*, Gordon & Cremonesi, London, 1977.

KAPLAN, Cora, 'Radical Feminism and Literature', *Red Letters*, No 9, 1979.

KAPP, Yvonne, *Eleanor Marx: Famly Life 1855–1884* (Vol I), Virago, London, 1979.

KLEIN, Viola, *The Feminine Character: History of an Ideology*, Routledge & Kegan Paul, London, 1946; reprinted University of Illinois Press, Urbana, 1972.

LAMPRECHT, Sterling (ed), *Thomas Hobbes's De Cive*, Appleton-Century-Crofts, New York, 1949; reprinted Greenwood Press, Westport, Connecticut, 1982.

LANE, Anne J. (ed), *Mary Ritter Beard: A Source Book*, Schocken Books, New York, 1977.

LANE, Margaret, *The Brönte Story*, Fontana, London, 1953; reprinted Greenwood Press, Westport, Connecticut, 1971.

LEASKA, Mitchell, *The Pargiters by Virginia Woolf: The Novel Essay Portion of The Years*, Hogarth Press, London, 1978; New York Public Library, New York, 1977.

LEAVIS, Q.D., 'Caterpillars of the Commonwealth Unite', *Scrutiny* 7, September 1938, pp 203–214.

LECKY, W.E.H., *History of European Morals from Augustus to Charlemagne*, Longmans, London, 1869.

LEIGH SMITH PAPERS (Barbara Bodichon), Girton College Library, Cambridge, England.

LEMONS, J. Stanley, *The Woman Citizen: Social Feminism in the 1920s*, University of Illinois Press, Urbana, 1975.

LIDDINGTON, Jill, and Jill NORRIS, *One Hand Tied Behind Us: The Rise of the Women's Suffrage Movement*, Virago, London, 1978.

LONGE, Julia (ed), *Martha, Lady Giffard: Her Life and Correspondence 1664–1722*, London, 1911.

MacKINNON, Catherine, *Sexual Harassment of Working Women*, Yale University Press, New Haven and London, 1979.

MANN, Katia, *Meine ungeschriebenen Memoiren*, Elisabeth Plessen and Michael Mann (eds), Fischer Verlag, Frankfurt a/Main, 1974.

MARCUS, Jane, '"No More Horses": Virginia Woolf on Art and Propaganda', *Women's Studies* 4, 1977, pp 264–289.

MARCUS, Jane (ed), *The Young Rebecca: Writings of Rebecca West, 1911–1917*, Macmillan, London, 1982.

MARDER, Herbert, *Feminism and Art: A Study of Virginia Woolf*, University of Chicago Press, Chicago, 1968.

MARSH, Margaret S., *Anarchist Women 1870–1920*, Temple University Press, Philadelphia, 1981.

MARTIN, Theodore, *Queen Victoria as I Knew Her*, Blackwood, London, 1980.

MARTINEAU, Harriet. See Select Bibliography, page 74.

MASSEY, Gerald, 'Last Poems and Other Works of Mrs. Browning', *North British Review*, 1862, pp 271–281.

McHUGH, Paul, *Prostitution and Victorian Social Reform*, Croom Helm, London, 1980; St. Martin's Press, New York, 1980.

McQUEEN, Simpson Alan and Mary (eds), *'I Too Am Here': Selections from the Letters of Jane Carlyle*, Cambridge University Press, Cambridge, England, 1977.

MILL, John Stuart, *The Subjection of Women*, 1869; reprinted MIT Press, Cambridge, Massachusetts, 1970; Oxford University Press, Oxford, 1974.

MILL, John Stuart, *Autobiography*, Longman, Green, Reader & Dyer, London, 1973; Columbia University Press, New York, 1924.

MILLER, Jean Baker, *Toward a New Psychology of Women*, Penguin, Harmondsworth, Middlesex, 1978; Beacon Press, Boston, 1977.

MILLETT, Kate, *Sexual Politics*, Jonathan Cape, London, 1970; Doubleday, New York, 1970; Abacus, Sphere Books, London, 1971.

MITCHELL, David, *The Fighting Pankhursts*, Jonathan Cape, London, 1967.

MITCHELL, David, *Queen Christabel*, McDonald & Jane's, London, 1977.

MITCHELL, Juliet, *Woman's Estate*, Penguin, Harmondsworth, Middlesex, 1971; Vintage Books, New York, 1973.

MITCHELL, Juliet, and Ann OAKLEY (eds), *The Rights and Wrongs of Women*, Penguin, Harmondsworth, Middlesex, 1976.

MOBERLY BELL, E., *Josephine Butler: Flame of Fire*, Constable, London, 1962.

MORE, Hannah, *Strictures on the Modern Female System of Education*, T. Cadell Jr. & W. Davies, London, 1799; reprinted Garland Publishing, New York, 1974.

MORGAN, David, *Suffragists and Liberals: The Politics of Women's Suffrage in England*, Basil Blackwell, Oxford, 1975.

MORGAN, Elaine, *The Descent of Women*, Souvenir Press, London, 1972; Stein & Day, New York, 1972.

MORGAN, Robin (ed), *Sisterhood Is Powerful: An Anthology of Writings from the Women's Liberation Movement*, Vintage Books, New York, 1970.

MORGAN, Robin, *Going Too Far: The Personal Chronicle of a Feminist*, Vintage Books, New York, 1978; Penguin Books, Harmondsworth, Middlesex, 1979.

MORRELL, Caroline, *'Black Friday' and Violence Against Women in the Suffragette Movement*, Women's Research & Resources Centre Publications, London, 1981.

MYERSON, Joel, *Margaret Fuller: An Annotated Secondary Bibliography*, Burt Franklin, New York, 1977.

MYERSON, Joel, *Margaret Fuller: A Descriptive Bibliography*, University of Pittsburgh Press, Pittsburgh, 1978.

MYERSON, Joel, *Critical Essays on Margaret Fuller*, G.K. Hall, Boston, 1980.

NAREMORE, James, 'Nature and History in *The Years*', in Ralph Freedman (ed), *Virginia Woolf: Re-evaluation and Commentary*, University of California Press, Berkeley, 1979, pp 241–262.

NICOLSON, Nigel, and Joanne TRAUTMAN (eds), *The Letters of Virginia Woolf* (6 Vols), Chatto & Windus, London, 1975–80; Harcourt Brace Jovanovich, New York, 1975–80.

NIELD, Keith (ed), *Prostitution in the Victorian Age: Debates on the Issue from 19th Century Critical Journals*, Gregg, Farnborough, 1973.

NIGHTINGALE, Florence, 'Cassandra', in Ray Strachey, *The Cause: A Short History of the Women's Movement in Great Britain*, 1928; reprinted Virago, London, 1978, pp 395–418; reprinted Kennikat Press, Port Washington, New York, 1969.

OAKLEY, Ann, *The Sociology of Housework*, Martin Robertson, Oxford, 1974; Pantheon Books, New York, 1975.

OAKLEY, Ann, *Women Confined: Towards a Sociology of Child-*

birth, Martin Robertson, Oxford, 1974; Schocken Books, New York, 1980.

O'BRIEN, Mary, *The Politics of Reproduction*, Routledge & Kegan Paul, Boston and London, 1981.

OKIN, Susan Moller, *Women in Western Political Thought*, Princeton University Press, Princeton, 1979.

PANKHURST, Christabel, *The Great Scourge and How to End It*, Woman's Press, London, 1913 (currently out-of-print; available for reference from Fawcett Library, City of London Polytechnic, London).

PANKHURST, Christabel, *Unshackled: The Story of How We Won the Vote*, Hutchinson, London, 1959 (out-of-print; available Fawcett Library).

PANKHURST, Sylvia, *The Suffragette*, Gay & Hancock, London, 1910.

PANKHURST, Sylvia, *The Suffragette Movement*, Virago, London, 1977.

PARKES, Bessie Rayner (later Belloc), *Remarks on the Education of Girls*, J. Chapman, London, 1854.

PAUL, Alice. See Select Bibliography, page 294.

PERCIVAL, Alice, Unpublished manuscript notes for an account of the Langham Place Group, to be called *A Remarkable Set*, 1973.

PERRY, Lewis, and Michael FELLMAN (eds), *Anti-Slavery Reconsidered*, Louisiana State University Press, Baton Rouge, 1979.

PETRIE, Glen, *A Singular Iniquity: The Campaigns of Josephine Butler*, Macmillan, London, 1971.

PHILIPS, Katherine, *Letters from Orinda to Poliarchus*, London, 1705.

PIPER, J.J., *History of Robertsbridge*, 1906 (obtainable Girton College Library, Cambridge, England).

PLESSEN, Elisabeth, 'Hedwig Dohm (1833–1919)', in Hans-Jürgen Schultz (ed), *Frauen*, Kreuz Verlag, Stuttgart and Berlin, 1981, pp 128–141.

PUGH, M., *Women's Suffrage in Britain 1867–1929*, Historical Association Pamphlet, London, 1980.

RAEBURN, Antonia, *Militant Suffragettes*, New English Library, London, 1974.

RAHM, Berta (ed), *Erinnerungen Hedwig Dohm: Hedda Korsch*, Ala Verlag, Zürich, 1980.

RAMELSON, Marian, *The Petticoat Rebellion: A Century of Struggle for Women's Rights*, Lawrence & Wishart, London, 1967; Beekman Publishers, Woodstock, New York, 1976.

REED, Joseph W. (ed), *An American Diary 1857-1858: Barbara Leigh Smith Bodichon*, Routledge & Kegan Paul, London, 1972.

RICH, Adrienne, *Of Woman Born: Motherhood as Experience and Institution*, W.W. Norton, New York, 1977; Virago, London, 1979.

RICH, Adrienne, *On Lies, Secrets and Silence*, W.W. Norton, New York, 1979; Virago, London, 1980.

RICH, Adrienne, *Compulsory Heterosexuality and Lesbian Existence*, Onlywomen Press, London, 1981.

RIVENBURG, Navrola, E., *Harriet Martineau: An Example of Victorian Conflict*, Philadelphia, 1932.

ROBERTS, Joan (ed), *Beyond Intellectual Sexism: A New Woman, A New Reality*, David McKay, New York, 1976.

ROGERS, Katharine M. (ed), *Before Their Time: Six Women Writers of the Eighteenth Century*, Frederick Ungar, New York, 1979.

ROSEN, Andrew, *Rise Up Women! The Militant Campaign of the Women's Social and Political Union*, Routledge & Kegan Paul, London and Boston, 1974.

ROSENBAUM, S.P. (ed), *The Bloomsbury Group: A Collection of Memoirs, Commentary and Criticism*, University of Toronto Press, Toronto, 1975.

ROSSETTI, Dante Gabriel, *Letters*, O. Doughty & J.R. Wahl (eds), Clarendon Press, Oxford, 1965-67; Oxford University Press, New York, 1965-67.

ROSSI, Alice S., *Essays on Sex Equality by John Stuart Mill and Harriet Taylor Mill*, University of Chicago Press, Chicago, 1970.

ROSSI, Alice S. (ed), *The Feminist Papers: From Adams to de Beauvoir*, Bantam Books, New York, 1974.

ROVER, Constance, *Women's Suffrage and Party Politics in Britain, 1866-1914*, Routledge & Kegan Paul, London, 1967.

ROVER, Constance, *Love, Morals and the Feminists*, Routledge & Kegan Paul, London, 1970.

ROWBOTHAM, Sheila, *Woman's Consciousness, Man's World*, Penguin, Harmondsworth, Middlesex, and Baltimore, 1973; Pluto Press, London, 1974.

ROWBOTHAM, Sheila, *Hidden from History: 300 Years of Women's Oppression and the Fight Against It*, Pluto Press, London, 1974; Vintage Books, New York, 1976.

ROWLAND, Robyn, *Women Who Do and Women Who Don't . . . Join the Women's Movement*, Pandora Press, London, 1983.

ROWLAND, Robyn, *Childfree* (forthcoming).

ROYAL COMMISSION UPON THE ADMINISTRATION AND

OPERATION OF THE CONTAGIOUS DISEASES ACTS, 1866–69, 1871 (C 408–1) xix.

RUSKIN, John, 'Of Queen's Gardens', in *Sesame and Lilies*, Vol XVIII, 1865; George Allen, London, 1905.

RUSSELL, Dora, Interview with Dale Spender, March; published in Dale Spender, *There's Always Been a Women's Movement*, Pandora Press, London, 1983.

SARAH, Elizabeth *et al.* (ed), *On the Problem of Men*, Women's Press, London, 1982; Merrimack Book Service, Lawrence, Massachusetts, 1982.

SCHENK, Herrad, *Die feministische Herausforderung: 150 Jahre Frauenbewegung in Deutschland*, Verlag C.H. Beck, München, 1979.

SCHREIBER-KRIEGER, Adele, *Hedwig Dohm: Vordenkerin und Vorkampferin neuer Frauenideale*, Märkische Verlagsanstalt, Berlin.

SCHREINER, Olive. See Select Bibliography, page 243.

von SCHURMAN, Anna, *The Learned Maid or Whether a Maid May Be a Scholar?* London, 1641.

SCOTT, Hilda, *Does Socialism Liberate Women? Experiences from Eastern Europe*, Beacon Press, Boston, 1974.

SCOTT, Hilda, *The Feminization of Poverty*, Pandora Press, London (forthcoming).

SHOWALTER, Elaine, *A Literature of Their Own: British Women Novelists from Brönte to Lessing*, Virago, London, 1978; Princeton University Press, Princeton, 1976.

SHULMAN, Alix Kates (ed), *Dancing in the Revolution: Selected Writings and Speeches by Emma Goldman*, Virago, London, 1983.

SIGSWORTH, EM., and T.J. WYKE, 'A Study of Victorian Prostitutes and Venereal Disease', in Martha Vicinus (ed), *Suffer and Be Still: Women in the Victorian Age*, Indiana University Press, Bloomington, 1972, pp 77–99.

SIMPSON, Hilary, 'A Literary Trespasser: D.H. Lawrence's Use of Women's Writing', *Women's Studies International Quarterly* 2:2, 1979, pp 155–170.

SMITH, Barbara, 'Toward a Black Feminist Criticism', *Women's Studies International Quarterly* 2:2, 1979, pp 183–194.

SMITH, Dorothy, 'A Peculiar Eclipsing: Women's Exclusion from Man's Culture', *Women's Studies International Quarterly* 1:4, 1978, pp 281–296.

SMITH, Florence, *Mary Astell*, Columbia University Press, New York, 1916,; reprinted AMS Press, New York, date n.a.

SOPHIA, A Person of Quality, *Woman Not Inferior to Man*, 1739; reprinted Bentham Press, London, 1975.

SPENDER, Dale, *Man Made Language*, Routledge & Kegan Paul, London and Boston, 1980.

SPENDER, Dale, *Invisible Woman: The Schooling Scandal*, Writers & Readers, London, 1982a.

SPENDER, Dale, *Women of Ideas – And What Men Have Done to Them from Aphra Behn to Adrienne Rich*, Routledge & Kegan Paul, London and Boston, 1982b.

SPENDER, Dale, *There's Always Been a Women's Movement*, Pandora Press, London, 1983.

SPENDER, Lynne, *Intruders on the Rights of Men: Women's Unpublished Heritage*, Pandora Press, London, 1983.

STAARS, David, *The English Woman*, Smith Elder, London, 1909.

STACEY, Margaret, and Marion PRICE, *Women, Power and Politics*, Tavistock, London, 1981; Methuen, New York, 1981.

STANLEY, Liz, Paper presented at British Sociological Association, Manchester, March 1982.

STANLEY, Liz, and Sue WISE, 'Back into the Personal, or, Our Attempt to Construct Feminist Research', in Gloria Bowles and Renate Duelli-Klein (eds), *Theories of Women's Studies II*, University of California Press, Berkeley, 1981, pp 98–118.

STANLEY, Liz, and Sue WISE, *Breaking Out: Feminist Consciousness and Feminist Research*, Routledge & Kegan Paul, London and Boston (forthcoming).

STANNARD, Una, *Mrs Man*, Germainbooks, San Francisco, 1977.

STANTON, Elizabeth Cady, Susan B. ANTHONY, and Matilda Joslyn GAGE (eds), *History of Woman Suffrage* (Vol I), Fowler & Wells, New York, 1881; reprinted Arno Press and New York Times, New York, 1969.

STEPHEN, Barbara, *Emily Davies and Girton College*, Constable, London, 1927; reprinted Hyperion Press, Westport, Connecticut, date n.a.

STERLING, Dorothy, *Black Foremothers: Three Lives*, Feminist Press, Old Westbury, New York, 1979.

STERNE, Madeleine B., *The Life of Margaret Fuller*, E.P. Dutton, New York, 1942.

STONE, Lawrence, *The Family, Sex and Marriage in England, 1500–1800*, Harper & Row, New York, 1977.

STONE, Luxy. See Select Bibliography, page 136.

STRACHEY, Ray, *The Cause: A Short History of the Women's*

Movement in Great Britain, Bell, London, 1928; reprinted Virago, London, 1978; Kennikat Press, Port Washington, New York, 1969.

STRACHEY, Ray, *Millicent Garrett Fawcett*, John Murray, London, 1931.

THE SUFFRAGETTE, Official Organ of the Women's Social and Political Union, October 1912–October 1915. Available for reference, Fawcett Library, City of London Polytechnic, London.

SUMMERS, Ann, *Damned Whores and God's Police*, Penguin, Harmondsworth, Middlesex, 1975.

SUMMERS, Montague (ed), *Aphra Behn: Works*, London, 1913; reprinted Phaeton Press, Staten Island, New York, 1967.

TANNER, Leslie B. (ed), *Voices from Women's Liberation*, Signet, New York, 1971.

TEALE, Ruth (ed), *Colonial Eve: Sources on Women in Australia 1788–1914*, Oxford University Press, Melbourne, 1978.

THOLFSEN, Trygue, *Working Class Radicalism in Mid-Victorian England*, Penguin, Harmondsworth, Middlesex, 1976; Columbia University Press, New York, 1977.

THOMAS, Keith, 'The Double Standard', *Journal of the History of Ideas*, No 20, 1959, pp 201–207.

THOMAS, Keith, 'Women and the Civil War Sects', in Trevor Aston (ed), *Crisis in Europe*, Basic Books, New York, 1968, pp 317–340.

THOMPSON, E.P., *The Making of the English Working Class*, Penguin, Harmondsworth, Middlesex, and Baltimore, 1968.

THOMPSON, E.P., and Eileen YEO, *The Unknown Mayhew*, Merlin Press, San Jose, California, 1971.

THOMPSON, William (in collaboration with Anna WHEELER), *Appeal of One Half of the Human Race, Women, Against the Pretensions of the Other Half, Men, to Retain Them in Political and Thence in Civil and Domestic Slavery*, Longman Hurst, London, 1825.

THOMSON, David, *England in the Nineteenth Century*, Penguin, Harmondsworth, Middlesex, and Baltimore, 1950.

TREVELYAN, G.M., *Illustrated English Social History* (Vol 4), Longmans Green, London and New York, 1942.

UPMAN, A.H., 'English Femmes Savantes at the End of the Seventeenth Century', *Journal of English and Germanic Philology* 12, 1913.

URBANSKI, Marie Mitchell Olesen, 'The Ambivalence of Ralph Waldo Emerson towards Margaret Fuller', *Thoreau Quarterly Journal* 10, July 1978, pp 26–36.

URBANSKI, Marie Mitchell Olesen, *Margaret Fuller's 'Woman in the Nineteenth Century': A Literary Study of Form and Content, of Sources and Influence*, Greenwood Press, Westport, Connecticut, and London, 1980.

VICINUS, Martha (ed), *A Widening Sphere: Changing Roles of Victorian Women*, Indiana University Press, Bloomington, 1977.

THE VOTE, Official organ of the Women's Freedom League, October 1909–November 1932. Available for reference, Fawcett Library, City of London Polytechnic, London.

WAGNER, Sally Roesch, 'Introduction' to Matilda Joslyn Gage (1893), *Woman, Church and State*, Persephone Press, Watertown, Massachusetts, 1980, pp xv–xxxix.

WALKOWITZ, Judith R., *Prostitution and Victorian Society: Women, Class and the State*, Cambridge University Press, Cambridge, England, 1980.

WATTS, Ruth E., 'The Unitarian Contribution to the Development of Female Education (1790–1850)', *History of Education* 9:4, 1980, pp 273–286.

WEBB, R.K., *Harriett Martineau: A Radical Victorian*, Columbia University Press, New York, 1960.

WEISSTEIN, Naomi, ' "Kinde, Küche, Kirche" as Scientific Law: Psychology Constructs the Female', in Robin Morgan (ed), *Sisterhood Is Powerful*, Vintage Books, New York, 1970, pp 228–244.

WEST, Rebecca, 'The Woman as Workmate', *Manchester Daily Dispatch*, November 26, 1912.

WESTON, Maria Chapman (ed), *Harriet Martineau: Memorials* (Vol III), Smith Elder, London, 1877.

WHEATLEY, Vera, *The Life and Work of Harriet Martineau*, Secker & Warburg, London, 1957; reprinted Richard West, Philadelphia, date n.a.

WHEELER, Leslie (ed), *Loving Warriors*, Dial Press, New York, 1981.

WHITTICK, Arnold, *Woman into Citizen*, Atheneum with Frederick Mueller, London, 1979; American Bibliographical Center–Clio Press, Santa Barbara, California, 1980.

WILSON, Elizabeth, *Only Halfway to Paradise: Women in Post-War Britain*, Tavistock, London, 1980; Methuen, New York, 1980.

WOLLSTONECRAFT, Mary, *Mary: A Fiction*, Joseph Johnson, London, 1788; reprinted Schocken Books, New York, date n.a.

WOLLSTONECRAFT, Mary, *A Vindication of the Rights of Woman*, Joseph Johnson, London, 1792; reprinted Miriam Kramnick (Brody) (ed), Penguin, Harmondsworth, Middlesex, and Baltimore, 1978; W.W. Norton, New York, 1967.

WOLLSTONECRAFT, Mary, *Love Letters of Mary Wollstonecraft to Gilbert Imlay* (with a prefatory memoir by Roger Ingpen), Hutchinson, London, 1908; reprinted Folcroft Library Editions, Folcroft, Pennsylvania, date n.a.

WOODHAM, Cecil Smith, *Florence Nightingale*, Constable, London, 1950.

WOOLF, Leonard (ed), *Virginia Woolf: Collected Essays* (4 vols), Hogarth Press, London, 1966.

WOOLF, Leonard (ed), *Virginia Woolf: A Writer's Diary*, Hogarth Press, London, 1966–67; Harcourt Brace Jovanovich, New York, 1973.

WOOLF, Leonard, *Downhill All the Way: An Autobiography of the Years, 1919 to 1939*, Hogarth Press, London, 1967; Harcourt Brace Jovanovich, New York, 1975.

WOOLF, Virginia, 'A Society', in *Monday or Tuesday*, Hogarth Press, London, 1921.

WOOLF, Virginia, *A Room of One's Own*, Hogarth Press, London, 1928; reprinted Harcourt Brace Jovanovich, New York, 1964.

WOOLF, Virginia, 'Introduction' to Margaret Llewelyn Davies (ed), *Life as We Have Known It: By Co-operative Working Women*, Hogarth Press, London, 1931; reprinted W.W. Norton, New York, 1975.

WOOLF, Virginia, *The Second Common Reader*, Hogarth Press, London, 1932; reprinted Harcourt Brace Jovanovich, New York, 1956.

WOOLF, Virginia, *Three Guineas*, Hogarth Press, London, 1938; reprinted Harcourt Brace Jovanovich, New York, 1963.

WOOLLEY, Hannah, *The Gentlewoman's Companion*, London, 1675.

THE WOMAN'S DREADNOUGHT, March 1914–July 1916, Published by East London Federation of the Suffragettes; renamed Workers' Suffrage Federation, March 1916. Available for reference, Fawcett Library, City of London Polytechnic, London.

THE WORKER'S DREADNOUGHT, July 1916–June 1924, Published by Workers' Suffrage Federation; renamed Communist Party of Great Britain, June 1919. Available for reference, Fawcett Library, City of London Polytechnic, London.

WYCHERLEY, William, *Works*, Montague Summers (ed), London, 1924.

YOUNG, G.M., *Portrait of an Age: Victorian England*, Oxford University Press, Oxford and New York, 1936; reprinted 1977.

Biographical Notes on Contributors

Naomi Black, Associate Professor of Political Science at York University, Toronto, is currently researching traditional women's organisations in Britain, France, the United States, and Canada.

Miriam Brody teaches writing at Ithaca College in upstate New York where she lives with her family. She is the editor (as Miriam Kramnick) of the Penguin edition of Mary Wollstonecraft's *A Vindication of the Rights of Women*, 1975.

Ellen DuBois, author of *Feminism and Suffrage: The Emergence of an Independent Women's Movement in America, 1848–1869* and editor of *Elizabeth Cady Stanton-Susan B. Anthony: Correspondence, Writings, Speeches*, is associate professor of history and women's studies at the State University of New York, Buffalo.

Renate Duelli-Klein is a Swiss biologist. She now lives in London, where she is doing research on the theory and practice of Women's Studies. She is the European Editor of *Women's Studies International Forum*, co-editor of the *Athene Series* and is co-editor with Gloria Bowles of *Theories of Women's Studies I and II* (Women's Studies UC Berkeley, and Routledge and Kegan Paul, London; 1980 and 1983).

Mary Evans was educated at the London School of Economics and the University of Sussex. She lectures in sociology at the University of Kent, and has taught in the Master's Program in Women's Studies at Kent, since 1980. She is the author of *Work on Women* (with David Morgan), *Lucien Goldman: An Introduction*, and the editor of *The Woman Question*. At present she is writing a study of Simone de Beauvoir.

Angeline Goreau was born in Wilmington, Delaware, in 1951. She received a double degree in French and English literature from Columbia University in 1973. Her study *Reconstructing Aphra: A Social Biography of Aphra Behn* (1640–1689) was published in 1980 by Oxford University Press; a documentary history of the 'feminine sphere' entitled *The Whole Duty of a Woman* is in progress. Ms. Goreau contributes frequently to the *Washington Post*, the *New Statesman* and other journals. She has been awarded fellowships from the National Endowment for the Humanities, the National Endowment for the Arts, and is currently Hodder Fellow, Council for the Humanities, at Princeton University.

Joan K Kinnaird was educated at Vassar College and Yale University and is currently Professor of History at Trinity College Washington, D.C., where her special field is seventeenth-century English feminists.

Ann J Lane, USA, is Professor of History and Director of Women's Studies at Colgate University. She has collected and edited two volumes of the writings of Charlotte Perkins Gilman, *Herland* and *The Yellow Wallpaper and Other Stories*, and is currently completing a biography of Gilman.

Jacquie Matthews teaches Women's Studies and French at Victoria University in Wellington, New Zealand. She is currently researching the links between English, French and American nineteenth-century feminists for a forthcoming book, *Feminists Abroad*. She is also completing a full-length study of Barbara Bodichon. She is the mother of four children.

Muriel Mellown was educated at University College, London, and is now Professor of English at North Carolina Central University, Durham, North Carolina. She has published articles on nineteenth-century English poetry and is currently working on the contributors to *Time and Tide*, and on a longer study of Vera Brittain.

Ann Oakley is the author of *The Sociology of Housework*, *Woman's Work* and *Subject Women*. She lives in London.

Elizabeth Sarah has written and edited articles and books on education and male power and is the editor of a special issue of *Women's Studies International Forum* which is concerned with a reassessment of the feminist movement earlier this century. She lives in England.

Alix Kates Shulman was born and educated in Cleveland, Ohio. She did graduate work in philosophy at Columbia University. In the late 1960s she became a feminist activist and began her writing career. Since 1968 she has published three novels, two books on the anarchist-feminist Emma Goldman (including *Dancing in the Revolution*), several books for young people, short stories and numerous essays on feminist themes. She has taught fiction at New York University and Yale University.

Dale Spender, born in Australia, is a writer and researcher in the fields of language, education and feminist history. She has taught women's studies courses and is editor of *Women's Studies International Forum*. She is co-editor of *Learning to Lose* (The Women's Press, 1980) and editor of *Men's Studies Modified* (1981); she is the author of *Man Made Language* (1980), *Invisible Women* (1982) and *Women of Ideas and What Men Have Done to Them* (1982). She lives in London.

Lynne Spender is the author of *Intruders on the Rights of Men: Women's Unpublished Heritage* and is completing a book on the myths of marriage and their historical origins. She lives in Australia.

Liz Stanley lives and works in Manchester, England. She has been involved in feminism since the early 1970s. Her recent research has been on obscene telephone calls. She has just finished editing the diaries of a Victorian maidservant (*Hannah's Places*, Virago) and hopes to continue writing on Olive Schreiner.

Jenny Uglow, born in 1947, was educated at Oxford and then began working in publishing. She now writes, teaches literature and Women's Studies and is the editor of the MacMillan *Dictionary of Women's Biography*. She has four children and lives in Canterbury where she is involved with local women's groups, the rape crisis line and the battered wives' refuge.

Marie Mitchell Olesen Urbanski is Associate Professor of American Literature at the University of Maine at Orono. She is the author of *Margaret Fuller's 'Woman in the Nineteenth Century': A Literary Study of Form and Content, of Sources and Influence*. Her recent publications include essays about Joyce Carol Oates and Henry David Thoreau. She edited the *Thoreau Journal Quarterly* from 1978 to 1982.

Gaby Weiner, a former primary schoolteacher, is currently researching Harriet Martineau and her attitude towards the education of girls. She has written numerous articles on the education of girls – and curriculum development – for educational periodicals, and is now at the Open University. She lectures in Women's Studies.

Leslie Wheeler was educated at Stanford University and the University of California at Berkeley, has worked as a teacher and in publishing. Her first book, a biography of former President Carter, was entitled

Jimmy Who? and her second book is *Loving Warriors; Selected Letters of Lucy Stone and Henry B. Blackwell, 1853–1893* (Dial Press). She has contributed articles to various historical publications and is currently working on an historical novel about three women living in mid-nineteenth century America.

Jean L Willis is Professor of American History at Fairleigh Dickinson University, Rutherford, New Jersey, where she teaches a course on Women in American History and Politics. She is the holder of an American Association of University Women Educational Foundation Individual Member Research Grant, awarded for the study 'Alice Paul: The Quintessential Feminist'.